FACING THE NATION

Facing the Nation

TELEVISION AND POLITICS
1936-1976

Grace Wyndham Goldie

THE BODLEY HEAD
LONDON SYDNEY
TORONTO

FOR F.W.G.

© Grace Wyndham Goldie 1977
ISBN 0 370 01383 2
Printed in Great Britain for
The Bodley Head Ltd
9 Bow Street, London WC2E.7AL
by Redwood Burn Limited,
Trowbridge and Esher
Set in Monotype Baskerville
by Gloucester Typesetting Co Ltd
First published 1977

CONTENTS

ACKNOWLEDGMENTS

Above all I must thank Sir Hugh Greene. When Director-General of the BBC he formally gave me permission to use its archives for the purpose of writing this book. That permission has never been rescinded and I have had generous help from BBC archivists, radio and film librarians, those in charge of files, as well as from a multitude of other friends and colleagues who once worked, or are still working (whether within the BBC or elsewhere) in broadcasting.

The present Director-General of the BBC, Sir Charles Curran, the Chief Secretary, Colin Shaw, the heads of legal, copyright and audience research departments—indeed all I approached—have shown goodwill, a desire to assist in every possible way combined, in the best BBC tradition, with a scrupulous avoidance of any wish to question the ways in which I might use the material they made available or influence the ideas and opinions I might express.

It is not easy to say in a few words how grateful I am also to the Warden and Fellows of Nuffield College, Oxford. To be made an Associate Member of the College for two years was an honour and the right of frequent residence a much appreciated privilege. Not only that. Both the Warden and David Butler have been good enough to read and comment upon the typescript at various stages and David Butler, who knows so much about politics and about television, has given me advice and valuable criticism at various times during the book's progress.

Dame Lucy Sutherland, when Principal of Lady Margaret Hall in Oxford, helped and encouraged the embryonic enterprise: another friend, Mrs Chester Wilmot, lent me papers and read the typescript: Mrs Adrian Eeles struggled vivaciously with my handwriting: Mrs Bootle kindly typed some of my manuscript and Mrs Rosemary Thurston has devoted her skills to keeping the material in secretarial order.

And now I must again thank Sir Hugh Greene. This time as a publisher. Having become Chairman of the Directors of The Bodley Head he has not only maintained his friendly interest in what I was

ACKNOWLEDGMENTS

trying to do but has given it a degree of personal attention for which I am deeply grateful. He, and all concerned at The Bodley Head, have been endlessly patient and considerate in assisting me to say whatever I wanted to say without ever trying to impose their own views. I must thank each one of them for the professional expertise from which I have so greatly benefited.

The responsibility for any mistakes I may have made, as for the opinions I have expressed is, however, mine alone.

INTRODUCTION

As more and more people watch television more and more people want to control it. Television, in fact, is increasingly regarded as power. In 1936 it was almost entirely ignored; in 1956 it was still being treated mainly as a method by which thousands could be supplied in their homes with trivial entertainment; in 1976, because it is watched by millions throughout the world, it is considered by numbers of groups with sectional interests to be an instrument which can be used to promote those interests, whether financial, social or political.

Few of those who regard television primarily as power, and want to lay their hands upon the levers of that power, ever seem to give adequate thought to the strange but undeniable fact that television's power rests ultimately on its programmes of enjoyment. People watch television because, for hundreds of different human reasons, they enjoy doing so: it extends their experience, gives them news, information, drama, an opportunity of seeing sport, dancing, clowns, circuses and funny men; anything, in fact, which interests them and which they enjoy.

It is enjoyment which enables television to enter the homes of individuals and, by doing so, offers to those interested in power a chance of influencing the attitudes of millions and persuading them to courses of action—whether of buying specific goods or supporting specific political policies—which, without that influence, they might not even consider.

Television as enjoyment is, rightly, what concerns the great majority of television viewers, producers of television programmes and critics of television output. But not many of those who are so properly preoccupied with this essential aspect of television, with ensuring that the enjoyment which television offers is of high quality and not merely the lowest common denominator of subjects, and treatments, which will attract the greatest audiences, are aware of the degree to which the whole television world which they enjoy, criticise, and in which they operate, is a bubble of fragility which can easily be pricked and destroyed by the decision of politicians.

The extraordinary truth, of which I became aware only gradually as a result of working in television for longer than perhaps I ought to feel it seemly to admit, is that television and politics are inextricably mingled: each influences the other in basic ways which, as yet, have neither been fully explored nor understood. My hope, in some respects, is that they never will be.

The investigations which have been conducted over many years and in many countries about the effect of television upon behaviour (for example upon delinquency and crime), in so far as I have examined the evidence and been able to judge, have produced minimal results; for the most part there seems simply to be an indication that, of those already disposed to behave criminally or violently who have had few other influences brought to bear upon them, some might have that predisposition increased by the frequent sight of violent or criminal action on television. Evidence of any specific effect of television upon the way in which citizens in this country vote is, happily, even more inconclusive. I say happily because it would seem to me to be disastrous if those who would like to control the political behaviour of millions could learn to pull the television strings so effectively as to turn voters in a democracy into political puppets.

Yet if the effect of television upon voting is, to say the least, still largely a matter of conjecture and speculation, there is no doubt that the treatment of political matters on television adds a new source of information to those already available to the electorate in democracies and may even, differently, influence governmental action in dictatorships. Moreover, the effect of political decisions upon television services is undeniable and can be observed in action in every country in the world.

These are among the reasons why I have written this book. It is, as any reader will find, not a thesis but a voyage of discovery, based on my own experience and therefore a very personal story. I have tried to set down, as they happened and in a rough sort of chronological order, the events which shaped my attitudes and the ways in which, during my own day-to-day operations, I gradually formed my conclusions. This, therefore, is the history of a process, and the subjects with which I have tried to deal, perhaps it might appear somewhat arbitrarily, have been selected because for me they played a significant part in that process.

It began in 1936 when I first heard of the experiments in television transmission which were taking place at Alexandra Palace in the north of London. I was then, as a result of a chance meeting in 1934 with the editor of the BBC's weekly journal *The Listener*, writing a regular column of criticism about radio drama. Rather to my own surprise I was fascinated by radio—particularly by its ability to appeal to the imagination and create pictures in the mind's eye. But as soon as I heard of the possible development of television I knew that radio would be eclipsed, and that television would become not only of national but of world-wide importance.

This seemed to me so obvious that I could not understand why such an evident fact was not universally recognised. Radio as a means of entertainment, propaganda and communication already mattered. If sight could be added to sound the communication would be more powerful, more complete. To listen without being able to see was, in a way, to be deprived; so, although it was possible to regret the loss of radio's ability to appeal to the imagination, I knew—and knew is not too strong a word for what I felt in 1936—that television was what counted.

I persuaded the editor of *The Listener*, Rex Lambert, not only to arrange for me to be present in Studio A at Alexandra Palace during the transmission of the first television programme to Radio Olympia in August 1936 but also to let me write about it and then, from 1936 to 1939, to add television to the subjects I was covering in my regular articles.

So for the next three years I saw most if not all of the programmes which were being produced at Alexandra Palace. But it was not until 1948 that I myself became a television producer. By then I had learnt something about production for radio and the workings of the BBC. Television was closed down for military reasons at the beginning of the 1939 war but towards the end of the war, in 1944, I was invited to apply for a vacant post as a talks producer in the BBC's Talks Department. This may well have been because the department was short of production staff since so many had left to join the forces. At any rate I was appointed, learned a lot, and met in the corridors of Broadcasting House a number of pre-war television producers—Mary Adams and George More O'Ferrall among them—whom I had encountered in television's early years. We talked nostalgically about their pioneering activities: and in 1948, two years after the television service had been re-started, I was asked to move from sound radio to television.

During the years I spent in television as a producer, head of a production department and, eventually, head of a group of departments, I was involved, enjoyably, in the creation of programmes which could be classed as programmes of enjoyment—travel, adventure, and the start of 'Monitor', that early endeavour to present on television some aspects of the arts—but, I suppose partly as a result of my previous training in history and politics, I gravitated towards the presentation of current affairs. This kept me in touch with what was happening in radio at the higher political levels and forced me to consider, day by day, the close and developing relationship between television and the processes of political persuasion.

That relationship is still developing not only in Britain but all over the world. May all go well: television, as I knew from the first and realised more fully in action, has its dangers; but so has electricity, and no one who has enjoyed the benefits of electric light would want to go back to lamps and candles for their sole illumination. Similarly few of those millions who have enjoyed television in their homes would be prepared to dispense with it entirely. Television, for good or ill, has come to stay. So, inevitably, has its relationship with politics.

[1]

Prelude : The Essential Decisions

1934 - 1936

Early in 1935 a National Government with Ramsay MacDonald
(Labour) as Prime Minister and Stanley Baldwin (Conservative) as
Lord President of the Council decided, with remarkable courage and
prescience, that a nation-wide television service should be started in
Great Britain. This decision was based on the recommendations of
the Selsdon Committee which had been appointed in 1934 'To consider the development of television and to report to the Postmaster
General on the relative merits of the several systems and on the
conditions under which any public service of Television should be
provided'.[1]

The members of the Committee were mainly experienced engineers and administrators working under the chairmanship of a
Conservative peer, Lord Selsdon, who, as Sir William Mitchell-
Thomson, had been Postmaster General from 1924 to 1929. Television was in a primitive stage. Experiments had been carried out in
many countries, including Germany and the United States. In
Great Britain a Television Society of the United Kingdom had been
founded and Licences for research and experimental work had been
issued by the Postmaster General.[2] These were necessary because,
technically, television broadcasting is a species of wireless telegraphy.
The Licence issued to the British Broadcasting Company in 1923
stated that 'by reason of the Telegraph Acts of 1863 to 1922 it is un-
lawful to establish any wireless telegraphy station or instal or work
any apparatus for wireless telegraphy in any place except in accordance with a licence granted in that behalf'.[3] And television was
defined, in the Licence of 1936, as 'the representation by telegraph
in transitory visible form of persons or objects in movement or at
rest'.[4]

Since television is an aspect of wireless telegraphy its operation, at
home and overseas, is intricately bound up with the handling of
communications by telephones and telegraphy. These are controlled

in Great Britain by the Post Office. Hence the fact that the unlikely figure of the Postmaster General was involved in all discussions about broadcasting and television.* It was successive Postmasters General who issued the various Licences to broadcast which legally permitted both the British Broadcasting Corporation and, later, Independent Television to transmit television programmes. It was the Postmaster General who answered questions on broadcasting in the House of Commons. The various Committees set up at intervals to review the work of the broadcasting organisations and to recommend whether, and on what terms, their Licences should be renewed, were appointed by him. And the first to deal with television, the Selsdon Committee, made the vital recommendations which were to determine the whole nature of television in Great Britain and to set it the continuing task of walking the tightrope between the abysses of total government control on the one hand and the grosser forms of commercialism on the other.

But the first question the Committee had to answer was whether there should be a television service at all. It had already been agreed that the British Broadcasting Corporation, which had the sole right to transmit radio programmes in Great Britain, should give facilities for a trial television service. And in the autumn of 1929 the Baird Company had carried out, both independently and in conjunction with the BBC, experimental transmissions. These eventually occupied two periods weekly of approximately thirty minutes each 'with accompanying sound on a separate wave length'.

In 1932 Baird showed television pictures in the Baird Laboratories in Long Acre on 'model home receivers' with screens of 9×4 inches, and in Paris he demonstrated two-way television between the offices of *Le Matin* and the Galeries Lafayette. A number of other firms were interested in developing and demonstrating diffe ent television systems and there was considerable pressure from them and from the manufacturers of equipment for a regular television service to be started.

But the prospects were far from good. Technically the quality of the pictures was poor. Most of the experiments had been in low definition with pictures built up on thirty lines, coarse in texture and giving little detail. Work had been done on systems which gave a

* The powers of the Postmaster General over broadcasting were later exercised by the Minister of Posts and Telecommunications and after March 1974 by the Secretary of State for Home Affairs.

higher definition but even these were mostly on standards of only
180 lines. From a financial point of view, things looked even worse.
After eighteen months of experiment in the United States the Columbia Broadcasting System closed its pioneering television station, W2
XAB, and it was reported that television 'as a commercial aspect of
radio broadcasting had been abandoned for the present by the
Columbia Broadcasting System'.

This was in 1933. The Selsdon Committee was appointed in 1934.
It made its recommendations in 1935. These, though soberly phrased,
were, in the circumstances, dashing. The Committee stated unanimously that a nation-wide television service in Great Britain was a
practical possibility; that the newly developed high definition system should be used; that transmissions should be on 405 lines; that
the two main rival systems, Baird and Marconi/EMI, should be
operated alternately so that any final decision about systems could
be made in the light of actual experience in comparable conditions;
that the service should start in the London area, where the radius
for reception would be approximately twenty-five miles, but that it
should gradually be made available, by building other transmitters,
throughout the country. Their recommendations were accepted by
the government and endorsed by the Ullswater Committee.[5] The
result was that the first regular high definition television service in
the world was started in London and was formally inaugurated at
Alexandra Palace on November 2, 1936 by the then Postmaster
General, Major G. C. Tryon.

Few people thought this of any importance. Only a handful of
enthusiasts possessed television sets. In the hope of increasing interest
in the new venture and persuading more people to buy television
receivers, special transmissions were arranged for the Radio Exhibition at Olympia in the August before the official inauguration in
November. One of the highlights of these programmes was a 'live'
revue called 'Here's Looking at You'.* Among its more successful
items was a well-known vaudeville horse-act in which a Griffith
brother who played the back legs of a pantomime horse kicked,
fraternally, the Griffith brother who played the front legs. Soon there
were other legs; the legs of chorus girls and dancers, the first in the
long line of girls and legs on television from the 'Television Toppers'

* I saw this transmitted from the Studio. Permission had been given for
me to be present because I was then writing criticisms for the BBC paper
The Listener. GWG.

to the girls who later took part in 'The Black and White Minstrel Show'. And I remember a playlet with the actors standing in a row since there was so little depth of focus that if they even made a gesture towards the cameras their hands and arms swelled grotesquely as if from a sudden attack of elephantiasis.

The idea that television would affect governments and that the ability to reach the voter through television would influence the choice of the President of the United States or the Prime Minister of Great Britain was remote from most people's thinking, certainly from that of politicians and political theorists, but also from that of the majority of those who worked in television or controlled it from Broadcasting House.

Yet, for all the flickering nature of its images and its lack of serious content, television in 1936 passed decisively out of the experimental stage and became a developing service. It was a new medium of communication with its own special characteristics which would inevitably shape the nature of what it could communicate; it was different from film; it was different from sound radio; it was totally different from newspapers and books. It was to sweep around the world and soon the statement that television was the most revolutionary change in methods of communication since the invention of printing became a cliché. In politics television was a new factor; one which offered new opportunities and new hazards to those in power, and to those aspiring to power. The governed, in their millions could, at a single moment, see and judge the governors; the governors could appear to millions of individuals simultaneously and sway their emotions not only by their voices but by whatever personal magnetism and visual authority they possessed.

Little or none of this was evident to most of those who in 1936 watched the first television transmissions. Critics, accustomed to the large size of cinema pictures and to the polish of cinematic performances, were contemptuous; television was crude stuff, home movies offering wavering shadows on cripplingly small screens. Others, including most of the administrators and production staff within the BBC, were equally contemptuous, but for different reasons.

The British Broadcasting Corporation, under its first Director-General, Sir John Reith, had shown a combination of enterprise and responsibility which had gained for it a unique position in the life of the country. This had been achieved with the help of a staff of unquestioned excellence. But their speciality was the use of words; they had no knowledge of how to present either entertainment or information in vision, nor any experience of handling visual material. Moreover, most of them distrusted the visual; they associated vision with the movies and the music hall and were afraid that the high purposes of the Corporation would be trivialised by the influence of those concerned with what could be transmitted in visual terms.

And some were jealous of the new medium; they had a vested interest in sound radio and felt their own positions to be obscurely threatened. Luckily the television studios at Alexandra Palace were a long way from Broadcasting House; few people from the sound services were sufficiently curious to come to see them in action. Television could be brushed aside; it was not a medium to be taken seriously; pantomime horses and chorus girls were its natural ingredients; it was not suitable for news or current affairs, let alone for important statements of policy or party political or election broadcasts and certainly not for such major occasions as the presentation of the results of a general election. All these were matters which must be dealt with in words, not vision. 'Television won't matter in your lifetime or mine,' the then Editor of the BBC's weekly *The Listener* said to me with some impatience in 1936. And even in 1948 a pioneer of education by radio, the late Mary Somerville, who knew that I was considering moving from sound to television, said, 'But why do you *want* to go? Television won't last. It's a flash in the pan.'

Such attitudes were widespread in the Corporation. They were deeply resented by the television pioneers and a marked hostility developed between the staff of the new television service and what they considered to be the dead hand of the old guard at Broadcasting House. This hostility continued even after the war. It was an irritant in the day-to-day handling of television affairs and in the production of television programmes. It was a cause of the explosive resignation from the BBC in 1950 of the then Controller of Television, Norman Collins, and was a factor of some importance in the breaking of the BBC's television monopoly in 1954.

But if many at Broadcasting House in the early days were culpably, unimaginatively and selfishly blind to the potentialities of television, the pioneers at Alexandra Palace did not sufficiently realise how important it was to the whole future of television in Britain that it had begun under the auspices of the British Broadcasting Corporation. They did not dwell on the harsh fact, which was fully understood at Broadcasting House, that one of the main reasons why it was possible to have a regular television service in Britain in 1936, whereas in the United States the CBS television experiment had failed in 1933, was that British television started under the umbrella of the BBC's monopoly; and that the early stages of television development were financed out of the ten shilling annual licence fee paid by listeners in Britain for the privilege of hearing sound radio programmes. This meant that British television was not dependent, as the CBS experiment had been, upon having a sufficient number of viewers to make it a commercially attractive proposition.

Other, and immense, benefits resulted from association with the BBC which few of the television production staff in the years from 1936 to 1939 really appreciated. The Selsdon Committee, in recommending that responsibility for the development of television in Great Britain should be given to the British Broadcasting Corporation, had said that the Corporation 'should exercise control of the actual operation of the television service to the same extent and subject to the same broad principles as in the case of sound broadcasting'. This meant that television in Britain had from the start two essential freedoms, achieved by few other television services as they developed around the world: freedom from government domination in its day-to-day running; and freedom from the domination of its output by commercial interests.

Television in Great Britain, in fact, inherited all the rights, duties and responsibilities which had been given to, and won by, radio broadcasting as a result of the struggles of Sir John Reith and the investigations of a series of imaginative and far-sighted Committees set up from 1923 onwards to consider the future of broadcasting. The recommendations of these Committees—Sykes and Crawford, Selsdon and Ullswater—had been embodied in a succession of Charters and Licences issued to the BBC, endorsed in White Papers and also by answers to questions in Parliament given by different Postmasters General of different parties in different governments. What emerged could be said to be a national attitude to broadcasting, which now embraced television. It was not to be abandoned to commercialism.

'It may be,' said the Sykes Committee in 1923, 'that broadcasting holds social and political possibilities as great as any technical attainment of our generation', and it went on, 'we consider that the control of such a potential power over the public opinion and the life of the nation ought to remain within the State and the operation of so important a national service ought not to be allowed to become an unrestricted commercial monopoly'.[6] And, in fact, even after the Television Act of 1954, which permitted commercial television, there has never been 'an unrestricted commercial monopoly' in Great Britain.

The public factor in television financed by advertising was ensured by the setting up of an Independent Television Authority which had powers and responsibilities comparable with those of the Board of Governors of the BBC. This body has been strengthened rather than weakened over the years. Following upon the report of the Pilkington Committee in 1962,[7] the Government took steps to see that the Authority should be in a position to deal more effectively than hitherto with the great commercial television companies. 'The Government proposes,' it was said in the subsequent White Paper, 'that the control of networking should pass to the Authority, which should generally take a much more positive rôle in the affairs of independent television. The Authority will chair a committee representing all the programme companies. It will also approve and supervise the arrangements for the buying and selling of programmes, so that this may operate in a manner which is helpful to all companies alike, large and small. Moreover, it will be responsible for the shape, content, balance and quality of the service as a whole.'[8]

This determination that British television should be free from the grosser forms of commercial exploitation can be compared with the powers and attitudes of the Federal Communications Commission in the United States. Mr Fred Friendly, Professor of Broadcast Journalism in Columbia University, an associate of the late Edward R. Murrow in producing some of the best actuality television programmes ever transmitted in America, has described the Federal Communications Commission as a 'tower of Jello on the Potomac'. And, though this may seem to some to be an extreme view, it is certain that the question of whether the Federal Communications Commission has any right in law to influence programmes has been constantly in dispute.

But if the early committees, supported by successive governments, were aware of the Scylla of unrestricted commercialism they were equally aware of the Charybdis of unrestricted government control. As early as 1926 Sir William Mitchell-Thomson said in the House of Commons when he was Postmaster General, 'While I am prepared to take the responsibility for broad issues of policy, on minor issues and measures of domestic policy and matters of day-to-day control, I want to leave things to the free judgment of the Corporation'. This statement of practice followed upon the recommendations of the Crawford Committee[9] which had rejected the idea of a State-run system in favour of that of a public corporation acting as a trustee for the national interest. This recommendation was endorsed by the Ullswater Committee[10] and accepted by the Government.

By 1936, therefore, the freedom of broadcasting from political interference in its day-to-day running was established. Television inherited that freedom. In 1946 this policy was described in a White Paper as being that 'best calculated to ensure freedom on the air and to remove from the party in power the temptation to use the State's control of broadcasting for its own political ends'. And in 1954 a similar freedom was granted to the Independent Television Authority.

This policy has been consistently supported by the national Press, which sees the freedom of broadcasting, however different it must be for technological reasons from the freedom of the Press, as being, nevertheless, related to it. And so any action which seems to indicate a move by political interests to manipulate broadcasting, whether radio or television, for their own political ends, comes under immediate attack. An example was the outcry in 1967 when two well-known politicians, Lord Hill, a Conservative peer who had been Chairman of the Independent Television Authority, and Lord Aylestone, formerly Mr Herbert Bowden, once the Labour Party's Chief Whip, were made Chairmen respectively of the Governors of the BBC and of the Independent Television Authority. The anxieties expressed in the newspapers had no apparent party political alignment: the fear was that these appointments indicated that broadcasting and television would be subjected to increasingly powerful pressures by political interests and that their freedoms would be diminished.

Nowhere more than in broadcasting is the price of freedom eternal vigilance; resistance to political pressures has to be constant and continuous. But it must be realised that such pressures are inevitable. For the aims of the political parties and those of broadcasting organisations are not the same. Broadcasting organisations, generally speaking, want to interest their audiences and to inform the electorate by presenting facts and opinions relevant to a particular situation regardless of any effect these may have on the future of the political parties. The political parties, generally speaking, want to use broadcasting, and particularly in recent years television, to persuade the electorate to support certain policies and people in order to win elections and gain power.

These differences become sharply evident when general or local elections are imminent or at moments of political crisis such as Suez. At such times accusations of bias, particularly in giving or denying members of the Opposition access to television, are freely thrown around and make headlines in the Press. On occasions of this kind, even although the freedom of the broadcasting organisations from political interference in their day-to-day running is agreed in principle by all concerned, successive governments have in practice brought pressures to bear, in direct as well as in more subtle ways, on broadcasting organisations in an attempt to increase their own share of broadcasting opportunities and to deny equal opportunities to the Opposition.

If the broadcasting organisations yield to these pressures they face attack from the Opposition; if they resist them they incur the anger of the Government. The issues are usually complicated and attitudes are seldom wholly factious, although they may sometimes be disingenuous. A Prime Minister may genuinely feel that he is speaking in a purely national capacity and that it is unnecessary, and even irresponsible, to turn a matter of national interest into a party political occasion by giving equal opportunities to a member of the Opposition. He may ignore, deliberately or subconsciously, a fact of which he is usually very conscious when in Opposition—that any appearance of a member of a Government has a party as well as a national aspect. A Leader of the Opposition may genuinely feel that it is his national duty, when opinion in the country is divided on a major issue of policy, to use television to put a case which is opposed to that of the Government, even although he may realise perfectly well that his appearance is likely to pay party dividends.

The broadcasting organisations are aware that their whole existence depends upon Parliament and in particular upon the Government of the day since the Postmaster General has, in theory at least, the power to revoke their Licence to broadcast and Parliament may refuse to renew the Charter of the BBC or may change its terms and can alter the Acts which govern the running of Independent Television. But the broadcasting organisations are in a position to resist governmental pressure since they know that they are enjoined to treat political matters with scrupulous fairness and that any failure to do this will mean that they are not performing one of the duties for which they were set up, and that any such failure would endanger their position in the long run since the Opposition will one day be the Government.

Freedom from political interference is not, therefore, a simple matter. It is maintained by a triangular system of checks and balances in which the rights of the Government, the rights of the Opposition and the duties of the broadcasting organisations all exist in a state of tension which prevents any one of them from dominating the other.

Among the reasons why this freedom has continued to exist and which has prevented broadcasting in Britain from becoming, as it has in many other countries—democracies as well as dictatorships— a mere tool of the government is partly the wisdom of the early committees which saw the dangers of unrestricted government domination and took steps to prevent it, thus creating a tradition of freedom which it has become difficult to break; partly the fact that the main political parties have been of relatively equal strength and neither wanted, when in Opposition, to be denied access to the powerful new medium. The result has been that each, when in power, has upheld in principle, if not in detailed practice, the rights of the Opposition to broadcast.

The third factor has been the record of responsibility with which the broadcasting organisations have performed their duties and exercised their discretion, a record largely the result of the standards originally set in sound broadcasting by the BBC under Sir John Reith. These standards were inherited by television and were applied in principle, though in detail they had to be adjusted to the demands of a medium which was visual as well as aural.

But if television inherited freedoms it also inherited the restrictions which had been imposed on sound broadcasting as a result of the recommendations of the early committees. For if these bodies were clear that neither governmental nor commercial interests should dominate the new media they were equally determined that no such domination should be exercised by the organisations set up to operate them. A variety of safeguards were devised to prevent this. From the beginning the Charters and Licences under which the BBC operated were issued for limited periods. Each renewal gave Parliament an opportunity of considering the use which had been made of the privilege of broadcasting. It could propose modifications in the

Charters and Licences. Moreover the Postmaster General could at any time revoke the Licence to broadcast should there be evidence of an abuse of the power which broadcasting organisations had been given.

These were latent powers, defences against misuse. But there was one positive instruction which was of great importance in the handling of politics and which television inherited from sound radio. This was that the BBC 'should not broadcast its own opinions in matters of public policy'.

Under the terms of the BBC's first Licence[11] the Postmaster General had certain large powers of veto ('The Postmaster General may from time to time by Notice in writing require the Corporation to refrain from sending any broadcast matter (whether particular or general) specified in such Notice'). It was under this general power that the Postmaster General issued his instruction that the BBC should not broadcast its own opinions on matters of public policy.* This instruction has remained. Each of the various committees set up to review the conduct of broadcasting, whether in sound or television, has advised that it should be continued. And, as a result of the Television Act of 1954, it was also imposed upon Independent Television.

This ban makes communication in political matters by sound broadcasting and television totally different from political communication by means of newspapers. Editors of newspapers, and journalists writing editorials, can, and do, advocate and attack specific political parties and specific political personalities. This possibility is denied to the broadcasting organisations and to those whom they employ in an editorial capacity.

The reason for the ban, originally, was an appreciation of the fact that technological circumstances limited the number of broadcasting organisations which could operate within the British Isles. Broadcasting used radio frequencies; the number of radio frequencies in the world is limited; many of these frequencies are suitable and necessary for purposes other than broadcasting; they are allocated by international agreement in order to prevent international chaos in communication. Those available for broadcasting in any one country are very few.

The technical position and its national implications were outlined

---

* The terms of the relevant memorandum issued under Clause 13 (4) of the Licence running from July 30, 1964 to July 31, 1976 requires 'the BBC to refrain from expressing its own opinion on current affairs or on matters of public policy'.

by the Sykes Committee.[12] 'All wireless telegraphy and telephony has to be conducted within a limited group of "wave lengths" which is already largely occupied with communications of the fighting services, the work of ship and shore stations and the commercial work of fixed stations. Every new wireless station takes up a certain amount of elbow room, technically called its "wave band", which no other sending station within a certain radius should be permitted to use. The wave bands available in any one country must therefore be regarded as a valuable form of public property; and the right to use them for any purpose should only be given after full and careful consideration. Those which are assigned to any particular interest should be subject to safeguards necessary to protect the public interest in the future. Should safeguards become necessary after definite allocation of this public property they may be found both difficult and costly.'

The use of this 'public property' was decided by the Postmaster General under the Wireless Telegraphy Acts. The right to broadcast was therefore a privilege; a donation of the power to persuade which was to be of great value commercially (Lord Thomson later called it in a famous phrase a 'licence to print money') and of great potential danger politically.

From the first the possible political dangers of the right to broadcast seemed to demand special safeguards. These were described by the Ullswater Committee. 'It is obvious,' the Committee said, 'that a medium whereby expressions of political opinion can be brought into seven or eight million homes needs very careful safeguarding if it is not to be abused. It would be possible for those in control of broadcasting to maintain a steady stream of propaganda on behalf of one political party or one school of thought. They could to some extent make or mar the reputations of politicians and by a judicious selection of news items and the method of their presentation they could influence the whole political thought of the country.'[13] And the Committee, while approving the discussion of controversial topics given that there was 'an impartial and representative balance', said, 'We think it right that the Corporation should refrain, as in the past, from broadcasting its own opinions, by way of editorial comment upon current affairs'.[14]

This ban, which now included television, seemed eminently reasonable, and indeed inevitable, in view of the BBC's monopoly. But when this monopoly was broken in 1954 as far as television was concerned, not only was the ban maintained but it was also enforced upon the Independent Television Authority. The ban was not, therefore, related to monopoly. It arose directly from the fact that the community, acting through Parliament, gave to a few organisations, necessarily limited in number, a unique and potentially dangerous power to persuade.

It is difficult to believe, even if a freer competition between more broadcasting organisations became technologically possible, that these organisations would be allowed by Parliament to broadcast their own opinions on matters of political controversy, to take up political attitudes and to advocate the policies of particular political parties and so have an important influence in deciding who should be the next Prime Minister and what party should be in power. Even in the United States, with its history of much greater diversity of broadcasting organisations and its greater area which, technologically speaking, makes a greater number of separate stations possible, regulations of strict impartiality and balance in matters of political broadcasting are imposed. It is one thing for politicians to plead their cause on television: it is quite another for a television station to put forward its own political views or to support one candidate for the Presidency against another.

Politicians, moreover, are aware that television gives them an opportunity of direct contact with the individuals who make up the electorate and that this has freed them, to some extent, from dependence upon the Press and its reporting of their speeches. It is unlikely that they would be willing to give up a system in which broadcasting organisations are politically neutral in favour of one in which these organisations could take up partisan attitudes similar to those of the Press and upon whose favour the political leaders would become, differently, dependent.

It was against this technological and political background that television began in Great Britain in 1936. It was controlled by the British Broadcasting Corporation, a body which had been set up to act as a trustee in the national interest, whose function was to 'inform, educate and entertain'; it was ultimately responsible to Parliament; it was non-profit-making; it was financed by fees paid by listeners and eventually viewers; it was permitted, even encouraged, to deal with controversial topics but enjoined to do so with scrupulous balance and fairness; and it was forbidden to put forward its own views in matters of public policy.

[2]

Pre-War Television

1936-1939

In these first years, though few of them realised it, the handful of men and women working on television programmes were fortunate in that they were almost completely ignored; by the public, by politicians and by the British Broadcasting Corporation itself. It was a tiny operation. Even in 1939 when, at the start of the war, the television service was closed down for security reasons, only twenty thousand people owned television sets. Reception was limited to a radius of anything between twenty-five and forty miles round London. Television was therefore not a national service but was confined to the south-east of England. Politically it was supremely unimportant. Moreover during the years between 1936 and 1939 the country was occupied with greater matters: the depression and unemployment; the Spanish Civil War; the rise of Nazi power; the parades of Sir Oswald Mosley; the abdication crisis; and, very soon, with Munich, Civil Defence and the threat of war.

Sir John Reith, the formidable Director-General of the British Broadcasting Corporation, was also preoccupied: with the rôle of sound broadcasting in national affairs, with the rôle of corporations within the State, and with his own personal position. His achievements and those of the BBC under his leadership were generally and admiringly acknowledged. He was a Scot whose towering height, craggy features and bushy eyebrows made him a gift to the cartoonists. He came from a religious background and his high standards of moral and religious rectitude had been enforced in sound broadcasting. His word was law. There must be no light entertainment or political controversy on the Sabbath; no breath of scandal must touch any member of his staff; the dignity of the Corporation must be maintained at every point; announcers, even although they were not seen, must wear dinner jackets in the evening.

His training had been that of an engineer and he had entered the world of radio in 1922 when he was made Managing Director of a company set up by a group of manufacturers of radio equipment. It was called the 'British Broadcasting Company' and licensed by the Postmaster General to 'establish and work a system of broadcasting'. It was not allowed to carry advertising or to pay annual dividends of more than $7\frac{1}{2}\%$, was responsible for providing a broadcasting service 'to the reasonable satisfaction of the Postmaster General' and was financed by a complicated combination of licence fees and tariffs.

By 1923 this sytem was already under review. The Government set up two Committees to look into broadcasting in all its aspects. These were the Sykes Committee (1923)[1] and Crawford Committee (1925).[2] They recommended that 'a public corporation should be set up to act as Trustee for the national interest in Broadcasting' and that it should be financed from licence fees paid by listeners.

And so on December 20, 1926, the British Broadcasting Corporation came into being as a result of a Charter of Incorporation granted by King George v. The members of the Corporation, who were responsible to Parliament for its conduct, were called Governors and were to serve part-time. The Chairman and Vice-Chairman were appointed by the King in Council and were to be paid (though there was provision for change) £3,000 and £1,000 a year respectively; other Governors £700. Normally the chief executive officer of the Corporation, the Director-General, who was responsible to the Board of Governors, was to be appointed by the Board. But the first Director-General was named in the first Charter. He was John Charles Walsham Reith—soon to become Sir John Reith.

The Corporation's first Charter and Licence were issued for ten years. And in 1936, after ten years of operational experience, the Ullswater Committee was appointed by the Postmaster General to consider 'the constitution, control and finance of the broadcasting service in this country'.[3] The Committee was almost fulsome in its praise of the work of the Corporation and recommended that 'in view of the widespread approval of the broadcasting service in this country, in which we fully concur, the Charter of the British Broadcasting Corporation should be extended for a term of ten years from the 1st of January 1937'. It also endorsed the recommendation of the Selsdon Committee that the BBC should be charged with the setting up of a television broadcasting service.

In spite of all this praise and in spite of the new responsibilities of television, Sir John Reith was restless. In a phrase which he was to repeat very often, he did not feel 'fully stretched'.* He believed that he had capabilities which should be employed in positions of greater power than that of a Director-General of the British Broadcasting Corporation. If he were to stay in broadcasting perhaps it should be as Chairman of the Board of Governors. But there were surely other places where his abilities could be of service? Why, for instance, should he not be Viceroy of India?

Meanwhile there were internal problems. The BBC's treatment of its staff had not only been questioned implicitly in the Ullswater Report[4] but was brought spectacularly into the open by a slander action which Richard Lambert, editor of the BBC's weekly *The Listener*, brought in a private capacity against Sir Cecil Levita.† This was in connection with remarks made by Sir Cecil about Mr Lambert's suitability to be a Governor of the British Film Institute. Mr Lambert had been nominated to this position by the British Institute of Adult Education but had had to get the consent of his employers, the BBC, in order to serve. Lady Levita was also a Governor of the British Film Institute and, in time, she took exception to some of Mr Lambert's attitudes. Sir Cecil Levita invited Mr Lambert's immediate senior in the BBC, Mr Gladstone Murray, to lunch and made statements about Mr Lambert which were the subject of the slander action.

The problems of Mr Lambert's position and the possibility of an action for slander dragged on within the BBC throughout 1936 and Sir John Reith was forced to become involved. Mr Lambert wanted to bring the action. He was pressed not to do so by the BBC and a memorandum was written to him which could be interpreted as threatening him with dismissal if he did so. Lambert brought the action. The case was tried in the King's Bench Division on October 4, 5 and 6, 1936. It had odd overtones which caught the fancy of the public and the Press—the happenings on a remote farm in the Isle of Man where a mongoose was alleged to talk became relevant to the evidence; and so, under the title of 'The Mongoose Case', it

* See *Into the Wind*, Sir John Reith's autobiography (Hodder and Stoughton, 1949). The phrase was also used repeatedly in broadcasts on television when Sir John Reith was interviewed by
(a) John Freeman in 'Face to Face' on October 30, 1960,
(b) Malcolm Muggeridge on November 23 and 30, 1967.

† Chairman of the LCC 1928–9: a member of the Consultative Committee which advised the Home Office on matters of film censorship.

filled daily columns in the newspapers. Mr Lambert, a conscientious and talented man with an almost obsessive interest in civil liberties and the rights of the individual, won the case and was awarded the then almost unprecedented sum of £7,500 in damages.

The question, as far as the BBC was concerned, was whether it had brought improper pressures to bear on a member of its staff to forgo his rights as an individual citizen. These anxieties had been so publicly canvassed that the Prime Minister, Stanley Baldwin, appointed a Special Board of Inquiry[5] to look into the Lambert v. Levita case as it affected the British Broadcasting Corporation. The Board was appointed on November 11, 1936, just a week after the formal inauguration of the BBC's television service at Alexandra Palace. Sir John Reith, among others, was asked to give evidence. Although the Board of Inquiry attributed blame for the situation pretty equally between the BBC and Mr Lambert, it used in its report such humiliating phrases as 'We have said that it does not follow that because the BBC were honest in what they did they were also wise'. It was equally humiliating for Sir John Reith that the Corporation, which had achieved so much, should be recommended by the Board of Inquiry to take notice of the helpful advice of the Civil Service in staff matters, and to have Mr Baldwin put on record in his Minute of March 1937 on the Report of the Board of Inquiry that the Prime Minister 'has learnt with satisfaction that the Corporation welcome this offer of assistance'.

The winter of 1936-7 was, therefore, not a good one for Sir John Reith. It was the winter of the first television programmes but this development was overshadowed by the fact that it was also the winter of the abdication crisis. Edward VIII had come to the throne in the previous January; by October gossip about his relations with Mrs Simpson was widespread; by November Stanley Baldwin was issuing warnings to the King about the possible consequences of the situation; in December came the abdication and Sir John Reith drove down to Windsor so that he himself should announce Edward VIII's final broadcast to the nation. He describes the occasion vividly in his autobiography. He does not mention the inauguration in November of the first television service in the world under the auspices of his own creation, the British Broadcasting Corporation.

To Sir John Reith broadcasting was sound—not vision. He has said that he was frightened of television from the start but this clearly did not mean that he felt incapable of managing or running a television service. He was frightened of television, he implies, because he believed that communication by means of vision would be an evil which would be damaging to the country and to the world. In answer to a question put by Malcolm Muggeridge in a television interview about whether he had seen the potentialities of television, he himself asked a question: 'Has the introduction of television been to the hurt of this country, of the world?' The answer which he himself would have given was plain. It was to the hurt. Yet he had been in a position to influence, in the most powerful fashion, the development of the new medium. The standards which he had set for the British Broadcasting Corporation were to have their effect in later years upon the television services of the world. But in the summer of 1938 he was able to abandon this vital rôle and to leave the BBC when television was in its infancy because he did not feel 'fully stretched'. It is difficult to believe that he had really been aware of the potentialities of television.

He had other and more important anxieties. Ever since 1933 he had been involved in discussions about the rôle of the BBC in the event of war. War now seemed imminent. In war, the BBC and its Director-General would have to work under a Minister of Information. In November 1937 Reith had offered to resign from his post of Director-General of the BBC. He did resign in June 1938.

In comparison with these personal and national preoccupations the development of television seemed of negligible importance. So, with few people interested and practically no one watching, television producers were free during these first years to experiment with programmes and to discover what the possibilities and limitations of the new medium actually were.

The conditions in which they operated were extraordinary. There were two television studios, one using the Baird system and the other Marconi/EMI, though as early as February 1937 the Baird system was dropped as being the less effective. The studios were built in a corner of Alexandra Palace, a vast nineteenth-century edifice constructed on high ground north of London to be North London's answer to South London's Crystal Palace and a centre of entertainment and culture for the northern suburbs. Its huge echoing halls contained a roller-skating rink and an immense organ; its empty corridors were full of mouldering statues to the Victorian virtues. Working there was like attempting to creat the most modern form of visual communication in a deserted railway station. It was wind-swept and shabby; the offices were primitive; the control gallery of the main studio was a tiny creaking platform reached by climbing a dangerous iron ladder; ancillary services were minimal.

Yet experiment went on. There was an abounding enthusiasm. Most of this was directed to the production of plays. Week after week between 1936 and 1939 the main efforts of the new television service, of producers and designers, lighting men and studio managers, costume and make-up departments, as well as money and energy, went into the production of studio plays, mostly stage plays adapted, effectively or otherwise, for television. The plays were ambitious: *Hassan* and *Murder in the Cathedral*; *Journey's End* and *The Duchess of Malfi*; *The Emperor Jones* and *Androcles and the Lion*; *Candida* and *The Insect Play*; *Cyrano de Bergerac* and *Julius Caesar*. These were seen at home by viewers on screens of about ten inches by eight. Transmission hours varied but were approximately from 8.30 p.m. to 10 p.m. A typical evening's viewing consisted of a play transmitted 'live'; a Gaumont-British or Movietone newsreel and a Walt Disney cartoon film. As the service developed there were other ingredients. Famous entertainers began to appear; viewers at home were able to see Arthur Askey and George Robey, Ruth Draper and Lupino Lane, Bea Lillie and Nelson Keys; the Russian Ballet danced 'Les Sylphides'; there were turns from cabaret; there was a Noël Coward revue.

But the main preoccupation was with drama. This was partly due to the practical circumstances of television. With limited studio space, money and effort, it was convenient to be able to fill an hour or more of television with a single production. A more varied output made greater demands on studios and on resources generally. But the overwhelming interest in plays was also the result of the pre-occupation of producers and of the backgrounds from which they had been recruited. There was no pool of experienced television producers on which to draw. This was the first regular television service in the world. Production staff came therefore largely from the theatre, from films and from sound radio. They arrived trailing with them the attitudes which had been shaped by their previous experiences. Both the theatre and the cinema were visual media; sound broadcasting was not. The men from the cinema and from the theatre seemed, and indeed felt themselves to be, professionals in visual communication and despised the people from sound radio as

33

inexperienced amateurs. Communication by means of talk was generally considered to be poor television and news continued for many years to mean newsreels.

By 1939, however, if news was still lacking and drama still dominant, television had revealed itself to be a democratic medium. The use of electronic (as distinct from film) cameras made it possible for television viewers at home to see distant events at the moment when they were actually happening. Privileges hitherto available only to the few were extended to the many. Viewers did not have to wait for a newspaper report of a football match or a horse race to know the results; nor did they have to rely upon the verbal descriptions of a radio commentator. They had first-hand, not second-hand, knowledge; and were less dependent upon what they were told by others since they could check the accuracy of any report against their own experience. This was television's unique contribution to communication; it made television different from any other medium and was the basic cause of television's profound impact upon any system of representative democratic government.

But that was for the future. Between 1936 and 1939 politicians and politics scarcely impinged upon the television screen. Current affairs programmes were few and simple, limited in the main to short, informed commentaries, mostly on foreign affairs, given by J. F. Horrabin and illustrated by maps which he himself drew; to occasional talks by the author-traveller, Peter Fleming; and to some illustrated lessons in British history given by Harold Nicolson.

Nevertheless the service as a whole had made an impact. It was hoped that the Radio Exhibition, planned to take place at Olympia in August 1939, would result in a breakthrough in the sales of television sets and that by the following year there would be 80,000 instead of the current figure of around 20,000. But war came first. On August 31, 1939, women and children began to be evacuated from London. Television signals could act as direction finders for enemy bombers. So, on September 1, the television service was abruptly closed down in the middle of a Walt Disney cartoon film. War was declared two days later. The trained television staff was dispersed; Alexandra Palace was put to military uses; television equipment was wrapped in dust sheets. The first television service in the world ceased to be operational and was not started again for nearly seven years.

[3]

Television Starts Again

1946-1950

At first sight it seems extraordinary that a group of eminent men, many of whom were closely concerned with the conduct of the war, should be asked in the midst of war to give time to consider how Britain could be provided with television programmes after the war.

Yet as early as September 1943 the Lord President of the Council, Clement Attlee, set up a committee under the chairmanship of Lord Hankey 'To prepare plans for the reinstatement and the development of the television service after the war'.[1]

The reasons were, however, far from frivolous. They had nothing to do with the quality of television entertainment nor with any appreciation of the potentialities of television as a means of political communication. The development of post-war television in Britain was simply an aspect of general post-war planning. Britain had established an early lead in television and the manufacture of television equipment was an industry which might be capable of expansion. It could perhaps help Britain's balance of payments and provide employment for demobilised men.

So the Hankey Committee was asked to give special consideration to the guidance which should be given to manufacturers 'with a view specially to the development of the export trade'. A flourishing export trade, it was considered, would have to be built upon a growing home market and this in turn upon a successful television service. To ensure these the Committee was instructed to prepare a plan 'for the provision of a service to, at any rate, the larger centres of population within a reasonable period after the end of the war'.

The fact that any such expansion was bound to make television politically significant was ignored by the Hankey Committee. A service which was confined to some 20,000 viewers in the south-east corner of England mattered little in national politics. But as soon as television had anything like a national coverage its potentialities as a method of political communication were bound to be discovered

35

and used. Both the Director-General of the BBC, Sir William Haley, and its Deputy Director-General, Sir Noel Ashbridge, were members of the Committee. It is not surprising therefore that any political problems should have been dismissed by recommending that the BBC should run the post-war television service and that the Minister responsible for sound broadcasting should also be responsible for television. It is more surprising that it allowed its financial and technological recommendations to be so largely governed by what was to prove a will-of-the-wisp—the possible showing of television in cinemas.

Cinema interests were understandably afraid that television would affect attendances in cinemas. This was particularly likely when great sporting and national events, the Derby, a Coronation and so on, could be seen by viewers at home at the moment when they were happening. Before the war a few cinemas had attempted to project television pictures of such events on to large screens so that audiences in the cinema could see them. But the definition of television pictures was not suitable for cinemas. So the Hankey Committee, bemused by the importance of having television in cinemas as well as in people's homes, said that television must try to develop a line standard suitable for cinema viewing. They declared that 'the aim should be to approach cinema standard. We think that the definition should eventually be of the order of 1,000 lines and that the introduction of colour and stereoscopic effects should be considered'.

They were assured that once such a line standard had been achieved cinemas would want to show television transmissions. This would make it possible for cinemas to be charged a special licence fee. The prospect of such a source of revenue was very welcome. For the problem of how to pay for a service as expensive as television and how to provide the capital sums necessary if television were to be extended throughout the country obviously defeated the Committee.

They had examined the possibility of sponsoring, but did not find it to be the answer. In an interesting comment they said, 'It is quite clear that until the television service is well developed commercial interests would not be willing to incur large expenditure . . . owing for example to the limited audience served'. They recommended that viewers should be asked to pay a special television licence fee of £1 in addition to the licence fee they paid for receiving sound radio programmes. But for some years television audiences would be small and the revenue from this source inadequate. They also recommended a cinema licence fee—but noted that the amount of such a fee and the date of its introduction would have to be considered later.

So the Hankey Committee took the remarkable course of recommending an immediate start for the post-war television service and its rapid extension throughout the country without giving any clear indication of how such a service should be paid for. It merely expressed the pious hope that the aim should be to make the television service self-supporting 'although it will clearly not be possible to achieve this in the early stages of development'.

If the Hankey Committee failed to solve the problem of television finance it failed even more remarkably to understand the fundamental difference between communication by means of television and communication to a cinema audience. Fundamental to television is that it is received at home. Millions of individuals may be viewing simultaneously; but the individual viewer watching in his own sitting room is not physically aware of those others. The communication appears to be to him. So television is a much more personal and direct medium of communication than the cinema. Television viewers could, and do, watch at home with pleasure on their small screens some of the products of the film industry. But the direct personal approach which suits television does not suit audiences viewing in a cinema.

It was this personal approach which made the success on television of the Richard Dimblebys and the Cliff Michelmores and, in the USA, of Edward R. Murrow. And it was because a direct and personal approach to the viewer suited television that it was bound to be used by politicians in ways which the cinema had never attempted.

Fortunately the failure of the Hankey Committee to understand the nature of television communication did little actual harm, for the only one of its recommendations which was effective in practice was that the post-war television service should start as soon as possible. This meant on 405 lines; that it would operate again from Alexandra Palace, inconvenient and unsuitable though it was; and that reception at the outset would once more be limited to forty miles or so around London. But it also meant that television's future line standards, its relationship to the cinema and to politics, were developed by people working in television and not as considered theoretically desirable by a Committee of busy men whose members

were largely ignorant of anything but the technological and administrative aspects of television.*

The Hankey Committee reported on December 29, 1944. In July
1945 there was a General Election and a Labour Government with
Mr Attlee as Prime Minister came into power. In October 1945 the
new Government accepted 'in substance' the recommendations of
the Hankey Committee. Television was to start again as soon as
possible and was to be under the control of the BBC. And on June
7, 1946 the post-war television service, operating from Alexandra
Palace and on 405 lines, went on the air in time to show the Victory
Parade with Richard Dimbleby giving the commentary.

But it was not until a month later that the Labour Government
issued its White Paper on Broadcasting Policy[2] which included not
only the Government's proposals for the reorganising of broadcasting services after the war but also its plans for the financing of
the television service. The broadcasting situation was urgent since
the BBC's current Charter and Licence were due to expire in
December 1946. The Attlee Government contended that during
much of the period of the current Charter and Licence the BBC had
been operating under abnormal war-time conditions. There was
also, it considered, too little time for a Committee of Inquiry to
make a thorough investigation. It therefore proposed that the
BBC's Charter and Licence should be renewed for five years without
waiting for a report from a Committee of Inquiry. Such a Committee
would, however, be appointed as soon as possible—it was eventually
to be the Beveridge Committee—and would report before the end of
the five-year period.

The Government's proposals were hotly contended. Winston
Churchill tabled a motion in the House of Commons which opposed
any extension of the BBC's Charter without a report from a Committee of Inquiry. Churchill's motion was supported by a hundred
members of Parliament. The BBC, though riding high as a result of
the acknowledged success of its war-time operations, was seen to be

* None of them had any experience of making television programmes
There were two representatives of the Post Office and one of the Treasury;
two scientists of great reputation, Sir Edward Appleton and Sir John Cock-
croft, and the Deputy Director-General of the BBC who was that eminent
engineer, Sir Noel Ashbridge. The Director-General, Sir William Haley,
who might have been expected to represent programme attitudes, was a
journalist from Reuters and the Press Association who had come into the

politically vulnerable. Its future and that of the broadcasting standards for which it stood might depend upon the view the Beveridge Committee took of the evidence given by those who wanted at almost any cost to break the BBC's monopoly. In comparison with those great issues the development of television seemed of minor importance.

With hindsight it can be said that those in charge of sound broadcasting during these post-war years were repressive and unenterprising in their treatment of television. Their attitudes were due to a number of separate factors. One was money. A second was the enormous self-confidence built up during the war within the BBC's sound services. A third was the character and approach to television of the Director-General of the BBC, Sir William Haley. All these had some bearing upon the development of television in Great Britain and upon its use for political communication.

Money was important. The Government had accepted the recommendation of the Hankey Committee that the post-war television service should be controlled by the BBC. Not only that, in its endeavours to solve the problem of financing television it had arrived at a method which in fact ensured that the television service would be financially dependent upon the sound services. The cost of television was estimated as being around £2 millions a year. The White Paper of 1946 stated that 'Initially the cost of this service will not be covered by the issue of special television licences, and the cost of the service during the development period will have to be met to a substantial extent from the proceeds of ordinary sound broadcasting licences. The Government consider that this course is justified, since the development of television will ultimately be of direct benefit to a substantial proportion of broadcasting licensees.' In the circumstances, the Government raised the cost of wireless receiving licences for sound programmes from ten shillings to £1 and issued an additional £1 licence for receiving television programmes. This arrangement suited the BBC; as one body, financially speaking, it was the better able to ensure that its standards were observed in television as in sound radio.

These standards included the handling of political broadcasting. In the White Paper of 1946 the Government had said that it did not

---

BBC only in 1943, four years after the pre-war television service had closed down.

'think it desirable to attempt to reduce to written rules the principles which should govern the Corporation in regard to political broadcasting. It must be the responsibility of the Corporation to maintain an impartial balance between political parties and in exercising this responsibility the Corporation will, no doubt, act in concert with the representatives of the political parties, as was done in the pre-election period in 1945 when the Corporation provided facilities to nominated spokesmen of the main political parties and studiously avoided in its own programmes any expression of political opinion.'

The principles which governed the Corporation in regard to political broadcasting would apply also to television. But television was generally considered to be a light-weight service and it was not evident in 1946 either to politicians or to most of the seniors at Broadcasting House that it was a suitable medium for political communication. Their view was shared by many at Alexandra Palace.

Nevertheless, as early as June 1946, Mrs Mary Adams, who was now in charge of television talks, put forward a scheme for controversial political discussions on television. The idea was taken up by Maurice Gorham, the Controller of Television, who asked the views of the Director-General. Sir William Haley replied on June 23, 1946:

'I think there are many other things we should concentrate on developing on television before we get around to political discussions. The main purpose of such discussions must be to inform a large democratic audience and at present television does not possess that. I am most anxious that we should concentrate on the serious side of television talks in fields which will be most fruitful and constructive and I don't think political discussions (to which in any case television can add nothing) are high on such a list.'

If television, in the opinion of the Director-General, could add nothing to political discussions, it was even less suited, he considered, to the presentation of news. During the months of preparation before the post-war television service started, Maurice Gorham sent in a suggestion from a television producer that *Illustrated News* would be possible as a regular part of television programmes. In addition to a daily or weekly newsreel, which television should itself make instead of being dependent, as before the war, on cinema newsreels, it would be possible to present the sound radio news bulletins with suitable illustrations. Maurice Gorham had seen a demonstration. 'I now feel,' he wrote, in a memorandum of June 1946, 'that it would be possible for us to have very slight alterations in an existing news bulletin and yet make it interesting in vision.'

The suggestion eventually reached the Director-General, who replied crushingly in August:

1 'I doubt whether the implications of a completely visual news *bulletin* have still been fully comprehended.

2 'There is all the difference between a news bulletin and a news reel. The first is a vital public service charged with responsibilities of all kinds. The second, in essence, is entertainment.

3 'The fact that the text of the bulletin would have to be received some hours in advance of transmission time (even with the possibility of late editions) shows the necessity that would arise to subordinate the primary functions of news to the needs of visual presentation. Any such subordination would prejudice all sorts of values on which the BBC's great reputation for news has been founded.

4 'I would like to re-iterate that I see no objections to the development of news reels (if they are thought worth developing) as an ingredient in television so long as they supplement and do not supplant the primary news bulletin.*

5 'The whole development of television is surely the right order of priorities. I should have thought that whatever manpower, time, thinking and effort we have available could be devoted to many other things that would more certainly benefit both television and its viewers.

6 'The matter can be re-opened when that more essential development has taken place.'

The cautious attitude at Broadcasting House to television news was rooted in a long history. From the beginning of broadcasting there had been special anxieties about broadcast news. These sprang from two sources—the jealous fears of the Press that broadcast news would affect the sale of newspapers, and the very proper fear which had been felt by the early Committees that it would be all too easy to broadcast irresponsible or slanted news.

Ever since 1923, therefore, the presentation of broadcast news had

---

* This was a radio bulletin which was given on television in sound only, at the end of the television evening.

been hedged about by safeguards. The British Broadcasting Company, under the terms of its first Licence, was allowed to broadcast 'only such news as is obtained from news agencies approved by the Postmaster General'. An arrangement was made under which the news from these agencies was pooled and supplied to the Company upon agreed terms. As a result of pressure from the newspapers the supply was subject to the condition that it should not be broadcast until after 7 p.m. This was to prevent the broadcasting of news earlier in the day affecting the sale of evening newspapers.

Three years later the Press was still representing to the Crawford Committee that broadcast news should not be transmitted 'earlier than the present hour (7 p.m.)' and that it should be supplied only through news agencies. The Crawford Committee did not agree that this stranglehold should be imposed, though it wrapped its decision in vague phrases. But as a result of the determination and tact of Sir John Reith, the BBC began to supplement the news service of the agencies from its own sources and to send its own correspondents abroad. This practice was approved in 1936 by the Ullswater Committee.[3] It recommended that the Corporation should continue to have freedom of choice as to the sources of news which it used and wanted no bar to developments which might be required in the future. 'Television, for example, must be free from restrictions as to hours.'

But though the Ullswater Committee recommended freedoms it also issued words of warning. 'The influence of broadcasting on the political life of the country is brought to bear not only by speeches, talks and reports, but also by the provision of news. It is therefore of the utmost importance that the news distributed by the BBC should be a fair selection of items impartially presented.' And again, 'We regard it as vital that the BBC should maintain a strong and impartial editorial staff. In the presentment of news, simplicity is desirable and the BBC should be as impersonal as possible.'

The recommendations of the Ullswater Committee were endorsed in the new Charter issued to the BBC in 1937.* This stated that one of the objects of the Corporation was 'to collect news of, and information relating to, current events in any part of the world and in any manner that may be thought fit and to establish and subscribe to

---

* The Draft Charter and Licence was presented to Parliament by the Postmaster General (Major G. C. Tryon) in December 1936 (Cmd. 5329).

news agencies'. But in exercising these rights the BBC remained highly conscious of the warnings of the Ullswater Committee. Its editorial staff must be strong and impartial; news must be presented simply and impersonally. Moreover the war had increased the BBC's sense of the immense responsibility and importance of broadcast news and by 1946 the News Division at Broadcasting House began to seem to be custodian of everything the BBC stood for. News was sacred and must not be imperilled.

In my own early days as a producer in sound radio this was quickly made clear to me. A famous man who was a highly successful broadcaster did not want to come to London to give a talk after the Sunday 9 p.m. news. He would like to record the talk earlier in the week. There was no difficulty about that. The problem was that he did not want it known that the talk had been recorded. One of the BBC rules was that if a broadcast were recorded the fact had to be stated. He said that in his view this was quite unnecessary; the public would react differently to his broadcast if they knew it was recorded, not 'live'; they liked to feel he was actually there talking to them at that moment. And no one would be able to tell the difference; recordings were now so good. He was determined and important. I took the matter higher. Was it possible, on this occasion, to break the rules? No. I took it higher still. I was told that the BBC could not accept the argument. Even if only two people knew that he was at home and not in the studio this would undermine faith in the word of the BBC when either explicitly or implicitly it said that a broadcast was 'live' and not recorded. Once you undermined faith in this way there was no telling where it would end. Trust was integral. Any breach of faith with the public, I was told in what was practically a hushed whisper, might mean that people would not believe the BBC news.

I found this argument convincing. It was upon attitudes of this kind that the standards of the BBC had been built and the worldwide reputation of its news services during the war had rested. I was to use it again and again in television when the question was discussed of whether it should or should not be made clear, even if only in the small print in the *Radio Times*, that a programme had been recorded. It affected my attitudes to arguments about whether acted scenes could be used in a documentary in combination with scenes of direct actuality. It was to be central to certain famous disputes such as those which reached the headlines on the occasion of a report in 'Panorama' from Scotland when the question of whether some incidents had or had not been faked to make a point in a current affairs programme was passionately debated. The central position, with which I agreed, was always that the BBC must keep faith with its public. There could be discussion about interpretation but none about the principle.

It was possible, therefore, to have some sympathy with Broadcasting House when it showed what seemed a lack of enterprise in relation to television news. Standards must be maintained, and the presentation of news in television in ways which were simple and impersonal as well as impartial was not easy. In one sense television could present instant news in a way not possible in any other medium. By using outside broadcast cameras television could let viewers see events at the moment they were taking place. But getting outside broadcast units to any particular places was a complex business; it took time and the areas from which they could transmit were limited. For events known well in advance, Royal occasions, football matches and race meetings, they were excellently suited. But for unpredictable developments, news which broke suddenly anywhere in the world, outside broadcasts were useless and were to remain largely so.* Many years later when a BBC outside broadcast unit was in Moscow preparing the first live coverage of the May Day Parade it caught, ten days before the first vision tests, the arrival of Major Gagarin after his orbit of the earth. But even in 1962 that was a rare combination of luck and enterprise. In the years between 1946 and 1950 it was an impossibility.

If the news were to be visually presented and outside broadcast cameras were not generally suitable there remained film. But that was slow. It had to be processed and edited and was out of date before it got to the television screen. And film was not as instantly malleable as words. If, in the opinion of an experienced news editor, a news story merited only twenty seconds but there was some specially shot film of it which could not really make its point in less than half a minute, what should he do? Abandon news values and show the film even if this meant cutting the length of another and more important news story of which there was only meagre film

* It took a long time for light-weight outside broadcast colour cameras to become practicable but by 1973 they were being used in light-weight outside broadcast units. Their future possibilities are discussed in an article by G. D. Cook in No. 96 of *BBC Engineering*, November 1973.

illustration? But that would be an abandonment of BBC news standards.

News in television, as Sir William Haley had feared, would be governed by its visual interest and by what had been shot and edited rather than by judgment of its real importance. That was unthinkable. But what was the alternative? The news reader could be seen reading the news. But that was certainly not keeping the news impersonal. In sound radio the most fantastic steps had been taken to keep the personalities of the news readers out of the news. They did not write it themselves; it was written for them: they merely read it. They were enjoined to use the same tone of voice in announcing the death of a famous politician as in announcing the results of a football match. Anything else would be comment on the news and this was not what the BBC should do.

To these attitudes there was added the temperament of the Director-General, Sir William Haley, who, like Sir John Reith, was more in sympathy with communication by words than by visual means. It was impossible, or at least I found it so, not to admire him. He was a strong Director-General, one of those who have made British broadcasting, by its adherence to high standards, an example to, and in many respects the envy of, the world. He conveyed a sense of total reliability; of being trustworthiness personified. In everything he did or said there was revealed the combination of qualities which made him remarkable. He was high-minded, yet homespun. He had a strong sense of moral responsibility but his decisions were rooted in reality. At meetings where programme policies were decided and which were attended by his senior staff, he would raise a subject of importance and lay it open for discussion. The talk was often as brilliant, as glancing and as subtle as that of an Oxford high table. He would let it run for what sometimes seemed excessive length, listening carefully but taking no part himself. Then, suddenly, he would thank the meeting, say that the discussion had been very helpful and that it was now clear to him what the course of action should be. He outlined it. His decision, cutting through the dialectic, went to the heart of the matter, and usually seemed so sensible as to be inevitable. He did not wait for comment but went on to the next subject.

His whole impressive approach to broadcasting might have been summed up by some words of Sir John Seeley which Sir William Haley himself quoted in a lecture[4] he gave to the Manchester

Literary and Philosophical Society after he had left the BBC. 'Public opinion is necessarily guided by a few large, plain, simple ideas. Where the great interests of the country are plain, and the great maxims of its government unmistakable, it may be able to judge securely even in questions of vast magnitude. But public opinion is liable to be bewildered when it is called upon to enter into subtleties, draw nice distinctions, apply one set of principles here and another there.' He quoted this with approbation. And, in so far as I myself saw him at work, he seemed to be guided in action by an exactly similar concept. He was possessed always with the desire to use broadcasting to transmit 'a few large simple ideas' and was impatient of 'subtleties and nice distinctions'. It was not that he himself was unsubtle or that he could not make nice distinctions if he chose. But he was concerned with communication to millions.

This was as true of television as of sound broadcasting. Yet he could not see it. Television was his blind spot. He appeared to distrust and dislike it and his attitudes, like those of Sir John Reith, seemed to be rooted in a moral disapproval of the medium itself. If his approach to television had been different, if he had seen the potentialities as well as the problems of television communication, commercial television, for good or ill, might not have come in Great Britain, or at any rate not at the moment when it did. He was opposed to commercial television and yet the policies he pursued in relation to the BBC's own television service helped to bring it about.*

The strict control of the administrators and accountants at Broadcasting House over television administration and finance was maintained and, on the programme side, there was a policy of integration: heads of programme output departments at Broadcasting House would also control departments which had a similar output in television. These measures would ensure that the standards which had been built up with so much devotion in sound broadcasting would not be jeopardised by the brash young television service; it would also mean that as television expanded there would be jobs for those made redundant by any decline in sound broad-

* Norman Collins deeply resented Sir William's failure to appreciate the importance of television and also his own treatment by the BBC. These were the main causes of his resignation. A result was that he became a driving force behind the campaign to break the BBC's Television monopoly. Lord Hill in *Behind the Screen* says that it was to Norman Collins of ATV 'more than anyone else the creation of Independent Television is due'.

casting. And schemes of training were initiated so that seniors from sound radio would gain some knowledge of television operations with a view to the eventual integration of the sound and television services.

It soon became clear to those working in television that 'integration' in practice would mean that trusted figures from Broadcasting House, whose whole experience had been in sound radio, would become overlords of television as well as of radio departments. Personal and professional hackles rose. This was not only for selfish reasons. Promotion, certainly, would be denied to television people if the top jobs were all to be given to those working in radio at Broadcasting House. But the despair felt at Alexandra Palace was mainly professional. Television producers did not believe that those in control at Broadcasting House would ever understand that television was a different medium from sound broadcasting. They were afraid that they would be asked, even ordered, to produce television programmes which could not possibly work.

The failure of the BBC to give more independence and responsibility to its television service was to be criticised later by the Beveridge Committee and became a factor of some importance in the campaign to start commercial television. Meanwhile the battle for independence was valiantly and to some extent successfully fought by Norman Collins and Cecil McGivern, whom Sir William Haley himself appointed in 1947 to be respectively the Controller of Television and the Head of Television Programmes.

[4]

Television Gets Closer to Politics

1947-1950

Appointing Norman Collins and Cecil McGivern to run the television service during a policy of integration between the radio and
television services of the BBC was rather like appointing a couple of
generals to crush a rebellion only to find that the generals promptly
joined the rebels. Both were experienced radio producers, one in
talks and the other in features. They understood programme production, devoted their great energies to developing the expression of
ideas and information in the medium of television, were at one in
their determination to increase what they called 'the intelligence' of
the television service and so lessen its dependence upon drama and
purchased films, to strengthen talks output and bring television
closer to the actual world where its unique strengths lay.

It is often said of the mass media that the public do not know the
people who really run them, who determine their policies and harness
their power to specific ends. This is certainly true of broadcasting
and perhaps even more true of television. The faces of the men in
real authority do not appear on the screen; their names are not on
the credits at the end of programmes. Millions of people who would
have recognised a Richard Dimbleby would have been hard put to
it to name the Chief Assistant to the Director-General or the Head
of Television Programmes.

So, in the years between 1947 and 1950, when Richard Dimbleby
was already becoming a familiar television figure, few people knew
anything of the powerful influence on television of Norman Collins
and Cecil McGivern. Yet these two men more than any others
shaped the television service of the BBC, set it moving along new
paths and made it a force which in time affected the nature of
Independent Television.

Collins and McGivern were very different and did not always see
eye to eye. Collins was very much aware of politics and of the relationship of politics to power. McGivern disliked politics and believed

that their broadcasting coverage should be left to sound radio. He had come up the BBC ladder, first as a contributor to programmes in the North; then, in London, he had written and produced some of the best sound radio features ever transmitted by the BBC. Collins, still only forty, was a successful novelist. He had come into the BBC in 1941 and worked in overseas talks. By 1944 he was responsible for all broadcasting to the Forces. In 1945 he had succeeded Maurice Gorham as Head of the Light Programme. Now he had again succeeded Gorham as Controller of Television. He was in charge of the service as a whole. McGivern was responsible to him for television programmes.

To the television veterans of 1936–9 they were interlopers from Broadcasting House who knew nothing about television and precious little about film and who had come to teach their grandmothers to suck eggs. So for Collins and McGivern there was, at the beginning, a constant fight to persuade the television service to accept the new management; to get producers to realise the need for greater professionalism in programme output; to get servicing departments to give better service to the production departments. The result was that the Controller of Television and the Head of Television Programmes seemed always to be asking for the impossible when already everybody was over-driven, when resources were inadequate and conditions appalling.

Conditions certainly *were* appalling and resources certainly inadequate. When Norman Collins and Cecil McGivern asked me in 1948 to move from Broadcasting House to television they suggested that I should spend a few days at Alexandra Palace before making up my mind. I went; I saw the faces, grey with fatigue, of other television talks producers. I climbed the dangerous iron ladder to the small crowded control gallery of Studio A. I was bewildered by the complexities of television production. I found that my office would be a tiny attic room reached by going into the open air in the rain and the wind, past the mouldering statues of Alexandra Palace; that it had no window, only a skylight; that it was warmed by a spluttering gas fire; and that I would share it, at first at any rate, with another producer, four telephones, two secretaries and two clattering typewriters. I discovered that though producers of plays were given the help of designers in getting sets for their productions, no such assistance was available to talks producers who had to make their own selection from stock sets in the store. There were two. One was the Charles the Second set. The other was the Louis XV set. Both were damaged and dirty from over-use.

I came back and wrote a formal refusal of the much appreciated offer to work as a producer in television. This was in spite of the fact that I had wanted to go. I had always, as Collins and McGivern knew, been interested in television. I believed that television, being a more complete medium than sound radio, would be of importance to the world. I had seen the first television programme produced in Studio A at Alexandra Palace in the summer of 1936 and had written regularly about television in *The Listener* between 1936 and 1939. But now, in the conditions of talks production at Alexandra Palace in 1948, I was afraid that I would not be capable of enduring the sheer physical strains of working there even if I could master the difficult techniques of television production.

Cecil McGivern persuaded me to change my mind. But in the following years I often wondered whether I had been mad to change the civilised decorum of Broadcasting House for an existence which frequently seemed intolerable, which meant working late into the night in underground film cutting rooms at the back of Alexandra Palace, returning along interminable dark corridors with an escort carrying an electric torch to keep off the rats and then, wearily, taking an infrequent bus down the hill to the underground station at Wood Green. It was not surprising that the members of the television service found the constant demands of McGivern and Collins for more and better programmes, more and better services, sometimes difficult to endure.

They won support largely because they identified themselves with the service. If they were fighting television people in order to achieve more professional standards they were also fighting Broadcasting House for more independence for television within the BBC; for more money and more resources for television programmes; a greater freedom from the rigid administrative and policy rulings which had grown up within sound radio but which could not be applied to television.

The battle at Alexandra Palace was tough, but at least it was fought on their own territory and they were in a position of strength. The battle with Broadcasting House was different; here they were in a position of weakness; sound was the father figure, established and responsible, television the spendthrift and tiresome adolescent. It could not pay its way and yet made incessant demands for more money. Its management, though enterprising, could never really be trusted to understand that the BBC, in spite of its tremendous war-time achievements, was vulnerable and that a political gaffe on television could damage the whole great edifice of the Corporation.

This attitude affected the television service in great as well as small ways. In December 1947 only a few months after Collins had been appointed Controller of Television, there was a reorganisation of the higher echelons of the BBC. A Board of Management consisting of five Directors was created to assist the Director-General. Controllers were subordinate to Directors. A number of Controllers were upgraded to be Directors. The Controller of Television was not one of them. He had no seat on the Board of Management; he was responsible, for programmes as a whole and the running of the television service in general, to the Director of Home Broadcasting; for everything to do with politics, current affairs and other policy matters to the Director of the Spoken Word. Television engineers were responsible to the Director of Engineering; questions of finance, recruitment and payment of staff and all general services came under the Director of Administration.

I myself met some of the pinpricking administrative obstinacy which was the result of centralising the control of all services at Broadcasting House. Sometimes the situations were so ludicrous that it was impossible to believe them. I had started, for instance, with the full approval of the Controller of Television and the Head of Television Programmes a new discussion series based on theses put forward in published books. It was necessary to have half-a-dozen copies of each book so that everyone taking part could have a copy to study simultaneously, and other copies had to go to design and graphic departments to be enlarged for backgrounds, used to make captions and so on. I had found that the 'props' department could supply pretty well anything from a performing giraffe to a brass band so I simply ordered on my 'props' list half-a-dozen copies of the required book. I was told that it was quite impossible for 'props' to supply these: they could provide everything else which was ordered; they could supply whole bookcases full of imitation books, but not real books for actual use. These could be bought only by the librarian at Broadcasting House. The librarian refused. Why could not a single copy be passed from hand to hand? And it was quite out of the question for a book to be destroyed as the result of the action of a graphics department. Memos went to and fro.

I daresay that in time I could have got my six books from Broad-casting House but I had no time. The programme had to go on the air. Its budget ran into hundreds of pounds; the cost of six books, in comparison, was negligible. I went out and bought them; broke the rules and fiddled the expense account. These affairs, however trivial, were grit in the machinery.

Television producers were getting a reputation at Broadcasting House for being difficult. To television producers the authorities at Broadcasting House seemed to be totally ignorant of the practicali-ties of production in a visual medium.

It was difficult for those close to the day-to-day struggle, as by this time I was myself, to appreciate what was at stake. Television was soon to be a national service. By the autumn of 1948 about 60,000 television licences were in force. That meant that there were about three times that number of viewers. In 1949 the Government approved the BBC's development plan as a result of which television would be available to 80 % of the population and so give television coverage within the next five years to nearly forty million people. Was this new nation-wide service to operate with the standards and attitudes which had made the sound radio services of the British Broadcasting Corporation so remarkable and so universally admired? Anything else would seem to be a betrayal of everything the BBC stood for and a denial of the trust of Parliament, which had appreci-ated the potential power of television and had placed it under the control of a body which had proved itself to be imaginatively respon-sible in the handling of that other, but related, medium of mass communication, broadcasting in sound only.

The problem for the authorities at Broadcasting House during the next few years was how to ensure the observance by television of BBC standards without destroying the vitality of a new and rapidly expanding service. To those working in television the problem seemed rather different; how to convince the authorities at Broad-casting House, few of whom had any practical experience of the television operation, that television was a different medium from sound broadcasting; that political comment could be made as effec-tively by a shrug of the shoulders as by a written statement; that the straight talk, which was the accepted method for all direct political communication in sound radio, was difficult in television; and that the nature of editorial control in current affairs programmes had to be totally different when vision was an ingredient as well as words.

I became involved in discussions of this kind because during the next few years I began to specialise in the television treatment of current affairs. It was Collins rather than McGivern who encouraged me to do this. McGivern's interest lay in programmes which dealt with human rather than with political situations. He wanted to develop television documentaries. He was tortured by his sense of responsibility to the viewing public for the quality of what went on the screen. He watched television output with an obsessive passion, infuriated by any shoddiness in thought, in feeling, in style or in the detail of production. His praise was generous. His criticisms were ruthless. Producers winced when they received, the morning after a programme, his withering memoranda detailing exactly what was wrong and demanding improvement. Both his praise and his criticisms were respected. The whole service knew that they were never based on self-interest, and never malicious. They were always rooted in his conviction that what the service was doing, even down to the most trivial detail, mattered because human beings were watching it and they deserved the best.

Norman Collins was increasingly occupied with the bitter battle which he was fighting within the BBC for more freedom and more resources for television. But he was also determined to make television output more topical. The result was that the period between June 1947, when he was put in charge of the television service, and October 1950 when he abruptly resigned, showed remarkable developments in the relationship between television and politics. One was the growth of television journalism. A second was the start of regular discussions about political matters in which Members of Parliament took part. A third was the reporting in television of political events—notably the results of the General Election of 1950.

I myself was closely concerned with two of these developments—the growth of television journalism by the regular reporting of foreign affairs in 'Foreign Correspondent' which began in 1949 and the presentation on television of the results of the General Election in February 1950.

'Foreign Correspondent' was made possible by the BBC's decision to produce its own newsreels. The small existing film department was enlarged, a new complement of film cameramen, film editors and script writers was recruited; and the first television newsreel was transmitted on January 5, 1948. The BBC's newsreels were very popular. But they were not news. Nor were they current affairs

53

reporting. And this was what Norman Collins now asked me to attempt. By 1949 I had learnt how to handle television studios and television control galleries and I had persuaded such experienced radio broadcasters as Alan Bullock and Francis Williams and George Woodcock to try their hand at illustrated television argument. The idea behind these programmes was that personally selected visual material would be used as evidence by each person arguing. I felt then, as later, that vision was part of argument, not outside it. And I was interested in having visual material, particularly actuality film, used not as a representation of total truth but as an aspect of truth selected by a particular observer. So I was hostile to what I felt to be the documentary tradition of the cinema where the attitude of one man—the film-maker—was presented as an unchallenged truth rather than merely a selection, however good and well-intentioned, of one aspect of reality chosen by a single person from all the different possible aspects which might have been chosen by others.

I was not concerned, therefore, with making films but in the use of visual images on celluloid as one among many visual tools in the hands of those who were discussing, or reporting upon, events, ideas and places. I would have preferred to use outside broadcasts for this purpose. They were more essentially television instruments and were less hung around with the mystique of the cinema and with the sociological hangover of the Grierson documentary tradition. But for current affairs coverage in television, as for news coverage, they were too cumbersome, too inflexible, and too expensive. Film was more suited to what we wanted to achieve.

The project started very simply. Among the newsreel cameramen was Charles de Jaeger. He had had some journalistic experience and had worked in the BBC's overseas services. He was not so much a film-maker as a kind of cameraman-journalist. He had a European background, spoke a number of languages and knew the European ropes. He was an early advocate of the hand-held camera and this offended some of the technical purists within the film department where he soon became restive. Norman Collins suggested to me that we might send de Jaeger abroad with a silent camera. He could film scenes in, say, Paris and Rome and we could give British viewers a vicarious experience of foreign travel. The programmes could be simple and cheap. There need be no fuss, no elaborate consultations with foreign affairs experts. But they should not merely be travelogues

in the cinema style. Couldn't some of the BBC's former war correspondents provide commentaries? People like Edward Ward were
now freelancing and working for BBC sound features. It should
not be difficult for them to learn the job of giving commentaries
to film.

There was then no cadre of trained television reporters. It was
essential to our plan that reporters in 'Foreign Correspondent'
should appear in the studio; be able to use visual apparatus such as
maps and diagrams as well as know how to handle film. But neither
the BBC's radio correspondents nor newspapermen had experience
of this kind. Even the BBC's newsreels did not need reporters with
these varied abilities: the film men controlled the content: film
cameramen, film editors and the heads and assistant heads of the
film department, most of whom had been trained in the film industry,
decided what film stories should go into the reel: and at what length.
A commentary writer was then employed to write the required
number of words to suit the timing of each shot. He had no hand in
the shaping of the material for which he wrote. He merely provided
words to match a product whose style and content had been prescribed by others.

We were trying to do something different. We hoped to get the
film-makers and the reporters to work together as a creative team
without any of them dominating the other. The visual reports were
the result of co-operation between the cameraman, the reporter, the
film editor and the television producer. The ideas of the reporter
therefore helped to shape the film sequences upon which he commented.

We planned in the first instance simply to visit six European
capitals and 'Six Capitals' was to have been the title of the series
until, on the instructions of Norman Collins, we changed it to the
more resounding 'Foreign Correspondent'. This was something of a
misnomer. These were not political reports though they were
planned with some awareness of the political situation in Europe.
What we were trying to do, in those days of the Marshall Plan and
the Cold War, was to move across Europe from west to east, showing
how Marshall Aid was affecting the countries in the west and how
countries in eastern Europe were able to live under the threat of a
possible Communist invasion.

So we attempted to show something of life in Paris and Rome and
Copenhagen, in Athens and Vienna and Helsinki. The portrait of

each capital started with the usual scenes which any tourist would see, then went on to discover how life was lived by people to whom these cities were home; what they ate and drank; what they paid in rent; how they went to work; what education was possible for their children; what, if any, were their political preoccupations. The idea was not to treat foreign affairs at the ambassadorial or expert level but to let viewers in Britain see for themselves that people who lived in other countries were human beings who bore little resemblance to the caricatures by which they were often represented.

Our second series was more specifically political. Its aim, starting with the Benelux experiment, was to look at the prospects of Western Union and the possibilities of European integration. I felt the need for more informed advice and persuaded Alan Bullock,* who had worked in the BBC's overseas services during the war and was teaching history in Oxford, to act as overall political adviser, to take part in some of the programmes and to help plan the series as a whole. The commentator in the first series had been Edward Ward. In the second he alternated with Chester Wilmot, also an ex-BBC war correspondent. Both were busy men. Chester Wilmot was engaged in writing *The Struggle for Europe*. Edward Ward was much occupied with other work, principally for sound radio.

None of us was satisfied with either series. By later standards they were crude affairs. The film was silent; commentaries were read 'live' by the reporter as he watched the film on a studio monitor. We all lacked experience. Some of the experts who appeared in the studio to discuss the reporter's findings were nervous. Nevertheless 'Foreign Correspondent' was the direct precursor of 'International Commentary' and 'Race Relations in Africa'; 'India's Challenge'; 'Panorama' and 'Tonight'; 'Gallery' and 'Twenty-Four Hours'. Reporting in television on current affairs had come to stay.

Even during the early days of 'Foreign Correspondent' we found that we had to ask ourselves some of the fundamental questions. Television was broadcasting, sight added to sound. What could sight add to political communication? Vision was more concrete than sound; words were better suited than vision to conveying ideas. But could not the very concreteness of vision increase understanding

---

* Later Master of St Catherine's College, Vice-Chancellor of Oxford University and (eventually) Lord Bullock.

of the actual world if it could be added to words? And was it not possible that vision could convey truths which words disguised?

Chester Wilmot crystallised this feeling one day. In a sudden moment of revolt against the euphemisms being used to hide the uglier aspects of war and political oppression, he said, 'I'd like to start a television series which dealt with words. After each word I'd show the reality which lay behind it. And I'd begin with the word "liquidate".'

The shock of seeing the reality behind the words was to be evident in much future television reporting: spectacularly so in the reporting of the war in Vietnam; of race riots in America; of student demonstrations all over the world; of the assassination of President Kennedy, of Martin Luther King and of Robert Kennedy. This is partly because visual reporting in television takes on something of the air of being an outside broadcast of an actual event. It gives the viewer a sense of seeing for himself what is actually there rather than receiving impressions at second hand from somebody else.

In 1949 we were already finding this. Our use of film was influenced by the nature of television. The essence of television was that it could let viewers see for themselves people and places at a distance. Viewers were accustomed to watching on their television screens aspects of the actual world. Outside broadcast units using electronic cameras were too cumbersome for current affairs reporting of the kind we were attempting. But film could be a substitute if it were used with the fidelity of the outside broadcast; if we tried to let the viewer see what he would have seen if he were actually there. This meant that the reporter took the place of the outside broadcast commentator. He identified people and clarified what was happening but did not come between the viewer and what the viewer could see for himself.

Chester Wilmot, himself a brilliant descriptive radio journalist, embraced this new rôle with characteristic insight and enthusiasm. During the second series of 'Foreign Correspondent' we were trying to see how Yugoslavia was recovering from the devastation and paralysis of war. Wilmot, with Charles de Jaeger as cameraman, had managed to get their film out of Yugoslavia uncensored. We looked at the rushes. There was a superb shot taken from the top of a high building and panning down the whole length of the main street of Belgrade. The only moving vehicle was one horse-drawn cart. 'This is the end of descriptive journalism,' said Chester, 'I need only say "Look" and everyone will be able to see for themselves.'

But visual reporting of this kind carries with it immense responsibilities. Even outside broadcasts could be 'slanted'. I had pointed this out in 1947 in a section of a book[1] on the mass media. 'The flavour and importance of television is that we do seem to be seeing for ourselves, and to a great extent that is true. Nevertheless the cameraman must select, as he goes along, the things we shall see. And it might be possible, by a deliberately tendentious, or merely careless, use of the television camera to give a false picture and create prejudices in the viewer's mind. If, for example, a cameraman, in giving a teleview of an election meeting, deliberately picked out for close-ups of the audience the faces of the disgruntled and the objecting and the bored, he might (though there would be correctives which he could not easily control) give a bias to the teleview. And this would be more dangerous in television than in, say, pictures in a newspaper since television feels like seeing for ourselves and therefore more like the truth than anything seen in a newspaper or a cinema film.'

If this were true of outside broadcasts it was even more true of film used in the style of an outside broadcast since film could undergo a sea-change during the processes of editing. And even with total intentions of integrity there were difficult detailed decisions to be made every day. In these early 'Foreign Correspondent' programmes, for instance, we were using silent film. The sound film cameras of those days were too large and heavy for visual current affairs reporting. There were therefore no actual sound effects recorded on the spot. But if the viewer had been there himself he would have heard, say, the music and the tramp of marching feet as a military band went past. Were these sounds not, therefore, part of the actual situation which we were trying to present? So we should surely be closer to the actual if we dubbed on to the film the appropriate sounds from the BBC's sound effects library. But what if the exact sound which we wanted had not been recorded? Would it be permissible, if we saw a bell tolling on a church in Switzerland and there were no available recordings of the bells of that particular church, to dub on to the film a sound which was reasonably like it even if it had in fact been recorded in Copenhagen?

In later years we were to be occupied with much larger problems of integrity in visual reporting than these. But the questions in a sense were always the same: how to apply the standards which had been developed within the BBC to the practical difficulties of a visual medium. This endeavour was complicated in the early days by the fact that most of those within the television service who were professionally competent in the handling of film had grown up within the film industry. They knew little or nothing about the history of the BBC and had little understanding of the reasons behind its attitudes. To those experienced men the television producers who came from sound broadcasting and attempted to use film in their programmes seemed incompetent amateurs. This caused difficulties on both sides.

I came back, for example, after a holiday at the end of the first 'Foreign Correspondent' series to find that Cecil McGivern had asked the film department to use the film which Charles de Jaeger had shot for this series to make some summer programmes on holidaying abroad. I discovered, with perhaps over-righteous indignation, that scenes we had had taken in a Viennese night-club to show the sleaziness of night life in an occupied city were being used in the holiday series to illustrate the attractions of a weekend in Paris. I protested. My grounds were that those viewers who had seen both programmes would not be sure whether the scenes had in fact been shot in Paris or in Vienna and that they therefore would not believe any future reporting in such current affairs series as 'Foreign Correspondent'. It was in essence the argument which I had heard in sound radio in relation to recording and news. If the public were confused about the accuracy and truth of what they were seeing no serious programme would be taken seriously and nothing would be believed.

These problems were solved gradually; partly by the eventual and painful decision that the film department should service the production departments and not itself be a department which created programmes; partly by the emergence within the television service of new men who regarded film simply as one among many tools of visual communication; partly by the change within the television film department itself so that a fresh generation of cameramen and film editors grew up who had been trained within television and who began to use film in ways which were suited to television rather than to presentation in cinemas. With these changes came a new acceptance of standards which were essentially those of the BBC so that the use of a shot taken for a current affairs programme in Vienna to make a holiday programme about Paris became unthinkable and no longer had to be argued.*

The development of television journalism was interrupted by the General Election of 1950. In the autumn of 1949 I was so occupied with 'Foreign Correspondent' that I was scarcely aware that plans for the handling of the election were already being discussed within the BBC. By July 1950 the Labour Government would have been in power for five years. There would have to be a General Election before that. In addition to plans for sound broadcasting there was the question of what part, if any, television should play.

The first phase when, in Sir William Haley's words, television could not reach 'a large democratic audience' was coming to an end. Television was expanding fast. By August 1949 nearly 160,000 television licences were in operation. In November the BBC bought thirteen acres of ground in West London, part of the old White City exhibition site and, with the agreement of the London County Council, was planning to build a great television centre there. In the meanwhile, to supplement the resources of Alexandra Palace, they had bought the Gaumont-British studios in Lime Grove, Shepherds Bush. These had been closed and were now to be converted to television. By December the powerful new transmitter at Sutton Coldfield in the Midlands was bringing television programmes to a near-national audience. By the spring of 1950 it was estimated that television would be within reach of a million viewers.

The lively television outside broadcast and film department at Alexandra Palace had already considered ways of presenting the election campaign. As early as 1948 the Assistant Head of the department, Ian Orr-Ewing (later Lord Orr-Ewing) sent Cecil McGivern a suggestion for covering the campaign by means of outside broadcast cameras and film. The coverage would include the adoption of candidates, canvassing, party meetings, scenes at Town Halls when votes were being counted and also in Trafalgar Square where crowds would be watching a public presentation of the election results on large screens.

---

* This was a crude example of lack of integrity in the making of documentaries, and certainly nothing as crude as this survived. But there were other more subtle problems which continued: one was highlighted in an exchange of letters in *The Times* in August 1975 between Sir Rudolf Peierls, FRS, Robert Reid, a documentary producer, and others, about the integrity of a BBC programme on the making of the Atomic Bomb.

McGivern put these proposals to George Barnes who, at the time, with the strange title of Director of the Spoken Word, was responsible, under the Director-General, for questions of policy and particularly of political matters. George Barnes replied that the suggestion was premature. In October 1949 McGivern presented revised proposals. But George Barnes and the Director-General were more concerned about whether to offer the political parties an opportunity of using television for party election broadcasts, and if so in what form, than in reporting the election campaign. They were, however, influenced by the suggestion that outside broadcast cameras might be put into political meetings. Eventually it was decided to offer each of the three main parties outside broadcast coverage on television of a main election speech given at separate mass meetings in the London area. This would be the equivalent of one television election broadcast for each party.

On December 14 and 15, 1949, plans for the use of broadcasting in the election were discussed with the parties. In a memorandum of December 20, George Barnes reported to Norman Collins, 'The Parties unanimously rejected the idea of televising any of the election broadcasts either by means of an outside broadcast of political meetings or in the studio. Every effort was made to interest them but the matter in their view did not even admit of argument.' The television service was therefore instructed to carry the party election broadcasts in sound only. Moreover, in order to implement the spirit of the attitude of the parties to television, newsreels were not to report election speeches and cameras were not to be taken inside a hall in order to report political meetings.

Since television could carry the election broadcasts only in sound and was prevented from covering the campaign visually, it would seem to be ignoring a major political event. Norman Collins was dissatisfied with this situation. What, for instance, should be shown on the television screen on the night of the poll? There could certainly be a special edition of the newsreel transmitted after the polls had closed at 9 p.m. But could nothing be done about the results? He called meetings of senior staff to discuss this. Most of them thought that the results should be left to sound. Television could add nothing to the detailed reading of figures. There was no point in putting a camera in front of an announcer and watching him read. Also the television service normally closed down around 11 p.m. and it was said to be difficult, even dangerous, from the engineering point of view, to keep the transmitters going much longer. Very few results would have come in by eleven. Anyone who could not wait to see the results in their morning papers could always go over to sound radio at the end of the television evening.

Programmes in television tend to grow out of one another. The eventual presentation on television of the results of the General Election of 1950 arose largely from 'Foreign Correspondent' and the enthusiasm of Chester Wilmot. He put his recollections on paper at the time. His notes state that:

'On Jan. 11 Attlee announced the date of the election.* I was lunching that day with Grace Wyndham Goldie, who produced for Television the Foreign Correspondent series to which I contributed three programmes last year. As soon as I saw her I asked what the Television Service was doing about the election. She said that nothing was planned and that the general opinion at Alexandra Palace was against doing anything except perhaps an outside broadcast from Trafalgar Square or Piccadilly. I said I thought that this was an opportunity that should not be missed and that television should set out to present the results visually as they came in on election night and should also show the way the election was developing through commentaries illustrated by charts and diagrams. Grace is a pioneer by instinct and foresaw the possibilities immediately. As soon as we had finished lunch, we cleared the table and settled down to work out a plan. We drafted the outline of a scheme which Grace duly presented to the Controller of TV Programmes, Cecil McGivern.'[2]

Cecil McGivern was not impressed. He saw innumerable complications, technical and political, and he still was not inclined to do more than have an outside broadcast from Piccadilly or Trafalgar Square. Chester Wilmot and I had proposed that in addition to having an Outside Broadcast unit in Trafalgar Square we should have two other OB units either at the main Party headquarters or, better still, at two Returning Offices where the votes were being counted. The latter plan was ruled out. The Returning Officers would not agree. They felt that the security of the poll might be prejudiced if we were to televise the counting. The Party headquarters plan was also ruled out because it was felt that we could

* The date was February 23, 1950.

not have cameras at the Tory and Labour headquarters unless we could also have an O B unit at the Liberal headquarters and a third O B unit was not available. McGivern's objections were supported by the Head of Outside Broadcasts and the general feeling at Alexandra Palace was that the chances of a fiasco were so great that the plan we proposed should not even be attempted.

Norman Collins, however, asked that anyone who had attended his meetings and had anything to suggest should send him, in a favourite phrase, 'a piece of paper'. So I sent in a revised plan taking into account some of the objections which had been raised. Norman Collins called a further meeting which was attended by Cecil McGivern, the Head of Outside Broadcasts, some other programme staff and some engineers. McGivern and most of those at the meeting were still against the plan. Norman Collins adjourned the meeting and said that we would continue the discussion that evening. When I went to Norman Collins' office as arranged about seven o'clock Cecil appeared; but no one else. I said, 'Isn't anyone else coming?' Norman Collins replied, 'Were they to come? I don't think we need anyone else.'

Norman Collins thereupon proceeded to discuss the difficulties. He said that he did not want to argue the policy questions and added, 'I know you don't agree with the plan, Cecil, but if we did decide to go ahead with it could you, for instance, manage to alter the existing evening programme?' He took the technical objections one by one and at last Cecil McGivern admitted that they could all be solved more or less satisfactorily. After about two hours the telephone rang. Norman's car had arrived. He got up and said, 'I'm afraid I must go now. Thank you very much, Cecil. I think we are all agreed that this plan is practicable. We'll go ahead with it. Goodnight.' Before Cecil could reply Norman was out of the door.

Chester Wilmot could not carry the programme alone. Moreover I was aware that Broadcasting House would not accept him as an expert on British Parliamentary affairs. It would be sufficiently difficult for them to accept any kind of commentary on the results. In sound radio election results were read by an announcer from a prepared paper. Comment was considered to be dangerous. But in television, if we were able to show the results, we could not have, say, a blank screen and music between them. There must be something or somebody in vision. In the original plan which Chester Wilmot and I had put forward there was to be an expert who would indicate general trends and particular points of interest. The whole project now seemed to turn upon finding someone sufficiently qualified and sufficiently neutral (in the party political sense) to be able to do this.

In a situation of this kind it was then inevitable that any member of the BBC staff should turn to academics. Journalists tended to be identified with newspapers which had political alignments and might be felt by the public, rightly or wrongly, to be partisan. Academics, rightly or wrongly, were considered to be more objective because more removed from the day-to-day battle. Some of the academics who were experts in political behaviour were coming to be regarded almost as professional neutrals. A study of the 1945 General Election had been written by R. B. McCallum, of Pembroke College, Oxford, which seemed to put him into the expert but professionally neutral class. I went to see him and explained the proposed programme. He was courteous but reluctant. He knew nothing about television. He was not prepared to give instant comment on individual results. This was not his métier. At last he said he would take part on two conditions. One was that he would be asked to give only two or three considered comments during the course of the evening. The other was that a young man who had worked with him on the book about the 1945 election and who knew, he said, a great deal more than he did about detailed facts and figures, should appear on the programme too. This was David Butler, then a student and later a Fellow of Nuffield College.

David Butler threw himself into the enterprise with characteristic energy. He was not only highly informed about the machinery and history of elections; he had a prodigious memory for detail, a taste for statistics, a total lack of nervousness of television cameras and an immense constructive and practical interest in methods of presentation. He suggested visual devices for showing swings and trends; a grid system for the enormous studio map which Chester and I had devised so that results could take the form of black or white squares painted in during the programmes as the information about the seats won and lost arrived. He was able to produce volunteers who would work out election statistics as the results came in. So, with his energy, Chester Wilmot's enthusiasm and Norman Collins' determination that something should be done about presenting the results of the election on television, the plan grew.

The Election Results programme soon began to acquire a momentum of its own. Studio hands practised running in gym shoes from one studio to the other to see how quickly they could get results from Studio A to Studio B; secretaries volunteered to help with typing and checking; senior studio managers offered to operate the State of the Parties board and keep it up to date. Instructions came pouring in from Broadcasting House. There had never before been running comment on election results as they came in. It must be very careful and strictly factual. There must be absolutely no prediction. Norman Collins became anxious about speed and whether the results on television would lag behind those on sound. Meanwhile Cecil McGivern held himself disapprovingly aloof from the whole enterprise. The only thing he considered to be worthwhile were the cameras in Trafalgar Square, which might give the occasion a little humanity. For the rest he thought it a waste of the limited resources of television to let a few people know tonight instead of tomorrow which politician had lost his seat and who had got in for East Walthamstow.

After a dummy run rehearsal we went on the air at 10.45 p.m. on the night of Thursday, February 23, 1950. It was an anxious moment. We had made careful and detailed plans and these had included planning for the unexpected and the impromptu. We could not plan the results, the order in which they would arrive or the pace. A great deal depended on the enthusiasm of amateurs operating newly devised machinery. And Chester Wilmot was the only one of the three commentators who had had any television experience. Norman Collins stayed in Alexandra Palace watching the programme on a monitor in his office. A great deal was at stake. He had backed this enterprise against much powerful opposition both from within the television service and from Broadcasting House. The whole thing could have gone wrong organisationally; disastrous political mistakes could have been made either in the presentation of the facts or in the comment. In the current political climate, with the future of the BBC being considered by the Beveridge Committee, any mistake could do the BBC great harm and the responsibility would be his.

Yet he remained totally calm. Just before the programme started he came to the studio control gallery and said that he would be in his office if I wanted him. We had not planned an exact time for the end. I asked him if he would come down to the gallery and let me know when to stop. It was difficult to tell, in the excitement of the

65

actual business of production, when the programme was becoming boring. He came up behind me around midnight and said 'Keep going'. A little before 2 a.m. he came down again and said 'I think you could go into your closing routine now'. That was all. It took courage.

The whole endeavour was too dependent on improvisation and volunteer effort. The service was not manned to handle such a large scale operation. But there had been no political gaffes and the results had been shown quickly as well as clearly and accurately. The accuracy was due to the checking at every point by Michael Balkwill, who was lent by News and became an integral part of the team: the clarity to the excellence of the caption writers: the map had worked and Chester Wilmot had used it well. His force, integrity, detailed preparation and television experience held the programme together. And David Butler had been immediately impressive. His extraordinary memory, his knowledge of political facts, personalities and past records, his assistants with their slide rules, had allowed him to pour out, without self-consciousness and throughout the night, a continuous flow of informed comment.

We learned a lot. I had tried to separate the clutter of the operation from the personalities of the commentators. The result was that the total effect was almost too tidy and clinical. We discovered that it would be better in future to let the public see the telephones, the runners, the caption artists. And going to Trafalgar Square had proved a mistake. The results were shown there untidily on a great screen, and were confusing because they came in a different order from ours. And they were interspersed with crude cartoons of political figures at which the crowds roared with laughter but which we could not show since they were personal political comment.

But after 1950 no one was ever to say again that the presentation of the results of General Elections had better be left to sound. And the methods we hammered out then were to be the basis of the later and much more sophisticated presentations of the results of General Elections in 1951, then again in 1955, 1959, 1964, 1966, 1970 and 1974.

The importance of the presenting of the results on the night of February 23, 1950 went far beyond the election night programme itself. The television service had proved that it could deal with events which the BBC considered to be politically dangerous by using, without any disastrous consequences, methods which were different from those of sound radio. Producers were learning how to handle political occasions in ways which suited television without departing from the duty of the BBC to be fair, impartial and to refrain from expressing its own opinions.

But there was more to it than that. The General Election Results programme of 1950 was a watershed in the handling of politics in television. Till then many people not only at Broadcasting House but at Alexandra Palace supported Cecil McGivern's view that politics should be left to sound and that political matters were not suited to a visual medium. The Results programme demonstrated that television could present to the nation the compelling drama of a great national political occasion in which every voter had participated by putting his cross on the ballot paper. Millions of individuals could see how the battle was going. They did not have to wait for others to tell them what they had decided and what their next government would be. They could see for themselves. So no one, not even a Macmillan or an Attlee, a Gaitskell or an Alec Douglas-Home, a Wilson, a Heath or a Margaret Thatcher, whose whole future and that of their parties depended upon the result, knew what it would be earlier than a shepherd in the Highlands or a housewife in Islington. The privilege of the few had once again been extended to the many. And this time in politics.

[5]

'In the News' and Pressure
from the Parties

1950-1954

No sooner was the election over in February than Norman Collins, continuing his pressures to make television more relevant to the day-to-day scene, was determined that a regular series of topical discussions should be started on television. Such discussions ought, he felt, to be run by the television talks department. But no senior talks producer was sufficiently free from other commitments to undertake this work.

Collins brushed these difficulties aside. It would be a very simple operation. All that was required was a more or less permanent team of informed people who would regularly discuss matters in the news. If the talks department could not undertake it he would make other arrangements. He considered that it should be possible to hire people from outside the television service and get them to work on contract. Edgar Lustgarten, for instance, a former news analyst and successful broadcaster, could be responsible for getting the people together and could possibly take the chair himself. John Irwin, an experienced television director, now freelancing, could be employed to direct the programme. The head of the talks department, Mrs Adams, could keep an eye on the policy.

So 'In the News', which was to run for years, be an immense success, cause the BBC considerable trouble politically and arouse the interest of politicians and the political parties in the possibility that appearances on television might be of personal and party advantage, was started without any very clear purpose except to be good television and without the editorial responsibility for it being clearly defined.

The first programme was transmitted on May 26, 1950. There was a team of four speakers who were in some kind of political balance. Two of them were Members of Parliament: a Conservative,

Robert Boothby, and a Labour member, Michael Foot. A third was W. J. Brown, who had sat in Parliament as an Independent. The fourth was Donald McLachlan, then an assistant editor of *The Economist*.

There was another edition of 'In the News' in June and three in August with a different assortment of speakers though with Michael Foot and W. J. Brown among them. And by October 'In the News' was to be established as a weekly series with a regular team consisting of Robert Boothby, Michael Foot, W. J. Brown and the Oxford historian, A. J. P. Taylor.

But during the months between May and October the rift between Norman Collins and those in authority at Broadcasting House was widening and the battles for more independence for television within the BBC becoming increasingly bitter. The BBC had decided that, with the growing importance of television, its head must not be merely a Controller, as Norman Collins was, but must have the status of a Director with a seat on the Board of Management. The appointment of a Director of Television was being considered at high level. The first of the autumn series of 'In the News' was transmitted on October 6, 1950. On October 12 the Director-General informed the Board of Management that a Director of Television had been appointed. It was George Barnes. Norman Collins resigned. On October 13 he made a statement to the Press which was in essence an indictment of the BBC's handling of its television service. He then called the senior television staff to his office at Alexandra Palace, said goodbye and left. George Barnes immediately took over.

It was inevitable that 'In the News' should be a matter of immediate concern to the new Director of Television. George Barnes was not by nature politically minded; his inclinations were scholarly and literary. Indeed some of the politicians with whom he had to deal found his approach to the practical problems of politics academic and unrealistic.[1] But, as Director of the Spoken Word at Broadcasting House, he had had to conduct negotiations with the political parties and was highly aware of the pressures which they sometimes brought to bear upon the BBC. This combination of temperament and experience made him wary rather than courageous in his handling of the relationship between television and politics during the next few years.

'In the News' had run into difficulties even before Barnes took over from Collins. The precarious arrangement by which Mrs Adams was to keep an eye on the policy of 'In the News' but without any clear executive authority had proved unsatisfactory. So Norman Collins suggested to Michael Balkwill of the News Division, who had been active in the Election Results programmes of 1950 and was now writing commentaries for television newsreels, that he should add to his other work the vague task of keeping an eye on the policy of 'In the News'. It need not mean much, he was told; only having dinner once a week with Edgar Lustgarten in his pleasant flat in Albany and discussing with him the topics for the next programme.[2]

Michael Balkwill knew Lustgarten and so this ill-defined relationship worked smoothly enough. But it was basically unsatisfactory since Balkwill's function had never been firmly stated and he considered that decisions about who should take part in the programme were not within his brief. This was the more important because Lustgarten was a freelance operating outside the normal BBC departmental structure and it was not clear to whom he was answerable for his selection of speakers. He was paid on contract to act as 'Editor in Charge' and to be responsible 'for all preliminary work in selecting and contacting speakers'.[3] And it was in regard to the choice of speakers that the continued political problems caused by 'In the News' were to arise. The result was that lists of proposed speakers came increasingly to be supervised, agreed or rejected by George Barnes himself or by Cecil McGivern, acting on Barnes' behalf, sometimes with Michael Balkwill acting as the intelligent but uncomfortable go-between, sometimes directly with Lustgarten.

The difficulties over 'In the News' arose not only as a result of its rickety organisational structure but also from the fact that while it was not originally intended to be of political significance it rapidly became one of the most important political programmes regularly transmitted by the BBC. It was also immensely popular. The regular team of Boothby, Brown, A. J. P. Taylor and Michael Foot seemed, in combination, to provide a remarkable effervescence of wit, commonsense, intellectual honesty and political passion. Week after week matters in the news were discussed by intelligent men who seemed to be thinking independently, not merely mouthing the clichés of routine party politics. But, paradoxically, since in creating a team which would discuss topical subjects it was felt necessary to maintain some sort of balance of political alignment, with Boothby and Brown considered to be roughly on the Right and Taylor and Foot roughly on the Left, the discussions quickly took the form of arguments of Right versus Left.

The question then arose of whether Boothby and Brown were representative of the Right in politics and Taylor and Foot of the Left. Party headquarters thought not; if there were to be Right-versus-Left discussions on television they felt that representatives of the 'solid core' of party opinion ought to be given a hearing and that the expression of political views should not be confined to two Members of Parliament who were on the fringe of their respective parties as Boothby and Foot at that time undoubtedly were. So pressures were brought upon the BBC to ensure that some solid party men were included in the 'In the News' team. George Barnes was well aware of these pressures. In a peremptory memorandum to Cecil McGivern in February 1951, he said, 'From the start of my time here I have emphasised in correspondence and in directives to Balkwill and Lustgarten that failure to use on occasion representatives of the main core of opinion in the two parties will lead to interference and will endanger the programme . . . Interference has begun and I must therefore insist that my directions are carried out.'[4]

But by the time Barnes had been appointed Director of Television the winter series of 'In the News' programmes had already started. From a producer's point of view the prior booking of a permanent team of proved ability is an immense advantage. As far as Lustgarten was concerned the system could not be bettered. The favoured team of Boothby and Foot, A. J. P. Taylor and W. J. Brown could be signed up for a whole forthcoming series. On any occasion when one or other of them would not be available or when it seemed in advance to be desirable to replace a member of the regular team by an invited guest this could be arranged in plenty of time and the substitute speaker could be chosen without last-minute panic. The result was that it became possible to have a highly topical discussion with subjects finally decided only shortly before the programme went on the air but which could nevertheless be planned well in advance and be given adequate publicity.

From Cecil McGivern's point of view 'In the News' was a remarkably successful television programme of the 'intelligence' which he had wanted to see on the television screen and he wished to retain it as far as possible with minimal changes in the team since it was upon the regular team that the programme's success appeared so largely to depend.

To George Barnes it was a constant anxiety and potentially a source of danger not only to the television service but to the BBC as a whole and the entire future of public service broadcasting. The political situation was extremely delicate. The Labour Government, with Mr Attlee as Prime Minister, had been returned to power in February 1950 but with such a fragile majority—only seven over the Conservatives with fifteen Liberals swinging in the wind—that it could not last long. Already by April 1950 the BBC was considering how it should handle the next election, which could not be far off. Meanwhile the Beveridge Committee was finalising its report. This was eventually published in January 1951. It recommended, subject to all kinds of safeguards and new procedures, that the BBC's monopoly of both sound and television broadcasting should continue. But the strength of the movement to break the monopoly had been revealed in, for example, the evidence of Geoffrey Crowther, then editor of *The Economist*, and of the well-known scientist, Sir Robert Watson-Watt. And one member of the Beveridge Committee, Selwyn Lloyd, an influential Conservative, had dissented from its findings in a minority report.

The BBC had never been so vulnerable. Whatever the attitude of the existing Labour government to the recommendations of the Beveridge Committee might be, the future was uncertain, since no one could tell what government would be in power when the fateful decisions about the future of British broadcasting were made. It all depended on the date and outcome of the next General Election. This was brought nearer by the resignation from the Cabinet in April 1951 of the powerful Minister of Health, Aneurin Bevan, and of Harold Wilson, the young President of the Board of Trade. The Bevanite revolt split the Labour Party. Michael Foot was a Bevanite. If he appeared on 'In the News' as frequently as he had done in the past and without any balancing personality from among the non-Bevanites in the Labour Party the BBC might seem to be taking sides with the Bevanites against the Government.

The split in the Labour Party had weakened the already weak position of the Attlee government. If the BBC appeared to be favouring the Bevanites it could be accused not only of departing from the prescribed standards of impartiality but even of helping to bring down the government of the day. The BBC must not, with the whole future of broadcasting in the public interest at stake, create a situation in which accusations of bias could be made to appear to have some justification.

During the long arguments in regard to 'In the News' large questions about political broadcasting were raised. One was whether any Member of Parliament appearing on television should be regarded as speaking as an individual or as a representative of the party to which he belonged. Another was whether in arranging political discussions the BBC should have regard in its choice of speakers not only to differences between the parties but to divisions of opinion within the parties. A third was whether it was proper for the BBC, by inviting a few individual Members of Parliament to appear very frequently, 'to allow particular personalities to be built up to the extent that would be involved'.[5] Another was what degree of consultation, if any, there should be with the parties on the choice of speakers.

These questions were to continue to arise in relation to many political broadcasts in television and in connection with programmes quite other than 'In the News'. The situation in 1950 and 1951 however was peculiarly intense because 'In the News' was the only regular programme in which politicians regularly appeared. There were then no party political broadcasts on television in which representatives of the parties chosen by the parties themselves could present their views. There were no programmes such as 'Press Conference' or 'Panorama' or 'Gallery' or 'Tonight' in which politicians appeared frequently and which could offset the regular appearances of Robert Boothby and Michael Foot so that these two would not seem to carry so great a weight of political communication upon their shoulders.

Altogether it is not surprising that the parties made representations and not surprising that the BBC took heed of them. In January 1951 the Director of Television demanded a statement from Michael Balkwill giving the number of appearances of everyone who had taken part in 'In the News' since the previous October. This showed that Michael Foot had appeared thirteen times and Robert Boothby ten. No other Member of Parliament had appeared as many as four times; others mostly once or twice.[6]

During the early months of 1951 George Barnes brought continual pressure on Michael Balkwill to see that representatives of the 'main core of opinion' in the two major parties should be included in the team. But he was now on a highly slippery slope. For who was to decide who the representatives of the 'main core' of party opinion actually were? Balkwill and Lustgarten considered the problem and Balkwill consulted his colleagues at Broadcasting House. Then Barnes began to ask some senior members of the political parties for suitable names.[7] The idea was not to sacrifice the regular team but to balance the appearances of Michael Foot and Robert Boothby by occasional appearances of other Members of Parliament who would be considered by the political parties to be more representative.

But there were few Members who did not deviate on some matter or other from the orthodox party line and a number of those who were invited to appear on 'In the News' as a result of George Barnes' consultations with the parties made it clear that they did not want to be considered as representatives of a party or of any one section of a party. Among them, Michael Balkwill reported, were David Eccles, J. B. Hynd and John Boyd-Carpenter. There was a pretty general feeling that Members of Parliament who took part in such programmes as 'In the News' should appear in their own right as 'practitioners of controversy'.[8] Indeed anything else could mean an intolerable restriction upon the freedom of Members who might come to be denied access to this increasingly important medium unless they were approved by a party hierarchy with whose views they were not necessarily in total agreement.

With all these difficulties it is surprising that 'In the News' was continued in the autumn of 1951. The BBC was editorially responsible for everything it transmitted. Yet, as a result of the way in which the organisation of 'In the News' had been improvised to suit the television situation of early 1950 the BBC, almost by accident, had handed over much of the editorial control of the most important political programme in television to a freelance contributor. Edgar Lustgarten was passionately opposed to any policy which affected the frequent appearances of the regular team. Together, he argued, they produced a brilliance of dialectic which no other combination of speakers could equal. If the team were diluted by substituting too often a 'solid party man' the programme would suffer and lose its popularity. He therefore fought a continuous rearguard action to prevent the alterations to the selection of speakers upon which George Barnes was insisting.

The effect therefore in the early part of 1951 of Lustgarten's contractual position and of his attitudes to the choice of speakers for 'In the News' was that the BBC was being hindered in exercising editorial control over a political programme for which it was editorially responsible. There was little chance of altering the situation before May 1951. The current series was to end triumphantly on May 25 with the regular team of Boothby and Foot, Taylor and Brown. Then it was due for a summer break. There was almost certain to be a General Election in the autumn of 1951. This could have been an excellent excuse for dropping 'In the News' from the schedules after the summer. There would then have been no need to renew Edgar Lustgarten's contract and the situation could have been reconsidered when the Election was over.

But such drastic action was not in George Barnes' character. It was almost more difficult to kill 'In the News' than to keep it alive. There would certainly be resistance from within the television service itself. Here was a new Director of Television straight from Broadcasting House and one of his first actions, it might be said, was to put an end, as a result of pressures from the political parties, to an intelligent and successful television programme. There were other problems. Lustgarten and the four members of the regular team were all highly vocal and each in his own way was a notable public figure. The impact of their views would be all the greater because of their success in 'In the News'. Any decision to stop 'In the News' would almost certainly be taken by them to mean a denial of free speech as a result of the BBC submitting to party political pressures. It was unlikely that they would consider the point, which Barnes was bound to consider, that the giving of free speech regularly on television in political discussions to a small privileged group including two particular Members of Parliament meant that others equally, or more, deserving of being heard were denied similar opportunities.

George Barnes therefore compromised. He tried to ensure that some of those others were included in the 'In the News' team. And, dangerously, he continued to consult representatives of the political parties about who should be included. This last was all the more astonishing in that it was contrary to the expressed instructions of the Board of Governors of the BBC.

In 1951, after having received a full report of the progress of discussions about 'In the News', the Board of Governors said firmly that:

'In the circumstances did they think that the choice of speakers should pass from the BBC to the Parties by means of lists approved by the Whips or by any other means.'[9]

In spite of this George Barnes, in December 1951, was consulting the Conservative Chief Whip, Patrick Buchan-Hepburn, and asking for advice about 'promising Conservative Members who might take part in the weekly political discussion on television entitled "In the News" '. Barnes and Buchan-Hepburn met on February 13, 1952 to discuss possibilities and on the following day Buchan-Hepburn, as a result of 'another talk with the Whips and the Central Office', sent George Barnes an amended list of possible speakers.

By June 30, 1952 Cecil McGivern, aware of the pressures and after discussion with Lustgarten, was proposing to Barnes that the original 'In the News' team of Boothby, Brown, Foot and Taylor should appear only once a month in the series beginning in October and that there should be other teams consisting of 'elder statesmen' such as Walter Elliott; from time to time a 'Ladies' Night'; a 'House of Lords team' and a 'non-MP team'. This was agreed by Barnes on July 9, 1952. On August 6 he wrote to Buchan-Hepburn saying 'I have just approved the arrangements for this coming session and I hope that the Parties will consider that they are satisfactory. A complete change has been made.' Buchan-Hepburn replied, 'I am very interested to hear that "a complete change" has been made in the arrangements for the coming session and I too hope that everyone will be satisfied.'

In the struggles over 'In the News' George Barnes was a lonely figure. Few people saw as he did that what was being raised was not merely a matter of the BBC either resisting or giving way to party political pressures but the whole question of the rôle of a corporation such as the BBC in the political life of the country. If the BBC used its unique position to give, through television, a regular near-nationwide prominence to the views of two individual Members of Parliament, Robert Boothby and Michael Foot, who did not carry an equivalent authority within their own parties, was the BBC not in fact by-passing the democratic process?

On May 22, 1951 Barnes wrote to Michael Balkwill: 'It is clear to me that the BBC cannot allow the only directly Party political programme in its Television Service to be composed of a single team particularly if that team has MPs in it.' This was a statement of principle which the BBC's television current affairs producers always subsequently recognised. After the demise of 'In the News' there were no further attempts to present on television discussions of current affairs by a permanent team who expressed their own political opinions. In the same memorandum Barnes reminded Michael Balkwill—who did not need reminding—that the BBC's obligation was to be above all impartial in party politics and went on to enunciate another principle: 'This impartiality does not consist only in maintaining a balance over a period between members of the Parties . . . It consists also in maintaining a broad impartiality within each Party and avoiding the publicising of one section of a Party at the expense of other sections.'[10]

This principle also came to be absorbed into the continuing attitudes of the producers of television current affairs programmes. There were many occasions in the future when the differences within the main political parties were of more significance than the differences between the parties. The BBC expected its current affairs programmes to reflect this situation. It was often difficult, as in 1951, when political circumstances were changing to know which Member of Parliament at any moment belonged to what section of a divided party. But it had been made clear by George Barnes that no current affairs producer must deliberately, for any reason, including that of entertainment value, give prominence to members of any one section of a party which was known to be a section, as the Bevanites were in 1951, as against other members of the party who did not belong to that section.

In his insistence, in spite of any opposition, upon these principles, the Director of Television was acting responsibly and courageously. His methods were less defensible. By his quasi-formal consultations with the political parties about the names of Members of Parliament who were considered by the Whips to represent the 'solid core' of party opinion he was putting the political independence of television in jeopardy. The danger was not now the gross threat of the domination of political expression on television by the government in power —as it was to be later, for example, in de Gaulle's France and in Czechoslovakia after the Russian invasion. But it was, though a lesser evil, the creation of the dangerous precedent of giving the main political parties some right to nominate Members of Parliament who would take part in the television political discussions which were supposed to be under the editorial control of the Corporation.

A bolder man than George Barnes might have preferred to make public the conflict with the parties over 'In the News'. As it was, though Barnes' policy made 'In the News' less and less a matter of controversy with the political parties, it also, as Lustgarten had foreseen, made it less and less effective as a television programme. The result was that it eventually disappeared from the schedules, not with a bang but with a whimper.

[6]

Members of Parliament as
Television Commentators

1950-1959

We were now entering upon a period in the relationship between television and politics which, looking back, seems strange but which at the time seemed natural enough. As a result of 'In the News', Members of Parliament were already taking part in television discussions about political matters and two of them, Robert Boothby and Michael Foot, had become well-known television personalities. The new development during the years between 1950 and 1959 was that a number of other Members of Parliament began to appear regularly on television not in discussions but as expositors, commentators and interviewers.

The era of the MP as television commentator began in August 1950 when Christopher Mayhew made his first television appearance in a special programme on the Korean War. The occasion was unplanned and accidental. Soon after we had presented the results of the General Election in February 1950, Cecil McGivern asked me to produce a new current affairs series of the 'Foreign Correspondent' type. He wanted six half-hour programmes at fortnightly intervals. He would like the series to start in October.

The practical problems were complicated by the fact that I was already beginning to plan the television coverage of the next General Election. Moreover David Butler had been such a success in the Election Results programme of 1950 that I was talking to him about a possible series of television interviews. Both he and I were interested in getting men of authority to explain the realities as distinct from the theory of the ways in which they operated. He was teaching politics in Oxford at Nuffield College and his interest was part of his professional approach. And I had discovered, when working in the Board of Trade during the war, how surprisingly different the practice was from the theories I had learnt as a student of history and of politics.

The Butler series was eventually transmitted under the title 'Men of Authority'. In it Lord Samuel, an ex-Cabinet Minister; Sir John Maud, then Permanent Secretary to the Ministry of Education; Lord Lyle, Chairman of the great sugar firm, Tate and Lyle; and Lincoln Evans, secretary of the powerful Iron and Steel Workers Union, answered with astonishing frankness the questions which David Butler and I had prepared. Though the actual interviews were impromptu and unrehearsed we had told each participant the sort of questions we would be asking and each said not only that he was prepared to answer them but would welcome the chance of doing so.

Lord Samuel talked in detail about how as a Minister he would set about getting rid of a Permanent Secretary who disagreed with his policies; Sir John Maud about how he would react in such a situation; Lord Lyle about how industrialists brought pressure to bear on Ministries; and Lincoln Evans on how the unions brought pressure to bear on industrialists. The new quality in this series was that of personal testimony. This was what television could provide. It was quite different from a journalistic or academic assessment of what had probably gone on. It was a statement by men who had taken part in action of what, in fact, occurred.

In the middle of all this I was now asked to try to get together a new set of 'Foreign Correspondent' type programmes. It would have to be more far-reaching than the previous series. World attention was shifting from the Cold War in Europe to a possible hot war in the Far East. In China the Communist forces led by Mao Tse-tung had defeated the armies of Chiang Kai-shek. On January 5, 1950, Britain recognised the Communist regime as the *de facto* government of China. But the United States had not done so. A representative of Chiang Kai-shek occupied China's seat in the Security Council of the United Nations. In protest the USSR representative, Mr Malik, had from January 1950 boycotted all meetings of the Council. The attitude of the USSR to Europe was now clearly linked to its attitude to China and the Far East generally. American forces were in occupation in Japan. The temporary post-war settlement which had divided Korea along the line of the 38th Parallel between the communist north and the non-communist south was beginning to look precarious.

Then on June 25 the North Korean forces invaded South Korea. The United States asked for an immediate meeting of the Security

Council. Malik, continuing his boycott, was not present. In his absence the Security Council by a majority of nine votes to none called on North Korea to withdraw its forces to the 38th Parallel. On June 27, with Malik still absent, the Council recommended Members of the United Nations to give South Korea such assistance 'as may be necessary to repel the armed attack and to restore international peace and security in the area'. On July 18, United Nations forces landed in South Korea. The Korean War had begun.

With the help of Alan Bullock, I was by now trying to get together a special expository programme on the Korean situation which we hoped would be ready for July 5 but which was eventually not transmitted until September 8. I had asked the United Nations film section, through our own film department, for a small amount of illustrative material. But thousands of feet arrived. I looked at it. What had been sent was in fact film of the crucial meetings of the Security Council at Lake Success on August 2 and 3. Mr Malik, after his seven-month boycott of the Council meetings, had told the Secretary General, Mr Trygve Lie, on July 27 that he intended to take the chair at the meetings in August when, under the system of rotating chairmanship, it was the right of the representative of the USSR to be President. During the August meetings he demanded, from the chair, discussions about peace in Korea in which representatives of the Chinese communist government and of North Korea would take part.

There were angry exchanges with the British representative, Sir Gladwyn Jebb, and with Warren Austin, who represented the United States. Both declared that it would be impossible to invite the North Koreans in view of the fact that they had deliberately defied the Security Council and had put themselves into a state of hostility with the United Nations. Then the matter was put to the vote.

Even seen through the long-winded speechmaking and the formal procedures of the United Nations the situation was electrifying. A possible new world war in which nuclear weapons might be used hung in the balance as men of different nationalities decided whether to support a war in Korea waged by an international force in the hope that by doing so world peace would be maintained. Malik's resolution was defeated by seven votes to two. The Korean War would go on.

By the time the film reached us the decision was already known.

And it did not show the trafficking in the corridors, the backstairs conversations, the pressures of the Great Powers and all the other influences which go to make up decisions at the United Nations. But it still seemed to me to be worth presenting a shortened version of this film as a special programme. The faceless representatives of Ecuador or India or Norway suddenly, in vision, became men; the speeches of Sir Gladwyn Jebb were seen to have a passionate conviction; the international flavour was conveyed not only by the faces of those sitting round the great table but by the styles and languages in which they spoke.

All this needed length, as well as vision, if it were to be communicated. In a news or newsreel snippet it would only have added to the boredom which all international conferences seem to create in the viewing public. But it also needed an interpreter; someone who knew the United Nations and could guide the viewer through the procedural maze; point out the significance of the occasion and of the speeches; indicate the pressures and the practical consequences which might affect those who were watching.

I said all this to Cecil McGivern. He agreed that I should have a half-hour at eight-thirty on the following Monday, August 8, for a special programme. But who was to be the interpreter? The matter was urgent. I telephoned a number of people who I thought might possibly undertake, at short notice, this difficult job. Among them was William Clark, then Foreign Editor of *The Observer*. He couldn't do it himself but asked if I had thought of Christopher Mayhew, who had been Under-Secretary of State for Foreign Affairs, knew a great deal about the United Nations and was now out of politics since he had lost his seat in the General Election in February.

I did not know him. But I telephoned him and explained the situation. It was now Friday evening. If the programme were to be transmitted on the following Monday it would be necessary to be at Alexandra Palace early on Saturday, work all day and possibly all the weekend as well as on Monday. That was no problem. Was he prepared to advise me on the content, write any necessary introduction and studio linking material, and speak it to camera? Certainly. Had he any previous experience of television or of working with film? No, but he could learn. He sounded brisk and confident. He arrived early on Saturday, bounding up the steps to the entrance hall at Alexandra Palace. My first impression was that he was likeable, totally lacking in pomposity, full of energy and enthusiasm.

We worked all day editing, with stop watches in our hands, the transcripts of the speeches, sending them down to the film editor, lunching off sandwiches and cups of canteen coffee, viewing rough cuts, writing links. His knowledge of the background and the people was invaluable. He took to television instantly and was not in the least nervous of the lights and cameras in the studio. On transmission he was an immediate success; lucid and informed yet showing in his relation to the audience a disarming friendliness. He could talk straight to camera—that is to the individual viewer—from his carefully prepared notes with an air of complete spontaneity. It was clear that we had in him a possible new television commentator on foreign affairs.

This soon became important. While I was planning and presenting the programmes on Korea, Cecil McGivern continued to demand an autumn series on international affairs. His insistence was due to the apparent dangers in the world situation. As a result of the victory of Mao Tse-tung, the two great powers of China and the USSR, not yet split by ideological differences, seemed in 1950 a unified block; immense, expansionist and threatening. The situation in Europe was precariously balanced. Another move by the USSR in Berlin or elsewhere could come at any time. The uncertain régimes in many Middle Eastern countries appeared to be peculiarly vulnerable to communist pressures and to infiltrating groups. In the Far East there was not only a United Nations war in Korea but a French war in Indo-China. There was guerrilla warfare in Malaya. There were large communist parties in Italy and France. Communism seemed to combine the historic imperialistic urges of great nations such as Russia and China with the revolutionary ideas which might destroy the West from within.

It was impossible to try to put this huge canvas on to television. To do anything at all with our limited resources was sufficiently daunting and could appear impertinent. Yet McGivern pressed me to try to do something. He was still not interested in politics. But he cared desperately about the quality of television output and its relation to life. While men were fighting and dying—British troops among them—we could not simply present the viewing public with cabaret, light entertainment and soap opera. That would be an abdication of responsibility. The film department was sending cameramen to Korea to cover the situation there for the newsreel. But we ought to be doing more. So he wanted a fortnightly series on the lines of 'Foreign Correspondent' but more specifically political than the previous series had been.

Any new series would have to deal with the East and not confine itself to Europe. Chester Wilmot had gone for a time to his native Australia and was not available. I knew of no one with sufficient television experience who could even attempt programmes of this kind. But now here was Christopher Mayhew, informed, interested and immediately free. I began to discuss possibilities with him. I knew from experience that on television it was useless to try to convey great world concepts. It was necessary to present specific and concrete examples. What began to emerge from our talk was a series of studies, illustrated by maps and diagrams and film, of the present situation in a few countries which were on the periphery of the USSR and of China. These were possible world danger areas— of the kind that Berlin and Korea had been. We would look to the future not the past. Were the dangers real? How did they seem to the inhabitants on the spot as compared with the attitudes of politicians and commentators considering them from the comparative safety of London and New York? Was communism within these areas a threat or a hope? Did resistance to infiltration depend on the nature of the existing régime; or to nationalism; or to religious feeling? Or to all of these factors?

On August 31 1950 I sent Cecil McGivern a memorandum outlining these rough ideas. Any new series would be very different from 'Foreign Correspondent'. Christopher Mayhew was an analyst and a commentator rather than a reporter. Although for many years he was remarkably successful on television he was essentially a man of ideas and he rated communication by words more highly than communication by vision.

Combining these two kinds of communication is never easy and remains one of the central problems of television. Words cannot be the master of vision and vision must not use words as a slave. If either of these alternatives is pursued the result is hack-work. Poor words used to express poor ideas will destroy the effect of the most magnificent visuals. On the other hand if the best film you have to illustrate the political problems of Burma in 1950 is a set of close-ups of elephants hauling timber, it is no use putting a commentary over these pictures which outlines the political history of Burma since the end of the war. People, in these circumstances, will look at the elephants and find the commentary irrelevant. Vision, in a visual medium, will always defeat words. What is necessary, therefore, is a great deal of hard thinking in advance of shooting the film to ensure, as far as you can, that the specific and concrete visual material will reinforce rather than destroy, or be irrelevant to, the general thesis which is being presented.

Such integration between the visual and the verbal requires respect by the visual men, the film editors and the cameramen, for the ideas and the words; and respect by the ideas and words-men for the importance of visual communication. The two can complement each other and the result be more effective than either alone. To achieve this it is essential to create a team which will work together. In the early days Christopher Mayhew was apt to want to state in a film commentary general concepts which did not relate to the visual material. He would say, airily, to a film editor, who pointed this out, 'All I want there is a montage'. The film editor, wearily, would provide it. What we saw, as a result, was a series of bitty, meaningless pictures which conveyed nothing. The words alone, spoken to camera in the studio, would have been more effective. So we threw out the montage and persuaded Mayhew to rewrite the commentary. But it was often necessary, too, to throw out pictures which the cameraman had obtained with infinite difficulty because, however effective in themselves, they were irrelevant to the main theme of the programme. And in these early days I often discarded, wounding the cameraman and perhaps the film editor too, glamorous pictures of cherry orchards in flower, or girls in local costume, or flocks of bleating lambs or children dancing in school playgrounds, because, though improbably, useful in a travelogue, they did nothing to add to a study of, say, the relationship of Yugoslavia to the USSR, or of the Burmese government to the disturbances in the north of that country.

We learned to accommodate ourselves to the team idea and Mayhew was soon firmly established as a successful television commentator. He was joined later by other Labour politicians: Aidan Crawley, Woodrow Wyatt and John Freeman. We had arrived, without intention and simply because they were all free and effective, at the extraordinary situation in which four of the most successful commentators and interviewers on television were four men who had all been Junior Ministers in the Attlee administration of 1945-51— Christopher Mayhew, Under Secretary of State for Foreign Affairs, Aidan Crawley, Under Secretary for Air, Woodrow Wyatt, personal assistant to Stafford Cripps in his Cabinet mission to India in 1949 and Under Secretary for War in 1951 and John Freeman, Parliamentary Secretary to the Ministry of Supply in 1951. He resigned this post to succeed Kingsley Martin as Editor of the *New Statesman* and, in the television series 'Face to Face', showed interviewing skills comparable with those of Edward R. Murrow in the United States.

All four looked to television as a method of expression when they lost their Parliamentary seats or turned away from politics. Christopher Mayhew had been defeated in the General Election of February 1950. Aidan Crawley lost his seat in the General Election of 1951 and soon started producing for the BBC a remarkable television series called 'India's Challenge' which he himself filmed. Woodrow Wyatt lost his seat in the General Election of 1955 and became a regular contributor to 'Panorama'.

This situation, which was eventually to be politically embarrassing for the BBC, was one with which I was very much concerned. It arose partly by accident and partly because in the early 1950s it was hard to find commentators on current affairs who were sufficiently knowledgeable and sufficiently free from other commitments to master the complicated television process. A number of politicians, journalists and academics were ready to air their views and earn useful fees by appearing in television discussions which required a minimum of preparation. But they were seldom able, or willing, to undertake a regular series of television programmes which involved travelling abroad for considerable periods of time; embarking on the arduous business of understanding filming and film editing; learning how to write film commentaries; how to conduct interviews whether on film or in the studio and how to use the various kinds of visual apparatus which television made possible.

But just at the moment when television needed people who were both informed about current affairs and sufficiently free to give time to a new medium, such men became available as a result of the political reverses of the Labour Party in 1950, 1951 and 1955. Energetic young ex-Ministers such as Christopher Mayhew and Aidan Crawley suddenly found themselves with nothing to do. They were able to contribute to political communication by television something quite different from what was already being done by journalists and dons.

Its quality was realism. They showed a greater understanding of the difficulties of government than the more theoretical critics. If political communication on television depends largely on the contentious statements of politicians in Party Political or Party Election broadcasts, or discussions of political subjects which are contentious also, and on interviews in which politicians are critically questioned, the danger is that too much emphasis is placed on the element of dispute in public affairs; and this tends to produce, I believe, in the minds of viewers not only confusion but a sense of disillusionment with politics and politicians.

This notion was in my mind in relation to the Mayhew 'International Commentary' programmes and also to the later Crawley 'Viewfinder' series. I wanted to aim at elucidation rather than dispute. I thought it harmful that a disproportionate emphasis was often laid on the fringes where there were party differences rather than on the frequently much larger areas of agreement. In the early 1950s this was particularly true of foreign policy. On many subjects there was little real difference between the attitudes of the political parties. By concentrating on these it was possible to have exposition by a single individual, even an ex-Labour Minister such as Christopher Mayhew, without involving the BBC in party political battles. It was therefore not only Christopher Mayhew's background which determined the fact that his first television programmes all dealt with questions of foreign policy. It was also because the political circumstances of the day made it easier to handle foreign than home affairs in this way.

But the whole situation would have been impossible if Mayhew and, after him, Crawley and Wyatt and Freeman had wanted to use their television opportunities for party advantage. In fact they all understood the position of the BBC and realised that they could not continue with their television programmes unless they did so. They willingly accepted the need to be fair and impartial. They all, in a sense, had cross-bench minds. This is demonstrated by their subsequent histories. Mayhew ultimately rebelled against the defence policy of the Labour Party, resigned from his post of Minister for the Navy and much later, joined the Liberal Party. Crawley left politics for a time to concentrate on television, left the BBC to start Independent Television News, crossed the floor of the House to become a Member of Parliament on the Conservative side and in 1968 gave up politics for television when he became Chairman of a commercial television company. Wyatt became known for his differences on many matters of policy with the leadership of the Labour Party.

Freeman abandoned the party political scene to become first, British High Commissioner in India, then British Ambassador to the United States, and later returned to television as Chairman of London Weekend Television.

Nevertheless from the first there were complaints from the Conservatives. I was pressed by the BBC to find the Conservative equivalent of Christopher Mayhew. It was not that Conservative leaders alleged that Mayhew was partial or biased in any party political sense in his presentation of foreign affairs. Lord Woolton, then chairman of the Party, certainly did not do so. Yet one day when I was staying in his house in Sussex he said to me a little bitterly, 'You know, you've *made* Christopher Mayhew,' and went on to suggest possible Conservative alternatives.

By the middle of 1951, when Mayhew had already given two television 'International Commentary' series, the need to persuade Conservatives to try their hand as television commentators had become urgent. This was partly because Mayhew, in June 1951, fought and won a by-election in Ernest Bevin's old seat, Woolwich East. He was back in the House of Commons and George Barnes immediately wrote me a memorandum asking me to take note of the fact that 'Mayhew is an MP now'. This meant that the practice of balancing broadcasts by Members of Parliament now applied to him; however impartial he might be on television each of his appearances was chalked up on the Labour side and must be matched by an equal number of appearances by Conservatives.

The urgency was increased by the approach which Aidan Crawley, another ex-Labour Member of Parliament, made to the BBC. As a result of the loss of his Buckinghamshire seat in the General Election of 1951 he was out of Parliament. He wrote to George Barnes, whom he knew, in October 1951, and suggested he might do some work in television. He had a certain amount of film experience. Between 1936 and 1939, using a 35 millimetre camera, he had made educational films mainly in Palestine. Early in 1952 he and his American wife, Virginia Cowles, decided to go to India for four or five months to study the working of democracy there. He would take his own 35 millimetre camera, travel in a station wagon with an English-speaking Indian driver and make a series of films as he moved through the villages. George Barnes asked me to meet him and discuss the project. What emerged was a proposal for six television programmes. Crawley saw India as one of the keys to the whole future of Asia. India was trying to operate a democratic system of government. The degree to which this was successful in solving the problems of poverty would be compared all over Asia and perhaps all over the world with the situation in Communist China. His films would try to show what was happening. And he hoped to interview on film a number of Indian politicians, financial experts and industrialists. I was asked to get out a costing and to consider the whole enterprise.

George Barnes had already written to Cecil McGivern saying that he thought the series should be accepted. But I had been doubtful about the political implications. Certainly Aidan Crawley was no longer a Labour Member of Parliament. But I said in a memorandum that I was going ahead with the Crawley series on the understanding that D.Tel.B.* 'had accepted the political implications of putting on a series of programmes on international affairs given by so prominent a Labour Party personality as Mr Aidan Crawley after a series by Christopher Mayhew with only a two months (approximately) gap between them'.[1] George Barnes agreed to accept the political implications,[2] given that we endeavoured to place a Conservative series on foreign affairs between the Mayhew and the Crawley series.

News of the projected Crawley series on India had, however, already reached high places in the Conservative Party. On May 30, 1953, the Prime Minister, Mr Churchill, when making a general complaint about the BBC's use of Labour candidates in its programmes, gave as an example the fact that the prospective Labour candidate for Buckingham, Aidan Crawley, was in India preparing a series of television programmes which would be transmitted by the BBC in August. Mr Churchill had been misinformed. Aidan Crawley was certainly in India preparing a series of television programmes but he was not the prospective Labour candidate for Buckingham. In fact a Dr Evans had been officially adopted. I reported this and said that 'Mr Crawley is not a Labour candidate anywhere (i.e. he has not been adopted for any constituency and is not at the moment seeking one)'. I also said that he had told me privately that he had no political plans at the moment though he was not proposing to give up politics and if a suitable by-election came along he would consider it.

* George Barnes.

The BBC made Crawley's position clear to Churchill and said that it was not their policy to go into the question of whether the commentators employed by them were, or at some future time might be, candidates for Parliament. There was an understanding with the parties, but not, it was emphasised, an agreement, that broadcasts by Members of Parliament should be roughly in proportion to the ratio established for Party Political Broadcasts. At the time the agreed ratio between the Labour and Conservative Parties was 50/50. But this was in relation, the BBC declared, to Members of Parliament and did not refer, or apply to, candidates.

The BBC stood firm; but Conservative pressures mounted. Many Conservatives felt that however impartial Mayhew and Crawley might be on television their success must be of some advantage to the Labour Party. And indeed, paradoxically, the more impartial Mayhew and Crawley were, and the less inclined they seemed to grind party political axes on television, the more they appeared to be statesmanlike as compared with those politicians who seemed to want to use television mainly for party political wrangling.

But it was right, as well as expedient, to try to find some Conservative members who might be just as effective on television as Mayhew and Crawley and just as prepared to be impartial. I did my best to do so. But in the process I discovered that, during these years at any rate, the attitude of most Conservative Members of Parliament to political communication by television was quite different from that of such members of the Labour Party as Mayhew and Crawley, Wyatt and Freeman. These four were interested in communication for its own sake. I sensed in them all a certain disillusionment with the party political battle. They had gone into politics in the immediate post-war situation with a burning enthusiasm. The Labour Party had been triumphantly in power for five years but the millennium had not arrived. The split in the Party which had helped to bring it down in 1951 still existed. They found in television a new means of expression, not of party policies but of the driving force which had sent them into politics in the first place. They delighted in its technicalities and wanted to explore its possibilities. They were prepared to accept its disciplines and to work generously as part of a production team of which each was only a member. They found no problem in travelling great distances with cameramen and sound recordists; working long hours in film cutting rooms with producers as they wrote commentaries; discussing maps and diagrams with designers; preparing cues into film; learning to talk to the right camera in the studio.

This was not at all the Conservative approach. Television in itself did not interest them. Most were busy men with a variety of outside interests. The fees which television paid were negligible in comparison with what they could earn elsewhere. They were prepared to give time to television if this were considered to be of advantage to the Party. They could see the point of political discussions such as 'In the News' where they could argue a party case, but they could see little point in going to all the trouble of being an expositor in a series of television programmes in which they would have to be politically impartial. They did not want to be quasi-professional television commentators of the Mayhew-Crawley kind. It was not for this that they had gone into politics. If they had any time to spare from their parliamentary duties they would rather give it to their own affairs, or to their families, than to television.

We did succeed eventually in placing two television series by Conservative Members of Parliament. Those who were persuaded to undertake them worked hard. As did we all. But they were not successful. Our failure to find the Conservative equivalents of Mayhew and Crawley was one of the reasons why the era of the MP as a television commentator gradually came to an end. But others were purely practical: as the television machine grew larger it became increasingly difficult to fit such television work as filming abroad into the changing demands of a political timetable. So though the Wyatt-Freeman-Crawley-Mayhew era went on for many years— and was of great value to television communication—it was replaced by the era of the full-time professional television journalist. There are many excellent professional television commentators and interviewers. But I believe that television current affairs programmes have been poorer since they lost men of the calibre of Mayhew and Wyatt and Freeman and Crawley who had had personal experience of the responsibilities of government.

[7]

The First Television Party
Election Broadcasts

1951

From 1950 onwards politicians were taking part in television discussions such as 'In the News' and in such expositions of foreign affairs as 'International Commentary' but there was no attempt by the political parties to use television to make a direct appeal to the electorate until the autumn of 1951.

The initiative came from the Corporation. The BBC considered that it was both inevitable and in the public interest that television should not only develop its own current affairs programmes but that it should also be used for the formal type of political communication hitherto confined to sound radio.

It is necessary here to differentiate between the two main kinds of broadcast programmes which may affect political behaviour—those which are under the editorial control of the broadcasting organisations and those which are under the editorial control of the political parties. In all the discussions and controversies about political broadcasting it became increasingly important to see that the line between these different types should be sharply defined so that the public would be aware whether it was being appealed to by a representative of a political party or whether it was being presented with a report or a discussion which was intended to be politically impartial.

It was not always easy to achieve this differentiation. The report of the Ullswater Committee in 1936, upon which much practice was built, put the point succinctly, but not very clearly, in its Summary of Recommendations:

'The BBC should regularly consult the Parliamentary parties on major political issues.'[1]

Consultation with the parties had already proved embarrassing in relation to 'In the News'. But an overall pattern was beginning to emerge. This was that in matters of political broadcasting the BBC had editorial control over the news and the whole range of transmissions roughly categorised as current affairs, which may include discussions or interviews or feature programmes or reports concerned with political matters.

But, so that the political parties could use the new medium for political communication, the practice had grown up of having a limited group of programmes over which the political parties themselves had editorial control and for which the BBC merely provided time, facilities and any technical and professional advice which might be required. In such programmes the BBC was the instrument of the political parties who were the arbiters of content. Programmes of this kind fell into four main groups. There were Party Election broadcasts, given by the political parties between the dissolution of Parliament and Polling Day. The number and allocation of these were decided at a special meeting called ad hoc when it became evident that there would be a General Election in the near future. There were also Party Political broadcasts put out between elections. These came to be called within the BBC the 'annual series' since negotiations about them took place every year at a meeting, usually held in March, which was attended by senior representatives of the political parties and of the BBC. There were also Budget Broadcasts. These were a curious hybrid, not classed as Party Political broadcasts but governed by a mixture of party political considerations, the programme needs of the BBC, and the wishes of the Chancellor and the Shadow Chancellor themselves.

There were, in addition, and most important of all, the addresses to the nation broadcast from time to time by Ministers of the Crown and usually called 'Ministerials'. These last, and the ways in which their use was regulated, including any right of reply by Members of the Opposition, were key factors in the relationship between broadcasting and a democratic system of government. Yet it was not till 1956 that the political parties agreed that Ministerial broadcasts could be given on television. They decided in 1951, however, that television was suitable for party election broadcasting.

The date of the 1951 election was to be Thursday, October 25. It was agreed that in addition to the thirteen Party Election broadcasts on sound radio each of the three main parties should give one fifteen-minute broadcast on television. These were to be transmitted on the nights of October 15, 16 and 17. I was instructed to produce all three.

My first step, I was informed, should be to contact the Party Whips and let them know that I was producing the television broadcasts and also that I would be available for consultation if there were any professional or technical matters about which they would like advice.

It was already apparent to me, and became more so, that the handling of Party Election broadcasts in television was bound to be very different from that of sound radio. Party Political and Party Election broadcasts in sound were given by a single speaker who read from a script. From time to time the question had been raised of whether a second speaker could take part in such broadcasts and whether it would be possible to use recordings of speeches and other material to illustrate the arguments being put forward. But there had never been any agreement on these points and such methods had never been used.

In comparison with the strictly controlled situation in sound radio the instructions in regard to television were wide and loose. I had merely been told that each party was to decide what it wanted to do with its fifteen minutes on television and that the resources of the television service should be put at their disposal. This position had been made clear to me during a series of conversations I had had with the Director of Television and with the Controller of Television Programmes. Somewhat disturbed by the fact that in action I found myself making a number of decisions which might be the subject of later argument, I was at pains to put on paper in a memorandum the position as I saw it. I said:

'As all my instructions have been received verbally, I thought it would be as well to put them on paper as I have understood them and as I am interpreting them in practice.

1 Each Party to have fifteen minutes. Each Party to decide themselves what they want to do with their time on the air.
2 The resources of the Television Service to be put at their disposal to implement whatever they want to do.
  In interpretation, and after discussion with C.Tel.P.,* I have taken this to mean that if the Parties want more than one speaker they are perfectly free to have them. If they want captions—whether ordinary or animated—we should offer them the assistance of our

* Controller of Television Programmes.

caption artists. If they had captions made outside, they were to be at liberty to use them. Similarly, if they wished to use film, we should do what we could to enable them to put film on.

3 The professional advice of the producer was to be available to each Party if they wished to make use of it.

4 The rehearsal time given to each Party was to be the normal amount required for the presentation of the particular type of programme which they chose to present. For example, a talk with a single speaker would get the amount of rehearsal that a talk with a single speaker normally required. But if the Parties chose a more complicated type of presentation they would be given the normal amount of rehearsal for that type of programme.

5 The BBC should not provide transport to and from Alexandra Palace.

6 Reasonable hospitality between rehearsal and transmission should be given.

I informed, as instructed, the offices of all three Party Whips that I would be producing the three programmes and told them that if they wished to consult me on technical matters I was available for consultation.

At their request, I have now seen representatives of all three Parties—Lord Samuel;* Sir Hartley Shawcross and Mr Mayhew;† and Brigadier Hinchcliffe and Mr Colin Mann, who saw me on Mr Eden's‡ behalf.

Two out of the three Parties wish to use two speakers and captions; in both cases, animated captions. This has raised one of the delicate problems which we foresaw, and which was one of the reasons why, on my advice being asked before these arrangements were made about ways in which absolute impartiality could be guaranteed, I advised that on this particular series, and until we had a little more experience of programmes such as these, captions should not be among the facilities which the BBC should make available. [My advice on this point had been disregarded.]

The situation is this: one of the two Parties has approached privately, and without my previous knowledge, one of the experienced freelance caption artists who is an experienced manufacturer

* Liberal.
† Labour.
‡ Conservative.

and operator of animated captions for television. The other Party approached the same man, but later. He consulted the Party which had approached him first and on a purely hypothetical basis asked whether they would object to him doing similar work for one of the other Parties. They did object and he has accepted their decision. The Party which he had to refuse has come back to us and asked whether the BBC would have the captions made and animated. I thought that we obviously must do so, under the terms which we have offered, and I am making arrangements accordingly.

I think it is likely, however, that the work of the freelance in these fields may be better (since he is a specialist) than that of our own caption artists, whose normal work is of a much more general character.

I don't think this situation can be helped in any way and in a sense it has nothing to do with us. But I think you should be aware that there may be some criticism of the animated captions made by the BBC in comparison with the others which are being made by the outside freelance.

Grace Wyndham Goldie.'[2]

The freelance whose name I did not wish to give in this memorandum because he had given me information on a confidential basis, was Alfred Wurmser. The situation as it developed was to be the cause of more trouble than I had envisaged.

Lord Samuel was to appear first. By tradition the party in power when a General Election was announced had the last word. In 1951 this meant that the Mayhew/Shawcross television broadcast would be transmitted on October 17, the Conservative broadcast by Mr Eden on the preceding evening, October 16, and the Liberal broadcast by Lord Samuel on October 15.

I went to see Lord Samuel.

It was already evident that one of the most difficult tasks in television, particularly for politicians and men of authority speaking on important occasions, was to talk direct to the lens of the television camera—that is direct to the individual viewer. And already we had discovered that the simplest situation in which to place someone inexperienced in television was that of being interviewed by someone more experienced.

Although the choice of an interviewer for party political occasions

96

was a difficult one I strongly advised Lord Samuel to choose the interviewing technique for his presentation of the Liberal case. He agreed. His experience in 'Men of Authority' had shown him how successful it could be. I was reassured: I thought that he did not sufficiently realise the difficulties of talking to camera, of keeping to time and of taking cues. If he over-ran, the BBC could be accused by the other parties of lacking impartiality in that the Liberal Party would have had more than its agreed fifteen minutes. And if, as a result of the difficulties of talking from notes, there were practical problems about cueing and so on it would be the BBC which would seem to be at fault.

In the event both these things happened. For Lord Samuel changed his mind. He let me know that he had decided, after all, to speak alone to the camera. He would not use a script, but would speak from notes. Now one of the minor but important difficulties for a producer when a speaker is speaking from notes is to know when he has finished. As the talk goes on and the minutes tick by, every pause may be the end. If in such a case the producer does not fade out promptly the speaker is left staring foolishly into the camera. But if the producer fades out and it is *not* the end, the speaker's final peroration may be cut. There are a number of ways of dealing with this situation. One is for the producer to have a copy of the notes so that the final words are in front of him. The other is even simpler. If the speaker agrees to say 'Goodnight' to the audience when he has finished, these words act as a cue to the producer who can pronounce immediately the magic formula 'Fade sound and vision' and the programme is over.*

Lord Samuel did not wish to let me have a copy of his notes; he said he would depart from them and that it was therefore not safe to use them as a text. And he did not wish to say 'Goodnight'. How, then, was I to know when he had finished? He said that when he came to the end of his talk he would put his notes down on the table in front of him. That would be the signal. He was too distinguished, too old, too courteous and too determined for me to insist.

This was the first party political broadcast ever to be given on television in the history of Great Britain. I went up to the control gallery to direct the programme, nervous but hoping for the best. I

* All broadcasts at this period were 'live'. The problem does not exist when programmes are pre-recorded.

learnt that evening that hoping for the best was never good enough. Lord Samuel over-ran. The fifteen minutes grew to sixteen and seventeen. I had decided that it was impossible on this first party political broadcast to signal to him to end as I would have done in an ordinary programme. He was unaccustomed to taking cues and it might flurry him. He came to the end of a sentence. There was a pause. His notes were on the table. He looked down and shuffled them about. Was this the signal? I decided that I could hold him in vision no longer and faded the picture and the sound. But he had *not* finished. It emerged later that he had simply lost his place in his notes. And his final peroration had been cut.

It was an unhappy moment, but in a sense it did not matter. He had seemed on television to be what he was—a statesman of distinction, wisdom and experience; a man of undoubted quality. And in a sense too, in spite of the practical problems which his decision to talk direct to the camera had caused, he was right to do so and ignore the advice I had given him that he should be interviewed. The interview technique can be a help in programmes such as 'Men of Authority' where the speaker is completely willing to communicate the facts and attitudes which the interviewer, for the information of the public, wishes to elicit. But this is seldom the situation in a party political or party election broadcast. Here the speaker is presenting a case. The opposing case will, it is reckoned, be put by the other political parties in their own party political or party election broadcasts. So it is seldom felt to be sensible by any political party that it should give part of its own time to the provision of opportunities for awkward questions which a politician might well prefer not to answer.

This was to be a continuing dilemma for parties and politicians. Many interviewers were not prepared to put only those questions which politicians wanted to anxwer: they considered it their duty to put the questions which they believed the public would have in their minds as they watched and listened. So when the parties chose to use the interviewing technique they were often faced with difficult decisions. Should they expose their main speaker to the searching and sometimes awkward questions put by an informed interviewer? Or should they try to find an interviewer who would put only those questions which had been prepared for him so that he would become an aid to the politician in presenting party political arguments rather than someone who questioned them?

In 1951 the Conservatives chose the second alternative. Mr Eden was to be interviewed by an experienced television interviewer, Leslie Mitchell, who was employed by the Conservative Party for this purpose. The questions and answers were carefully prepared and carefully rehearsed. On the screen this was all too apparent. This was the 'finger on the trigger' election and a whole front page of the *Daily Mirror* had been filled, menacingly, with a photograph of a hand holding a revolver. 'Mr Eden,' said Leslie Mitchell earnestly, 'it has often been said in recent times that the Conservative Party is a war-mongering party. Is there a shred of truth in that?'

But it was not only the choice between interviewing and 'straight to camera' talks which created difficulties in 1951. Both the Conservatives and the Labour Party wanted to experiment with the use of visual aids in the presentation of their respective cases on television. Part of the Conservative case was the accusation that the cost of living had risen sharply since the Labour Government had come into power in 1945 and that this was not due, as the Labour Party was said to claim, to the Korean war but to 'Labour muddle, mismanagement and misrule' including Dalton's policy of inflation, the nationalisation of coal, transport, electricity, gas and steel and the devaluation of the pound. A graph, based on figures from the London and Cambridge Economic Service showing a steeply rising line for the cost of living between 1945 and 1951, had been printed in Conservative election leaflets and was used in the Conservative Party Election broadcast.

Christopher Mayhew and Sir Hartley Shawcross were to appear on television the night after Anthony Eden and Leslie Mitchell. I knew that the Labour Party spokesmen wanted to refute, if they could, the points put forward on the previous evening by the Conservatives. And I thought it likely that Christopher Mayhew would try to make this refutation visual as well as verbal.[3]

He did. With his usual enthusiasm, energy and refusal to accept difficulties, he asked on the morning of the Labour Party Election broadcast that a new graph should be drawn to refute the graph used by the Conservative Party on the previous evening. He would provide a set of figures and all that was necessary was to translate those into a graph. Mayhew's whole argument was that the Conservative graph made the rise in the cost of living since 1945 look steep because of their juggling with the vertical and horizontal axes of the graph. He wanted to demonstrate that by using identical figures but drawing the graph out horizontally it was possible to flatten the steepness of the rising curve so that it appeared almost a straight line. He also wanted to show that by using neither of these pieces of electoral trickery it was possible to produce what he called an 'honest graph' showing the reality of the situation.

All these arguments were to be criticised later in the Press and in letters to the newspapers. In the meanwhile my own problems were practical. Our caption artists were skilled in lettering, but they were not statisticians and had no experience of translating figures into graphs.

By this time Christopher Mayhew and I had worked together for about six months on 'International Commentary' and had become colleagues and friends. He had said that the drawing of the graph from the figures he had provided was easy and that anybody could do it. Why then could he not do it himself? I thought he would understand the difficulties and agree readily. But no. He stood on what he considered to be his rights as a party representative. The BBC ought to carry out this work. I said that if he would translate the figures into a graph we certainly would. He said that if I continued in my refusal to translate the figures into a graph he would ring up the Director-General. I said that I would be delighted if he did. At long last, and with the disarming cheerfulness which made him a pleasure to work with, he agreed to draw the graph. And I agreed that the caption artist would copy this on to a caption card.

Next morning the newspapers were full of what they called 'The Battle of the Graphs'. *The Economist*[4] in a long article under the title of 'Contest in Curves' examined the various arguments. In a surprising sentence it said of the graph used in the Eden broadcast, 'It is true that the draughtsman made the curve steeper than it need have been by not using the whole of the horizontal axis, but some sharpening of emphasis is accepted practice in election broadcasts'. One was tempted to ask—accepted by whom? This was the first television election. Few television viewers would be likely to be aware of or understand the sophisticated attitudes of *The Economist* when it stated that 'to represent the rise in prices by an upward curve is, after all, merely symbolic, and no one gradient is right'.

What, almost certainly, would impress most television viewers was the appearance of the graph on the screen and the way in which it was presented to them. If a reputable statesman such as Anthony Eden said in effect, 'Look: just see how steeply the cost of living has risen since the Labour Government came into power. This graph represents not my figures but those of a group of independent investigators', and showed a steeply rising line, the viewer would tend to accept this as evidence that prices had in fact risen steeply.

The 'Battle of the Graphs' in this first television election showed that visual material used in election propaganda sharpened the personal responsibility of political leaders for the material they presented. If a politician like Anthony Eden used a graph on television which could be accused of being a fake and which could be publicly attacked as inaccurate his own reputation was involved—not merely that of the party machine which had produced it. In a pamphlet a graph had a certain air of anonymity and was merely part of the vast output of paper with which electors are deluged at election time. But a misleading graph used by one of the leaders of a political party to support his arguments on television was quite another matter. This was highly personal and electors who were viewing would be more likely to trust the evidence of the graph because of the calibre of the man presenting it than they would a semi-anonymous leaflet. The tools of political propaganda on television became therefore more personal than such other tools as print because on television the politician himself was seen to be using them and in a sense was acting as a guarantor of their validity.

If the television broadcasts of the 1951 election made it evident that politicians who used television to appeal to the electorate must take some personal responsibility for the television tools which they used, it also made evident, to me at any rate, that there must be a much clearer definition of the relationship between the responsibility of the BBC's television producer and that of the political parties for the effectiveness on television of what the parties wanted to present. The differences with Christopher Mayhew over the graphs were not sensible and could have been avoided.

They arose not only from the lack of facilities for the making of graphs within the television service at that time but also from the fact that neither the political parties nor those at Broadcasting House who conducted the high-level negotiations had given serious thought to the nature of television as a method of political communication. The seniors at Broadcasting House understood radio and were knowledgeable about microphones, scripts and the production of talk. They were at sea in anything to do with television. The political parties, even more at sea, found television a nuisance.

This was particularly true during a General Election campaign. Television was simply one more thing which party headquarters had to bother about and an added burden for party leaders. It was outside the experience of the officials who ran the campaigns. And it demanded of politicians a new kind of expertise which few of them possessed and some of them despised.

These attitudes remained long after 1951. The result was that negotiations between the BBC and the parties about the use of television for Party Political and Party Election purposes were conducted on a high plane of ignorance and impracticality. The handling of political broadcasting in television could not be regulated in detail as it was in sound radio because none of the senior negotiators understood the detail. So the precedents of 1951 remained. Each political party was to do what it pleased with its agreed television time and resources of the BBC's television service were to be at its disposal.

This was basically a healthy situation. It was ludicrous that in a democracy the political parties contending for the support of the electorate should not be able to use to the full the variety of new methods of communication which television made possible. In sound radio if one political party wanted to use a second speaker or an illustrative excerpt from previous political speeches in a political broadcast this had to be considered at the formal yearly meeting between the political parties and the BBC. But in television any one party could decide at will whether it would have a dozen speakers in a television studio together with music, films, maps, diagrams, drawings and the use of outside broadcast cameras. Their decisions were not subject, as in sound, to what was effectively a veto by another party.

But this greater freedom inevitably caused strains, and left a great deal of decision-making about practicalities to the television producer assigned to the broadcast. He or she might well find it necessary to say to the officials from Labour and Conservative Headquarters, or even to party leaders, that it was technically impossible to implement the broadcast in the manner in which they had planned it. Or to advise that though technically possible the result would be ineffective and that the points they wished to make would not register. Or that, in spite of their wishes to have outside broadcast cameras in a suburban home so that the householders and their friends could be seen to be asking questions of a politician in a television studio, the request had come so late that it was almost impossible to implement without disrupting a sports programme and depriving millions of viewers of a scheduled football match.

These were some of the questions which developed as a result of the experimental Party Election broadcasts in 1951. Summarised, they were a greater freedom for any political party to use the new methods of communication for political purposes; a greater responsibility for television producers of political programmes than for those of sound radio with greater consequential possibilities of friction; and an increasing concern within the political parties about the attitudes and abilities of the television current affairs producers who were responsible for Party Political, Party Election and Ministerial broadcasts.

[8]

The Breaking of the BBC's Television Monopoly

1952-1954

Discussions about the future uses of television for Ministerial and Budget broadcasts were taking place at the very moment when the new Conservative Government was considering a political decision about television which was the most momentous in the history of British broadcasting since it started in 1926. A broadcasting system for television, differently financed and differently motivated, was to be set up which would be in competition with the BBC.

The matter had not been one of the subjects debated by the parties during the election campaign of 1951. It was a decision made by the leaders of the Conservative Party. Five years later Randolph Churchill wrote bitterly in the *Evening Standard*,[1] 'Never let it be forgotten that it was a Tory Cabinet which, during the illnesses of Sir Winston Churchill and Sir Anthony Eden, took the decision to thrust Commercial TV upon our country. The presiding genius at that Cabinet was the party's outstanding Mr R. A. Butler. Let credit be given where credit is due.'

But in fact the new government had revealed the nature of its intentions almost immediately after its victory in the 1951 election. A powerful group had grown up within the party which was determined to break the BBC's monopoly. The BBC's current Charter and Licence were due to expire on December 31, 1951. Although the Attlee government had stated in a White Paper[2] in July 1951 that the best interests of British broadcasting required the 'continuance of the Corporation substantially on the present basis', no action to renew the Charter and Licence had actually been taken before the election. The way was therefore wide open for the start of a commercial television service. And the commercial television lobby found the political support it required among members of the Conservative Party.

The split between the political parties over commercialism in broadcasting was not due to any liking in the Labour Party for the BBC nor to any interest in the development of television. Clement Attlee, invited with his wife by George Barnes to see an evening of television, sat, obstinately silent and disapproving, watching, with some of us in attendance, television output on a monitor at Lime Grove. At the end he briefly compared the BBC television service unfavourably with the excellent work done by the Workers' Educational Association and departed as coldly as he had come. Labour opposition to commercial television was mainly a question of principle. The party was opposed to power being given to commercial interests in a medium which could affect men's minds.

Behind Conservative Party attitudes to commercial television, on the other hand, lay a good deal of suspicion and dislike of the BBC, which made them inclined to support any move to break the monopoly. The defeat of Winston Churchill and the party he led in the General Election of 1945 and again in the General Election of 1950 had been a shock to Churchill and to the Conservative Party as a whole. They could not believe that the country would have rejected Churchill, the architect of victory, for what they felt to be the lesser figure of Clement Attlee unless subversive influences had been at work. They sought for scapegoats. Among them was the BBC. Many Conservatives were convinced that the BBC had fomented a radical attitude in political matters and that, as an organisation, it was biased against Conservatism. Winston Churchill himself believed that the BBC was infiltrated by communists. The minutes of the regular meetings between the BBC and the political parties reveal his almost obsessional preoccupation with this idea.[3]

No one knew better than Churchill that during the war it had been necessary for the British government to ally itself with whatever groups in Europe and elsewhere were opposed to Hitler and Nazi domination. Were there communist sympathisers among them? They were all anti-Nazi: all against Hitler: all fighting for the same cause as British troops everywhere and as Winston Churchill. But, after the General Election of 1945, a suspicion grew in Churchill's mind that if, during the war, there might have been communist sympathisers in the BBC's Overseas Services, similar attitudes might have existed within its Home Services. He persisted in this belief whatever the denials of the BBC; whatever its conduct of enquiries and its presentation of the result of those enquiries to the political parties. And some leading Conservatives, however much they criticised Churchill's leadership of the Conservative Party, and however little they believed that the BBC was 'infiltrated by Communists', found it convenient to consider that, at the very least, the BBC as an organisation was, in a favourite phrase, somewhat 'left wing'.

So, within the Conservative Party those campaigning for commercial television and the breaking of the BBC's monopoly found receptive ears. All the more so because a commercial television service could be presented as a stroke for private enterprise and an attempt to give the public what it wanted rather than what those running a monopolistic service considered to be good for them.*[4]

The result, inevitably enough, was that one of the first actions of the new Conservative Government which came into power in October 1951 was to reject the recommendations of the Beveridge Committee and also the Labour Government's proposals as set out in the White Paper of July 1951.[5] Instead of giving the BBC a new Charter and Licence for fifteen years, it issued a Charter and Licence for only six months; this would last from December 31, 1951 to June 30, 1952. And in May 1952 the Conservative Government issued a White Paper[6] which was its own comment on the report of the Beveridge Committee. There were the usual tributes to the BBC. The White Paper said:

> 'The Government recognise that this effective monopoly has done much to establish the excellent and reputable broadcasting service for which this country is renowned and that the BBC have become an important fact of the structure of our national life. Their services must remain intact and the BBC should be the only broadcasting organisation having any claim on the revenue from broadcasting receiving licences.'[7]

At the end of June 1952, when the six-month Charter and Licence expired, the BBC should be given a new Charter and Licence, though for ten, not fifteen, years as the Labour Government had proposed.† There were regrets that the national post-war economic situation had prevented the capital investment necessary for the

* Mr Selwyn Lloyd, MP, a Member of the Beveridge Committee, who became a Minister of State in the 1951 Conservative Government, had disagreed with the majority of the Committee and had argued the case for breaking the BBC's monopoly in a powerful Minority Report.

† The new Charter and the new Licence were duly issued in June 1952.[8] The new Licence was for the first time non-exclusive.

BBC to pursue various developments in television and high frequency broadcasting: and pledges that it should have the first call on labour and materials when these became available.

But a profound change of attitude was apparent in paragraph 7 of the White Paper. It said:

'The present Government have come to the conclusion that in the expanding field of television provision should be made to permit some element of competition.'[9]

The green light had been given to those advocating commercialism in television broadcasting. The decision made in 1952 proved irreversible. For good or ill, broadcasting in Great Britain would no longer be a public service monopoly. Once the principle had been abandoned in the case of television there was no logical defence for continuing it in sound radio. Implicit in the start of a commercial television service was the start of commercial radio whenever this appeared to interested groups to be sufficiently profitable.

Politically, however, the new service would be unimportant. Although a political decision brought it into existence, it was expressly forbidden to deal with political matters in its television programmes. The White Paper of 1952 said:

'the new stations would not be permitted to engage in political or religious broadcasting.'[10]

The concept of the future of British broadcasting as held by the Conservative Government in 1952 and as outlined in its White Paper seemed to be of a national broadcasting system of proved responsibility and repute (the BBC): this would continue to handle political matters. From now onwards it would merely be supplemented by a profit-making commercial television service financed by advertisers, probably specialising in light entertainment, forbidden to deal with politics and religion and supervised by some sort of controlling body since 'It would be necessary to introduce safeguards against possible abuses.'[11]

But the processes of opinion-making and the national attitudes to the powers, danger and privileges of broadcasters which had created and shaped the BBC during the 1920s and 1930s now began profoundly to affect the simple concept of a second and competitive commercial television service as set out in the White Paper of 1952.

In November, 1953 the Conservative Government issued a second White Paper on Television Policy.[12] This, clearly, was a result of the criticism of the policy which had been set down in May 1952.[13] The new White Paper said:

'Many of the fears lately expressed as to the Government's policy arise from a misconception of the form competitive broadcasting might take in this country: and it is in order to inform Parliament of the Government's views in greater detail that this further White Paper is being issued.'[14]

But what the White Paper of November 1953 revealed was not an amplification of the scheme as outlined in the White Paper of May 1952. It was a total change of policy. What was now being proposed was not a second television service forbidden to deal with serious subjects such as religion and politics but a second Corporation which was virtually a mirror-image of the BBC. The controlling body, which the 1952 White Paper declared to be necessary as a safeguard against abuses, was now to be a public corporation. It would be set up by Statute for an initial period of ten years and, like the BBC, would operate under Licence from the Postmaster General. This new Corporation, the Independent Television Authority, would be governed by a Board of Directors, very similar to the BBC's Board of Governors.* Like the BBC, it would be given independence in the handling of day-to-day matters including individual programmes.

Since commercial broadcasting was to be under the control of a public corporation there was now no need (said the White Paper) to ban it from producing programmes about religious or political matters.[15] But the special position of the BBC was formally recognised:

'The proposal that there should be competition with the BBC is in no way a criticism of that body, of whose achievements the whole country is justly proud. It has been made clear throughout that the BBC would continue to be the main instrument of broadcasting in the United Kingdom.'[16]

The White Paper was issued on November 13, 1953. In March 1954 the Postmaster General issued a Licence to the Independent

---

* There were some differences. The BBC's Board of Governors were appointed by the King (and after the Queen's accession by the Queen) in Council. That meant, in practice, by the Prime Minister. The Board of Directors of the IBA (later called Members of the Authority) were appointed by the Government. Such an apparently minor distinction could have significance in a constitutional crisis.

Television Authority. On August 4, 1954 the Television Act, which allowed a commercially financed television service in Great Britain for a period of ten years, became law.

The decisive change from the ideas put forward in the White Paper of 1952, altered in the White Paper of 1953 and formalised in the rules laid down in the Television Act of 1954, was that the new service was not to be one of 'unrestricted commercialism'. Public anxieties about the possible abuse by commercial interests of their right to enter people's homes in order to persuade had resulted in a number of safeguards being written into the Act. The most important was the ruling that advertisers should not be allowed to control or influence the form and content of television programmes. They could buy television time and make television 'commercials'. But these advertisements had to be distinguishable from ordinary television programmes and could be placed only at certain points during transmissions, for instance at the beginning and end of programmes and in the so-called 'natural breaks' within programmes as, for example, between the acts of a play. Moreover detailed regulations were laid down about the amount of advertising which could be permitted in relation to programme time and which could be allowed in any 'clock hour'.

The Television Act was also more specific than the White Paper of 1953 in regard to the political coverage allowed in commercial television broadcasts. It forbade the inclusion of matter 'designed to serve the interests of any political party'.[17] This made it impossible for the political parties to buy time on television which they could use, for instance at times of elections, for party purposes. But the Act permitted the inclusion in commercial television of 'relays of the whole (but not some) of the BBC's party political programmes'.[18]

The result was that the usual procedure in regard to party political and party election programmes came to be that these were produced, as before, in co-operation with the parties, by the BBC and were 'relayed' by the commercial companies on the same days and at the same times as the BBC transmissions. The use of word 'relay' was significant. It seemed to indicate the pre-eminence of the BBC in matters of party political television. It also appeared to endorse the statement in the White Paper of 1953 that the BBC would continue to be the 'main instrument of broadcasting in the United Kingdom'. Also, in order to make these 'relays' practically possible, representatives of the Independent Television Authority were present at the meetings between the BBC and the political parties at which the length, number, placing and timing of party political broadcasts were agreed.

But since the impact of political pronouncements in formal party political broadcasts was declining and the impact of appearances of politicians in ordinary television current affairs programmes was increasing, the arrangements under the Act of 1954 about the relaying of party political programmes were less important than other factors in determining the effect of the new service on politics. One of these was that the commercial companies were specifically permitted by the Television Act of 1954 to present 'balanced discussions and debates where the persons taking part expressed opinions and put forward arguments of a political character'. This opened the way to the appearances of politicians, including Prime Ministers and Leaders of the Opposition, in commercial television current affairs programmes.

Looking back it seems astonishing that so few of us at the production level were aware of the danger to the whole existence of the BBC which had become evident as a result of the attitudes to broadcasting within the new Conservative government and of the pressure groups acting upon it. The truth is that few of us really believed that a commercial television service would be started or that, if it were, it could be successful. It was obviously absurd for politicians to say as they did[19] that the BBC would not be affected if its monopoly were to be broken. But it took a considerable time for most of us to realise that the long-term question was whether the BBC and the standards for which it stood could survive at all.

The possibility of the extinction of the BBC as we knew it was brought home to me sharply one day when a Junior Minister came to lunch with some of us at Lime Grove. Our audience figures had dropped alarmingly as a result of the first impact of commercial television. I asked him what would happen if the figures dropped still further; if for instance only 20% of the television audience watched BBC television and 80% watched ITV. He said briskly that in such a case the government could not possibly insist that the BBC's licence fee should continue to be paid. Politically it would be impossible to ask 80% of the viewing population to pay for the benefits enjoyed by only 20%.

This may not have been government policy though it made obvious commonsense in a democratic political system. I had not really expected any other answer. We must, I knew, keep up our figures if we were to survive. But I was taken aback by the apparent cheerfulness with which a politician who had some authority in broadcasting matters could envisage the end of the BBC's contribution to the national life. And though startled myself, I was glad that some of the television producers who were present were able to hear the brutal truth from someone more influential than I was. A number of experienced television producers were then honourably— but perhaps a trifle myopically—mainly interested in creating programmes of cultural importance designed for minorities and it was vital that they should realise that unless their programmes were popular as well as valuable their chance of producing valuable programmes in the future might vanish altogether.

But the other danger was equally evident. If the television service of the BBC maintained its audience figures and yet the standard of its programmes and the values which animated them seemed no different from those offered by commercial television the public was bound to ask another question. What could any government reply to a statement which ran 'There seems no difference between the kind of programme we get from the BBC and from commercial television. If we can obtain programmes like this free, why should we pay licence fees so that the BBC can supply us with exactly the same kind of stuff?' Politically any government in such a situation would find it difficult to enforce the payment of licence fees to the BBC.

The almost impossible task, therefore, which faced the BBC's television service during the next few years was to maintain the audience figures and yet produce programmes of a standard which would be sufficiently different from that of commercial television to ensure that the public could be asked to support the payment of licence fees to the BBC.

Some intellectuals, and many who wished to ensure the continued existence of the BBC because they thought that it provided a service which was socially valuable, pressed it to pay more attention to minority interests; to patronage and promotion of the arts; to educational programmes; to religious matters; and that it should ignore audience figures. We, who were in the business, realised bitterly that if we did so we should rapidly become a small specialised channel which would not be supported by the mass public and would not therefore be entitled to a licence fee paid by the public, but which, if sufficiently useful in its minor way, might be maintained as a government service, government subsidised and therefore in the long run government controlled. The broadcast freedoms which had been won so painfully would disappear. And television, losing them, might in the long run carry the BBC's sound services down too so that they also would be controlled by the government. The reality of broadcasting would be elsewhere. And the unrestricted commercialism which the Sykes Committee had rejected in 1923 would exist in Great Britain as it did in the United States.

We understood, therefore, that everything the television service did had to be in a precarious state of balance. We could not expect to get many programmes of purely minority interest into peak hours. If a programme couldn't make the figures would it at least add to our prestige and so justify the payment of our licence on the grounds that we were clearly not pandering to commercialism and interested only in the size of our audiences? Public relations became more important. Presentation had to be brighter. And always we had to remember that the BBC and commercial television were judged by different standards.

Many years later I heard a denunciation from a pulpit of a particular BBC programme. Afterwards I asked the preacher why he had not denounced equally an ITV programme which I personally had found far more distasteful. He said 'Oh, but we don't expect that kind of thing from the BBC.' This was true from the beginning. The BBC was generally expected to be more socially responsible than commercial television and yet to compete equally for audiences.

It took time for us to realise all this. There were other more immediate effects. One was the increased power of television vis-à-vis Broadcasting House. We could always say and often did, in relation to some new idea which was a departure from BBC precedent, 'Well, if *we* don't do it, *they* will.' The second was the brain drain. There was no cadre of experienced television personnel in Britain other than those trained by the BBC. The television companies had to buy BBC production staff and engineers either with the prospect of greater personal opportunities or of larger financial rewards, or both. This had various results: one was that the standards of the BBC infiltrated commercial television; secondly, and it was a related point, that there was a camaraderie at the lower levels between the television staff of the BBC and those of commercial television, however cut-throat the competition became at the top. Thirdly, there was a sense of expansion within the BBC. It lost many valuable people, but with them went some dead wood. As a result channels of promotion were opened up; there were more opportunities for the young, a greater receptivity for new ideas.

With all this, and perhaps it was the greatest justification for the start of a competitive television service, was the new sense of freedom among television personnel. If the BBC didn't like them, or if they didn't like the BBC, they could go elsewhere and, with their television expertise, find a living in some other group in which television played its part. This was more important to the permanent television staff employed by the BBC than to the actors, entertainers, writers and speakers to whom it gave contracts. Actors could, and did, move between the theatre, television and films. This was equally true of entertainers who could appear not only in television but on the halls and in cabaret. Writers who provided scripts for television could write plays for the theatre, or books, or articles for the Press, according to their particular talents. But those who specialised in television production and television operations had few other outlets. Their new freedom was important to them. And because they were free to go many stayed in the BBC with a new spirit. They themselves decided that their hearts were in what the BBC television service was trying to do; there was therefore a new enthusiasm which could be harnessed.

But a price had to be paid. The BBC was forced to do something, even if painfully and gradually, to see that its Civil Service-like staff and salary structure became more related to television market values. Wages and salaries went up. And the fees paid to everyone who appeared on television rose astronomically. Vast fortunes could apparently be made by people who invested in the new commercial television companies. Those who made this possible, the musicians, the entertainers, the writers, the actors, the stars which television itself had produced, as well as the owners of racecourses, football clubs and organisers of sporting occasions, all wanted a greater share of the television wealth which now seemed to be around. Television in Britain was no longer simply a public service which could not afford to pay its stars the sums they could earn in the theatre or on films or even in Fleet Street. It had become a great money-making machine.

This changed the whole climate in which television operated. Serious speakers and politicians, hearing of the high earnings of others, began to ask why their own fees should not be raised. Few politicians, even those who had backed the introduction of commercial television, appreciated the fact that, in a commercial system, time on television is a commodity and that in the United States, for example, it was not normal practice for politicians to be paid for their appearances on the air. Rather the reverse. They were considered fortunate if they did not have to buy time. The BBC had always maintained that a politician should be treated like any other contributor and paid at the same rates. So, as fees went up, appearances on television had a double attraction for many politicians: not only could they reach a wider audience than in the House of Commons, the sums they earned could be a very welcome addition to their incomes.

But a more important result of rising costs was the effect they had on the relation between the BBC and the Government. A member of the Independent Television Authority once said to me jovially and triumphantly, 'Your trouble is that you can't increase your revenue as costs go up whereas we can.' This was, and is, true. Among the broadcast matters over which the Government retained control were the number of broadcasting hours and the size of the licence fee. As television costs rise it is possible for the commercial companies to put up their advertising rates. But the BBC cannot itself increase the licence fee upon which its whole existence depends.

Any increase in the licence fee is certain to be unpopular. No government wishes to take unpopular decisions which may be politically damaging and so the BBC's need for a higher revenue in order to pay for a rapidly expanding and increasingly costly television service caused fresh strains in the relationship between the government and the Corporation. Moreover, however little any government might wish to interfere with the BBC's day-to-day management, it was bound, when dealing with a request for an increase in the licence fee, to ask for figures to justify the demand. The result was that the BBC, accustomed to the periodic investigations of official Committees whenever its Charter and Licence were due for renewal, was now forced, because of the uneasy situation caused by a fixed licence fee at a time of rising costs, to face some kind of government investigation whenever it needed a higher revenue to maintain the services—including a second television channel and the development of colour—which were expected of it. The Corporation therefore became more vulnerable; and this inevitably meant some diminution in its hard-won independence from government interference in its day-to-day running.

[9]

Developments in Television
Political Broadcasting

1952 - 1955

In spite of the publication in May 1952 of the Government's White Paper which foreshadowed a competitive television service and in spite of Sir William Haley's departure* in June, the BBC pressed on with its plans for more political broadcasting on television.

The very existence of television forced the pace. We discovered that if Ministers felt that, with advantage to themselves, their parties and their policies, they could appear on television when invited to do so by the BBC, even in the unprecedented circumstances of their being asked to reply impromptu, and in public, to unrehearsed questions put by journalists, then they would do so. So although in March 1952 the parties had formally refused to have either Budget or Ministerial broadcasts on television, nevertheless on July 11, 1952 a senior Minister, the Chancellor of the Exchequer, Mr Butler, took part in the first television 'Press Conference'. He had never before appeared on television and no Chancellor of the Exchequer when in office had ever taken part in a television programme. And for the next two years, though the parties continued to reject the BBC's offer of television time and facilities for Ministerial broadcasts, Ministers of the Crown and Leaders of the Opposition appeared regularly on 'Press Conference'.

Such appearances were not considered to be Ministerial broadcasts in the formal sense and were not subject to the rules agreed with the Parties and set down in the Aide Mémoire of 1947. I put on paper in February 1953 some of the rather fine distinctions between formal 'Ministerial' broadcasts on television and the appearances of Ministers and Opposition Leaders in 'Press Conference'. This memorandum was written because I wanted to invite Mr

---

* He became editor of *The Times* and was succeeded by Sir Ian Jacob.

Macmillan, then Minister of Housing and Local Government, to appear in 'Press Conference' on April 22, 1953. Two permissions had to be sought. No Minister could broadcast without permission from the Prime Minister. And since the Director of the Spoken Word, now Harman Grisewood, had the responsibility of clearing this with the officials at No. 10, all invitations to Ministers had to have his agreement. In my memorandum I said:

'I obtained in June 1952 permission from D.Tel.B. (George Barnes) to invite Mr Eden to take the main part in the first Press Conference programme and if Mr Eden should refuse, permission to approach Mr R. A. Butler.*

Permission was given on the understanding that these appearances should not rank as Ministerial broadcasts but as programme appearances. The decisive factors which made them distinguishable from Ministerial broadcasts or Party Political broadcasts were the following:

(i) That the Ministers should be invited to take part in exactly the same way as any other personality. They would not themselves decide when to appear and would obviously have no right of appearance.

(ii) That the subject and handling of the programme would be determined by the BBC and not by the Ministers. In "Press Conference" they would have to be prepared to answer unscripted such questions as the journalists should ask. (The general area of questioning and the nature of the approach are, in fact, decided by the producer in conjunction with the journalists.)'

We had recognised from the first that if Ministers were to appear on 'Press Conference' there would be special problems both for us and for them. There were no rules of the kind which governed formal 'Ministerials' and which laid down conditions for any right of reply from the Opposition. But we were under the general obligation to be fair and impartial. We interpreted this as meaning that we ought to try to preserve an overall political balance, so that if we invited the Chancellor of the Exchequer and he accepted, we should, at the same time, plan for the appearance of the Opposition spokesman on financial affairs, then Hugh Gaitskell.

* Mr Eden accepted in principle but developed jaundice and could not appear.

I wanted, however, to avoid a Party Political type of tit-for-tat. I thought this would be bound to occur if, say, a Butler 'Press Conference' were followed immediately by a Gaitskell 'Press Conference'. Interest, I believed, would then inevitably be diverted from an encounter between the Press and the chief speaker to what the speaker in the second programme would reply to the speaker in the first. So I planned a kind of four-programme cycle with a Minister of the Crown being followed by a foreign statesman such as Ernst Reuter, the Mayor of Berlin, or a Commonwealth statesman such as Roy Welensky, then a figure from a different world, such as the Trade Union leader, Jack Tanner, or a philosopher such as Bertrand Russell, and only in the fourth programme a representative of the political Opposition.

We did not expect, or wish, the pattern to be as rigid as this. But it gave us a rough scheme upon which to work. In the event, because of the practical difficulties of fixing dates which would suit the other commitments of the main speakers as well as the need for the programmes to be topical, it was seldom possible to follow the scheme. So although the Chancellor of the Exchequer appeared in 'Press Conference' on July 11 1952, we could not arrange for Hugh Gaitskell to appear until November.

It was known, however, that we had invited Gaitskell and that the difficulty was only one of fixing dates. This was important. What we hoped to achieve, and gradually did, was that politicians and spokesmen for the political parties should realise that we wanted to present a politically balanced series, but over a period of time, so that there would not be an instant demand for a right of reply if a Minister appeared on television.

This was helped by the fact that 'Press Conference' was a questioning programme and not a platform for a single speaker. Expressions of critical, if not opposing, views were already built into it by the choice of the journalists who appeared. And it was not till 1954, when Peter Thorneycroft, then President of the Board of Trade, was alleged to have been given such a soft type of questioning by journalists that the Opposition protested and demanded a compensating programme.*

* Plans were made for a special fifteen-minute interview with Harold Wilson. These were dropped for practical, not theoretical reasons and Wilson appeared in 'Press Conference' at a later date.

If achieving political balance without the strict procedures laid down for 'Ministerials' was largely our problem, 'Press Conference' created a different set of problems for Ministers. Certainly they did not have to face the practical difficulties involved in trying to present their cases without the help of a written script; they need only answer questions, and this was a situation with which they were familiar and for which their training had equipped them. But now they were answering questions in an unfamiliar context, one which was not governed by the procedural rules of the House of Commons; nor were they in the privileged position of being the man on the platform dealing with hecklers down below. They were talking to a few knowledgeable newspapermen who were sitting beside them and asking questions which were often penetrating. The answers had to match the questions in seriousness if Ministers were not to seem lesser and lighter men than those who were questioning them. Moreover evasive replies were immediately seen to be so by the millions who were watching.

Yet it was often difficult, and could be against the national interest, for a Foreign Secretary or a Chancellor of the Exchequer to answer frankly some of the questions which were bound to be asked by informed and information-seeking journalists. These were not briefing sessions where a Minister could give background information to journalists on a non-attributable basis. He was seen to be saying whatever it was he said. And he would be watched not only by ordinary viewers but also by representatives of the Commonwealth and foreign Press so that a slip of the tongue or an insufficiently considered reply given tonight could make headlines in the newspapers of the world tomorrow.

The pyschological and political difficulties for Ministers appearing on 'Press Conference' were those of taking part in what looked like a reasonably private and friendly encounter but which in fact was immensely public, within sight of a viewing audience which expected frankness when frankness was often impossible, and in the kind of close-up which made evasiveness easily detectable.

To run a programme like 'Press Conference' it was necessary to appreciate some of the strains it imposed on Ministers who were appearing on it. Without prescribed methods or rules of procedure we had to work out our own. Their object was to see that the situation was not made impossible for Ministers who might be in the middle of delicate international or financial negotiations but which would still allow programmes to be genuinely unrehearsed and unscripted. These rules were pragmatic, flexible and never written down; but they became part of the unwritten practice of programmes of political interrogation on television.

The first was a matter of attitude. We hoped that the questioning process conducted in vision would reveal something fresh about the aims and personal attitudes of a Minister. If journalists felt that they were being fobbed off with an evasive or a merely routine answer to a serious question, they would pursue it. But there was no wish to set traps. And we made this clear to those we invited. In the early days some Ministers wanted to be told in advance what questions they would be asked. We always refused to do this. The programme would no longer be spontaneous and its whole purpose would be defeated. We might as well have the journalists read out their questions and the Ministers read their answers.

Moreover there was the professional reputation of the journalists to be considered. If we gave Ministers a list of questions they would be certain to try to exercise some kind of censorship over them, to say that they did not want this or that question to be asked since it would be embarrassing, and not in the national interest, for them either to answer it or not to answer it. But the journalists knew, and we knew, that if they did not put the key questions on matters which had already been canvassed in the Press and which the public would expect them to ask, they would appear to be either ill-informed or to have submitted to censorship. They were, rightly, not prepared to be put in either of these categories.

We tried to overcome these very real difficulties by two main methods. Though we refused to give Ministers (or any other figure who appeared on 'Press Conference') a list of the questions which were to be asked, we were prepared to indicate in general terms the areas within which there would be questioning. This was simply commonsense. It would be ridiculous to expect a Foreign Secretary, for instance, at a time when public interest was centred on the dangers of the Cold War in Europe or the position of the oil companies in Persia, to have at his fingertips the detail of negotiations currently being conducted in Latin America or Indonesia. There was therefore every sensible reason not to put a clever question which would force the Minister to reveal that he was not fully aware of the latest developments in such negotiations.

No responsible journalist wanted to put trick questions of this kind. But journalists were bound to put questions which Ministers might find it embarrassing to answer in a session as public as 'Press Conference'. If our advice were asked we suggested to Ministers that it was better to refuse to answer than to be evasive. Better still would be to make it clear in replying that the journalist asking the questions must know that it was impossible for a Minister to answer such a question at this moment. Unless such an answer clearly was an attempt to evade legitimate questioning most journalists accepted this type of reply.

Ministers were differently and often revealingly adept in dealing with situations of this kind. One example was Aneurin Bevan. He appeared in 'Press Conference' on March 26, 1953 and was questioned by Andrew Shonfield, who often acted as participating chairman; an American, Ed Newman, who was London correspondent of the National Broadcasting Company; Malcolm Muggeridge, formerly Deputy Editor of the *Daily Telegraph* and then Editor of *Punch*, and Trevor Evans, then Labour Correspondent of the *Daily Express*.

Bevan, since his resignation from the Cabinet in 1951, had, in a sense, been in the wilderness but was a powerful rival to Hugh Gaitskell for the leadership of the Labour Party. He had attacked the Gaitskellite policies, particularly in matters of defence. A key question was whether he could also afford to quarrel with the Trade Unions. It is worth noticing the differences between radio and television as a method of communication on such occasions. Bevan was not a successful radio broadcaster, largely because he had a stutter. But when I first met him I was at once aware that his immense vitality and the warm generosity of his attitudes would, on television, make his stutter irrelevant. Silences, or impediments in speech, are of the utmost importance in sound radio. If a pause is longer than usual, while, for instance a speaker is trying to consider how to answer a question, the listener is apt to think that something has gone wrong and begins to fiddle with the controls of his set. But on television nothing is more fascinating than to look at a person who is thinking, who is revolving a question in his mind and trying to decide how to answer it. This is a genuine situation, real and immediate; and the message of the act of thinking is conveyed visually by the expressions on the face of the man who is answering. Programmes of interrogation are, therefore, on the whole more successful on television than on sound radio. There is no interruption of communication; sight supplements the spoken word.

In a sense this is true also of impediments in speech. A stutter on radio can be embarrassing. Communication depends on being able to hear what is being said and a stutter becomes, so to speak, an interference in communication. But this is not true of television. Communication is not cut off since it is possible to watch the speaker as he struggles to communicate verbally. And if he is not embarrassed neither is the viewer. Moreover, for reasons which I do not fully understand, a stutter can in fact add to, rather than detract from, the effectiveness of communication in vision.

This is what happened in the case of Aneurin Bevan. He had a reputation for being both formidable and destructive. On 'Press Conference' we had been prepared for this. But on this occasion he decided to be genial and avuncular. He steered the questions into paths which suited him and chased enormous hares down long corridors of irrelevancy. The questioners failed to pin him down and became exasperated. Then Trevor Evans asked an explosive question: 'Why is it that your group has been so free in denigrating personalities among the Trade Union leaders?' Bevan said, 'This is a mere repetition of newspaper headlines.' Evans replied, 'Not at all, not at all.' Bevan demanded, 'Where has there been a denigration?' Evans said, 'Well, the latest example was the criticism of Lincoln Evans for accepting the knighthood. Do you concur with that attack?'[1]

If Bevan said that he did not concur he was denouncing those of his own followers who did. But if he said he did concur he would offend powerful colleagues in the Trade Unions.

In the control gallery we waited, tense, to see what would happen. He looked reproachfully at Evans; and said, 'No. No. No.' Then he smiled broadly, lifted his finger, shook it in Evans's face and said, 'You have been very naughty, as you know. You must not try to inveigle me into personal attacks on my colleagues.'[2] There was a burst of laughter. It was impossible to pursue the question. He had handled the television situation with the superb skill with which he had handled others elsewhere.

I maintain that such television broadcasts were and are valuable. It was clear to anybody watching that he was skating, however successfully, over some very thin ice; that he was not going to accept the logic of journalists or any other logic except that of his own devising. But it was also clear why he was so powerful a figure in British politics. This was no mean conspirator or stabber in the back, but a determined, skilful and generous man who pursued ends which were not ignoble with passion and humour through whatever channels were open to him.

I do not know, and did not care, whether Aneurin Bevan's appearance on 'Press Conference' helped or hindered him in his struggle for the leadership of the Labour Party. I was only concerned to try to see that television revealed him, as faithfully as possible, to be what he was. The millions who watched, and judged, were accustomed to assessing character. This was part of their own expertise; a talent they had to exercise in their daily lives, in making up their minds about who they should marry, how to deal with a foreman, a relative or a managing director. The basic approach of those producing programmes such as 'Press Conference' was always that the public were good judges if they were given material upon which to judge. And television could add one more facet to those already existing; to the records of action; the newspaper profiles; the reports of speeches. That, in the main, was what 'Press Conference' was about.

Until 1953 television coverage of political matters was largely confined to 'Press Conference' and other current affairs programmes initiated and controlled by the British Broadcasting Corporation. The only formal use made of television by the political parties had been the three experimental Party Election broadcasts in the election campaign of 1951. But on March 24, 1953, the parties accepted the BBC's offer of television time and facilities for both Party Political and Budget broadcasts. The problems of Ministerial broadcasts and any future Party Election broadcasting were referred to a working party which was set up to consider them and to make recommendations before the next annual meeting between the BBC and the parties in March 1954.

The need to make immediate arrangements for Budget and Party Political broadcasts and the setting up of the working party to study the use of television for Ministerial and Party Election broadcasting made television people like myself sharply aware of the complex relationships between the BBC and the political parties; in particular of the importance of the annual meeting with the parties; of the Aide Mémoire of 1947 and the disputes which had taken place from 1947 onwards about the interpretation of its rules in regard to Ministerial broadcasts and about such ancillary agreements as the 'fortnightly rule'.

The history of the Aide Mémoire is very curious. This vital document* was a record of the agreements reached between the BBC and the political parties as a result of conversations in 1944, 1945 and 1946 about the resumption of controversial broadcasting after the end of the Second World War. During the war and while the Coalition Government under Winston Churchill was in existence there was no party political broadcasting and the BBC's own current affairs broadcasting had come under the general jurisdiction of the Minister of Information. By May 1945 the Coalition Government had been replaced by the Caretaker Government with Mr Churchill as Prime Minister. A General Election was imminent. The end of the Ministry of Information was in sight. Broadcasting would once more be used contentiously in party political battles. Under these circumstances talks between the political parties and representatives of the BBC were inevitable. But the talks took place in a restrictionist atmosphere.

Sir Ian Jacob, when Director-General of the BBC, wrote a paper for the Board of Governors in preparation for the annual meeting with the political parties in March 1953, in which he said that in 1946 and 1947 it was felt that senior politicians were so opposed to any freedom in the handling, however impartially, of political affairs by the BBC that there was a real danger that the parties might come to an agreement that the Corporation should not undertake any political broadcasting other than the set Party Political broadcasts by Government and Opposition. 'To avoid this,' he said, 'and to preserve some freedom for broadcasting the BBC had accepted various restrictions, including the fortnightly rule.'[3]

The BBC from the first had been restive about the terms of the Aide Mémoire and had made representations to the political parties about the desirability of making changes both in regard to the 'fortnightly rule' and the definitions of 'Ministerial' broadcasts. The political parties argued that the Aide Mémoire was a binding agreement which could not be broken without the consent of the parties and certainly not unilaterally by the BBC. The BBC contended that the Aide Mémoire, as its name implied, was simply a record of agreements made in discussion at a particular time. They quoted, in support of their case, a letter which Mr Greenwood, when Lord Privy Seal in the Labour Government, had written on January 3, 1946 and which referred to the Aide Mémoire. It said:

* See Appendix A, p. 341.

'The Government do not think it desirable to attempt to reduce to written rules the principles which should govern the BBC in regard to political broadcasting. The principles to be adopted must depend upon good sense and goodwill, and it is as impossible to formulate exhaustive principles on paper as it is, for instance, impossible to define what conduct is unbefitting to an officer and a gentleman. The few short principles indicated should therefore be regarded as a mere aide mémoire of the conversation.'[4]

Nevertheless at annual meeting after annual meeting the political parties refused to accept changes suggested by the BBC. The matter came to a head over the so-called 'fortnightly rule'. Senior politicians in both Government and Opposition had been anxious that broadcast discussions of political affairs should not result in broadcasting becoming an alternative forum of debate to Parliament. So paragraph 6 (iv) of the Aide Mémoire of 1947 ran:—

'No broadcasts arranged by the BBC other than the normal reporting of Parliamentary proceedings are to take place on any question while it is the subject in either House.'[5]

The vagueness of this paragraph made the rule almost impossible to administer and in July 1948

'Government and Opposition agreed with the BBC that 6 (iv) should be construed as:

(a) that the BBC will not have discussions or ex parte statements on any issues for a period of a fortnight before they are debated in either house:

(b) that while matters are subjects of legislation MPs will not be used in such discussions.'[6]

The Corporation continued to find the rule restrictive and, in practice, difficult to operate. It affected all topical programmes and was creating difficulties in television discussions such as 'In the News'. Information about precisely what subjects were to be debated in Parliament within any particular fortnight was not always easy to obtain and some topical broadcast discussions, arranged before the Parliamentary timetable had been finalised, had had to be cancelled at the last moment. The Corporation therefore continued to argue that the 'fortnightly rule' should be abolished. But the parties continued to refuse.

The long struggle over the fortnightly rule revealed the weakness of the BBC when faced with a united front by the main political parties. This was demonstrated by subsequent events. The Corporation eventually came to the conclusion that it need not accept restrictions unless they were laid down in its Charter and Licence and decided that it should use its own discretion in regard to broadcast discussions about political matters which might be debated in Parliament. The political parties were informed of their intentions. The result, as revealed in the exchange of correspondence between the BBC, Herbert Morrison (Lab.) and H. F. C. Crookshank (Con.), was to produce what can only be considered to be a threat to the BBC by the political parties. The Corporation was warned that it was inadvisable to get into a position of public dispute with the Leaders of all parties in the House of Commons.[7]

More important than the discussions about the 'fortnightly rule' were the arguments over the definitions of 'Ministerial' broadcasts as laid down in the Aide Mémoire of 1947. The question here was not that broadcasting might become an alternative to Parliament as a forum for debate but that Ministers might use broadcasting to bypass Parliamentary procedures. If a Minister, particularly a Prime Minister, could make his statements on domestic or foreign affairs not to Parliament but by broadcasting, directly, personally and unchallenged, to individual members of the electorate the whole system of democratic representative government could be undermined.

Parliament therefore was highly suspicious of the development of Ministerial broadcasting. That way could lie dictatorship, or at least an increase in the power of the Executive in relation to the Legislature. So in the Aide Mémoire of 1947 the right of Ministers to broadcast was acknowledged but careful definitions were laid down about the use of these rights and provision was made for giving the Opposition a right of reply. Paragraph 2 of the Aide Mémoire ran:

'In view of their responsibilities for the care of the nation the Government should be able to use the wireless from time to time for Ministerial broadcasts which, for example, are purely factual, are explanatory of legislation or administrative policies approved by Parliament; or in the nature of appeals to the nation to co-operate in national policies such as fuel economy or recruiting, which require the active participation of the public. Broadcasts on State Occasions also come in the same category.'

The rights of Parliament were apparently secured. Ministerial broadcasts were to be mainly explanations of legislative or administrative policies already approved by Parliament or innocuous appeals for public co-operation which came to be known within the BBC as the 'Post Early for Christmas' type of Ministerial broadcast.

And the rights of the Opposition were also made clear. Paragraph 2 of the Aide Mémoire went on:

> 'It will be incumbent on Ministers making such broadcasts to be as impartial as possible, and in the ordinary way there will be no question of a reply by the Opposition. Where, however, the Opposition think that a Government broadcast is controversial it will be open to them to take the matter up through the usual channels with a view to reply.'

The Aide Mémoire went on to specify in detail the procedures for a right of reply:

> 'As a reply if one is to be made should normally be within a very short period after the original broadcast, say three days, the BBC will be free to exercise its own judgment if no agreement is arrived at within that period.'

An extraordinary situation was thus created. The political parties in effect insisted that the British Broadcasting Corporation, itself ultimately responsible to Parliament, should adjudicate between the parties when they were in dispute about whether Ministers of the Crown had made a proper use of their right to use broadcasting to address the nation.

The position of the BBC was made all the more difficult because Ministers themselves did not adhere to the definition of Ministerial broadcasts and rights of reply as set out in the Aide Mémoire. This was true of both parties. As early as 1948 Sir William Haley was pointing out some of the problems. The Minister of Health (Aneurin Bevan) at the time of the doctors' plebiscite on the Health Service had wished his Chief Medical Adviser to broadcast and had demanded from the BBC an assurance, before they had even seen the script, that the Opposition would not be accorded a right of reply. The Director-General felt that it was impossible to decide in advance that a broadcast on a controversial subject, however factual and objective it might be, was not to be regarded as controversial[8].

In 1952 Sir William Haley, in an internal memorandum in

preparation for the meeting with the parties in March, stated that the definitions of Ministerial broadcasts laid down in the Aide Mémoire (and he had been a party to the discussions which had led up to it) were laid down by way of illustration rather than intended to be a limiting definition of them.[9] He quoted a remark of Winston Churchill's which seemed to support this view. Haley said that when the BBC had pointed out how many Ministerial broadcasts there had been in the first years of the Labour Government, Mr Churchill took the initiative and said, 'The King's Government must be carried on and broadcasting is a proper means to help to do this.'

In practice leaders of both political parties continued to use the agreed rights of Ministers to broadcast not so much in terms of the definitions set down in the Aide Mémoire as in the spirit of Winston Churchill's pronouncement. The discrepancy between actual practice by Ministers in 'Ministerial' broadcasting and the narrow definitions laid down in the Aide Mémoire of 1947 left the BBC in a difficult position. In cases of dispute its decisions were liable to be attacked by whichever Party felt aggrieved. Feelings often ran high. Explanations were demanded. Protests were registered. And everything had to be done at speed since a reply, to be effective, had to be given within a few days of the original broadcast.

For some time television was not directly involved in these troubles. But it was inevitable that Ministers, particularly those who had had some television experience, would soon want to use television as well as sound radio when making important statements to the nation. This happened in the spring of 1954. On May 31, Mr Anthony Nutting, Minister of State at the Foreign Office, wrote to Sir Ian Jacob suggesting that the Foreign Secretary, Mr Eden, should give a talk on television after his return from Geneva about some of the issues which had been raised there. When asked to comment I proposed an appearance by Mr. Eden in 'Press Conference' on either June 11 or 18 or 30 and discussed these possibilities informally with the Foreign Office.

It was made clear to me that this proposal was not likely to satisfy Mr Eden. I was asked whether it would not be possible for the Foreign Secretary to be interviewed by a single person as, by 1954, was the practice for Budget broadcasts. But the method we had devised for Budget broadcasts was intended to suit an occasion when differing views were put forward on successive nights, starting with the Chancellor of the Exchequer, followed by the Shadow Chancellor on the second night. What Mr Eden was now suggesting was that he should use the same style but without any prearranged expression of Opposition opinion. It seemed to me, therefore, that he was in fact asking for a Ministerial broadcast.

I reported this within the BBC. On June 2, 1954, Sir Ian Jacob wrote to Anthony Nutting and pointed out that the political parties in March had once again rejected the BBC's offer of television for Ministerial broadcasts and had felt that all Ministerial broadcasts should be confined to sound.[10]

So, by 1954 it had become clear that Mr Eden wanted to use television to address the nation but did not wish this to occur in circumstances where he would have to answer the questions of journalists some of whom might be hostile. Indeed, though after Sir Ian Jacob's letter the proposal for a television appearance by Mr Eden in June 1954 was dropped, it was revived in November. Mr Eden wished to be interviewed on television on November 24 or 25 by one person with whom he would discuss the line of questioning in advance. These attitudes were a foreshadowing of the difficulties there were to be about Ministerial broadcasting during the Suez crisis. But that was not until 1956. And now I must go back to the early months of 1953 when my own immediate concern was the devising of methods for handling the first television Budget broadcasts.

The matter was urgent. These broadcasts were the result of the decision of the political parties in March 1953 that though Ministerial broadcasts should not be given on television yet television should be used for Budget as well as for Party Political broadcasting. And by March the Budget was almost upon us. Budget Day was to be April 14. But already by March 27 Sir Ian Jacob had written to Patrick Buchan-Hepburn saying, 'We understand that the Chancellor is thinking in terms of a television broadcast on the third night.' This meant that the Chancellor, Mr Butler, would give a sound radio broadcast on the evening of Budget Day as was the established custom. Mr Gaitskell, the Shadow Chancellor, would broadcast his reply, also in sound, on the following evening. But on April 16 there would be a television broadcast by the Chancellor and on the 17th by Mr Gaitskell.

I was asked to suggest the form which the television Budget broadcasts might take. Aware that neither Mr Butler nor Mr Gaitskell would want to give a straight talk and aware too that both had appeared on 'Press Conference' and were familiar with its format, I suggested that for each of these Budget broadcasts we might mount a special 'Press Conference' with William Clark of the *Observer* as participating chairman and the rest of the team balanced in the party sense and chosen with regard to their background of interest in economic affairs.

This proposal was put forward by the Director-General. But the Chancellor and Mr Gaitskell preferred to have only one questioner, the same for each. The Budget broadcasts would therefore take the form of interviews. And it was almost inevitable that the interviewer should be William Clark. He had worked with me on 'Press Conference' from the beginning and, though not an expert in economic affairs, was politically well informed, known to both Mr Butler and Mr Gaitskell and by now highly experienced in television.

The format was agreed. But the practical arrangements were complicated. The Chancellor would have to slip out of the House of Commons for two brief periods, one for a preliminary lighting session so that we could try out the camera shots, and later for the broadcast interview itself—which would be 'live'. We had no television studio within the Palace of Westminster or indeed anywhere near it. The easiest arrangement for the Chancellor would be for the interview to take place in his own study in Number 11 Downing Street. But this would mean making an Outside Broadcast Unit available. It was not easy to achieve this. These units made heavy demands on technical manpower and required a great deal of time to instal. It would be necessary to run cables into Number 11, bring in cameras and fix lights and microphones in the Chancellor's study during what was probably the busiest week of his year. Moreover Outside Broadcast Units were in great demand for ordinary programme purposes. Nevertheless this first television Budget broadcast by a Chancellor of the Exchequer was a special occasion and it was eventually agreed that an Outside Broadcast Unit and director could be made available. The van, which was the equivalent of a television control gallery from which the programme would be directed, could be parked at the back of the Downing Street gardens near the Horse Guards Parade; and cables could be run through the garden of No. 11 into the Chancellor's study.

The question then arose of the milieu for Mr Gaitskell's broadcast on Friday evening. He would not have to be in the House of Commons. There was no reason, therefore, why he should not come to

Lime Grove. He was very anxious, however, not to do so. He would like the interview to take place in his house in Hampstead. I, too, hoped to arrange this because it would be proper to treat the Shadow Chancellor as nearly as possible in the same way as the Chancellor.

But it was not possible. I asked the Outside Broadcast department whether the Unit which we were using on Thursday, April 16, in Downing Street for the Chancellor's broadcast could be moved to Hampstead in time for Mr Gaitskell's broadcast on Friday, April 17. They said that it could not be done. Quite apart from various other technical problems, it would be impossible to de-rig the Downing Street installations and re-rig them in Hampstead by the following evening. And a second Outside Broadcast Unit could not be made available without disastrous disruption of ordinary programmes.

These were the decisive arguments. But in any case the Outside Broadcast Department could not see the point of going to all the expense and the effort of using an Outside Broadcast Unit to broadcast a short television interview from an ordinary room in an ordinary house. The broadcast from No. 11 was an historic occasion with the Chancellor of the Exchequer answering questions about the Budget in the traditional residence of Chancellors of the Exchequer. In such a setting Outside Broadcast cameras could reveal visually something of the significance of the occasion quite apart from anything that was said. But an ordinary Hampstead drawing room could be reproduced perfectly well in a studio at Lime Grove with much less trouble and at a much smaller cost. Mr Gaitskell, faced with this situation, reluctantly agreed that his broadcast should take place in a television studio.

The arguments of the Outside Broadcast Department were full of practicality and commonsense. But in fact the circumstances in which an interview takes place change in subtle ways the manner in which it is conducted. If Outside Broadcast Units are used on political occasions the man in office usually has an advantage over the man in Opposition. Even if we had been able to arrange that Mr Gaitskell's Budget broadcast came from Hampstead the Chancellor would still have gained from the fact that the whole apparatus of visual transmission would show him to be a senior Minister of the Crown. The historic settings of No. 10 or No. 11 in themselves clothe a Prime Minister or a Chancellor of the Exchequer with an authority which does not exist visually in a drawing room or a studio.

And this affects the interviewer, however little he may intend it to do so. In a Downing Street interview he is seen to be asking questions of a man whose surroundings proclaim that he has been entrusted by the nation with power. If he seems brash or discourteous he will lose the sympathy of the viewer. Interviewers adjust themselves to such situations not in the content of what they ask but almost imperceptibly in the manner of their asking. This is not calculated. It is simply an instinctive reaction to the circumstances.

And there is also the question of the host–guest relationship. Mr Gaitskell, like other Opposition Leaders, had no official residence such as No. 11 Downing Street and so he was bound to lose in this respect as compared with Mr Butler. But if the broadcast had taken place from Hampstead he would have been the host and the interviewer his guest, just as Mr Butler was in Downing Street. Interviewers in such circumstances are aware that they appear as guests. Their function is to ask questions on behalf of the television public; but they must behave as guests to their host since that is the rôle in which they are cast by the circumstances in which they appear. In a television studio they are more at home than the politicians and so their rôles are changed in small, subtle ways which are not deliberate. Mr Gaitskell was right, therefore, to think that the place from which his broadcast took place was of importance.

This question of the milieu for political broadcasts on television continued to be a problem. It was raised again in relation to the Budget broadcasts of 1954 and caused some difficulty later when Sir Alex Douglas-Home as Prime Minister was interviewed in No. 10 Downing Street and Mr Wilson as Leader of the Opposition in a studio at the Television Centre. The differences were normally not in the content of the questions but in the fact that on television a slightly greater courtesy of manner was evident when a Prime Minister in No. 10 Downing Street was being interviewed by people who were his guests than in an interview conducted by the same interviewers in a television studio.

Negotiations about the Budget broadcasts were not conducted with representatives of the Party organisations. Two groups of people, I found, were involved in relation to the Chancellor's television appearance. There were those representing the Treasury and those concerned with Mr Butler's timetable and with the practical arrangements for installing cameras, lighting equipment and so on in No. 11. The Treasury discussions were with the Head of the Treasury's Information Services; those about the Chancellor's time-table and the practical problems at No. 11 with the Chancellor's Private Secretary and with the various people responsible for the household.

An advantage, I discovered, in trying to produce Budget broadcasts was that in the last resort one man made the decisions. The Chancellor might take all kinds of advice, but his wishes were paramount. And in the end the discussions about methods and television styles took place directly between him and the television producer—myself. And so it was for Mr Gaitskell. But Mr Gaitskell was in a more difficult position than Mr Butler. He could not prepare his sound radio or television broadcasts until he had heard the Chancellor's speech in the House of Commons. And he had none of the cushioning apparatus available to the Chancellor: Treasury officials to provide figures; Private Secretaries to answer telephones and fend off the Press.

On the day of his television broadcast, I lunched with him and with William Clark in the latter's flat in Albany. We had to devise for these interviews a method which walked delicately between the cross-examining style and the over-helpful stooge type of questioning. We did not want to echo, much less to forestall, the debate which was simultaneously taking place in the House of Commons. What we could do, taking advantage of the Press and radio coverage since Budget Day, was to put to the Chancellor and Mr Gaitskell some of the critical points which had been made of their respective standpoints and get each to comment upon them. That was what happened. It was a limited, but I thought a sensible, objective and did constitute an opportunity for viewers to see under questioning two influential politicians whose views and actions could affect the national economy and the lives of individual citizens.

They came over very differently. Mr Butler, urbane and confident, obviously taking pleasure in being one of the long line of Chancellors of the Exchequer and in succeeding those others in No. 11. Mr Gaitskell in a Lime Grove studio, pale, strained and a little tense; almost desperately sincere. Then, as on later occasions, I noticed the different look of the men in power from the men in Opposition. The whole apparatus of office creates a sense of ease and authority. Mr Butler swept up to No. 11 from the House of Commons in an official chauffeur-driven car. There were policemen outside the door; inside were his secretaries and assistants from the Treasury. William Clark and I and the cameramen and lighting and sound engineers from the Outside Broadcast Unit were waiting. We had all been anxious, during the preparations, not to disturb the household more than was necessary, not to trouble the doorkeeper with over-much coming and going, not to damage the furniture as it was moved around so that the cameras could get the most effective shots of the Chancellor and of William Clark and yet give some impression of the surroundings in which the interview was taking place. The whole atmosphere was in a sense hushed. Everything in the attitudes of doorkeepers and policemen and secretaries and members of the household made us aware that we were in the residence of the holder of an historic office, a man who by virtue of his position must be protected and cared for.

Not so for Mr Gaitskell. If he did not wish to drive his own car from Hampstead to Lime Grove (where parking was difficult) we were prepared to send a car for him. This was costed against the programme and set down by the producer as part of his budget. When Mr Gaitskell (or any other Opposition figure) arrived he would let the receptionist know that he wanted the producer to be told. I would then come to meet him, take him into one of the reception areas on the ground floor where he and I and William Clark would make any final arrangements; then up to the studio so that he could see the setting and so that the lighting engineer could adjust the lights and the sound engineer give him a voice test. The No. 11 broadcast was, so to speak, custom-built for the Chancellor. At Lime Grove Mr Gaitskell fitted into the complex machine of television production.

These differences applied, of course, equally to the world outside television where none of the secretaries, cars, research facilities, official residences and civil servants available to Ministers were available to Leaders of the Opposition. But, since television is a visual medium, this difference tended to be reflected in the general air of those taking part. Jane Austen's Emma said to Mr Knightley that she could tell the difference between the bearing of those who arrived in a carriage from that of those who arrived on foot. I began to think that I could tell the difference between the bearing of those Leaders of the Opposition who appeared in a television studio and those Ministers who were interviewed with the help of an Outside Broadcast Unit in their official residence.

By the time the Budget broadcasts were transmitted I had started negotiations with the Conservative Central Office about the first television Party Political broadcast. On sound radio there were normally twelve party political broadcasts each of fifteen minutes in any one political year (i.e. between April 1 in one year and March 31 in the next). They were allocated at the annual meeting in a ratio determined by the proportion of votes cast at the last General Election. In 1952 the allocation for sound radio broadcasts was 6 for the Conservatives, 5 for Labour and 1 for the Liberals. There was no possibility of television, with its limited transmission hours, being able to accommodate as many as this. So it was agreed that in addition to their sound broadcasts the Conservative and Labour Parties would each have 2 television broadcasts and also that each would have the right to take 2 of its quota of sound broadcasts as television broadcasts. Each therefore, if it wished to do so, could have 4 television party political broadcasts between April 1, 1953 and March 31, 1954. The Liberal Party, which was not represented at the annual meeting, was entitled to 1 party broadcast only. The meeting decided that they should have the right to take this on sound radio or on television or on both simultaneously.

These arrangements were announced by the BBC on April 22, 1953. But by then the Conservative Party had already decided that it wanted to have its first television Party Political broadcast on May 1 and I was already discussing with Mark Chapman-Walker of Central Office the form it would take. Our prediction at the meeting on December 19, 1952 that politicians and party organisations would want to present complex programmes on television had been correct. We had thought in terms of possible future election programmes, but it was immediately true of this first television Party Political broadcast. And I was soon alarmed by the unrealistic complications which the Conservatives were planning to introduce into their programme.

The subject was to be housing. The chief speaker in the studio would be the Minister of Housing and Local Government, Harold Macmillan. Mr William Deedes, Conservative Member of Parliament for Ashford, a well-known journalist, would also appear. And Mr Macmillan's Parliamentary Private Secretary, Mr Ernest Marples, who had been a building contractor, would present a specially shot film showing the new building methods which were being used to speed up the housing programme. In addition there would be stills, other short film sequences and introductory music. All this in twenty minutes. At the meeting with the Parties on March 24 no decision had been made about the length of television Party Political broadcasts but, though Labour would have preferred thirty minutes, the Labour and Conservative parties finally agreed that for the first year, as an experiment, Party Political broadcasts on television should last twenty minutes only.

Within the BBC we had come to some general conclusions about the responsibilities of the producer and of the Corporation in regard to those political broadcasts in television over which the parties had editorial control. The content was the responsibility of the parties though the producer could and should give any professional and technical advice which was required. As a result of my experience over the 'Battle of the Graphs' in 1951 it had been agreed that any stills, graphs and other visual aids should be provided by the parties themselves. Similarly any film sequences which they wanted should be provided (and paid for) by the party organisations and not by the BBC's film department. This was mainly because we had insufficient film resources for our own current affairs and newsreel programmes. If we had to make films at short notice at the request of the political parties, and to their brief, we could only achieve this by disrupting our own programmes. Moreover, given the ignorance of film at Party Headquarters, it was highly unlikely that their brief would be realistic and I could see endless possibilities of friction because the film we shot and edited might well not match the ideas which officials and politicians conjured up in their mind's eye. So we thought it better for them to get any film they wanted made by an outside commercial film company. We would give advice and be responsible for the transmission of any such film: not for its manufacture.

But there were a number of other areas in which responsibilities were far from clear. I outlined these, and the situation generally, in a memorandum which I wrote on April 21, 1953. It included the following points:

'(a) On receiving my instructions to look after the programme, I was told it was in the hands of the Conservative Central Office. Mr Chapman-Walker asked me if I would first discuss the proposed programme from the technical point of view with Mrs Crum-Ewing* and a young man (who has, I believe, been through our training school) whom they have got in as their technical television adviser, Mr Kneebone. They brought with them a draft script which had been devised, I understand, at high level within

* The Conservative Party's 'television officer'.

the Conservative Party, and which they were merely told to discuss with me in technical terms. It presented a number of technical and practical problems on which they wanted urgent discussion.

My own view was that the whole scheme for the programme was misguided. It tried to get too much into twenty minutes; having too many ingredients it would almost certainly be scrappy; it asked far more of amateur speakers (in using stills, in cueing in films and in commentary live to film) than I would have risked asking of similar speakers in an ordinary programme.

I let Mrs Crum-Ewing know that I thought the script was too complicated, but there was no point in discussing it in detail with her since she had no authority except to implement it. The script has since been greatly simplified, but it still, in my view, asks far too much of amateur speakers and runs considerable risks, therefore, of being technically untidy.

(b) I have today seen Mr Chapman-Walker. He told me that the script had taken this complicated form for two reasons:

    i The Prime Minister* himself was taking a great interest in the programme and wanted to try out the technical tricks of television.

    ii Mr Macmillan was anxious not to do anything in the "Press Conference" style since he did not want the questioning to be hostile and a programme of this kind with "stooge" questioners would compare unfavourably with existing "Press Conferences". He therefore wanted to try something quite different and with a good deal of illustration.

I said that I thought that he was running into grave dangers in attempting anything as complicated as the script they proposed with amateur speakers. He said that this was an experimental programme and they were prepared to have a flop. I said that, unfortunately, it would be the BBC who would be blamed for the flop—if there should be one—not the Conservative Party, since the flop would take the form, to the public, of technical deficiencies (e.g. the film not appearing when the speaker obviously expected it) which would look to the outward eye like a failing on our side—not theirs.

He took the point, but is very anxious indeed not to have the

* Winston Churchill.

script changed or revised in any way. I feel myself, however, that we must be firm about this. I am aware that the situation is delicate. On the one hand we want to interfere as little as possible—this should be *their* programme which we merely put on. On the other hand it would, I think, be disastrous if we gave an impression of incompetence on an occasion like this, merely because the Party script was unrealistic.'

I added a long list of minor decisions which I had made and, in a postscript, said:

'Since dictating this, Mr Chapman-Walker has asked me to come tomorrow morning at 10.30 to meet Mr Macmillan, Mr Marples and Mr William Deedes.'

I went. This was a Party occasion. A Minister was the chief speaker but his Ministry was not involved and Civil Servants were not present at our discussions. Indeed Civil Servants tended to treat these Party appearances of Ministers with a kind of lofty disdain. To most of them their Minister had, so to speak, two separate faces. One was that of their master, the head of their Ministry. To him, whatever they thought of his abilities, they behaved as loyal servants. But there was also the other face, that of the party political propagandist. They owed no official loyalties to him in this regard, washed their hands of all responsibilities, and left them to the party organisations.

Our meetings about television Party Political broadcasts in which Ministers were concerned took place therefore not, as in the case of the Chancellor's Budget Broadcast, in the Treasury or at No. 11 Downing Street, but at Party Headquarters. And it was clear to me that no one single person seemed to be in a position to make a final decision about the content and style of the broadcast. I soon discovered that television Party Political and Party Election broadcasts are usually a compromise, painfully arrived at, between a number of very differing points of view. Party officials like Mark Chapman-Walker had to consider any particular broadcast in relation to party strategy as a whole; to political speeches which were being made elsewhere; to the grass roots views of party workers; to the need to mould what was being said in a television broadcast to specific political events—forthcoming local elections, or a by-election, or a current crisis in regard to the farmers' or the miners' vote. In all these matters they were responsible to the Chairman of the Party, then Lord Woolton. Often, even within the Party organisation itself, there might be conflicting views about what was best for the Party at any one moment. And sometimes, as in 1953, the Prime Minister, then Winston Churchill, might have views which could not be ignored.

Neither Lord Woolton nor the Prime Minister took part in any of the discussions at Party Headquarters about this first Conservative television Party Political broadcast. But it was apparent that Mark Chapman-Walker's unwillingness to change the plan for the broadcast was largely due to the fact that it had been difficult to get agreement either on content or presentation and that having achieved it he did not want to start the process again on the basis of a revised plan.

I found, however, that the attitudes of Mr Macmillan and Mr Marples were different from those of the party officials. On this occasion they were Party men speaking on behalf of their Party. But they were also politicians wanting to make a personal success of their television appearances. They were anxious, therefore, to have any professional advice which might help them and were prepared to take notice of it even if this meant making drastic changes in the proposed programme. They asked for my views and I gave them. Or at least some of them. At this stage, ten days before the broadcast, it was no use saying that I thought the whole programme unconvincing, even, in some respects, ludicrous; that the title 'Winning Through' was calculated to make viewers switch off rather than continue to watch; that an introductory film sequence presented by William Deedes, showing a house made of playing cards first falling down and then building up again, seemed unnecessary and more likely to make cynical viewers think that all promises made about housing were cardboard rather than excite their imaginations. These devices, bits of film, stills, diagrams and title sequences, had been agreed, commissioned by the Party and were in process of being manufactured by various firms and individuals. It was difficult to get them altered at this late date. In any case my rôle was to help the politicians and the party organisation to do whatever they wanted to do, not to change it. So I merely emphasised the practical difficulties for those appearing if they had to cue in so many different visuals.

As a result the script was again simplified. The transmission took place on the evening of May 1 after a preliminary rehearsal of the speakers at Conservative Party Headquarters and a studio rehearsal at Lime Grove. There was nothing impromptu about this programme. It was highly rehearsed and highly predictable. Mr Macmillan, predictably, had style, though the style was slightly histrionic and his Edwardian manner not very suited to television. Mr Marples, also predictably, was sharply professional, a man who knew about building. Mr Deedes was casually at ease. The visuals were adequate. There were no disasters. But the programme had that curious air of falsity which clings to Party Political and Party Election television broadcasts. It was impossible to believe it.

This is a basic dilemma for the political parties when they try to use television for party political communication. The sense of falsity is far more important than any lack of professionalism. It is largely the result of the contrast between the appearances of Ministers and Leaders of the Opposition in Party Political broadcasts and their appearances in ordinary television current affairs programmes. When a Minister appeared in 'Press Conference' and was questioned by journalists, he might answer the questions well or badly, but he showed that he was aware that such questions were in the public mind and that he must try to give an answer. If, in a Party Political broadcast, he blandly ignored the existence of the problems about which he would have been questioned by journalists in 'Press Conference' it became difficult to respect him or believe what he said. The public knew that such problems existed; that the Minister's policies in regard to them were being canvassed in the Press, discussed on radio and television and queried by the Opposition. The Minister must also know this. When he could put his own case on television why did he not deal with them? Questions do not disappear from the public mind because a Minister does not choose to have them put.

But it is not easy in a Party Political broadcast to query the policies of your own Party. That is the job of the Opposition. It could reply in its own television time. And often did. With the result that most Party Political broadcasts became black versus white statements with neither side admitting any weakness in its own case and each denouncing the other as black and representing themselves as whiter than white. In consequence the politicians who took part in such broadcasts seemed less credible, less sensible and less statesmanlike than they did when they appeared in ordinary television current affairs programmes.

What was gradually emerging was the difficulty of transferring to television the traditional methods of party political campaigning without debasing the political currency and undermining the reputation of political leaders. Traditionally in a political campaign each party puts forward its own case. It is normal to leave the other parties to draw public attention to the weaknesses in yours and it is not thought dishonourable to leave out of party manifestos facts which do not support the party line any more than it would be for barristers to do so in a court of law. The public, like a jury, has a chance to hear the different cases put by experienced pleaders in the great political debate. And, like a jury, it can make its own choice between the cases presented to it. The conventions are so well understood that no one considers it odd that the government of the country should be entrusted to men who have won an election by the half truths and highly selected facts of their election manifestoes and public communications.

But television is different, largely because on it political communication is so continuous, so personal and so domestic. Political leaders appear regularly in all kinds of programmes. They are not distant figures on a platform or even the disembodied voices of radio. They are here in close-up in the sitting room. Viewers get to know the Home Secretary and the Minister of Defence and the Leader of the Opposition, are able to recognise their faces and their mannerisms, get used to the way they stand up to questioning. The individual viewer may like or dislike them, feel they are trustworthy or otherwise, agree or disagree with their attitudes; but they are individuals, all of a piece. You know them. When they suddenly put on their Party Political masks and tell you palpable half truths they are at once different and diminished.

In sophisticated circles the double image of the politician is understood and accepted. He can be both a man who is using all the available tools of controversy in order to achieve power and also a responsible statesman who can be trusted, when in power, with the life and death and happiness of millions of individual citizens. But this double image is neither understood nor accepted by the majority of those who watch television and whose judgments are simpler and more human. Here is a man whom you have often seen on the television screen. He has carried, or may carry, great responsibilities. He is asking you to trust him with power over your life and that of many others. Why, if he is trustworthy, does he lend himself to what seems at best a pointless and unconvincing piece of window-dressing and at worst an attempt to deceive the public by presenting what he must know are half truths and a biased presentation of facts?

Moreover the methods used by party and other officials to organise political broadcasts tended to emphasise the mask-like qualities of those appearing in them. A senior Labour politician,* retreating in obvious disgust during the preparation of a Party Political broadcast in which he was taking part, revealed to me that he had only then had his section of the script given to him; that he had had no hand in writing it; that he did not agree with it and that he did not want to speak it. But he did. A party committee had been set up to handle the broadcast and he was persuaded that it was now too late to make any changes.

A leading Conservative speaker,† due to give a major broadcast on a complex subject, arrived at the studios for rehearsal and was handed a script which, it appeared, had been prepared laboriously during the previous three weeks by a number of Civil Servants from the different departments involved—including the Foreign Office and the Board of Trade, by officials from the Conservative Central Office and by representatives of their women's section since the reaction of women was thought to be important. It was written in Civil Service language, stuffed with statistics, and the largely incongruous paragraphs, inserted to satisfy special interests, had been stitched together with unlikely linking sentences. The greatest television professional alive could not have put it across. At a moment during rehearsal, when the speaker was trying to read a peculiarly fatuous paragraph, a young man from one of the government departments who was in the control gallery with me and with the other 'advisers', murmured complacently, 'I put that in because I thought it would get the women.'

Nothing could have been done to alter the script to make it even tolerable. So it had to be torn up. Work on it was started afresh by the principal speaker an hour or two before the broadcast though three misspent weeks had already been devoted to its preparation by a group of people who had different axes to grind and who did not understand television. And the speaker was forced to spend a good deal of his precious remaining time in smoothing the ruffled feathers

* Richard Crossman.
† Edward Heath.

of those whose cherished sentences had been thrown into the waste paper basket.

Many politicians disliked taking part in broadcasts of this kind and, in particular, believed Party Political broadcasts to be ineffective and a waste of time. The party organisations were aware that they were floundering in a medium which they still did not fully understand; found them both expensive to produce and a strain to organise; the administrators in BBC television thought them a nuisance because they made sudden, unpredictable demands upon BBC resources and disrupted programme schedules; television producers tried to avoid handling them because they were not themselves in control and had to be responsible, as I had been in May 1953, for the production of a programme which others had devised; which they knew could not achieve what it was setting out to do; and which it was not in their power to alter in any basic way without seeming to interfere in its political content which was strictly not their business.

There were three main reactions to this unsatisfactory situation. The first was that the parties, instead of devising new styles of programmes for themselves, tried to present imitations of the most successful types of BBC current affairs programmes. This rose to a climax in the 1959 Election when all the Labour Party election programmes were a deliberate imitation of that most successful magazine programme 'Tonight', with, at the Labour Party's request, the deputy editor of 'Tonight', Alasdair Milne, in charge of production.

The second was a movement within the parties, supported by a number of senior officials inside the BBC, to abolish Party Political broadcasts altogether and leave party political communication, at any rate between elections, to the appearances of politicians in the ordinary current affairs programmes of the BBC. I was one of those who opposed this idea. It seemed to me, as with 'Ministerials', that it was both wrong and dangerous to create a situation in which the leading politicians of the country could use the new medium of television to put their case to the country only when they were invited to do so by the producers of television programmes.

The third was a much more profound reaction. As individual political leaders found that they could make frequent and less regulated appearances in ordinary television current affairs programmes and came to believe that these were more effective than appearances in television Party Political broadcasts, they readily accepted invitations to appear not only in 'Press Conference' but in the other current affairs programmes which were developed from 1952 onwards. Most of these programmes were interrogatory. Questions were asked of Ministers and Leaders of the Opposition either, as in 'Press Conference', by a group of journalists or, as in later programmes, by interviewers employed on contract by BBC producers. And, in so far as these interviewers were asking the questions which they thought were in the public mind and trying to elicit answers on subjects about which they thought the public should be informed, they were in fact usurping some of the functions of the elected representatives who sat in the House of Commons.

In this situation a number of members of Parliament, including notably some leaders of the Conservative Party, came to believe that the only solution was to televise Parliament itself. Though the proceedings of Parliament were conducted in public and the individual citizen had the right to watch them, it was in practice difficult to do so. You either had to seek the privilege of being given a special entry card by a Member of Parliament or wait in a queue, shepherded by policemen, in the hope of getting a place in the public gallery. You, who had given these men power by your votes, were treated very much as intruders in a private club for the élite. And, to exercise even these poor rights, you had to be in London. So most people got their impressions of what went on in Parliament at second hand through the eyes of journalists. In a television age this was anachronistic. Television could give you a privileged seat and a first-hand view of all kinds of public events. It was inevitable that this should be required in regard to politics also.

This inevitability lay at the back of the increasing development of television current affairs programmes. Without any deliberate intention but simply by following the trends which the existence of television demanded, these filled the gap created by the failure of the political parties to use television effectively for political communication. In such programmes politicians were no longer an élite at whose activities you were allowed occasionally to peep from a public gallery in the House of Commons. Any individual voter, whether he lived at Land's End or John o' Groats, could sit in his privileged seat in his own sitting room and watch them being questioned in public.

But in a sense the position was intolerable. I felt this most deeply when senior politicians seemed to feel that their appearances in current affairs programmes were so important that they found it necessary to drop hints that they would like to be invited. Sometimes more than hints. I was approached at a reception one evening by a senior politician, a man of great distinction and an ex-Cabinet Minister, who asked me why it was that he had not been invited recently to appear in any television current affairs programme. I said that I would mention his feelings to the producers responsible. He said he would be most grateful.

Incidents such as these made me feel that something must be changed. And, as a long term solution, I became one of those who felt that Parliament should be televised. But for this to be effective the proceedings of Parliament would have to be altered. And Parliament itself was not yet ready for change or willing to be televised.

In the meantime an enormous responsibility rested on the television current affairs programmes in which politicians appeared; and on the shoulders of the producers who were responsible for them.

[10]

The Power of the Producer

1952-1955

Two factors affected in important ways the kind of television current affairs programmes which were produced during those years and the kind of producers who were put in charge of them. One was the attitude to television of the BBC's news department; the other was the continuing dependence of television in matters of staffing upon the senior administrators at Broadcasting House.

The Editor of BBC News at this time was a journalist from New Zealand with the Maori name of Tahu Hole. He had been appointed in 1948; he did not understand the techniques of television production and appeared reluctant either to venture into the presentation of television news or to welcome the attempts being made in television to produce current affairs programmes. He held a position of great authority. During the war the BBC's overseas services, then under the ultimate control of the Ministry of Information, had fought and won a hard battle to defend their right to present accurate news even when this might seem to be against British interests, for instance by publishing abroad news of British losses and defeats. It came to be accepted that, even in war, the traditional integrity of broadcast news must be maintained. News should not be 'slanted'. News bulletins must not be edited to suit the changing needs of war-time policy or say one thing in one place and something else in another. To do so would destroy their credibility. And by the end of the war the accuracy and truth of BBC news and its effect upon the underground movements in Europe had become a legend.

When at the end of the war the Ministry of Information was abolished the tradition that the BBC's news services must not speak with different voices lived on and came to be interpreted within the BBC as meaning that the control of all the Corporation's home news output must be centralised. There could be only one Editor of News. If news were sacred, BBC news, by intention and reputation, must uphold the doctrine with special fervour and in 1952 Tahu

Hole appeared to be accepted by many of the seniors at Broadcasting House as its embodiment.

The situation was not a healthy one. Whatever the excellence of the Corporation's motives in regard to its news services; whatever the integrity of Sir Ian Jacob, its Director-General; whatever the value of the strict codes of impartiality which the Editor of News imposed upon his staff, it was not sensible that all news broadcasting in Britain should be effectively under the control of a single individual.

The television service escaped almost by accident from some of the rigidities of this centralised system. The vacuum created by the apparent inability of the Editor of News to create news services which were suitable for television was filled by the development of programmes over which he could exercise only a minimal control. He was not able to offer an effective alternative to television's newsreels; all he could do was to make one of his news staff, Michael Balkwill, available as a liaison officer. He had not been able to prevent television presenting the results of the General Elections of 1950 and 1951; again all he could do was to allow Michael Balkwill to be the representative of the News Division on those programmes. Moreover, as a result of the precedents set by 'Foreign Correspondent' and 'International Commentary', current affairs reporting in television had come to be done largely by independent commentators such as Chester Wilmot and Christopher Mayhew, who were employed on contract by the television service and who were not members of the BBC staff under the control of the Editor of News.

The independence enjoyed by television in these matters was made possible because most of those in ultimate authority at Broadcasting House were aware that George Barnes, the Director of Television, Cecil McGivern, the Controller of Television Programmes, and people like myself who were concerned with television current affairs output, valued the standards which governed the attitudes of the Corporation to news and current affairs. What was in dispute was not the validity of these standards but the methods by which they could be implemented in television as distinct from sound radio. And so long as television audiences remained small as compared with those for radio, the authorities at Broadcasting House, still pretty ignorant of television, were inclined to leave the running of even its current affairs programmes to television professionals.

There were exceptions when party political pressures were brought to bear in relation to 'In the News' or by the need to find a Conservative to balance Christopher Mayhew. But in the main those working in television current affairs were left to adapt as best they could BBC standards of fairness and impartiality to the different circumstances of a new medium. The result was that by the time those in charge at Broadcasting House began to take a serious interest in the handling on television of current affairs a number of precedents had been created within the television service which were difficult to change; styles of programme different from those of sound radio had been developed and different attitudes to authority had emerged.

This spirit of independence was reinforced by the nature of the current affairs production staff recruited for television in the early 1950s. By accident, not by design, this recruitment was largely my responsibility. In the summer of 1952 Cecil McGivern was asking for more current affairs programmes than I could myself produce. He had wanted the various Mayhew series to continue, and we were already filming in South Africa, the Sudan and the Gold Coast for 'Race Relations in Africa', which was to start in November. He wanted the Crawley project for a number of programmes about India to go ahead. For political reasons he wanted a series by a Conservative Member of Parliament to be ready early in 1953. And he wanted 'Press Conference' fortnightly. He realised that to achieve all this as well as keep an eye on the developments in television of Party Political and Party Election broadcasting and also consider how to improve methods of presenting the results of the next General Election was more than could be expected of any one producer. But, officially, there was no establishment for any increase in the staff of the television talks department. Unofficially, he told me to find help. In this situation we could not use the official methods of recruitment. But if I could find the right people he would, he said, 'fiddle it somehow'.

At the time I felt the need to do my own recruiting simply an added burden. I approached one or two of my old colleagues in sound radio and asked if they would care to come and work in television for a time. I thought, I said, that we could fix it. They refused. It was not easy for them to risk possible chances of promotion for the hardships and uncertainties of television. Or to become learners at the bottom of the production ladder in a medium which many of them still despised. So I had to look elsewhere.

The 'fiddle' which Cecil McGivern proposed limited the field of choice. He could get round the establishment position by engaging on temporary programme contracts such assistants as I could find. They would not be members of the BBC staff. Whatever they were paid would come out of McGivern's programme allowance and be charged as a cost against the particular programme upon which they were working. This meant that we could offer no security and no permanence of employment. Moreover, the amount we could pay out of a programme budget was small. No one whose feet were already upon the rungs of any journalistic or academic ladder would want to abandon his chosen field for so precarious a situation in so unknown a world. Only young people at the start of their careers would be interested. We would have to look for those who had had a certain amount of training in political affairs and who would be attracted by the chance of experimenting with communication in a new medium.

I found three. One was James Bredin, a freelance journalist who had worked on the cinema current affairs series, 'The March of Time', and was writing occasional commentaries for the television newsreel. Another was Geoffrey Johnson Smith, who, after going on a university debating tour to the United States, had worked for British Information Services in California. The third was Michael Peacock, then twenty-three and still an undergraduate. I had written to a number of friends in the universities whose judgment I trusted and who knew something about television and told them what I was looking for. Among them was Robert McKenzie, then a lecturer in politics at the London School of Economics. He suggested Michael Peacock, who had had part of his education in the United States, had finished his military service, had done some work for McKenzie in connection with David Butler's book on the General Election of 1951, and was about to sit for his degree examination. An academic career would certainly be open to him. But McKenzie thought he was perhaps too extrovert a character to be satisfied by academic life. I invited him, with some others, to come to the new studios at Lime Grove and help with an experiment I was making in the use of hidden cameras for television discussion programmes. The experiment was genuine; but I hoped that it would also reveal a potential current affairs production assistant. It did. As we left Lime Grove I asked Michael Peacock whether he would like to come and work in television after he had graduated. He came on a three months' contract and stayed for sixteen years.

These three were the nucleus of what I was beginning to call my Current Affairs Unit. None of them had been through the broadcasting mill or had worked in sound radio. They found the rigidities of Broadcasting House remote, unreal and sometimes ludicrous. But those in command there were seldom encountered. In the meanwhile the three of them got on with the television job and, each in his own style and while still very young, became an experienced television professional. These were the new men; the younger generation. They, and those who were added as the Current Affairs Unit grew, belonged to television. To them, from the first, television was a natural medium of expression. Many, like Michael Peacock, came to television without having as their first loves radio or the theatre, or devotion to the written word. They were aware of power and enjoyed it. But they wanted to exercise it with responsibility.

Michael Peacock was the most ambitious. His abilities were obvious even during that first discussion session at Lime Grove. His years in America at school and college had had a great effect upon him; he had learned to be tough, but with good manners; he despised Oxford and what he felt to be the dilettante attitudes of Oxford men and revealed in action a clear mind, a respect for facts and a remarkable ability to express himself. The insecurity of a three-month contract did not seem to trouble him; he knew that he had ability; it would be interesting to try something new. If he didn't like it there would always be something else. He was much less personally creative than, for instance, Donald Baverstock, who was soon to come from the BBC's Overseas Services to be trained in television and who was attached to the Current Affairs Unit. But both were unusually talented. They went step by step upwards within the BBC's television service. And the complicated relationship between them, based on liking but streaked with rivalry, had a major effect upon television output within the BBC and, many years later, on Independent Television.

These very different men had one thing in common. They were all of unmistakable quality. It was impossible to believe that any one of them could behave meanly or with emotional or intellectual dishonesty. It is what people are rather than the subjects about which they make programmes which in television determines the value of the output. A religious programme produced by a man or woman of mean spirit will inevitably be coloured by that meanness. A news report, however outwardly fair and accurate, can have little value if it comes through the eye of an observer whose outlook is superficial and insensitive. That is why the choice of production staff and their relationship with the heads of programmes and all the hierarchical systems and personnel of a broadcasting organisation are of such vital importance. It matters far more than what became the practice after the start of commercial television—totting up the number of hours devoted to 'educational' programmes or drama or light entertainment which the BBC and ITV respectively had transmitted.

Within the BBC the power of the producer is enormous, largely because much of the work of programme origination is his responsibility. Certainly, there is a constant two-way process. Broad, and occasionally specific, ideas come down from the Director-General and through him from the Board of Governors or the General Advisory Council to the Directors of the various services and the Heads of Departments. And at all levels there is constant discussion of programme output between producers and Heads of Departments, at departmental meetings, at other regular meetings such as BBC Television's weekly Programme Board at which all the Heads of Departments review with the Controller of Programmes the achievements and failures of the previous week: the quality of the output, the lapses of taste, the allegations of inaccuracy or bias, the size of the audience as measured by Audience Research, letters from viewers, comments from the Director-General or the Board of Governors. And there is a constant flow of memoranda of praise and blame to individual producers from Heads of Departments, Directors of services and the Director-General. But basically the creative upward flow was from producer to Head of Department and the Controller of Programmes. And the programmes from which the Controller could choose were as good or bad as the producers who had been appointed to the output departments—drama and light entertainment; outside broadcasts, including sport and public events; talks, including current affairs, travel, science, documentaries and the arts.

Producers therefore played a vital part in shaping the programme decisions of the BBC television service. This was essential if the Corporation were to maintain the creativity in programme output which was the reason for its existence. It was therefore welcomed and desired. But the problem of how to relate the creativity of producers to the ultimate editorial responsibility of the BBC was central to all its work.

There was a special problem in relation to those producers who were concerned with politics and current affairs. It was essential that they, like all producers, should want to be fair and impartial rather than have those obligations thrust upon them and also that they should not wish to use their privileged position to persuade others to accept their own views in matters of controversy. Otherwise there would be continual tension. If they resented the restrictions which had been placed upon the BBC by its Charter and Licence it would be impossible to work with them. If they wanted to use their powers of persuasion in political matters they could do so by entering politics or in journalism; but not in broadcasting.

But there was more than that. Most producers and production personnel working on current affairs and political programmes not only understood but welcomed their obligation to be unbiased. That was one of the reasons why public service broadcasting attracted them. But the bias might be unconscious. The backgrounds from which they came, the education they had received, their friends and associates—all affected them. As did their youth. And because of the accidental circumstances which had forced me from the first to recruit young people for the television Current Affairs Unit most of those who were working in television current affairs were young. And since these young people, Michael Peacock and James Bredin and Geoffrey Johnson Smith; and, later, notably, Donald Baverstock and Alasdair Milne, had so quickly and successfully become television professionals it was not possible to put older men, untrained in television, over their heads; and it was difficult for older men, with experience in the world of politics or journalism, to work under such young people, many of whom had minimal experience of politics in action.

The youth of the producers of television current affairs created problems. The Ullswater Committee had pointed out in 1935 that

'There is an . . . inevitable tendency in the general programmes of the Corporation to devote more time to the expression of new ideas and the advocacy of change, in social and other spheres, than to the defence of orthodoxy and stability, since the reiteration of what exists and is familiar is not so interesting as the exposition of what might be.'[1]

This tendency was obviously increased when a large proportion of the producers who suggested programme ideas were young. We did not ask, when considering people for appointments, what their politics were. This would have been contrary to all the principles of the Corporation. We merely reminded them of the obligation of any BBC producer to be fair and impartial in dealing with matters of controversy. Unless they accepted this it would be useless to try to work in television current affairs. But unconscious bias was more difficult to deal with; it could be seen in choice of subjects, choice of spokesmen to appear in programmes, ways of editing a film report even when the producer had no wish to present a biased picture. It was impossible to eradicate altogether this unconscious bias. It could be pointed out when discussing programmes in advance with producers. And after production if the bias had been evident. But the impulse to create programmes which sprang from a vital interest in life could easily be emasculated by putting every programme idea under too powerful a critical magnifying glass. To control the relationship of creativity to responsibility, and in particular to the BBC's editorial responsibility, required an understanding of the creative impulse in television programme making, of the ultimate responsibility of broadcasters, and the obligations of the BBC under its Charter and Licence.

In practice I found that, pragmatically, one way of dealing with the question of unconscious bias was to see that as far as possible there was a balance of temperaments among the production staff. For the differences in the main were temperamental not political; not between those who were Conservatives or Labour or Liberals— though this was true of a few who ultimately left the BBC when their obligations to be impartial became too restrictive, among them Geoffrey Johnson Smith, who entered Parliament as a Conservative and Jack Ashley, who entered Parliament as a member of the Labour Party. But the differences between producers were more often those of being temperamentally conservative with a small c; liberal with a small l; and radical with a small r; and a proportion who were none of these but simply professional programme makers interested in making effective whatever they undertook.

Within the current affairs unit during those early years the problem of reconciling creativity with editorial responsibility scarcely arose. The new recruits were acting as my assistants and working on programmes which I, not they, had devised: Michael Peacock on 'Race Relations in Africa'; James Bredin on 'Press Conference;' Geoffrey Johnson Smith helping with preparations for the projected series to be given by Conservative Members of Parliament. All three were learning their trade; how to draw studio plans and calculate camera angles; how to handle the control gallery and give minute-by-minute instructions to studio managers and television cameramen; how to work with crews of technicians and reconcile the demands of good studio lighting with good studio sound; how to work within the limitations set by the technical situation in any particular studio; to operate with three cameras when, ideally, there should be four; to budget for specially shot film; make travel arrangements for film cameramen and the delivery of film stock to different parts of the world; get visas and permissions to film abroad from the embassies of countries it was proposed to visit; how to ensure that there should be meticulously timed cues into film sequences so that it was possible to move smoothly from studio to film; how to prepare opening routines so that they cushioned the change from a light entertainment programme to a study of racial problems in the Sudan without causing viewers to switch off; how to organise a complicated series such as 'Race Relations in Africa' with its specially filmed sequences, its studio maps and diagrams, its studio interviews and its 'straight to camera' links by Christopher Mayhew, as compared with the fast-moving impromptu question and answer techniques in the studio required by 'Press Conference'.*

Above all, they learned how to create programmes which started as an idea and must end up as a combination or vision and words which would hold the attention of an audience, not yet of millions, but of hundreds of thousands. This meant that it was necessary, as in drama, to give them form, shape and an element of suspense. But giving them form must not distort the thought upon which the programme or series was based. There was none of the dramatic licence which was permissible in a play or even, dubiously, in a 'dramatised documentary'. Current affairs programmes, like news, must stand up to any criticism of their accuracy and impartiality. They were a new element in the communication of actuality. They could reflect situations at home and abroad which, by the width of their reach

---

* Normally BBC producers were trained directors and many producers continued to direct their own programmes. I thought this important since in my experience producers who had been, or were, directors had a different creative approach to programme-making than producers who had never directed. In Independent Television producers, as a rule, were not allowed, mainly for Union reasons, to direct their own programmes.

across the world and the scale of the viewing audiences which they achieved, could affect public opinion and so the handling of political policies in both domestic and international affairs.

Television programmes of this kind raised new questions of editorial control within the BBC partly because they were not scripted. Detailed technical scripts were required in order that the dozens, and sometimes hundreds, of technicians involved in a complicated programme could play their necessary part in the action: teleciné operators required their cues; cameramen needed their shot lists; sound supervisors and lighting men and caption operators and switching centres all needed to know well in advance and with precision exactly what they had to do at what moment. But the words which were to be spoken 'live' in series such as Mayhew's 'International Commentary' were not written down in advance. The general line had been discussed with the producer and agreed. But there was no written script which could be scrutinised before transmission by a senior official of the Corporation.

In radio, 'straight talks' were scripted. The normal method by which the BBC exercised editorial control over them was that after a decision about the subject and the speaker had been taken the handling of the talk was discussed by the producer and the speaker. It was drafted and sometimes modified in the light of further discussion. An agreed text was then available and could be read before transmission by a senior in the department. If he were in any doubt about possible slander he could consult the BBC's legal department; if he thought that it might be transgressing the Corporation's Charter and Licence, for example if it could be accused of being a statement of the BBC's own views in a matter of controversy, he could refer it higher, if necessary up to the Director-General. And there were the more difficult matters of the BBC's own editorial responsibilities in matters of taste and the effect any particular talk might have upon its audiences. If there were a written script all this could be considered before the talk was transmitted and, in the last resort, with all the difficulties which this involved, the talk could be cancelled.

The three editorial controls over talks programmes which were exercised in sound radio were, therefore, choice of subject; choice of speaker; and scrutiny of a written document before transmission. Only the two first operated in television. So a greater weight of responsibility rested in television upon the choice of speaker and above all on the speaker/producer relationship.

All television production is a team job. The nature of the team varies from department to department and from programme to programme. In light entertainment the team may consist of a comedian such as Tony Hancock; writers such as Galton and Simpson who provide his material; a television producer who plans the whole operation and who is responsible within the broadcasting organisation for its success or failure. Behind this central triangle are, so to speak, the support troops: the production secretaries who are the producer's aides; the studio manager, in charge on the floor; the scenic designers; the costume and make-up specialists; the cameramen and the lighting and sound engineers; the technical operations managers who are responsible for the engineering effectiveness without which no viewer would be able to see or hear the programme at all. And behind these again are the linking machinery of Central Control and the centres of distribution which ensure that a Cup Final played at Wembley can be seen by every viewer in Britain and, if required, throughout Europe or even, by satellite, throughout the world. Failure by any single individual among the hundreds, and sometimes thousands, who are involved in a major television production can ruin the programme. But these individuals are not seen by the public. If the programme is a success it is the 'front man', the star, who receives the adulation and the high financial rewards; not the producer or even the writers of material.

Creativity in television depends upon the building up of teams of individuals whose talents are complementary and who, in combination, are able to make programmes which are more original, more effective and more valuable than any one of them can achieve alone. There is no simple recipe for the creation of such teams. And in a sense there are in-built tensions which can in time destroy a successful team. The classic example was that of Tony Hancock. He was a star whose greatest successes were on television. No producer could have taken his place or achieved what he did. But the adulation which a 'front man' of his calibre receives tends to make him believe that the public is right; that he alone is the source of the creativity which in fact is the result of a combination of talents. He begins to resent the control of the producer; of being a puppet in the hands of the writers of his material; to find it intolerable that a studio manager should ask him to move to the left so that a better shot can be obtained by camera two or to raise his voice at this point so that the microphone can get a clearer sound. The emotional demands made upon him in performance are, he feels, underestimated. He will no longer submit to his exploitation. He will go it alone. He throws aside the writers who have served him and the producer who has organised the series of programmes which have made him famous. He goes elsewhere. And so teams break up.

The suicide in Australia of Tony Hancock tragically dramatised a dilemma which is to some degree inherent in all television production teams. In current affairs programmes within BBC television the team situation takes special forms. The 'front man' contributes ideas as well as personality and performance. The contents of the programmes in which he takes part are not the work of independent writers but are hammered out between the speaker and the producer, who use the detailed research which is available to them as well as the necessary consultation with advisers. The content and the words in which it is expressed must match the personality and the reputation of the speaker since it is he who speaks them directly in vision to the viewer. Yet they have to be formulated in the light of the BBC's overall editorial policy and the producer's understanding of the television audience as well as the harsh realities of the television operation. They must suit the needs of lighting and of sound, the disciplines of film editing and the even more demanding disciplines of exact timing in every section of the programme.

By 1953 it was already clear that the work of preparing series such as 'Foreign Correspondent', Mayhew's 'Race Relations in Africa' and Crawley's 'India's Challenge' involved a very close creative partnership between the speaker and the producer in the content as well as the presentation of expository current affairs programmes. This meant a good deal of mutual understanding; about the general intention of the programmes; the fact that the producer was editorially responsible within the Corporation for whatever the speaker said and yet that the speaker had been chosen because of his individuality and the acumen of his views as well as for his expository skills. He must play a large part in shaping the ideas upon which the programmes were based. Yet he must respect, and work within, the editorial responsibilities of the BBC and, less obviously, accept the ways in which the Corporation interpreted these responsibilities.

Early in 1953 this last point caused a major difference of opinion between the Corporation and Christopher Mayhew. Although the various Mayhew series had all been planned well in advance of the news we had managed to achieve a good deal of topicality by a careful consideration of what developments were likely to take place in the world political scene in the foreseeable future. As a result we had been almost too topical in the planning of the 'International Commentary' programme on Persia in 1950 since the eruptions there had made it almost impossible to present the programme at all.

A difficulty of a different kind arose in 1953 in relation to the high degree of topicality of one of the programmes in 'Race Relations in Africa'. Since the problem in each area was different we had planned a somewhat different treatment for each. In the case of the Central African Federation different opinions were so strongly held that we had decided to have not one film report but three. The film was edited into three sections according to the wishes of three different commentators who would take part in the studio discussion. This meant that they would be able to make their different opinions known verbally but could also present different visual reports upon the situation as they knew it.

During the series it became evident that the programme on Central African Federation would coincide with a Conference on Central African Federation which was to be held in London. On Friday, January 2, we planned the scope of the studio discussion with the participants and arranged a further meeting with them for the morning of Monday, January 5, as a final session before the evening transmission. But by then I had been told by the Chief Assistant to the Director-General, Mr Grisewood, that the programme must be cancelled. I spent the week-end in argument with an angry Christopher Mayhew on the one hand and with a resolute Mr Grisewood on the other.

Situations of this kind cause tensions in the speaker/producer relationship and between the producer and the broadcasting organisation for which he works. It was not easy to understand why the Corporation insisted upon cancellation. The programme did not contravene the BBC's Charter and Licence. It was not the expression of an editorial view; it was simply a statement of fact and a presentation of conflicting opinions. Nor was it biased in any party political sense. Cancellation was bound to create the suspicion that the Corporation was giving way to governmental pressures. No Ministry likes public discussion of a matter while it is the subject of delicate political negotiation. Discussion in the Press is bad enough; but arguments in newspapers may cancel each other out. Broadcast discussions, whether on radio or television, are another matter. They reach a wider public. They are almost bound to over-simplify a situation as complicated as that of Central African Federation. They could do great harm. Surely it was better to leave questions of this kind to the professionals who had studied them for years and who were doing their best to find solutions?

Had the BBC been subjected to arguments of this kind? And even if there had been no direct pressure had the BBC itself been over-cautious in interpreting its responsibilities?

I found the arguments put forward within the Corporation as a justification for cancellation both vague and disingenuous. There was talk of the subject of Central African Federation being *sub judice*; but in fact there was no question of it being a matter for the courts. The shadow of the 'fortnightly rule' seemed to hang over us; but Central African Federation was to be discussed in a special Conference, not in Parliament. In a sense great issues were involved; the freedom of broadcasting from government interference whether explicit or implicit; and, in the absence of a written script, the trust of the Corporation in its own producers and in the commentators whom they employed.

These problems were to recur in television current affairs broadcasting but, as a producer, I never found it easy to be doctrinaire about them. The principles of freedom in broadcasting were and are of crucial importance. But in any particular instance the difficulty for a producer lies in estimating the degree to which a decision such as that of cancelling the programme on Central African Federation is due to a genuine fear that such a programme might diminish the chances of agreement in a serious political matter where disagreement could lead to bloodshed, or simply to the desire of a Government department not to be embarrassed by public discussion of a subject which officials prefer to deal with themselves.

Such a desire was understandable enough in the case of Central African Federation. The impact of a television programme could not be confined to Great Britain. However factual and impartial it was intended to be, and actually was, it could possibly arouse passions among different groups in Africa as a result of its very impartiality on the grounds that who is not with me is against me. Moreover any broadcasting organisation has to consider not only its own sense of what is right for it to do but also the attitudes of which it may be accused. If the Conference on Central African Federation failed, the BBC could have been faced with accusations that it was partly to blame and that it had not acted with a proper sense of responsibility.

A producer in these circumstances is bound to consider the motives of those who make decisions such as that of cancelling the programme on Central African Federation. Here the whole relationship between the individual producer and the organisation for which he works is crucial. If it is one of mutual trust the problems are not grave. As a producer in 1953 I had no reason to believe that those in authority within the BBC were anything but determined to maintain the independence of broadcasting from government interference in its day-to-day operations. I could not imagine them quivering at the shake of a Ministerial finger. So I did not feel, as a producer, that I was being asked to acquiesce in the kind of dictatorship over broadcasting which became typical of, say, the French television service under General de Gaulle or, differently, of Czech television after the Russian invasion.

I did not agree with the decision to cancel the Central African television programme. But I was prepared to trust the judgment of those in control of editorial policy at Broadcasting House. This was partly because I was very conscious of the hazards involved in television reporting upon a complex political subject. However well researched a programme might be, however many authorities had been consulted, however impartial and honest its intentions were, I knew that such reports were conditioned by all kinds of practicalities: by the time available, by cost, by the availability of transport, by the ability of those interviewed on location to speak English: above all by the inability of the commentators or the film camera crews, even if they had been on the spot and had seen the events and the people with their own eyes, to be certain that what they had seen was really representative.

Knowing all this I could not believe that the cancellation of a single programme such as that on Central African Federation was a major disaster which must be resisted at all costs. I would have felt differently if, in my opinion as a producer, the cancellation had been due to the BBC giving way to official pressures and that as a result there had been a suppression of essential truths. But I did not believe that this was so.

The programme was not transmitted. This decision was much resented by Christopher Mayhew who believed that he had been invited to broadcast less frequently in 1953/4 than he had in the years 1950/3 and that this was due to the cancellation of the programme on Central African Federation. In March 1954 he wrote both to the Chairman of the Board of Governors (then Sir Alexander Cadogan) and the Director-General (then Sir Ian Jacob) suggesting that there was a connection between the decrease in the number of his broadcasts and the cancellation of the programme. He asked if this were so and wanted an explanation.

Sir Alexander Cadogan agreed in his reply[2] that there had been a diminution, particularly in television, in the number of his appearances but said, 'This, I think, is a natural result with an MP who for a period does a great deal. There is bound to be a diminution for a time because of the need to preserve balance and because we have to avoid an undue building up of a political reputation.'

This reply did not satisfy Christopher Mayhew; nor could it satisfy any producer who, like myself, simply wanted to produce programmes of high quality and hoped for the co-operation of whoever could undertake this task most satisfactorily. Yet I believed, above all, in the need to preserve the freedom of the BBC from government interference in its day-to-day running; and if, in order to achieve this, those in charge of BBC broadcasting believed that it was necessary to preserve the clumsy device of 'MP balance', I was prepared to accept their decision.

Christopher Mayhew and I argued a great deal over this and other matters, but seldom quarrelled; and the Race Relations series continued happily even after the troubles about Central African Federation. His television appearances certainly became more and more rare; but I knew that this was due to quite other factors than 'MP balance'. New commentators were appearing in magazine programmes such as 'Panorama' and 'Tonight' and there was now competition for the resources, particularly of film cameramen and film editors, which hitherto had seemed almost to belong to those who, like Christopher Mayhew, were presenting the major current affairs series. But above all the problems involved in adjusting the plans of a developing television service to the changing situation which was the result of Mayhew being a Member of Parliament were increasing. He had decided, as a result of growing pressures from within the Labour Party, to pay more attention to politics and less to television. So we had to try to plan filming sessions to suit Parliamentary recesses; editing and rehearsals to the days and times when he was not required at Westminster. It grew too difficult.

Differences of opinion between commentators, producers and

those in editorial control of the BBC changed to some extent in later years as a result of the start of television news and the handling of current affairs in a wide range of programmes such as 'Panorama', 'Tonight' and 'Gallery'. Any subject as important as that of Central African Federation would have been treated in different ways in such programmes. The fact that they were run by different editors and intended for different audiences reduced the danger of political pressure in relation to any one programme. If there were doubts about the treatment of a subject say in 'Panorama', other aspects had been dealt with in other programmes, other voices heard and other people seen. This proliferation of current affairs programmes meant that in the future no single programme had to carry as great a weight of responsibility as the Mayhew Central African Federation programme seemed to do in 1953.

Nevertheless the problem continued. Commentators employed on contract by the BBC did not always agree with the editorial decisions of the Corporation. Producers sometimes shared their anxieties. And the immediate, and very strong, reactions of producers and commentators if they suspected that any BBC decision relating to their programmes was the result of political pressure became a continuing factor in the day to day struggle to maintain the independence of broadcasting from political interference.

Political pressures took a variety of forms. In the reporting of foreign affairs the most crucial was the attitude of governments in the areas into which it was proposed to send film camera teams. Countries in which standards of living are low when compared with those of highly industrialised states are usually reluctant to allow pictures to be taken which show poverty, or, in general, conditions which might be considered in technologically advanced countries to be backward. These could seem an indictment of the government responsible and be used as propaganda by its enemies.

This was to be a continuing difficulty when any attempt was made to present foreign affairs on television. Few nations or governments really like accurate and objective representation of conditions within their borders. Most want praise for their achievements, acknowledgment of their qualities and a boost for their tourist industry. In many countries the Ministry of Information is not only responsible for giving permission to film but is also the Ministry of Tourism. It can exercise control over television reports in various ways. These range from the granting or withholding of visas for camera crews and commentators to the use of customs regulations to prevent, hinder or make impossibly expensive the admission of film equipment or film stock, unwillingness to allow exposed but undeveloped film to be sent back without having been seen by those in authority, or complaints by Ambassadors and High Commissioners after transmission.

Such methods can be used effectively as a form of censorship. In my own experience during the years between 1953 and 1956 they made objective film reporting for television virtually impossible in the USSR, in the People's Republic of China, in most of the Iron Curtain countries, and sometimes caused difficulties in Italy, in various areas of the Far and Middle East and even in Australia. Filming in the USA was difficult, not for political reasons but because of trade union attitudes and high costs.

These problems had already been encountered in running 'Foreign Correspondent' and 'International Commentary'. In 1952 the BBC's television service decided to accept in principle an even more delicate adventure. This was a series of six 45-minute programmes by Aidan Crawley on the problems facing the government of a democratic India.

Somewhat to our surprise the Indian High Commissioner in London not only welcomed the series but did everything in his power to make it possible. So did the Indian government in Delhi. Crawley had his own silent 35 mm. camera, did his own filming and had been given a refresher course by the BBC's film department in order to make this possible. But for the essential interviews with Indian politicians he relied upon the use of Indian Government studios and newsreel units. These were made available. There was no attempt to censor the material. It was sent back to Alexandra Palace for processing, editing and commentary writing without anyone in India having seen it.

Though Indian authorities were happy, British representatives in Delhi expressed some alarm. In the spring of 1953 the BBC's Delhi representative wrote to say that the Deputy British High Commissioner would be returning to England in the near future and would be glad to give advice 'policy-wise' upon the whole series. In making this offer the BBC's representative emphasised the importance of the series being 'as well balanced as possible'. This offer of assistance was sent to Cecil McGivern, who asked me to comment. In a memorandum dated March 5, 1953 I answered that we would be delighted to have any advice which the Deputy High Commissioner cared to offer us but that we could not delegate editorial responsibility for the series.

We had to be wary of offers of advice from a government department. The battle for the freedom of broadcasting from government interference in its day-to-day running had been won. It was important that in television we should not allow this freedom to be eroded. So though we welcomed advice from High Commissioners and Ambassadors we were not bound to accept it and we wished to make this clear. But it was necessary on all such occasions to understand the anxieties of the representatives of the British Government and also of BBC representatives abroad. These, like Ambassadors and High Commissioners, had to form their own connections in the countries in which they were stationed and deal with complex and difficult relationships. In any kind of delicate situation—and most to which television camera teams were sent *were* delicate—they were afraid that television commentators and camera teams might come blundering in and cause resentments with which they would have to deal.

BBC representatives had a special difficulty in that few people abroad really believed that the BBC was independent of the British Government. This attitude was in part due to the powerful effect of the BBC's radio transmissions during the Second World War when the voice of the BBC was unmistakably the voice of Britain. And the changes made after the war in the relationship between the BBC and the British Government were subtle and complicated. The BBC's external services remained part of the Corporation's responsibilities but they were financed, not out of licence fees paid by listeners and viewers, but by an annual government grant-in-aid. They formed a separate division of the Corporation with a separate Directorate. They had a special relationship with those government departments—for instance (then) the Foreign Office, the Commonwealth Relations Office and the Colonial Office—which were concerned with areas overseas. They could expect the interest and guidance of these departments in regard to overseas broadcasting. This guidance did not have to be accepted and sometimes, notably at the time of Suez, was rejected. They had, therefore, a considerable independence in regard to the policy of the government of the day. But their relationship with government departments was closer than that of the Corporation's home radio and television services which had been assured that there would be no government interference in their day-to-day running and which managed to maintain this independence not only in theory but in practice. This made it possible for the BBC's television service to be free to accept or refuse any advice which was proffered by a government department or even by the BBC's own external services.

But it was not to be expected that foreigners would understand these complexities, distinguish between the BBC's external, home or television services or be aware that each of these had a considerable degree of autonomy. Abroad the BBC was simply the BBC. And if a series such as 'India's Challenge' were factually incorrect or showed bias and caused resentment in India, the BBC's representative in Delhi would be expected to reply to criticisms and there might be some embarrassment for the British High Commissioner. It was no answer for them to say that they did not control the content of television programmes and that their advice, if given, could be ignored by the BBC's television service. They simply would not be believed.

In this complicated situation the BBC, to preserve its freedom from government interference, could not afford to make many mistakes. If there were allegations of inaccuracy or bias from informed quarters it had to be able to justify its programmes. This meant that it had to be able to rely upon the integrity, as well as upon the ability of its producers and of the commentators which it employed. When Cecil McGivern asked for my comment on the offer of policy advice from the British Deputy High Commissioner in Delhi he was in a sense asking me for a guarantee that he would be able to defend the programmes which Aidan Crawley was making and for which I was responsible to him and he, ultimately, to the Board of Governors of the BBC and through them to Parliament.

The BBC, editorially responsible for the output of the creative people and independent commentators which it chose to employ, had to give these the maximum of responsibility and the minimum of detailed supervision if they were to continue to be creative and independent. But the BBC policy-makers were entitled to ask for reassurance from producers in return for allowing them to exercise such a high degree of responsibility and power. The memoranda which were exchanged between Cecil McGivern and myself in regard to the offer of advice from the British Deputy High Commissioner in Delhi placed, within the BBC, the responsibility for the impartiality and accuracy of 'India's Challenge' firmly on my shoulders. And, as a producer, I, in my turn, had to rely upon the impartiality and the accuracy of the observations of Aidan Crawley.

This was simply one example of the vertical interdependence of the policy-makers at the top of the BBC's structure and its production staff, commentators and reporters. Without the trust shown in producers and commentators there would have had to be control in detail which, given the speed of television operations, would have been almost impossible to implement. Nevertheless the power of the producer within the BBC was still remarkable and it took nerve in the higher management of the BBC to allow it. The whole system relied in practice upon mutual trust; trust of the BBC by producers and commentators; and trust in producers and commentators by the BBC management. And since producers normally chose the commentators the key factor in control was the quality of the production staff.

This meant that the ultimate responsibility for creativity in programme making and for the impartiality and accuracy of programmes depended upon the proper selection, appointment and promotion of producers. In my view this was the most important work carried out by Heads of Departments. It was peculiarly necessary for them to interest themselves in the appointment of production assistants, then the lowest level of the production hierarchy. All being well, production assistants would eventually be producers, executive producers and go on to be Heads of Departments, Controllers of Programmes and Directors of Services. The calibre of such men (or women) determined the quality of BBC output. In a sense they *were* the BBC. Within the Corporation the division between 'management' and 'men' did not exist in the form common in industry. The flow was as much upward as downward. Producers created programmes. They and the Heads of Departments and Controllers of Programmes helped in a consultative process to shape BBC policy. But because of the nature of television programme-making, there was bound to be a great deal of devolution of authority particularly to those working in the field in distant parts of the world. A failure of judgment by a single producer, particularly in the realm of current affairs, could jeopardise the whole future of the BBC and its hardly won freedoms. 'India's Challenge' fortunately did none of these things and by the end of 1953 Crawley had become one of the BBC's regular and valued television commentators on current affairs.

The coverage on television of current affairs and matters of political concern was by now considerable. But it was not systematic and very little of it was topical. Party Political programmes continued during 1954, so did Budget and Party Election broadcasts. All other television political and current affairs projects depended upon the acceptance or rejection by television's Controller of Programmes of ideas submitted to him by producers and Heads of Departments. This was true of 'In the News' and 'Press Conference', which continued to be the most successful programmes in which politicians regularly appeared. It was equally true of series about foreign and commonwealth affairs such as 'International Commentary' and 'India's Challenge'. And true also of documentaries such as 'Special Enquiry', which dealt in the main with social conditions at home.

But these programmes did not constitute a service. They were not planned in relation to each other in order to provide a balanced coverage of political affairs at home and abroad. They competed with drama and light entertainment and sport for television time, resources and money. The Controller of Television Programmes accepted or rejected them in relation to their costs, their demands upon studios and design efforts, their importance as part of the BBC's obligation to inform and educate as well as to entertain; and the likelihood of their attracting a large audience.

This last factor was important. No programme however well intentioned, factually accurate and intellectually respectable, had any value if nobody watched it. It had to be viewable. This meant that from the first it had to be conceived in television terms. Producers and commentators alike had to understand the nature and the technicalities of television communication; seize the opportunities it offered and accept its limitations; realise in practice as well as in theory that as a medium television was ephemeral; study the relationship between words and vision in a continuing sequence which embraced them both; keep always in mind the fact that though a television programme could be transmitted to millions it was received by those millions as individuals watching a small screen in a domestic setting.

The success of current affairs programmes showed that by using methods which suited television and a personal approach by skilled commentators it was possible to interest a large British public in problems of foreign and commonwealth affairs which had a bearing upon home politics but which might have seemed, at first glance, remote from the immediate concerns of the individual British citizen.

But programmes such as 'India's Challenge' and 'International Commentary' were the jam, not the bread and butter, of political and current affairs communications. They did not deal as a duty with the routine daily round of events; they concentrated on the plums, the subjects which happened to interest talented commentators, where the settings were exotic, where the light was good for filming even in the winter months, and where a useful number of politically relevant people could speak English.

Moreover they were not flexible and could not deal with sudden developments such as the Korean War. Topical events had to be covered on television by special ad hoc programmes, specially prepared, costed and placed by the Controller of Programmes with a consequent disruption of programme schedules. What the television service now required was a number of regular spaces with guaranteed finance and facilities which would accommodate regular information about current events at home and abroad and which would also make possible, without disruption of the schedules, a presentation of facts and opinion in regard to any major unexpected political development. These two requirements were met in the years between 1953 and 1955 by the start of television news and by the beginnings of topical television magazine programmes of which the first was 'Panorama'.

There were changes, too, in the organisation of the BBC's Television Talks Department which affected its handling of politics and current affairs. Mrs Adams, the Head of the Department, was made an assistant to Cecil McGivern: she was succeeded on January 1, 1954, by Leonard Miall, an outstandingly effective BBC news correspondent who had worked for many years in Washington but who had no experience of television production. I was appointed to a newly-created post—that of Assistant Head of Television Talks.

Preparations were already being made for the next General Election, which for television would be a much larger operation than in 1951, and we agreed that Leonard Miall should be in overall charge of Party Election broadcasts and that I, with Michael Peacock as my deputy, would continue to be responsible for the presentation of Election Results.

Meanwhile in the Palace of Westminster there was the Churchill cliffhanger. Churchill's eightieth birthday was to be celebrated on November 30, 1954. When he resigned he would inevitably be succeeded by Anthony Eden. Would Churchill resign in time for

Anthony Eden, as Prime Minister, to lead the Conservative Party to victory at the polls?

He did not in fact resign until April 5, 1955; Eden succeeded him as Prime Minister on April 6; and, by his decision, a General Election took place just over a month later, on Thursday, May 26. The Conservative Party won the election with a majority over Labour of 67 seats, 41 more than in the election of 1951. The new Prime Minister, Sir Anthony Eden, seemed firmly in the saddle.

[11]

The New Style : Eden
Succeeds Churchill

1953-1956

It is extraordinary that Winston Churchill, who had used sound broadcasting so effectively to give 'the lion's roar' during the war years, made no direct use of television for his communications to the nation. From 1951 to 1955, when he was Prime Minister, he had been seen frequently on television screens in Britain but only on public and news occasions, at party conferences and the like. He had never taken part in any television Party Political or Party Election broadcast. And he had never agreed to make a special television appearance in any of the BBC's own television programmes.

The one exception was on his eightieth birthday. Endless public and formal celebrations had been planned; speeches in Westminster Hall; the presentation of his portrait; a dinner at Buckingham Palace. The proceedings in Westminster Hall were televised, and all the comings and goings of the day were shown and recorded by the BBC's Outside Broadcast Department. But it was hoped that television would be able to present, in the evening, a more intimate personal programme.

The difficulty about such celebratory programmes is to prevent them from appearing to be obituaries. A small committee consisting of Donald Baverstock, Richard Cawston and myself was formed to work out a programme which would not seem to be an obituary but a tribute to a living man. We thought that this might be achieved if the programme were one of good wishes offered directly *to* Churchill by his personal friends upon which the British public would, so to speak, be eavesdroppers, rather than a programme *about* Churchill shown on television to viewers.

We hoped that Churchill would see it and even reply at the end of the programme to those who had sent him their good wishes. I was told that the best method of achieving this would be to contact

Montague Brown, Winston Churchill's private secretary. Would such a programme be welcome to the family? Would they watch it at the end of a crowded day? Could we install cameras in No. 10? Was there any chance that Winston Churchill himself might reply on television to the good wishes of his friends? And who ought those friends to be? The programme, in contrast to all the formal celebrations, should, we thought, be intimate and friendly. Montague Brown suggested that I should try to persuade Lord Ismay to interest himself in the idea. If Ismay backed it the battle was half won.

Lord Ismay was then Secretary-General of NATO and based in Paris. I asked for an appointment and flew over to see him. Lord Ismay was totally co-operative, delightfully informal and highly practical. He thought that Churchill would welcome the programme but must not be bothered about it beforehand. Keep Lady Churchill informed through Montague Brown and she would persuade Winston to watch it if anybody could. Lord Ismay drew up a list of Churchill's personal friends, beginning with Bernard Baruch, from whom he thought Churchill would like to hear on his birthday. He would write to each of them and explain the programme in which they were being asked to take part.

We proposed to record, on film, messages from Baruch in New York, Robert Menzies in Australia, and from others all over the world together with those from friends at home, among them Lord Alexander, Lord Freyburg, Sir Philip Vian and Lady Violet Bonham Carter. We would also have 'live' in the studio a group of people who had worked closely with Churchill—Sir Richard Pym, who had travelled with him during the war, Neville Duke, who had piloted him, Jo Sturdee, his secretary for many years. Each, whether on film or in the studio would recall some occasion which they specially remembered in their association with Churchill and give him their personal good wishes. Lord Ismay was prepared to come to London to act as compère and to record his commentary on the linking film.

Montague Brown enlisted the help of Lady Churchill. We could not, on such a day, create disturbances in No. 10 by trying to install television cameras. If, however, we could persuade the Chancellor of the Exchequer, R. A. Butler, to let us put them in next door, No. 11 Downing Street, it would only be necessary for the party from No. 10 to walk through a short internal passage to watch the programme. The Chancellor willingly agreed. I persuaded Huw

Wheldon, who had come to BBC television in the first instance as a press and public relations officer but who had since joined the Television Talks Department as a producer, to take charge of the Downing Street end of the production. Above all he was to keep in touch with me and let me know whether Churchill would watch the programme or not.

Churchill, after all, was eighty. He would have had an exhausting day of tributes and speeches in Westminster Hall. He had to go to Buckingham Palace. He might have neither the time nor the wish to watch a television programme. He would almost certainly be too tired to be bothered with any need to reply. So, with the help of Lord Ismay and Huw Wheldon, I planned three alternative endings to the programme: one for a situation in which Churchill neither watched nor spoke; one in which he was seen but did not speak; and one in which he would be seen and also reply.

I was directing in the studio control gallery at Lime Grove and could see on one of the monitors the pictures coming in from Downing Street. Just as Lord Ismay was about to start the programme, I saw on the Downing Street monitor, to my immense relief, a little procession moving into the room in No. 11 where we had installed cameras and a television set. Churchill, looking very old and uncomprehending, helped and followed by Lady Churchill, his daughters and his aides, sank into an armchair. Like an ancient tortoise withdrawn into itself and unaware of its surroundings, he gazed blankly at the television set. As the programme went on one or other of the family called his attention to someone on the screen. He neither moved nor responded. It was impossible to believe that he knew in the least what was happening. But when Lady Violet Bonham Carter, at the end of her message, said 'Courage, that is your greatest gift to those who know you', I watched, unbelieving, on my gallery monitor the ancient head move slowly from side to side in a gesture of negation and tears roll slowly down the leathery cheeks. Only we in the gallery saw this incredibly moving spectacle. And we were filled also with professional relief. He was registering something after all.

As the programme ended everyone round the mahogany table in the studio, gay with its candles and champagne, rose to their feet and raised their glasses. Ismay said 'Prime Minister—Happy Days'. And Churchill, coming suddenly to life like a statue from the stone age taking on humanity, started to speak straight to the television

camera in No. 11—spontaneously, clearly and masterfully. He
said:

'I have been entranced by the thrilling panorama you have presented to me of so many of my cherished friends who have been
given an opportunity of expressing their feelings of kindness to me,
and the memories that they have. I am fortunate indeed to have
met these men and women and to have worked with them in the
years of struggle through which we have passed. I am grateful
that modern science has enabled me upon my birthday to receive
in this amazing manner their friendly greetings and good wishes.'[1]

To Churchill, in 1954, making his first and last special television
appearance in Britain, television was still an amazing wonder of
modern science. To the next two Prime Ministers, Anthony Eden
and Harold Macmillan, it was an established method of political
communication. With the departure of Winston Churchill the relationship between television and politics in Britain changed. There
were new styles, new television methods. These were largely the
result of the personalities and attitudes of Eden and Macmillan.

Both rather fancied themselves as users of television. Each had
appeared frequently on the television screen. Eden was always nervous; but believed in his own style. This was not really successful.
He had charm and long practice in political communication; but he
could not achieve the personal relationship with the individual
viewer which television demands. It is incredibly difficult for a
politician to do this. A political communication in television is
received not only by the supporters and friends of the speaker but
also by his opponents and his enemies; by the sophisticated and the
unsophisticated alike, each reacting differently and individually to
the communication. To be able to hold the attention of all those
individuals simultaneously without resorting to the lowest common
denominator of platitude is as hard as trying to write an Ibsen play.
And requires as much insight into the reactions of individuals and as
great an understanding of technique. Ibsen could tell a story at
three different levels at the same time: at the simple level of dramatic
action; of the hinted complications which added an extra dimension
of which the sophisticated would be aware; and he could suffuse the
whole with symbolic overtones which were never so baffling as to
hold up the action but which added a vertical horizon to the play as
distinct from the horizontal plane on which the action took place.

A different but related skill is required by politicians who try to use television for political purposes. There must be the clear message; there must be indications which do not interrupt the message but will be picked up by the sophisticated and reveal the fact that the speaker is aware of the complexities of the subject with which he is dealing; and there should be overtones which convey the speaker's understanding of the way in which this particular subject fits into a larger and overall view of the national life.

In sound radio this had been done by Winston Churchill. Churchill took broadcasting seriously. He shaped each of his radio broadcasts with infinite care. For him communication was not a gimmick to be added to the message. They were one, and both were aspects of his own beliefs and of his own style of being. This unity between the message, the expression and the man was a major cause of the tremendous impact his broadcasts made.

In television a corresponding unity was not achieved by either Eden or Macmillan. Neither of them appeared to take television really seriously. It was a peripheral activity, sometimes useful, sometimes a nuisance; sometimes—especially and latterly for Macmillan—rather fun. But never important. They could not identify imaginatively with the individual viewer who was at the receiving end of their broadcast. Each in his own style tried to establish contact with those millions of others by tricks of communication added to the message. Eden addressed the television audience as 'My friends'. The very use of the plural showed that he was not conscious in making his communication that millions of individuals might be watching alone at home. Moreover he did not appear to appreciate that some of these individuals were his opponents and would not welcome being addressed by him as a friend.

Harold Macmillan, much easier to deal with, possessed of a much greater sense of humour and with a totally different style, tried other methods of identifying with the individual human beings he was meeting on television. He would for instance demonstrate his common humanity by talking about his grandchildren. He began one of his television political broadcasts in this way and showed it in draft to Huw Wheldon, who was the producer. Wheldon persuaded him to change it by pointing out that the individual viewer who was being asked for his vote wanted more of a Prime Minister than that he should be a grandfather; and that these references, though charming enough, were irrelevant to the situation and something of a waste of time.

But the major change in the relationship between television and politics which resulted from the change from Churchill as Prime Minister to Eden was that Eden, frustrated in 1954, was now determined to have Ministerial broadcasts on television. In 1955 he informed the BBC that he wished to announce the Dissolution of Parliament and the date of the General Election simultaneously on television and sound radio.[2] Sir Ian Jacob drew his attention to the fact that this would be a television Ministerial broadcast and that the parties had continued to refuse the BBC's offers of time and facilities for Ministerial broadcasts on television. The Chairman of the Board of Governors of the BBC, Sir Alexander Cadogan, had reminded the parties on April 10, 1955 at the special ad hoc meeting called to discuss the arrangements for broadcasting during the election campaign, of the position in regard to Ministerial broadcasts on television; and had said that the BBC would be grateful if the parties could keep this in mind for decision. But no decision had yet been made. In the meanwhile there could be no Ministerial television broadcasts. It was possible for the Prime Minister to announce the Dissolution of Parliament and the date of the General Election on sound radio but not on television.

Eden was angry. His anger was understandable. By the autumn of 1954 there were 3,500,000 television licences and these were increasing at the rate of 800,000 a year.[3] Television was rapidly becoming a more significant medium of political communication than sound radio. It was not really possible to maintain a situation in which a Prime Minister could use sound radio to speak directly to the nation but was forbidden by the decision of the political parties to do so on television. But nothing could be done until the next annual meeting. This took place in March 1956 when Hugh Gaitskell, by then Leader of the Labour Party, opposed the whole idea of Ministerial broadcasts, particularly on television. The Director-General of the BBC had conversations with Mr Gaitskell and at the meeting of the BBC's Board of Governors on April 12, 1956 he reported that he had received that morning[4] a letter conveying the agreement of the Opposition to a limited number of television Ministerial broadcasts. And the first formal Ministerial broadcast on television was given by the Prime Minister, Sir Anthony Eden, on April 27, 1956. The occasion was the visit to Britain of the Russian leaders, Bulganin and Khruschev.

Such was the position about Ministerial broadcasts when, in the summer of 1956, Sir Anthony Eden wished to use television during the Suez crisis to broadcast to the nation. There were a number of reasons why it was difficult to apply the rules of the Aide Mémoire of 1947 to Ministerial broadcasts of this kind. The Aide Mémoire stated that:

'it will be incumbent on Ministers to be as impartial as possible, and in the ordinary way there will be no question of a reply by the Opposition. Where, however, the Opposition think that a Government broadcast is controversial it will be open to them to take the matter up through the usual channels with a view to a reply.'

If no agreement had been reached within 'say, three days, the BBC will be free to exercise its own judgment'.

There were few precedents which could assist the BBC in exercising its own judgment in as explosive a situation as Suez. Moreover neither Sir Anthony Eden, nor after him Mr Macmillan, cared to be bothered with the Aide Mémoire, nor, indeed, with any rules which would affect their view that a Prime Minister had the right to use television to address the nation whenever he thought fit to do so. And neither could see any reason why a Leader of the Opposition should be granted a right of reply to a Prime Ministerial broadcast.* Both were therefore resentful if the BBC, under pressure from the Opposition, and exercising its judgment as it was enjoined to do in the Aide Mémoire, provided in such circumstances time and facilities for the Opposition to broadcast.

Pressures were certainly brought to bear and resentments were certainly, even violently, expressed over Sir Anthony Eden's Ministerial broadcasts during the Suez crisis. And, since he chose to give them on television, those of us who worked in television current affairs were necessarily involved in the tensions which developed between Government, Opposition and the BBC.

Sir Anthony Eden's first major Suez broadcast was given on television at 10 p.m. on August 8, 1956. August is usually a dead month as far as broadcasting is concerned and 1956 was no exception. The majority of television current affairs producers were on holiday; 'Panorama' was off the air; the Head of Television Talks was in the United States; in his absence, as Assistant Head, I was in charge of

---

* Mr (later Sir) Harold Evans made this absolutely clear to me when he was Press Officer to Mr Macmillan at No. 10 Downing Street. He told me that this was the Prime Minister's view, and that he himself shared it.

the department and of all television political and current affairs output. At Broadcasting House the Board of Management with the Director-General in the chair had met on July 30 but it had not met on the following Monday, August Bank Holiday. It did not meet again until August 13. Harman Grisewood, however, my chief point of reference on matters of political policy, was available for consultation.

The Suez Canal had been 'nationalised' by President Nasser on July 26 and we were presenting a few topical items about the takeover in 'Highlight', a nightly programme of interviews for which Alasdair Milne, deputising for Donald Baverstock, was responsible. Now I had to deal with the Ministerial broadcast. It was to be a 'straight to camera' address to the nation and Sir Anthony Eden was to come to Lime Grove to deliver it. We were desperately short of studios; the new Television Centre was still unfinished and all available studios were fully booked for regular programme purposes. So it had been decided, I discovered, that programmes such as political broadcasts which made limited, if sudden, demands upon resources should come from the temporary announcer's studio at Lime Grove which was more or less permanently arranged to suit a man sitting at a desk and talking to camera.

As it turned out this was an unhappy decision. I was directing and the makeshift control room was as tiny and cramped as the studio. Both were filled with the multifarious equipment and operators involved in a television transmission. In the studio there wasn't an inch of room for anything but the desk and chair and a monitor. There was no air conditioning yet the windows had to be kept closed and heavily curtained because trains ran past outside them every few minutes. In the August heat the small rooms were stifling and, since there was no lift, they could be reached only by climbing three flights of concrete stairs lit by naked hanging bulbs.

I did what I could: the technicians were alerted to the importance of the occasion: we discussed the lighting and other practical matters and, since it was impossible for any of those who were likely to accompany the Prime Minister to be in the studio or the control gallery, I arranged that the run-through should be transmitted to a reception room on the ground floor where they could watch it. And I made sure that, on this unbearably hot night, iced champagne should be available.

Sir Anthony arrived: he brought his wife and a number of aides. They expected, understandably, to be able to see the rehearsal in the studio. I had to explain why this was impossible and the alternative arrangements I had made. Then I had to ask the Prime Minister, who looked strained and ill, to come with me up those three flights of concrete steps to deliver a broadcast which was to reverberate around the world.

He did not comment upon the intolerable circumstances and remained politely courteous throughout this difficult evening. But the Suez situation was so delicate that he had to read his script word for word. In the glare of the studio lights this was not easy: he did not wish to be seen to be wearing glasses yet it did not seem possible to do without them. Perhaps a reading stand on the desk would help? But even with it the glasses still proved to be necessary and in this primitive little studio the use of the stand set limits upon the camera shots.

At last he read the speech with his usual practised confidence. The rehearsal over, he seemed less anxious. So, since there was bound to be a pause before transmission—the necessary technical processes at that time were lengthy—I suggested that to escape from the heat and discomfort of the studio he should return to the ground floor room where the others were waiting and had been watching.

He came. But the atmosphere there was tense. Nobody was satisfied, least of all myself. The content of the address was not my responsibility; but I felt ashamed, as I took Sir Anthony once again up those long flights of steps, that we had not been able to provide a Prime Minister with more suitable surroundings in which to make so momentous a broadcast.

That broadcast is now part of history. Sir Anthony, in 1956, seemed to be giving warnings which were echoes of 1939, Munich, and the evils of appeasement. He said that 'Colonel Nasser's' action had created 'a very grave situation' and that 'if it were to succeed each one of us would be at the mercy of one man for the supplies upon which we live. We could never accept that. With dictators you always have to pay a higher price later on, for their appetite grows with feeding'.[5]

Sentences such as these held serious implications of possible action by Britain to resist Nasser and foreshadowed the British military intervention. But my own preoccupations were with the next few days. Sir Anthony's broadcast was given on Wednesday. Two days later, on Friday, August 10, I was responsible for a routine television 'Press Conference' and had decided that in view of the Suez crisis we should depart from the usual pattern of four journalists questioning a single personality and mount instead a discussion with Peter Calvocoressi of the Royal Institute of International Affairs in the chair and with Kingsley Martin, editor of the *New Statesman* and Michael Curtis, editor of the *News Chronicle*, taking part. They would presumably be critical of the policies of the Government. On the other side were H. V. Hodson, editor of the *Sunday Times*, and the Conservative politician and journalist, Charles Curran. The programme ended at 10.30 p.m.

It was not until later that evening that I realised how important it was that, following upon the Prime Minister's broadcast on Wednesday, some anti-government opinions had been heard on television on Friday. This was not the case in sound broadcasting. Moreover the situation in sound radio was complicated by the fact that the Foreign Secretary, Mr Selwyn Lloyd, was due to broadcast, not on television but on sound radio, on the following Tuesday, August 14.

The Labour Party was restive about the reiteration on the air of the Government point of view without there having been any reply by the Opposition. Pressures were being brought to bear upon the BBC. But at the same moment quite different pressures were being exercised by the Prime Minister. Mr Menzies, Prime Minister of Australia and the senior Prime Minister of the Commonwealth countries, was in England. He would be taking part in an international conference to be held in London on August 16 which would endeavour to create an international system for running the Suez Canal. He was prepared to broadcast on the Suez situation as he saw it. This offer had been conveyed to the BBC. But the Corporation had declined it.

I learnt this late on Friday evening when I was telephoned after 'Press Conference' by William Clark, with whom I had worked on the start of 'Press Conference' and other television programmes, and who was now Press Officer to the Prime Minister. He said that Sir Anthony Eden was extremely angry with the BBC and had found its refusal of the offered broadcast by Mr Menzies quite intolerable. Clark was afraid that in his anger the Prime Minister might take some drastic action which would be permanently harmful to the BBC.*

---

* William Clark told me later that in the Prime Minister's then state of health and temper he had been unable to judge whether the threats of action against the BBC were likely to be carried out or not. At the time he had felt it necessary to take them seriously.

I was dumbfounded. William Clark knew well, even better than I did, that should the Director-General not be available the proper channel of approach to the BBC was through his Chief Assistant, Harman Grisewood. I said this; but I was told that the refusal to accept the Menzies broadcast had come from Harman Grisewood himself. William Clark, clearly alarmed by the whole situation, said that he had got in touch with me only because he knew me and thought that there was possibly *something* I could do to make the Menzies broadcast possible. Nothing else would placate the Prime Minister.

I could not understand the BBC's refusal to accept a broadcast by Mr Menzies: in view of his position in the Commonwealth and the active part he was playing in the Suez negotiations anything he could say would surely be a contribution to public information. And he was known to be an excellent and experienced broadcaster. William Clark said that he believed that the BBC's refusal to invite him to broadcast was the result of the attitudes of the Labour Party. If the BBC transmitted yet another broadcast in favour of Government policies on Suez—as any broadcast by Mr Menzies was likely to be—there would have been three Government-orientated broadcasts in succession; that of the Prime Minister on Wednesday, August 8; the Menzies broadcast for which a possible date was Monday, August 13; and the Selwyn Lloyd broadcast which was scheduled for Tuesday, August 14. During all this time no one would have broadcast the views of the Opposition.

I said that that might be true of sound radio, but it was not true of television. The Foreign Secretary's broadcast on Tuesday would not be seen on television; and we had transmitted on television that very evening in 'Press Conference' a discussion which included some anti-Government views. Apart from a series of factual reports in 'Highlight', television's Suez coverage so far had consisted only of the Prime Minister's broadcast on August 8 and the discussion in 'Press Conference'. In terms of a balance between pro- and anti-Government broadcasting on television it would, I thought, be perfectly proper for television to transmit a broadcast by Mr Menzies on Monday. And I offered to get in touch with Harman Grisewood and put this to him.

It was very late. But I had his home telephone number. As always, he was reasonable and co-operative. He had forgotten about television. And he had not seen 'Press Conference'. He confirmed

William Clark's understanding of the reasons why the BBC had rejected the offer of the Menzies broadcast. It would simply increase the already considerable anger of the Labour Party about the BBC's coverage of the Suez situation. But if the position in television were in fact different from that of sound radio and if, for example, Kingsley Martin had that evening been given an opportunity in television's 'Press Conference' of expressing the views of some of those who were opposed to the Government's policies over Suez, then perhaps this provided a way out of the impasse over the Menzies broadcast.

Could we in television provide facilities for a broadcast by Mr Menzies on the following Monday? If so, could I get in touch with Mr Menzies early on Saturday morning? He was staying at the Savoy. There followed, into the early hours of Saturday morning, a series of triangular telephone calls: from Harman Grisewood and myself to William Clark: from William Clark to the Prime Minister: from me to the television planners.

It might be possible, I thought, to cancel 'Highlight' on Monday and put the Menzies broadcast in its place. I got in touch with Alasdair Milne. Could he direct and be responsible for the practical arrangements? He faced the unexpected problem, as always, with admirable efficiency and coolness. He would call for me in a taxi at 9.30 a.m. We could go to the Savoy and see Mr Menzies. By now we had an appointment with him for 10 a.m. When we got there we were shown into the bottle-littered bedroom of Mr Menzies' public relations officer. There had been a party the night before. Then, in Mr Menzies' sitting room, in spite of the chilly atmosphere understandably engendered by the BBC's attitude to the offer that he should broadcast, we were able to make the necessary practical arrangements with Mr Menzies for his broadcast on the following Monday. He came to Lime Grove and gave his television broadcast to the British people at 7.10 p.m.

The points he made were almost identical with those which had been made by the Prime Minister on the previous Wednesday. But the style and manner in which he made them were very different. It is only necessary to compare two sections of the broadcasts for this to be clear. Sir Anthony Eden's final words include the following paragraph:

'So, my friends, the alternatives are now clear to see. If we all join

together to create an international system for the Canal and spend
its revenues as they should be spent, to develop it rapidly, that
can bring growing prosperity to East and West alike, the countries
that produce the oil and the countries which buy it. There will
then be wealth for all to share, including Egypt. There is no
question of denying her a fair deal or a just return; but if anyone
is going to snatch and grab and try to pocket what really belongs
to the world, the result will be impoverishment for all, and a
refusal by some countries at least to lead their life at such a
hazard.'[6]

Mr Menzies eschewed the use of such quasi-moral phrases as
'snatch and grab and try to pocket what really belongs to the world'.
More harshly, he presented the issue in terms of conflicting national
interests. He ended by saying:

'I do urge clear thinking on these matters. We're about to try to
deal by negotiation with a matter which is vital to the trade and
economies of a score of nations. To leave our vital interests to the
whim of one man would be suicidal. We in Australia applaud the
statement made by France, the United Kingdom and the United
States. . . . We can't accept either the legality or the morality of
what Nasser has done.'[7]

Between August and November 1956 there was extensive general
coverage on television of the developing Suez situation. In addition
to the almost nightly reports in 'Highlight', a documentary was
presented by René Cutforth on August 30 which gave the background to the crisis. On September 17 'Panorama' returned and
started with an outline of the latest Suez developments. On September 24 the Foreign Secretary, Mr Selwyn Lloyd, appeared in
'Panorama' and was questioned by Hugh Cudlipp, editor of the
Daily Mirror. On November 2 the Minister of Transport, Mr Harold
Watkinson, appeared in 'Press Conference' and was questioned by
Francis Williams and other journalists.

All these were ordinary BBC current affairs programmes. Ministers appeared in them at the invitation of the BBC. They were,
therefore, not 'Ministerial' broadcasts and the procedures of the
Aide Mémoire did not apply to them. But the Prime Minister now
asked for time and facilities for his second 'Ministerial' broadcast on
Suez. The rules of the Aide Mémoire of 1947 did apply here and also
the provisions for a right of reply by the Opposition. Sir Anthony

Eden gave his broadcast on Saturday, November 3. Israel had attacked Egypt; British and French forces were preparing to occupy key points on the Canal and were bombing military targets in preparation for the landing of ground troops. The Prime Minister's broadcast was in essence an attempt to explain and justify British military intervention.

The Labour Party immediately demanded a right of reply. The BBC now came under severe pressure from both political parties. There was no agreement between them that the Prime Minister's broadcast had been 'controversial' in the sense of the Aide Mémoire. So the BBC had to 'exercise its own judgment' about a right of reply.

Since the political parties had refused to bring the definitions of 'Ministerial' broadcasts up to date it could be argued that the kind of broadcast given by Sir Anthony Eden on November 3 lay outside the definitions as laid down in the Aide Mémoire of 1947. Even technically, therefore, the decision was not an easy one. It was complicated by the view of some Government supporters that in the Suez situation any broadcast by the Leader of the Opposition must simply be an appeal to the nation at a time of national crisis to reject the policies of an elected government.

The BBC, under stress, with time short and emotions running high, eventually agreed that Mr Gaitskell should broadcast on Sunday, November 4, the evening after the Prime Minister's 'Ministerial'. To those who supported Sir Anthony Eden's military intervention this could well seem a stab in the back. At a moment when British troops were fighting abroad for British interests the last word to the nation would have been given on television by the Leader of the Opposition, who opposed the action taken by the Government.

To the Labour Party the 'right of reply' seemed merely justice. The Prime Minister had already, on August 8, given his views to the nation in a 'Ministerial' broadcast. The Leader of the Opposition had certainly appeared subsequently on television in 'Press Conference'. But there he had been challenged and cross-questioned. The Prime Minister, unchallenged and unquestioned, had on November 3 given a second 'Ministerial' broadcast. Surely the Leader of the Opposition should now have the right to broadcast a reply? He would be speaking as the Leader of the Opposition, in terms defined by the Aide Mémoire. The subject was certainly controversial. The nation was divided about the Government's Suez policies; and there was division even among Ministers.

On Sunday, November 4, 1956, Mr Gaitskell was nearly as strained as Sir Anthony Eden had been on August 8. He was surrounded by advisers who, even at this last moment, gave him conflicting advice. He had been working at the broadcast all day and continued to work on it at Lime Grove. Meanwhile the crew of technicians, specially summoned for mid-morning, waited in the studio. As the minutes went by I began to feel that the continual comments from his advisers were worrying Mr Gaitskell as well as delaying him so, eventually, I asked if he would care to use an adjacent office where he could work alone. He accepted—apparently with relief. The broadcast, at long last and with everybody anxious, was recorded.

At the time every word seemed momentous. But in fact all was now over. What was being done about Suez was more significant that what was being said. The news of the cease-fire came in time to be discussed in 'Panorama' on Monday, November 5. Sir Anthony Eden, too ill to continue in government, went to Jamaica to recuperate and eventually resigned on January 9, 1957. He was succeeded next day as Prime Minister by Mr Harold Macmillan.

The full truth about Suez is not likely to be known until relevant documents, hitherto protected by the so-called 'Thirty Year Rule', are released for public scrutiny. Perhaps not even then. For who knows how much was decided during those torrid months as a result of private or telephoned conversations which were never recorded?

This is equally true of the pressures which were brought to bear upon broadcasters. In the absence of any decisive written evidence which may become available the most succinct statement about the intentions of the Prime Minister in regard to broadcasting at that time is made in an article in the *Sunday Times* of March 24, 1968. It quotes William Clark, by then a Vice-President of the International Bank, as saying 'Eden's plan was to control the overseas broadcasts particularly and force the BBC to allow Ministerial broadcasts whenever he wished without allowing the Opposition the right to reply'.

Most of the discussion about the pressures brought to bear upon broadcasters during the Suez crisis has been related to broadcasts in the BBC's Overseas Services in October and November 1956, after military operations against Egypt had begun. It is interesting, therefore, that William Clark also mentions the Prime Minister's attitude to Ministerial broadcasts. And I know from my own experience that as early as August 10, 1956, the anger of the Prime Minister, as reported to me by William Clark in his telephone calls about the Menzies broadcast, was already taking the form of threats—then vague—of action which might be taken against the BBC.

I thought at the time that these threats were simply the result of the heat, strain and possibly the obvious ill-health of a Prime Minister who felt that his reasonable wishes at a moment of national crisis were being thwarted by a stubborn and recalcitrant Corporation which was more concerned about its own independence than the national good. I believed William Clark when he told me that threats had been made. But they sounded, even at second-hand and over the telephone late at night, more like the outburst of an angry and exhausted man to a member of his own staff than a cold-blooded plan to take over the BBC if it did not obey his wishes. That such a plan actually existed or would be put into effect did not enter my head, and I had arranged for the Menzies broadcast in a state of fatigue, but pleased with the efficiency and coolness of Alasdair Milne and glad that the careful political balance we had maintained in television about Suez had made it possible to come to the rescue in a difficult situation which had, apparently, been caused by the lack of a similar balance in the sound services.

More precise threats of a take-over of the BBC were made, however, according to Harman Grisewood, in October 1956. He says in his autobiography *One Thing at a Time*,[8] published in March 1968, that William Clark told him 'towards the end of October' 1956 that Eden's reserves of patience with the BBC were fast running out and that 'the Prime Minister had instructed the Lord Chancellor (Lord Kilmuir) to prepare an instrument which would take over the BBC altogether and subject it wholly to the will of the Government'. A later paragraph contains the further comment 'The next I heard was that Eden had found Kilmuir's draft inadequate and he had been asked to prepare something stronger.'

Since the freedom of the Press and the freedom of broadcasting are intimately connected it is not surprising that these statements caused an immediate outcry in the Press and questions in the House of Commons. On April 13, 1968, Mr Boston, then Labour Member for Faversham, asked the then Postmaster General (Mr Mason) whether he would 'take a look at the hair-raising revelations contained in Mr Harman Grisewood's book about the pressures applied by the then Conservative Government in 1956? Does he not think there is a strong case for thorough investigations into these revelations?' Mr Mason said: 'No, because the BBC has always retained its independence in this respect.' And in May, on the motion for the adjournment, Mr Mason replying to Mr William Hamilton, said 'Once any government decides to control in some measure the programme content of a broadcasting service it sets off on a steep and slippery slope' and went on, since Mr Hamilton had suggested that new steps might be taken to prevent the BBC being threatened with the censorship of broadcasting, 'The BBC and the ITA are independent. This principle had been reaffirmed many times . . . there can be no great virtue in trying to get more of the facts, particularly as the outcome was that the independence of the broadcasting authorities remained complete and unqualified.'

These fresh assurances in 1968 of the importance of the 'complete and unqualified' independence of the BBC and the ITA were not related to the existence (or otherwise) of the 'instrument' which Lord Kilmuir is alleged to have been instructed to draw up in 1956: they were rather a re-statement of the general principles which had been established in order to govern the relationship between broadcasters and the political parties in Britain. It was upon these principles that broadcasters relied at the time of Suez, both in regard to Ministerial broadcasts and broadcasts by the BBC's External Services.

Established procedures, agreed by the main political parties as well as by broadcasters, had been created precisely in order to prevent broadcasting being dominated by whatever government happened to be in power at any one moment. It was these agreed procedures, giving the Opposition the right to claim a reply to a Ministerial broadcast, which resulted in the Prime Minister's broadcast on November 3, 1956 being followed by that of Mr Gaitskell on November 4, in spite of the fact that the Prime Minister would have preferred this not to happen: it was because the duty imposed upon broadcasters to be fair and impartial in handling matters of controversy had not been strictly interpreted by the sound services of the BBC that the broadcast by Sir Robert Menzies had had to be given on television rather than sound. Above all, it was because the BBC had not received formal instructions about the control of its External Services at a time when the country appeared to be being dragged into war without war having been declared that the Governors of the BBC decided that the Corporation should not depart from its duty to be impartial unless it were formally instructed by the Postmaster General to do so or a state of war was formally declared to exist.

This decision meant that the BBC allowed both pro- and anti-Suez opinions to be broadcast at home and continued to permit, in its regular External Service 'Press Review' programmes, the broadcasting, world-wide, of statements which were critical of the Government's Suez policies as well as those which were favourable—even though this course of action was known to be causing disquiet in Government circles.

The arguments about broadcasting during the Suez crisis remain valuable and relevant; the independence of the Press and of broadcasting are still living issues. Most governments at moments of international, or national, political stress would like to be in control of broadcasting and to ensure that only their own policies are heard by suppressing those of the Opposition. This is peculiarly likely to happen when governments are convinced that they are acting wisely and in the national interest. Suez is, therefore, a salutary warning of the lengths to which a political party may go, when in power, to prevent the broadcasting of any opinions but its own. It also reveals the importance of maintaining procedures, agreed in advance by broadcasters and the Opposition as well as by Government, to which the broadcasting organisations can refer when refusing to submit to government pressures exerted at moments of tension when emotions are running high.

[12]

'Panorama', the News and the Rise
of the Television Interviewer

1956-1959

In 1957, after Suez, the duty of broadcasters to be impartial in matters of controversy and the agreed procedures in regard to Ministerial broadcasts and rights of reply by the Opposition still remained: so did the 'complete and unqualified' independence of the broadcasting organisation which Mr Mason in 1968 was to welcome and endorse. There was, however, a dilemma for Ministers of the Crown and Leaders of the Opposition. As the number of ordinary television current affairs programmes increased they could either rely on invitations to appear on occasions when normally they would be challenged and cross-questioned by journalists and others or they could rely on the rules and procedures of the Aide Mémoire.

In the event, and with considerable political wisdom, both methods were retained. Ministers freely accepted invitations to appear on television current affairs programmes. But when such invitations were not forthcoming, or when Ministers preferred to give a direct address to the nation rather than be interviewed in a current affairs programme, the Government retained the right to demand a 'Ministerial' broadcast and the Opposition retained its right to ask for an opportunity to reply. And, on the difficult occasions when there was no agreement between the parties about whether a Ministerial broadcast had or had not been 'controversial' and whether, therefore, the Opposition should be granted a right of reply, the BBC continued to be saddled with the embarrassing duty of making a decision which would certainly be disliked by both parties.

Within the BBC, however, there was a major change. Sir Anthony Eden's insistence that there should be Ministerial broadcasts on television and his use of television for his Suez broadcasts on August 8 and November 3, 1956 made it inevitable that in the future

Ministers and Leaders of the Opposition would use television for important addresses to the nation. The sound of the Suez broadcasts was taken from television and transmitted to radio listeners. Television had decisively replaced sound radio as the main means of direct communication between political leaders and the individual voter.

The repercussions of this on political leadership and the status of Members of Parliament were, in 1956, very largely unforeseen either by politicians or by the BBC. But they proved to be great. For vision changed the nature as well as the style of the communication. It was no longer made by words alone. It consisted not only of what a speaker said but what he conveyed by his manner and bearing; by the turn of his head; by the lines on his face; by the way in which he used his hands; by the gestures and mannerisms which were part of him. Seen on television political leaders became at once more human and more vulnerable. On sound radio they were protected from the public gaze. Their talks were normally scripted. They could write and re-write them, rehearse and re-rehearse them until the result seemed a miracle of warm-hearted spontaneity.

On television things were different. Addresses to the nation could be, and often were, written and re-written, rehearsed and recorded. A Minister or Leader of the Opposition could, and sometimes did, record on video-tape several 'takes' of his broadcast. He and his advisers could look at them and decide which they thought most suitable for transmission. It even became possible, once video-tape editing could be done at speed, to select what they felt to be the most effective sections of several 'takes', have these put together and so transmit an optimum version of the broadcast.

Nevertheless, in the end, on television the man himself was there. Resolute words made little impression if the man who used them appeared irresolute. Generous sentiments verbally expressed could be denied visually by a cold eye. As a result a Party Political or Ministerial broadcast on television was judged not only by the broadcaster's verbal expression of his political opinions but by the viewer's personal assessment of the calibre and trustworthiness of the man who was uttering them.

Mr Grimond, when Leader of the Liberal Party, frequently attacked television on the grounds that it trivialised politics by emphasising personalities rather than policies. But judgment of political policies had never been divorced from judgments of the men who were advocating them and who would have to implement them. The change which television made was to extend the opportunity of making such judgments from the few to the many. In the past the chance of seeing political leaders regularly in close-up and in action had been limited largely to Members of Parliament, lobby correspondents, senior Civil Servants, party officials, and, generally, to a select inner ring of those in the know. The judgments of these few provided a basis for the personal assessments of political figures presented by daily and weekly newspapers. All this remained; but now there were other opinions. Millions of individual voters no longer had to depend upon these second-hand sources. They themselves could see political leaders regularly on their television screens and could make their own judgments as they watched, in close-up, Sir Anthony Eden, Harold Macmillan, Hugh Gaitskell, Sir Alec Douglas-Home, Harold Wilson, Edward Heath and Margaret Thatcher.

Their judgments were bound to be different from those of Parliament. Viewers might be shrewd judges of men, but few had experience of exercising the responsibilities of political power; of dealing with the strengths and weaknesses of a permanent Civil Service; of feeling the pressures of departments and Ministers within a Cabinet; of relating national interests to an international situation; of giving appropriate weight to political strategy and political tactics. Many Members of Parliament were as little experienced in these matters as the majority of viewers. But some, whether in the governing or opposition parties, had held office, so that a professional understanding of the problems of government sometimes tempered the equally professional hostilities of party politics.

Such professional understanding could not be expected of a television audience. Their judgments were more direct, more human and less informed. But the very fact that they could be made outside the regimented party system which operated in the House of Commons created a new kind of public opinion about political leaders which decreased, at least apparently, the dependence of the individual voter on the judgment of his elected representative in the House of Commons, and so diminished the importance of a Member of Parliament and increased the authority of the Executive. For from 1956 onwards any Minister who had something to say which might interest the public would almost certainly be invited to appear on one or other of the established television programmes which dealt with current affairs. 'Press Conference' was one such programme. But now there were others—of which, by 1955, 'Panorama' had become the most important.

'Panorama' started in 1953 but was not then a current affairs programme. It was a general interest topical 'magazine' which came out fortnightly and was largely concerned with the theatre, books and the arts. The first edition, transmitted at 8.15 p.m. on November 11, 1953, contained, in addition to book reviews and theatre notices, a section called 'Under Fire' in which officials and 'experts' were confronted by individual citizens who had grievances; there were interviews with 'People in the News'; and an attempt was made to present a television version of the type of topical cartoon which usually appears in a newspaper.

'Panorama' was not a success. Indeed it had such a bad press that it was immediately withdrawn for re-shaping. It did not return until December 9, 1953, and then with a new editor and a new compère. It was still struggling to find a style and an identity. On January 24, 1954, the television critic of the *Sunday Times*, Maurice Wiggin, wrote: 'Panorama is a perfect example of what is wrong with television'. On February 24, 1954, the *Manchester Guardian* said: 'Panorama is not as bad as it once was.'

It continued to run fortnightly for the rest of 1954 and well into 1955. One of its regular contributors was Malcolm Muggeridge. In an article in the *Radio Times* on October 15, 1954, the then editor recalled among the highlights of past editions Malcolm Muggeridge interviewing Billy Graham, a high-level laundry representative facing an angry housewife who flourished a ruined pillow slip in his face, and a girl having a tooth extracted under hypnosis at the very moment when Dame Sybil Thorndike was arriving to talk about her fifty years on the stage.

Cecil McGivern, though I was not then aware of this, was becoming increasingly dissatisfied. He did not feel that the programme was worth the demands it made on television resources and money. At a routine meeting with him in the summer of 1955 he told me that he was going to take 'Panorama' off unless I would take it over. Though I was Assistant Head of the Television Talks Department, which had the overall responsibility for 'Panorama', I had not personally been concerned with it. I was still busy with the various continuing Mayhew and Crawley series; with 'Press Conference'; with the development of a new series called 'Facts and Figures' which was intended to illuminate the statistics of economics; with the presentation of election results and, in general, with the output of the production staff of the erstwhile current affairs unit.

One of the difficulties about routine meetings with a television Controller of Programmes is that there never seems enough time for consideration. This was true of the decision about 'Panorama'. I had to say 'Yes' or 'No'. I said 'Yes': but only if I had complete freedom to decide its staffing. I wanted Michael Peacock as editor. And I wanted Richard Dimbleby, who had worked with us on the Election Results programme in May 1955, to be the compère. We all wanted to give 'Panorama' a new look; to make it harder, more concerned with the world outside Britain and outside the confines of the studio; to give it the kind of authority which had been achieved by the Mayhew and Crawley series; but to do this weekly. And we wanted to change the title. Effectively this was going to be a new programme. But McGivern would not agree. He insisted that as a title 'Panorama' was 'too valuable a property' to be discarded. So we devised the somewhat absurd sub-title of 'A Window on the World' to indicate the programme's new intentions; and also a new setting with a tower, rather like a lighthouse, where Richard Dimbleby would sit and call in from different parts of the world the different ingredients of the programme. This edifice got in the way of cameras; stage hands irreverently christened it 'The Dimblebox'; and, quickly, we abandoned it.

The new look 'Panorama' with Michael Peacock as editor and Richard Dimbleby as compère went on the air on September 20, 1955. Woodrow Wyatt, journalist and politician, in a rôle new to him, became its main television reporter. The first edition contained a film report by Wyatt on the then highly topical subject of the situation in Malta. There was a direct line to France using Eurovision and a series of filmed interviews with foreign tourists in Britain. The *Manchester Guardian* said: 'If it keeps up last night's form it may become the most important live news magazine of the week.'

'Panorama' in content, style and intention was a development of such previous current affairs programmes as 'Foreign Correspondent', 'India's Challenge' and 'International Commentary'. But these were series which ran for a period of six or eight weeks, after which there was a gap while another series was being planned and prepared. 'Panorama' provided continuity. And its magazine format made possible a degree of flexibility which had not existed in planned series which usually dealt only with a single subject. In any edition of 'Panorama' there were normally several items of varying degrees of importance. Most of these could be arranged in advance. Film reports dealt, in the main, with aspects of foreign affairs. But, if there were a sudden change in a home situation, it was possible to cancel or postpone one of the prepared but less topical items and substitute a studio interview, perhaps with a Minister.

'Panorama''s weekly coverage of current affairs offered the viewing public both variety and topicality. The ingredients of all television magazine programmes are pretty much the same; reports on film; interviews and discussions in the studio; the visual presentation of facts. What distinguishes one magazine programme from another is its style. Style must be consciously created. It depends upon consistency in the choice of items, the way in which these are linked, and the personality of the compère who presents them. All these depend upon the quality and outlook of the editor of the programme. The style of 'Panorama' was to be authoritative. Like any serious weekly it could not afford to omit major developments at home or in international affairs. And, on television, it was necessary, if at all possible, to interview those making vital decisions in regard to them. Such interviews frequently made news. What was said on 'Panorama' on Monday evening came increasingly to be headlined in Tuesday's morning newspapers. And an interview on 'Panorama' was soon accepted by politicians, including Prime Ministers and Leaders of the Opposition, as a suitable method of communicating with the nation.

The regular coverage of current affairs by 'Panorama' was all the more important because of the laggardly start and incompetent presentation of BBC television news. A popular newsreel had been transmitted on television since 1948. But, as Sir William Haley had pointed out, a newsreel was not news and was governed by quite other standards than news values. Nevertheless the existence of the newsreel complicated the problems of providing a service of television news. BBC news came under the control of the Editor of News, Tahu Hole, and it was considered within the BBC to be inevitable, as well as proper, that he should control any service of television news.

The practical problem was that neither Tahu Hole nor any of his staff had the faintest idea of how to present news in visual terms. They were men of words, mostly recruited from newspaper journalism, accustomed to writing news bulletins for sound radio, operating within all the established codes of Fleet Street and with many of the inhibitions of a lobby correspondent. They tended to despise television, suspect the use of vision in political communication, and be afraid of the problems it presented.

If they were governed by their newspaper traditions and their developed expertise in sound radio, so equally but differently entrenched was the head of the BBC's Film Department, Philip Dorté, who had come from Gaumont-British and who had created the Television Newsreel.

The long-drawn war between the News Division at Broadcasting House and the Film Department in Television was like a battle between a school of whales and a herd of elephants. There was no common ground upon which they could meet. Each guarded jealously its own status and their inability to co-operate delayed intolerably the presentation of news on BBC television.

By the end of 1950 the Television Newsreel had become more topical. There were three editions a week. The Editor of News at Broadcasting House had attached a senior news editor, Michael Balkwill, to be his representative on the newsreel staff and Michael Balkwill had worked closely with the newsreel producer, Richard Cawston, in an attempt to give the newsreel a 'harder' look.

Nevertheless to Broadcasting House this was still a newsreel and not news. The BBC regarded the provision of a service of 'hard' news as a sacred duty. Most 'news' is simply the selection by the editors of different newspapers and of different broadcast news programmes of reports of events which they consider will interest their readers or their listeners. Yet there is some consensus of opinion among newsmen in a free, as distinct from a dictatorial, society about what must be reported and what must not be suppressed. In war if a battleship has been sunk that is news and must be reported. In peace a major speech by a political leader is news and must be reported whether it is for or against the policy of the government. The duty and the right to publish this core of 'hard' news has been widely considered to be an essential aspect of political freedom. During the war the BBC had carried out this duty and exercised this right not only in its overseas services but in its national news. Yet on television the BBC was providing only a newsreel; there was still no news.

Although this was a battle of departments and of personalities it was also a battle for principle in regard to television news. Should news on television be considered primarily as entertainment and so-called 'news values' be subordinated to programme considerations? Or should it aim at being a public service in which 'news values' would be upheld even if programme attractiveness were diminished?

In 1953 the Director-General made a decision which ignored the practical difficulties of the dilemma. He announced in a memorandum issued on April 27, 1953 that:

'As it is not practicable to separate the responsibility for News from responsibility for Newsreels, both will be included in the service for which News Division will be responsible.'

The Editor of News at Broadcasting House had won. It was hoped that 'News and Newsreel' would start on January 1, 1954 but there were delays. These were caused in the main by the long series of experiments and 'dummy runs' which the News Division at Broadcasting House felt to be necessary. These were carried out in the television studios in an atmosphere of ridiculous secrecy. Television production personnel were excluded from the studios in which they were taking place. Neither help nor advice from the television service was invited. The News Division would go it alone.

When, on July 5, 1954, 'News and Newsreel' at last appeared on the screen it was pretentious, unattractive and lamentably amateurish compared with most television programmes being transmitted. It started with a pompous display of the BBC's coat of arms. This was followed by a series of printed captions, like paragraph headings in a newspaper. These were held in vision while an announcer, out of vision, read the appropriate item of news.

If the television newsreel had failed to be news it was at least competently presented. 'News and Newsreel' was neither competent nor an effective piece of television communication. The trouble was not only that the News Division at Broadcasting House was inexperienced in using visual material and of operating in television studios. It arose more profoundly from the fear of the Editor of News that any attempt to make news visual would mean a lowering of news standards.

His attitudes were understandable. They sprang largely from the highly respectable doctrine that, in a newspaper, news must be clearly distinguishable from comment. News was fact; comment was opinion. If a news reader were seen while giving the news, any change in his visual manner, a smile or lift of an eyebrow, might, however little this was intended, be interpreted as comment. The sacred dividing line between fact and comment could be blurred.

Then there was the different danger that news would be personalised. It would no longer be 'the news', an anonymous statement of facts given with all the authority and backed by the reputation of a famous newspaper such as *The Times* or of a great organisation such as the British Broadcasting Corporation: it could well seem 'the news according to' the particular news reader seen on the television screen, known by the public, liked or disliked, but essentially a fallible individual.

The Editor of News was also afraid of the possible infiltration of cinema standards into the handling of 'News and Newsreel'. Among the instructions which were intended to prevent this was a rule that the newsreel should use only the actual sound recorded when any event was filmed; nothing must be added from other sources. This rule created practical difficulties, particularly in the early days when sound film cameras were so heavy as to be relatively immobile. And it raised major questions of what was truth in the presentation of reality on television. Suppose, for instance, a royal tour were being filmed for the newsreel. Many of the occasions would have to be covered by hand-held silent cameras. Should the newsreel editor do as he was instructed and let these sequences run in silence even though the crowds had been cheering? Or should he try to find recorded cheers in the sound library which matched as nearly as possible those which had been heard by people on the spot? Which course of action would produce greater truth in the representation of what had actually happened?

This was a very real problem, one of which Richard Cawston and Michael Balkwill were much aware. They struggled to solve it with all the integrity and professional expertise they possessed. But they also had to struggle against Philip Dorté's conviction that they were making difficulties where none existed. And a number of others who had been trained in cinema newsreel traditions considered that extra sound should, of course, be dubbed on from any suitable source not only in order to increase the accuracy of the reel but also to enhance its effect. Music could increase the emotional impact of a visual scene; the excitement of a demonstration could be made more evident by adding some shouting and booing from a recording which had nothing to do with that particular event. A newsreel was art as well as a presentation of fact. The effect was what counted; the end was what mattered; not the means by which it was achieved.

But here was a highly slippery slope. Where was the line to be drawn? Would it, for example, be proper to add to the applause with which a political speech had been received if the recorded sound seemed inadequate? Or simply to increase the dramatic effect of an important statement? It was understandable that the Editor of News should not want to embark upon these perilous distinctions and that he should prefer to lay down a rigid rule based upon a clear principle, i.e. that nothing in the news or newsreel must be faked, and that adding to the sound track as it had been actually recorded was a species of faking and could not be permitted.

But his small knowledge of the problems of film-making prevented him from understanding the practical difficulties of the newsreel producers and, as a result of their trying to implement the strict instructions coming from Broadcasting House, the newsreel grew more and more arid. On October 18, 1956 the Director-General confirmed to the Editor of News that 'there is no Corporation policy which demands that there should be a programme called "Newsreel".' This meant that the Editor of News could not force the Controller of Television Programmes to accept the Newsreel if he did not wish to do so. McGivern accepted it as a daily programme until the end of 1956. But he decided that from January 1957 he wanted only two newsreels a week. Television's newsreel was being destroyed effectively by the News Division at Broadcasting House.

This was partly the result of their lack of professional knowledge of how to use visual material, particularly their ignorance of film, but it was due also to their wish to maintain the highest news standards and not to compromise with what they believed to be the lower standards of a cinema-type newsreel. Newsreels in any case were disappearing from cinemas and were an anomaly on television. A medium which made it possible for viewers to see a football match as it was happening and the results of a General Election as they came in could no longer tolerate the slow pace and the lack of topicality of a newsreel. In BBC television the vacuum created by the decay of the newsreel and the rigid attitudes of the News Division which prevented an adequate service of news was being filled largely by television current affairs programmes such as 'In the News', 'Press Conference', 'Panorama' and the presentation on television of the results of General Elections.

But a quite different factor had already affected the BBC's attempts to present news on television. This was competition from a rival system. 'Independent Television News', with Aidan Crawley as its first editor, had been launched in May 1955 as a non-profit-making company with its own staff, premises, studios and equipment. It was financed by the commercial television companies and its shares were owned by four of them, Rediffusion, ATV, Granada and ABC. Crawley regarded personalisation in the presentation of news as an asset to be exploited, not as a crime to be avoided. So, though BBC news readers remained what they were called, men who read the news and had no hand in writing it, Independent Television News employed not news readers but 'newscasters' who from the first not only read the news but helped to edit and prepare it.[1]

Though Aidan Crawley soon resigned from his post as editor of ITN and returned to work with the BBC, the standards which he had established and the battles which he had fought against commercial pressures were continued. The result was that Independent Television News, with its newscasters, interviewers and special current affairs programmes, became the most effective of all the challenges which the competitive system offered the BBC.

One of the results of the development of television news and current affairs programmes was that Ministers of the Crown and Leaders of the Opposition became increasingly willing to be cross-examined by television interviewers who had no political standing, who had not been elected and who were simply freelance operators working on contract for broadcasting organisations. These interviews took place outside Parliament; the procedures of Parliament did not apply to them; questions were put, not across the floor of the House of Commons under the impartial gaze of a Speaker, but in front of television cameras and within the sight of a million judging eyes.

The practical arrangements for such interviews were determined by the convenience of television programme planners and of television current affairs producers. There were no rules other than those developed by the broadcasting organisations themselves. Whether these encounters took place in a television studio or in No. 10 or No. 11 Downing Street, the physical circumstances, with the television interviewer seated beside the politician he was interviewing, seemed to give him equal status with, say, a Prime Minister or a Chancellor of the Exchequer. Moreover, since those who asked the questions had the initiative, it was difficult for politicians to prevent them from appearing to be the dominant figures.

So Ministers and Leaders of the Opposition, by their television appearances, often gave the impression that they were responsible for the conduct of the nation's affairs not to the elected representatives of the people assembled in Parliament but to one or other of the freelance interviewers employed by television current affairs producers. The questioning of Ministers on television, being so frequently seen, began to appear more important than Question Time in the House of Commons. The status of Parliament and, indeed, of political leaders, was thereby diminished.

This was all the more surprising in that the control of television producers and the interviewers they employed was the responsibility of two bodies, the Board of Governors of the BBC and the Independent Television Authority, each ultimately responsible to Parliament for the conduct of their organisations. Why, then, did Parliament accept such a diminution of its status? Why did Ministers agree to appear on television and be questioned by people who had no political authority?

A number of reasons are apparent. One is that the scripted form of direct political communication with the electorate which had been used by political leaders in sound radio was virtually impossible on television. All broadcast talk, because it is received by individuals in their homes, takes on a personal character. Like Queen Victoria, individual listeners do not want to be addressed by another individual as if they were a public meeting. So in sound radio immense pains were taken to write scripts not in a literary form suitable for publication, nor in that suitable for a speech in a public hall, but in the conversational style appropriate to informal conversation between individuals. And care was taken with the detail of presentation, for instance by preventing the rustling of the papers of a script, in order to preserve the pretence that this was personal and impromptu talk, not the reading aloud of a carefully prepared written document.

Vision prevented deception of this kind. The speaker, being seen, was seen to be reading. No illusion of informal communication could be maintained. It was contradicted by what the viewer actually saw. Yet on important occasions it was hard for a politician to do without a script. A slip of the tongue in an impromptu talk by a Chancellor of the Exchequer or a Foreign Secretary might have disastrous consequences. And there were the practical difficulties of continuing to look directly at the appropriate lens of the appropriate television camera (that is, directly at the individual viewer) while still being able to take cues manually given by the floor manager, and also keep an eye on the timing. These problems combined to make the 'straight' unscripted talk the most difficult of all forms of television political communication.

The interview offered a solution. It was easier to talk informally to an interviewer than to the glassy eye of a television camera. And the practical problems were shouldered by whoever was conducting the interview. Politicians could ignore the cameras and leave matters of timing, of maintaining continuity and of taking cues, to the interviewer. Normally the general areas of questioning would have been discussed in advance with the interviewer and with the responsible producer, though the actual questions would not have been disclosed. These could not, in any case, be pre-determined. The questions the interviewer asked had to depend upon the answers he got. He had to maintain a logical line and yet be ready for the unexpected reply. So he had to be flexible. And it was his responsibility to see that what was revealed would be intelligible to the viewing public and relevant to their interests. This was not easy for either participant. The politician had to be prepared to cope with delicate questions which he would rather not have been asked. The interviewer had to be careful not to antagonise the public by seeming bad-mannered; yet he must not accept evasive answers which did not deal adequately with matters about which there was public anxiety.

In the past the remoteness of Parliament from the ordinary voter had been supplemented and humanised by the appearances of politicians at public meetings where individual citizens could question and heckle their masters. The procedures at such meetings were far from being Parliamentary. The questioners were self-appointed, not elected. Anyone could shout at a Prime Minister and demand that his grievances be heard and his doubts resolved. The existence of television made it possible for this questioning to be done, not in a public hall with a maximum audience of thousands but in a television studio with an audience which could be reckoned in millions. The television political interview was therefore in a sense not new; it was merely the translation into television terms of an established democratic tradition.

But television changed the style and manner of these encounters. They were now done by proxy. The individual voter no longer shouted at a distant figure on a platform. He could sit at home and watch questions being put on his behalf to a Minister of the Crown. The setting had become domestic; there could be no violence, no rough ejections by stewards, no abuse, no rhetoric. The Minister, by coming, had agreed that he should be questioned and that the questioning should be impromptu; interviewers were bound, as in a private conversation, to be polite, but politeness must not become subservience. They were there to put the questions which were likely to be in the minds of the television audience. And this audience included opponents of the Government and critics of a Minister as well as his friends and supporters. Yet interviewers, when questioning a Minister, must not be voices of the Opposition, nor, when questioning a Leader of the Opposition, of the Government.

This delicate difference had been emphasised to me by the Chief Assistant to the Director-General, Harman Grisewood, on the occasion of Mr Macmillan's Budget broadcast in the spring of 1956. Mr Macmillan had asked that I should produce this.[2] The problem of conflicting advice being given to a political leader by a variety of people with different interests and some right to be heard, which bedevilled much Party Political and Party Election broadcasting, did not arise in a Budget broadcast. At our meeting in No. 11 Downing Street the Chancellor had his advisers, mostly Treasury men; but he was their master. They could give advice, but he could ignore it. This is what Mr Macmillan did. He listened courteously to what they proposed and thanked them. He would consider all the points they had made. Then he said that he had a few practical matters to discuss with me. He indicated vaguely that these concerned make-up and the times when he would be required for rehearsal. As the door closed behind them he turned to me and said, 'Now, let's talk about what I should really do.'

By 1956 the established practice for television Budget broadcasts was that the Chancellor of the Exchequer and the Shadow Chancellor should be interviewed on successive nights by a single, and the same, interviewer. Mr Macmillan, however, was anxious for something different. He did not want a single interviewer. He preferred the style of a television 'Press Conference' with a number of different questioners. Rightly, he did not want to get involved with visual illustrations. I myself felt that all too often politicians had been pressed by their advisers into using tools such as film and diagrams which were outside their experience and merely made them seem to be bad actors. Their strength lay in their ability to answer questions: particularly hostile questions; they knew how to handle hecklers at a public meeting and how to deal with awkward questions in the House of Commons.

The Chancellor rose to the idea of hostile questioning like a war-horse hearing the sound of trumpets. With enthusiasm he began to list newspapermen who might be approached. 'We must have Hugh Cudlipp,' he said. And he mentioned Donald Tyerman of *The Economist*. Eventually we arrived at a formula. As Chancellor he ought to give some of his time to speaking direct to the public and take advantage of the fact that the questioning was being done, at his invitation, in the historic surroundings of No. 11 Downing Street. He would therefore open with a brief talk, not longer than three-and-a-half minutes, in which he would make it clear that he had invited a number of journalists to question him on matters arising out of the Budget. The chairman would be Robert McKenzie of the London School of Economics, who was an experienced television interviewer. We hoped that Hugh Cudlipp and Donald Tyerman would accept invitations to appear. At the end of the question and answer session the Chancellor would once more turn to camera and, briefly, sum up. The whole broadcast was to last only fifteen minutes so three questioners were all we could accommodate.

Since this was a departure from the normal procedure for Budget broadcasts and since it had been arrived at in discussion simply between Mr Macmillan and myself, I felt it necessary to put the plan to Harman Grisewood.

Arrangements for the Budget broadcasts were urgent, so I telephoned Mr Grisewood and then dictated a note of what he had said. This was for the record and for the information both of Leonard Miall, the Head of Television Talks, and Huw Wheldon, who was to produce the Budget broadcast of the Shadow Chancellor, Harold Wilson.

Mr Grisewood approved the proposals for Mr Macmillan's Budget broadcast but made a number of points which crystallised much practice in regard to political interviewing. He said that though he agreed that the questioning of the Chancellor 'should be hard hitting, it should avoid taking the party line since the party line will be provided by Mr Wilson on the following night'.[3]

This was an important statement of principle which went far beyond this particular broadcast. Interviewing could be hard hitting but must never take a party line. Interviewers could challenge statements of fact; question assumptions; point out discrepancies between what a politician had said in the past and what he was saying now. But an interview was not a discussion, much less an argument. The interviewer was not there to put forward his own opinions nor those of a political party but to clarify, for the public benefit, the attitudes and policies of the man he was interviewing.

Television political interviewing was, however, soon affected not by doctrines such as these but by purely technological factors. A number of firms' developed devices, variously called teleprompters or autocues, which allowed politicians to read their talks from a written script while appearing not to be doing so. The principle of these devices was simple. By a system of mirrors, a specially typed script passed over the lens of a television camera so that it could be read by the speaker and yet be invisible to the viewer.

The art of using a teleprompter was to succeed in pretending not to be reading but to be talking directly and informally to the individual viewer. The speaker had to learn not to keep too static a pose nor fix his eyes too rigidly upon the words which appeared in front of him; that would make him seem unnatural and reveal the fact that he was reading. He must therefore simulate the movements of head and body which were appropriate to a man who was talking. A communication to the nation made by a politician who was using a teleprompter was therefore a visual lie. The truth that he was reading was denied by all the visual circumstances of television presentation.

On January 17, 1957 Harold Macmillan, now Prime Minister, used a teleprompter when he made a television broadcast from No. 10 Downing Street. The producer was Huw Wheldon. In preparation for the next annual meeting with the political parties producers were instructed to make a candid professional report upon the political broadcasts for which they had been responsible. In his report upon the Prime Minister's January broadcast Huw Wheldon said:

'The Prime Minister's statement from Downing Street on taking office was a "personally speaking" type of programme done on a teleprompter.'[4]

He went on to say:

'Teleprompters are a dangerous friend. They undoubtedly work, but the time will come when the present Prime Minister or others will want to come before the country as "Mr Sincerity". They won't be able to do without their teleprompters, and in a very real sense the use of this equipment will invalidate an approach of this sort.'[5]

On February 1, 1957, the Liberal leader, Jo Grimond, reluctantly used a teleprompter in a Party Political broadcast. The producer, Rex Moorfoot, reported:

'As is usual, Grimond was subjected to pressures from his colleagues in the House both as regards the style of the programme and the use of the teleprompter. It was only after a demonstration in his office at the House that he accepted the use of the teleprompter which he subsequently used brilliantly.'[6]

It is difficult to assess the effect of the teleprompter upon political communication. That teleprompters existed and were used was no secret. Indeed in later years, in answer to a question in a children's programme, there was a demonstration of how teleprompters were used by news readers. But, after all, news readers were known to be reading. They were therefore different from politicians, who tried to create the illusion that they were talking frankly and directly to the individual viewer. And the more effectively the politician's script simulated talk, the more brilliantly he delivered it to camera with all the simulated movements of a talker, the more effectively he deceived.

Viewers with some television experience, watching a politician in close-up, could deduce from the movements of his eyeballs that he was reading a script, not talking to the viewer. But even those less knowledgeable about the techniques of television were, I believe, obscurely aware that things were not quite what they appeared to be. However well written the script, it seldom sounded like impromptu talk. The speaker was too glib. His eyes were focussed differently from those of a man who was talking impromptu. He was looking at the surface of the camera lens over which the written script was passing rather than trying to look through the lens at the individual viewer with whom he was endeavouring to communicate. Moreover, viewers who were accustomed to seeing politicians being questioned

THE RISE OF THE TELEVISION INTERVIEWER

in 'Press Conference' or 'Panorama', when they were genuinely talking impromptu, were bound, even if subconsciously, to notice the difference. Somewhere there was pretence. Somewhere there was deception. And the more the talk had the appearance of being frank person-to-person communication, the deeper the sense of deception was bound to be. Politicians who used teleprompters were therefore in danger of seeming devious.

And teleprompters did not solve a major problem which faced politicians who wished to use television to make direct statements to the electorate: how to approach the television audience. Huw Wheldon outlined some of the difficulties in a report to the Head of Television Talks:

> 'As you know I went down to Downing St. last night in connection with the Prime Minister's Ministerial broadcast.
>
> The mechanics of the programme were as follows: a script was made available at 5.30 and typed on a special machine in order to be ready for the teleprompter equipment. The script (subject only to minor possible emendations) had already been distributed to the Press. The Prime Minister rehearsed it on the teleprompter at 9 p.m. Only very minor modifications were possible a) because it had already gone to the Press and b) because there would have been no time to have re-done a complete teleprompter script before transmission.
>
> Immediately after transmission I had an informal meeting or session with Harold Evans, the Public Relations assistant, Heath, the Chief Whip, one of the Prime Minister's secretaries and a further secretary whose name I did not get.
>
> In this session I held out very strongly that the script as written was totally inadequate. I pointed out, inter alia, that the script as written could not, in fact be spoken by one human being to another without embarrassment to both parties. This was easily demonstrable; and the demonstration undoubtedly disturbed the four people concerned. The script was in fact not directed at all but simply delivered into a void, and it was undoubtedly true that the Prime Minister could not possibly have read the script as it stood to any group of people in the world. This they acknowledged.'

He went on to say:

> 'This is not a matter of changing words here and there. Fundamentally it is a question of not taking the job seriously.' And:

'It seems to me this convention in ministerial broadcasts of speaking sentences into camera which no human being could possibly speak direct to a postman or a professor or a housewife or a child is made all the worse by the use of a teleprompter, which allows the whole statement to be given in much the same way as a Press communiqué. I touched on this factor but not in any detail.'[7]

The difficulties which Mr Macmillan found in presenting his ideas in a form which would be appropriate to their reception by any individual postman or philosopher or housewife were not peculiar to him. They coloured nearly all formal straight-to-camera television broadcasting by political leaders. This was partly, as Huw Wheldon pointed out, because few politicians took 'the job' seriously.

But it is worth while considering why this was so. 'The job', as Huw Wheldon and most producers of television political programmes saw it, was that of communicating with the electorate. But some serious political leaders (Sir Alec Douglas-Home among them) drew a clear distinction between the formulation of political policies and the conduct of political public relations. The formulation of political policies was what mattered. Public relations were simply a kind of salemanship and television was a peculiarly tiresome form of public relations in that political leaders were expected themselves to take part instead of leaving it to publicity departments and to advertising agents. Television appearances, therefore, did not need to be taken seriously by serious men. So political leaders allowed themselves to be badgered by their colleagues, advisers, and anyone who was considered to be knowledgeable about public relations, into using styles of presentation and forms of words which were totally unsuitable for communication through television with individual members of the electorate. More thought by responsible politicians might have changed this. But few politicians or their advisers wished to think about television; they merely wanted to use it.

Behind these easy attitudes lay something deeper. The circumstances of television reception, with viewers alone or in small groups watching a political leader apparently talking directly to each of them, created an expectation of personal communication which could not be fulfilled. Politicians were not interested in individual postmen or professors or housewives. They saw the electorate as a body of people who might be persuaded to support the party in its political struggle for power. The scale of the support was what mattered; the size of the television audience was what interested them. Postmen or philosophers or housewives were politically significant only in the mass; not as individuals. This was the reality of politics and had to be recognised. But it ran counter to the illusion created by television of a man-to-man relationship between the politician on the screen and the viewer in his home.

The disparity between what television caused the viewer to expect and the reality of what, through television, a politician could give, made for disappointment in both politicians and viewers. Politicians found their television addresses less successful than they had hoped: viewers became cynical about Ministerial and Party Political broadcasts. The 'straight' talk to camera, whether in a Party Political or Ministerial broadcast, and irrespective of whether the speaker was using a teleprompter or not, lacked credibility. It was not what television made it seem to be, a personal communication between a political leader and the individual viewer; it was an essay in persuasion. Half-truths were part of the technique of persuasion; and in Party Political and Ministerial broadcasts there was no one to question them.

In comparison, questioning programmes such as 'Press Conference' or interviews in 'Panorama' appeared more credible. The viewer was no longer a passive recipient of propaganda; he was a judge, not only of the personality and character of a political leader but of how the policies which were being advocated or defended stood up to questioning by newspaper or television journalists.

Moreover he could judge not only the politicians who were being questioned but also the calibre of the interviewers who were asking the questions. By 1959 these men (there were still few women among them) had become part of the political scene. They appeared constantly on television; they were known to millions and often seemed to have more political significance than the majority of backbenchers. They were a new factor in British political life. Who were they? How were they selected? Under what kinds of editorial control did they operate? What, in practice, was their power?

The short answer is that they were selected by television current affairs producers and paid on contract for their appearances in specified television programmes. Normally they were not, as producers were, permanent and salaried members of the Corporation's staff. Their contracts could be renewed or terminated. Their fees were subject to negotiation. Their position, in fact, was very like that of actors and actresses in programmes of television drama and of performers in programmes of television light entertainment.

A main difference was that whereas actors and actresses and entertainers had existed long before television and merely had to adapt their skills to the new medium, there was no similar group of trained interviewers upon whom the producers of television current affairs programmes could draw. The most likely were experienced newspapermen who had an extensive knowledge of politics and who were accustomed to asking questions. That is one reason why, in the first of the major questioning programmes which dealt with politics, 'Press Conference', the questioners were all newspaper journalists.

But interviewers were drawn also from other fields. There was no hard and fast distinction between television commentators and television interviewers. Current affairs programmes, or items in 'Panorama' presented by Chester Wilmot, Christopher Mayhew, Aidan Crawley or Woodrow Wyatt, usually contained interviews whether on film or in the studio; but such interviews were simply useful tools in the general exposition of the contemporary political scene. They were not what some political interviews later became, cross-examinations of British political leaders on behalf of the British public and therefore apparently a rival to Question Time in the House of Commons.

This strange development went unremarked only because it came about so gradually. The BBC had always been aware of the dangers of seeming in any way to be a rival to Parliament. Broadcasting organisations existed by the will of the people expressed in Parliament. They must not challenge that will or their own existence would be in jeopardy. The BBC's determination that its current affairs interviewers should not take a party line when interviewing political leaders was simply one aspect of this general policy. The party political struggle for power was conducted in Parliament; questions in the House of Commons were to some extent a continuation of this struggle. But political interviewing on television lay outside the party battle; questions were asked not to further party interests but for the information of the public. The questioners were not members of a political party which could form an alternative government; they were there to press a political leader in front of the television cameras to reveal facts and attitudes which were of national importance but which might otherwise have been with-held from public knowledge.

It can be argued that this non-party characteristic makes tele-vision political interviewing complementary to, rather than a sub-stitute for, Question Time. The strength of the Member of Parlia-ment as compared with the television political interviewer is accountability. He is responsible to his constituents; has been chosen by them and at the next general election can be dismissed by them. The television political interviewer is accountable directly only to the broadcasting organisation which employs him. That organisa-tion, certainly, is ultimately responsible to Parliament for the behaviour of everyone it employs and cannot afford to employ interviewers who are partisan or incompetent or ill-informed. But this is a general responsibility not a particularised one. However effectively the mass public may be able to judge the interviewers it sees on its television screens they cannot decide whether a particular interviewer should be employed or dismissed.

This means that the television political interviewer has no status. He represents nothing but the decision of a television current affairs producer and of a broadcasting organisation to employ him. They may believe that he is informed, impartial, and that he asks the questions which the public wishes to have answered. But these are merely opinions; based, certainly, on programme per-formance but without any constitutional validity. Yet by 1956/7 the questioning of political leaders on television by impartial inter-viewers had become established custom. Nevertheless the practice by which broadcasting organisations selected a number of inter-viewers by methods which seemed arbitrary and were seldom disclosed, caused legitimate resentments among politicians and the public.

Even in 1957 such matters were obviously of concern to anybody interested in the whole relationship of television to the societies in which it operated. But they were long term. In 1957 we were con-centrating on immediate matters. And for many of us the most immediate was the start of 'Tonight'.

[13]

'Tonight' and 'TWTWTW'

1957-1963

'Tonight' was the first major topical programme to be presented on television five nights a week by the BBC. It was created to fill the so-called 'Toddlers' Truce', the period between 6 p.m. and 7 p.m. during which there had been no television partly, it was said, to make it easier for parents to persuade their young children to go to bed. The commercial companies, anxious for more programme hours in order to be able to increase their advertising revenue, wished to fill this space. The BBC felt compelled to do likewise. In the competitive climate of 1956–7 it seemed important not to lose the early evening audience to 'the other side' in case they might keep it for the rest of the evening.

Just at this moment two relatively new members of the Talks Department production staff were about to be free from the pressures of other work. One was Donald Baverstock, a Welshman who had come to television by way of Oxford, teaching at Wellington College, and the BBC's overseas service. The second was Alasdair Milne, a Scot, who had been selected as one of a limited number of graduates called 'general trainees' who were recruited by the BBC for a period of two years. During this time they were sent on attachments to various departments and could apply for any permanent job which became vacant. Alasdair Milne applied for, and got, a post as production assistant in the Television Talks Department. He then worked with Donald Baverstock on 'Highlight'.

This had been called into existence in order to fill a gap in the schedules. It had poor studio facilities and a small budget. Partly because of this it consisted almost entirely of interviews. By the autumn of 1956 Baverstock and Milne were tired of trying to produce a nightly topical programme with such limited resources. So they were discussing with the Head of Television Talks a possible twenty-minute nightly programme which would need more resources than 'Highlight'. They were also discussing with me a possible

weekly half-hour programme which was to be called 'Man Alive'.*
This, in Donald Baverstock's words, would be 'on the side of the
audience'. He did not like 'Panorama', which he thought too much
the voice of authority, and wanted to create a programme which
would look at authority and authoritative policies from the point of
view of the ordinary man, the viewer.

During the discussions about 'Man Alive' we began to talk about
the 'Toddlers' Truce' and to wonder whether the 6–7 p.m. period
could be filled by a nightly programme which would make use of
some of the ideas we were exploring for 'Man Alive' and benefit by
the experience gained from producing 'Highlight'. Any such project
would have to be related to our assessment of what viewers would be
likely to be doing between 6 p.m. and 7 p.m. We made enquiries.
They would be coming and going: women getting meals for teen-
agers who were going out and preparing supper for husbands who
were coming in; men in the North would be having their tea; com-
muters in the South would be arriving home. There was no likelihood of an audience which would be ready to view steadily for
half-an-hour at a time. What seemed necessary was a continuous
programme held together by a permanent staff of compères, reporters, and interviewers, but consisting of separate items so that any
viewer who happened to be around could dip into it knowing that
something different would soon follow and that he had lost nothing
by not being able to watch from the beginning.

I thought that any such programme ought to be cross-
departmental. It would have to make use of outside broadcasts
which were the essence of television, so there ought to be an associate
outside broadcast producer; there would be a modest amount of
light entertainment but this ought to be professionally presented so
there should be an associate light entertainment producer; film
would be important and the new programme must have its own
senior film editor who would be seconded from the film department.†

I had always believed that the departmentalised structure of the

---

* Owing to the start of 'Tonight' this was never transmitted. The same
title was later used by the producers of a quite different programme.

† These appointments were agreed: and 'Tonight' gained Ned Sherrin
for Light Entertainment, William Cave for Outside Broadcasts and Tony
Essex for films. But the cross-departmental structure foundered on the
differences between the departments in regard to the assessment and

BBC's production departments was in a sense a barrier to creativity in broadcasting. It was based on a bricks-and-mortar mentality which had become out-of-date, a lecture room with visual aids for 'talks', a music hall for light entertainment. But in both radio and television the whole air was free for imagination and for a new appreciation that to most people in the electronic age it was possible to move easily from entertainment to politics. They could like both, and both could be combined in a single programme. This was the idea of 'Tonight'. In life people do not live in departments; they can enjoy both gluttony and abstinence; they do not have to be earnest all the time, nor frivolous all the time. Frivolity is a relief from earnestness and earnestness is a necessary complement to frivolity.

I put these ideas to Cecil McGivern. He reacted with a kind of cold impatience. A nightly programme of this kind could be done only if it had its own full-time studio. But no studio was available. I was aware, and should have been more aware, that the studio situation, for the time being, was difficult. The new Television Centre was still being built; the first of its studios would not be available until 1960. In the meantime the BBC's television service was having to make do with the converted film studios at Lime Grove and with a number of other converted buildings dotted about London. Already it was almost impossible to pack into them the major drama, light entertainment, talks and children's programmes which were the mainstay of the service. Cecil McGivern was therefore understandably irritated by being asked to consider an idea which demanded the full-time use of a television studio. I said at last, 'If I can find a studio, would you consider the idea?' He said, 'But there *isn't* a studio. We've been looking for one for months.'

I went away. Then I remembered that I had once seen a number of television exercises put on by students who were attending the BBC's television training school. I had watched these from a cramped control gallery. But there had been cameras and lights and engineers. Eventually I found that a small film studio in a Kensington cul-de-sac had been temporarily converted to television by Marconi's in order to train television engineers and cameramen for the start, in 1955, of commercial television. It had now been dismantled. The television equipment was piled in a corner under

---

rewards of production staff. So all these posts were eventually transferred to the Talks Department.

dust sheets. Marconi's lease of the premises was due to expire in three weeks' time. Their engineers had been dispersed all over the world.

But I discovered that the owner of the film studio would be willing to renew Marconi's lease and that Marconi's were willing, at a price, to re-mantle the studio and provide an engineering crew. BBC engineers knew and trusted Marconi's, BBC lawyers were willing to go into the question of the renewal of the lease; BBC administrators believed that they could supply, on a part-time basis, the necessary ancillary staff. By now I had told McGivern that we had found a studio. He asked me to provide, immediately, a scheme which would state programme intentions, plans, staffing and film requirements, and, above all, costing, including the costs of the hired studio with its crew. He would then consider it.

Donald Baverstock and Alasdair Milne were already working on programme ideas. Baverstock, typically, had listed forty different possible types of programme ingredients. I had seen, in the United States, some of the casually presented early morning programmes which included news, time checks, interviews with people who were pulled in off the street, combined with easy apologies for the non-appearance of someone who had failed to turn up. These apparently casual programmes were the result of highly professional skills and their styles were refreshing when compared with the more formal BBC presentation, not only of news, but of 'Press Conference' and 'Panorama'. This was what we wanted. A new style.

Styles in television programmes are the result, not of gimmicks, but of the attitudes to life of the production staff. The style of 'Tonight' was the result of the intellectual integrity and the human understanding of its editors, Donald Baverstock and Alasdair Milne. The production staff of 'Tonight', its reporters and commentators, were specially recruited with the intention of their working as a team with the editors.* They had, therefore, to be of like mind. This gave the programme a remarkable unity which was increased by the fact that for the first months of its existence 'Tonight' was produced from its own studio, operated by Marconi engineers and was therefore, to some extent, outside the centralised controls of the BBC's television service.

* The extension of programme hours was felt to justify an increase in the BBC's production staff.

But the actual start of 'Tonight' was the result of a most courageous decision made by Cecil McGivern. When he had received, for consideration, our papers giving programme plans and costs he called a meeting of senior administrative staff. I expected the meeting to be argumentative and hostile. This was a new venture, and it did not fit into normal BBC procedures. To my astonishment McGivern opened the meeting by saying that he had accepted the plan and now simply wanted to hear how it could be implemented. So 'Tonight', a forty-minute programme, began on February 18, 1957, for an experimental period of three months in what came to be called 'Studio M'.

For visual interest 'Tonight' depended largely on carefully planned film reports; for topicality mainly on studio interviews. During the course of 'Highlight' Donald Baverstock had given a great deal of thought to the nature and conduct of television interviews. Their purpose must be clear, and decided well in advance of transmission. There were dozens of different kinds of interviews, some intended to reveal personality, some to provide information, and those of the cross-examining type which challenged, for example, the assumptions of politicians. The nature of the questioning must be determined by the purpose of the interview. Production staff, under Baverstock's personal and detailed supervision, were responsible for the questions asked. So 'Tonight' became a kind of school for interviewers. There must be ease of manner. Cliff Michelmore, whom Baverstock had chosen, as a result of his 'Highlight' experience, to be 'Tonight's' compère, gradually developed this. So did Derek Hart and Geoffrey Johnson Smith. But, in spite of the easy style there must be tight control; not a second must be wasted; every word must make a point. Baverstock's attitude was that every television minute asked for a minute out of the individual lives of several million people. Lives were too important to be squandered on generalities or padding. Every interview must be pared to the bone in order to justify the demands it made upon human attention.

On September 28, 1958 the *Observer* newspaper published, with pictures, a full-scale profile of the 'Tonight' team. The writer remarked that 'Tonight' in a sense, had been a makeshift and that makeshifts tended to be suspected or patronised. He went on to say that 'Tonight' had suffered both extremes until gradually it dawned on people that here, for the first time in British television, was superb and regular journalism, five nights a week. He said, rightly,

that Baverstock and his colleagues, even before the programme
began, had developed a series of attitudes and principles: 'Politicians needn't be treated with awe, railwaymen with condescension.' It was necessary for interviewers and compères to be
relaxed, but never sloppy: 'try to show humility: don't try to fool
people'.

'Tonight' in general and in detail was based on respect for the
individual human being. Their importance and their intelligence
must never be underrated. And Donald Baverstock, deeply concerned with the moralities of broadcasting, insisted, in spite of
criticisms (mostly from within the BBC) of being irreverent and
anxious to 'take the mickey' out of anything, that 'Tonight' was
'basically and strictly moral'. In my experience this was true. Every
night, after each 'Tonight' programme, there was a ruthless post-
mortem. What was argued, sometimes hotly, was not merely the
effectiveness of an item and certainly not its possible effect on
ratings: it was the validity of presenting it on television to millions
of viewers. Baverstock is quoted in the *Observer* as saying:

> 'I assure you that what really hurts us after a programme is some-
> thing that is wrong, that is evil. Little things, where you put on a
> man you think is dishonest and he's made some witty remarks and
> the interviewer may have smiled in the middle and enjoyed it.
> You feel that's slightly immoral because you have endorsed this
> man's successful hypocritical projection of himself.'

And there were more subtle and complicated judgments. Donald
Baverstock mentioned those of Cynthia Judah,* a senior member of
the team, and quoted her opinions about an interview conducted by
Derek Hart. It was with Robert Frost, the American poet. Baverstock said:

> 'It was a superb projection of Robert Frost, the man came over
> as an angel. And yet there was still Cynthia coming in to bat and
> saying, after it, that he was so nice that it was *wrong* to invite him,
> because his niceness was a private niceness. It was a private thing,
> and in a sense in putting him on we were making public the
> private niceness.'

---

* Later married to Robert Kee, a distinguished broadcaster who worked
with the BBC and, later, for ITV.

By the autumn of 1958 'Tonight' had a nightly audience of around seven million viewers. Donald Baverstock and his team had won in 1957 and again in 1958 the Guild of Television Producers' Award for the best factual programme of the year and Cliff Michelmore had been chosen by the Guild as the television personality of 1958.

'Tonight's' approach to political interviewing was journalistic rather than reverential. Ministers and Opposition leaders were invited because they were in the news. Moreover an essential aspect of the 'Tonight' style of interviewing was that it was under strict editorial control. Interviewers were far from being merely mouthpieces. They all contributed ideas and attitudes as well as personalities. But, as the *Observer* pointed out, the questions that Derek Hart asked and the jokes that Cliff Michelmore made with such ease and timing might well have been written (and rewritten) by Gordon Watkins or Cynthia Judah. Interviewing, as everything else on 'Tonight', was a team job. And Donald Baverstock was very much in editorial control of the 'Tonight' interviewers and therefore answerable for them.

The result was that no 'Tonight' interviewer gained the personal ascendancy in political interviewing which was eventually achieved by Robin Day and some of his colleagues in 'Panorama'. Yet 'Tonight' had a great influence on the BBC's interviewing methods. This was not a result of its political attitudes: politically it was balanced and impartial. But its fundamental approach was egalitarian. Gardeners and housewives and eel-catchers were treated as seriously as Members of Parliament. Power, even the power endorsed by election in a democratic society, did not confer wisdom, and those who wielded it could be questioned. Even wealth could be laughed at; even millionaires mocked. And one of 'Tonight's' most successful reporters, Alan Whicker, as a result of his poker-faced presentation of the activities of the wealthy (in which they surprisingly co-operated), produced television reports which were in fact a kind of mockery. He did not comment. He was simply an interested observer from another world: the world of those who had never known, and would never achieve, wealth.

Whicker, in his own way, was a representative of the ordinary man. He was, as Baverstock had always intended the whole 'Tonight' programme to be, clearly and obviously on the side of the audience. And he remained one of them. He never altered the kind of clothes he wore, or his tone of voice, whether he were interviewing a Master of the Quorn or a Paul Getty or a woman who believed in leprechauns. His interviews were often sharply penetrating but never malicious. If millionaires could be laughed at, they were also treated with sympathy. They too were human beings.

The immense popularity of 'Tonight' was due, I believe, in part to a kind of national explosion of relief. It was not always necessary to be respectful; experts were not invariably right; the opinions of those in high places did not have to be accepted. In Britain, broadcasting, even television broadcasting, had seemed hitherto to be dominated by Reithian attitudes. These were suffused by intellectual condescension. Broadcasters knew the best when they saw it; it was their duty, with the help of the experts they selected, to pass on to the listening and viewing masses this privileged perception.

In the field of television current affairs 'Panorama' was communication of this kind. Its strength, still, was that it was authoritative. Because it was a serious programme dealing seriously with national and international affairs political leaders were willing to appear on it and to be questioned by interviewers who might ask embarrassing questions but who understood the political scene. It attracted a vast audience at a peak time because it was topical, dealt with a variety of subjects and was presented with professional competence.

'Tonight' was different. It stood, so to speak, the accepted communicative process on its head. It looked at those in power from the point of view of the powerless; it examined the effect of the judgments of experts upon specific cases; and of administrative policies upon the human beings who were at the receiving end of the administrative machine. Yet, though the appeal of 'Tonight' was regard for the individual, it was never sentimental, doctrinaire, or morally self-righteous. Realism prevailed.

It is never easy to know to what extent a television programme creates a national mood and to what extent it merely reflects it. What seems to happen is that, from time to time, a broadcast programme embodies a change in the mood of a nation. In sound radio this had been true of 'Itma'. In television it was true of 'Tonight'. By 1957 a number of influences, including that of television itself, had made the viewing millions impatient of paternalism. They could see, and judge for themselves, the performances of footballers, of politicians, of interviewers, of entertainers, of actors and actresses. They were no longer content to be the grateful recipients of the opinions of those who were supposed to know better.

'Tonight' was a reflection of this mood: it was not rebellious, far less revolutionary, but it was sceptical, particularly of theorists and 'experts'. If 'Panorama' with Richard Dimbleby had become the voice of authority, 'Tonight' with Cliff Michelmore was rapidly becoming the voice of the people.

Such an identification between the public mood and a television programme does not happen by accident. All television producers must, to some extent, have an affinity with the public for which they are producing programmes. During the preparation and rehearsal of a programme they must wince where the public is bound to wince, they must resent condescension which the public is bound to resent. This is a question of feeling, and, to a degree, of experience. Without it they are no good as producers. But 'Tonight' carried this normal requirement a stage further. Every spoken word was scrutinised to ensure that it was part of the process of identification. But the desire for identification sprang from passion, particularly from Donald Baverstock's strong personal feelings about the importance of every individual human being.

'Tonight', to those who worked on it, became a way of life. They were 'Tonight' people. They strutted about Lime Grove in a body, respecting the audience but despising other broadcasters. They were overworked and, in their own view, underpaid. They particularly resented the resources which were put at the disposal of 'Panorama' and of documentary producers. With a bitter pleasure they worked out tables showing the cost per thousand viewers of these productions compared with 'Tonight'. But they did not want to leave 'Tonight'. Why, they argued, should promotion and higher salaries not be achieved within the 'Tonight' structure rather than by leaving it for less competent enterprises?

Their fervent attachment to the programme was largely due to Donald Baverstock's editorship. He ran 'Tonight' with a mixture of authoritarianism and democracy which he called leadership. There was no nonsense about status and hierarchies. Nobody had to make appointments to see him or anyone else. In the rabbit warren of the 'Tonight' offices at Lime Grove everybody collided with everybody else, exchanging information and opinions as they did so. Every member of the team, secretaries, film editors, production assistants, producers, had their say: at planning meetings, at the noonday sessions where film was scrutinised, at the evening post-mortems when the programmes were nightly pulled to pieces. Anybody with anything intelligent to contribute was listened to, but they had to be quick. Time was short. And the editor's decision was final.

But if they did not want to leave 'Tonight' they did need change. The gruelling disciplines of a five-night-a-week programme with its never-ceasing demands upon inventiveness, became, at one time or another over the years, too much for most of them. Wives grew restive; their husbands left early and got home late; weekends were spent in telephoning commentators and camera crews in Singapore or Buenos Aires. But everybody resisted the wishes of Cecil McGivern (among others) who wanted this successful programme to move to a later time in the evening. Unless they were to be even more over-worked this would involve a shift system. And that would destroy the unity of the programme.

The strength of 'Tonight' was partly that it had not been con-ceived in a vacuum; it was not simply a programme 'offer' to be slotted in wherever the programme planners thought fit. It had been created to suit the needs of a particular audience at a particular time of the day. If McGivern wanted a new late-night programme we would create one, but this would not be achieved merely by moving the early evening 'Tonight' to a later hour. So 'Tonight' stayed where it was.

But something had to be done to give the team respite. One morning I walked into the sordid little office at Lime Grove which was shared by Donald Baverstock and Alasdair Milne. I was on my way to the airport for a fortnight's holiday. The Editor and the Deputy Editor of 'Tonight' were lying across their desks with their heads on their arms. Startled, I asked what was the matter. They did not raise their heads but simply said, 'You must take the pro-gramme off. We can't go on.' With a mixture of concern and alarm, I asked whether they could possibly manage for another fortnight. When I came back we'd sort it all out. Wearily they agreed. After an anxious holiday I rushed to see them to discover how things were. They couldn't even remember what I was talking about. 'Come up to the cutting room,' they cried, 'and see some marvellous film that's just come in.'

It was this regular alternation between despair and exhilaration which made it obvious that the kind of people who were responsible for the success of 'Tonight' needed an administrative organisation different from what was normal in the BBC. Holidays apart, their overwork and fatigue did not require a rest from creativity. They were creative people. What they needed from time to time was a change of tempo: an opportunity to use the talents they had developed on 'Tonight' for making films at speed and producing light entertainment with a topical edge, in an atmosphere of greater leisure than was possible on 'Tonight' and yet within the overall ethos of the 'Tonight' programme and under the guidance of its editors. They were still 'Tonight' people.

The result was that 'Tonight' became a kind of forcing house for new programmes which cut across the formal departmental structure of the BBC. The young film-makers who had worked with Tony Essex wanted to make longer programmes on film and believed that they could do this in half the time required by documentary producers who had been brought up in the Grierson tradition, and at half the price. John Schlesinger, then unknown but later an internationally famous film director, had been recruited by 'Tonight' as a free-lance contributor and, working with Donald Baverstock, had discovered that in television there were new uses for celluloid as part of the process of visual communication; Kevin Billington, who had come to 'Tonight' as a production assistant, made 'The Matador' about Cordobes, the Spanish bull-fighter who was illiterate, earned a fortune and was always accompanied by his priest; Jack Gold, who had been an assistant film editor on 'Tonight', made, with Alan Whicker and members of the Quorn Hunt, a programme about foxhunting called 'Death in the Morning'; Tony Essex, working with Alasdair Milne, eventually made a massive series about the 1914–18 War called 'The Great War' in which he used new techniques for stretching historic film so that it was slowed to normality and removed the tendency of film about the past, taken in the past, to make participants seem ridiculous because of the jerky speed of their movements.

All these, and others, bore the 'Tonight' stamp. Although they dealt with controversial subjects they did not plead a case. What united them was a wish, based on human curiosity rooted in human compassion, to understand the actions of politicians and of generals as well as to show the impact that these had upon soldiers in the field; to make clear the fascination of bull-fighting while never disguising its cruelty; to convey the excitement of the hunt and also the revulsion of those who hated blood sports. The drama of these situations was never muted but it was never contained, as so often in television, within a verbal confrontation. The conflict was of feeling, all of it strong, all understandable, and all of it expressed visibly in action.

By 1962 the 'Tonight' team were trying to find a fresh outlet for their programme inventiveness by creating a late night entertainment, 'That Was The Week That Was'. This, rather than any of 'Tonight's' more serious output, was to rock the BBC and raise, abrasively, the relationship between the BBC and the leaders of the political parties. It was a highly personal programme which dealt with politicians rather than with political principles and with the pretentions of men of religion rather than with religious faith. In spirit it was derived from current undergraduate humour—Cambridge University's 'Footlights' and their London West End success 'Beyond The Fringe' as well as from such night club enterprises as 'The Establishment'. The mood of these pieces was one of intelligent iconoclasm. They pleased the small coterie public for which they were intended. More surprisingly, when translated into television terms by 'Tonight's' light entertainment producer, Ned Sherrin, they delighted, late on Saturdays, an immense national audience.

'That Was The Week That Was' might never have got on the air in a different BBC climate. But the top management was changing. Sir Ian Jacob retired at the end of 1959 and was succeeded as Director-General by Hugh Carleton Greene who, since 1958, had been Director of News and Current Affairs. This was a new post, created partly in order to provide for both radio and television an 'overall co-ordination and editorial direction of topical output'.[1] He had jurisdiction not only over both sound and television news but over such topical television programmes as 'Panorama' and 'Tonight' and brought a new style to the relationship between those in policy control at Broadcasting House and the producers of television topical programmes. Sir Ian Jacob had tended to treat television producers as subalterns who were there to carry out orders issued by their seniors at Broadcasting House. Hugh Greene was prepared to discuss day-to-day problems with those who had the responsibility of presenting, on television, matters of political interest.

Essentially he was a newsman and a journalist, with experience of sound broadcasting in Germany as well as with the BBC's German service during the war. His outlook was international and adventurous rather than insular and restrictive. He did not approve of the rigidities of Tahu Hole's attitudes to news nor of his endeavours to control television current affairs programmes. He himself would have liked to see 'Panorama' and 'Tonight' make more use of news correspondents in the field. But there were to be no shot-gun marriages. He had a developed sense of humour and had enjoyed political satire in the cabarets of post-war Berlin. From the first, therefore, he relished the idea of 'That Was The Week That Was'. And gave it his support.

This was peculiarly important in 1962 since the BBC's television service was in a state of considerable administrative disarray. The general disturbance centred on the controversial figure of Cecil McGivern, who for over fourteen years had been in charge of BBC television programmes.

The then Director of Television was Gerald Beadle who had run, admirably, the BBC's West Region. He was thought, fairly generally, to be a stop-gap, in charge only until Cecil McGivern could be weaned away from his obsession with programme detail and be prepared to take responsibility for the television service as a whole. Meanwhile Cecil McGivern was made Deputy Director of Television and the current incumbent moved to another post.

It was expected that McGivern, clearly destined to succeed to the top television post as Director, would appoint a Controller of Programmes who would take programme detail off his shoulders. But he continued to refuse to do this. He wanted to remain in sole charge of television programmes but with the added authority he possessed as Deputy Director of Television. The situation dragged on interminably. At last the BBC decided that a Controller of Programmes must be appointed, even if Cecil McGivern did not agree. They chose Kenneth Adam, an ex-*Manchester Guardian* journalist who had worked both in the BBC and in Independent Television. McGivern's crusading spirit was outraged. He did not believe that either Gerald Beadle or Kenneth Adam appreciated the real responsibilities of television. Their decisions, he thought, were taken for reasons of expediency rather than principle. He felt boxed in between a Director of Television above him and a Controller of Programmes beneath him, who increasingly saw eye to eye, but not with his eyes.

For him it was an agonising moral dilemma. He could not relinquish responsibility for the television standards upon which so many millions depended for their information and perhaps for their guidance. But that responsibility, he felt, was being taken from him. He was no longer in control. He crumbled under the strain of his own sense of failure, left the BBC and died as a result of a tragic accident in his own home.

The new Director of Television was not, therefore, Cecil Mc-Givern, but Kenneth Adam. There were other new appointments. The Editor of Television News, Stuart Hood, was made Controller of Television Programmes. And Donald Baverstock was made Assistant Controller. The 'Tonight' team were jubilant. Donald Baverstock's editorial ability had been recognised. The importance of creativity in television broadcasting had been acknowledged. 'That Was The Week That Was', with the powerful backing of the Director-General and with Donald Baverstock, one of its main begetters, in a position of authority, went ahead.

By February 1962 Alasdair Milne and Ned Sherrin, with the overall guidance of Donald Baverstock, had sketched out plans for the programme. It was not to be a magazine on the lines of 'Pano-rama' or 'Tonight'. The difference was to be emphasised by the fact that 'That Was The Week That Was' would have its own jazz group and its own studio audience. Members of this audience would participate in controversial discussions started by journalists such as Bernard Levin. 'That Was The Week That Was' would be as topical as 'Tonight' but geared to the mood of viewers who had seen a week go by, could examine it, let it go, and relax before beginning another week on Monday. Very much a 'Tonight' adventure, it was not to be under the jurisdiction of the Television Light Entertainment Department. It would not rely on established comedians or depend upon elaborate settings. However well prepared, it must seem to be improvised and casual. And it must not be simply escapist. New writers, among them Gerald Kaufman, a well-known Labour Party supporter, were invited to take part; David Frost, an ex-'Footlights' figure from Cambridge, was tried out as the compère: the whole programme was to be infused by a sense of political awareness and social consciousness.

A pilot programme was recorded. Donald Baverstock invited me to see it. I found this first endeavour long (it lasted around two hours), amateurish in its endeavours to seem casual, and politically both tendentious and dangerous. In an attempt to mock the stereo-type of Conservative women, a member of the production staff had telephoned the Conservative Central Office and asked them to suggest names of ladies who were Conservative Party supporters and who might like to take part in an experiment intended to assist in the creation of a new television programme. The ladies turned out to be good-humoured, but made it clear that they would not want, on any future occasion, to be associated with a programme of this kind.

My own position was difficult. Leonard Miall had been moved from his post as Assistant Controller of Television Talks and Current Affairs to become Assistant Controller of Programme Services. In his place I had been made Head of Talks and Current Affairs. Formally, therefore, since 'Tonight' came under the Television Talks Department, its latest offshoot, 'That Was The Week That Was', was one of my responsibilities. But I knew that this situation was unreal. As planned, 'That Was The Week That Was' was even more cross-departmental than 'Tonight'. It was concerned with politics, but it was also show business. Its new approach to the provision of intelligent topical entertainment was the result of an alliance between Donald Baverstock, Alasdair Milne and Ned Sherrin. The last, who moved easily in the world of London's West End, had come to 'Tonight' as a specialist in light entertainment and as a studio director.

It would not have been sensible to try to impose on this team the organised disciplines of the BBC's departmental system, nor to ask Donald Baverstock, when Assistant Controller of Programmes, to operate, as far as 'That Was The Week That Was' was concerned, through me, the Head of the Television Talks Department. It was certainly anomalous that Alasdair Milne, who had been made Assistant Head (Current Affairs) of the Talks Department soon after I had become the Head of the Department, should remain responsible to me for the main part of his work and be responsible directly to Donald Baverstock for anything to do with 'That Was The Week That Was'. But I knew them both well and foresaw no difficulties. Donald Baverstock, the leader of the team which was in the process of creating 'That Was The Week That Was', must launch and run it. No one else could. Least of all myself.

The Director-General, however, wanted to be reassured about the channels of editorial control through which 'That Was The Week That Was' would operate. As a result Donald Baverstock wrote, on November 15, 1962, a memorandum to Stuart Hood. 'That Was The Week That Was' was due to start on November 24, and to run weekly on Saturdays until the end of April 1963. In his memorandum, Donald Baverstock made it clear that he did not wish to undertake the continuing detailed supervision of 'That Was The Week That Was'. This would not be compatible with his duties as Assistant Controller of Programmes. In his memorandum he said:

'As agreed with you the departmental supervision of this programme and the detailed responsibilities for its content will be in the hands of A. H. T. (C.A.) Tel. [This was Alasdair Milne].
Necessarily he will have to act as Executive Producer of the programme for the first few editions. Once the style of the programme has settled down and once the exact area of difficulty has defined itself, he will be able to withdraw a little and exercise a less close supervision. I have therefore asked him to regard his responsibility for this programme as an absolute priority over all his other duties until the New Year. In case of doubt about policy or taste it will be his responsibility to refer to me, acting as your deputy.'[2]

The editorial responsibility for 'That Was The Week That Was' was therefore placed firmly on the shoulders of Alasdair Milne. And if, after the New Year, the latter were able to 'withdraw a little' the development and control of this experiment in television programming would be in the hands of its producer, Ned Sherrin. In practice, and as a result of Ned Sherrin's attitudes to production, it became very largely an experiment in the devolution of editorial responsibilities to free-lance contributors.

Ned Sherrin, a brilliant director of fast-moving impromptu television programmes, had the gift of surrounding himself with writers, actors, singers and musicians who were willing to co-operate with him in the styles which he had devised for 'That Was The Week That Was'. As a result he was able to produce every week a new topical revue, with new sketches, new songs, new and barbed portraits of leading political figures and new lyrics which embodied sharp comments on the contemporary social scene. Sherrin was prepared to harness to the talents of his team not only his own skills as a television director but also all the resources which the BBC was prepared to make available. His disciplines were those of a professional. He did not want to be, far less appear to the team to be, an instrument of the policy control felt appropriate by the British Broadcasting Corporation.

The first edition of 'That Was The Week That Was' went on the air at 10.50 p.m. on Saturday, November 24, 1962 and had an audience of three and a half million. During the winter of 1962/3 audiences increased until they fluctuated around the eight to ten million mark. It might have been supposed that a late night programme such as 'That Was The Week That Was' would appeal only to a small sophisticated audience. But the vast British viewing public was aroused by its irreverence, impressed by its vitality as well as shocked by its mockery of leading political figures and of some aspects of religion. A number of viewers were surprised, as well as shocked, by its schoolboy sexual jokes and lavatory humour.

Its studies of politicians were full of carefully researched facts, frequently illustrated by large still pictures and usually accompanied by a hard-hitting commentary. They were particularly resented by the Conservative Party since the targets were often Conservative Ministers. An anti-Establishment programme tends to be anti-Government. In 1962/3 this meant being anti-Conservative. Most of the Conservative Ministers who were pilloried in 'That Was The Week That Was' took the attacks lightly. Some even seemed to enjoy the absence of what Donald Baverstock, quoting Mary McCarthy, called the 'slow drip of cant'. But the Conservative Central Office and many Conservative supporters in the country were bound to find that 'That Was The Week That Was' had an anti-Conservative bias.

On January 11, 1963, a member of the BBC's Secretariat reported that the Conservative Party was disquieted by the programme. They hoped, he said, that it would die a natural death or drop such a clanger that there would be a major libel action. A Party official was quoted as saying that:

> 'being anti-Establishment was one thing but it was hard to swallow a programme whose general bias was so extremely left wing, Socialist and pacifist.'[3]

This could have been expected. Much more surprising were the critical reactions expressed by Donald Baverstock to Alasdair Milne on January 14, 1963. A recent item had offended many orthodox viewers. It was a 'Consumer Report on Religions', a skit in the style of the assessments in consumer magazines of the merits of various kinds of consumer goods but applied to the advocates of various kinds of religious faith. Donald Baverstock defended this, saying:

'There were strong reasons for thinking that this item did have a place in the context of this programme.' But he continued, 'I would have been happier about it, however, if the programme as a whole had been better. In my opinion it was the worst yet.' He dealt, point by point, with the ingredients of this particular edition and said 'The Hailsham and North East item swiped at the Government with less precision than one would expect from the most ill-educated local Labour ward politician.'

Baverstock had brought from his Welsh background a great deal of sympathy with working class aspirations. But he demanded precision of thought as well as of execution in television programmes. There must also be honesty among producers and candour in their relations with authority. He ended his memorandum by outlining to Alasdair Milne a number of steps which should be taken to improve 'That Was The Week That Was'.

'1 It must be re-affirmed to Sherrin that the Corporation's restrictions on the use of swear words, blue jokes and obscene gestures applies, for obvious commonsense reasons, to this programme as to all others.

2 You must inform him immediately that he is henceforth expected to consult you on all matters of programme content in detail and with complete candour.

You must make it clear to Sherrin that your responsibility for the programme extends over all its aspects and is not limited to what is commonly thought of as 'policy'. Such a programme as this puts a great strain on the judgment of any one person. He must now be told that it is your judgment finally which the Corporation is having to trust. You can make the right judgments and at the same time assist him in all the ways in which he needs assistance only if he accepts this.'[4]

Donald Baverstock was dealing here with one of the perennial problems which face British broadcasting organisations. How can they ensure that the rules which Parliament has laid down in order to control the power of broadcasters are observed in practice and yet give creative people the freedoms they need if they are to continue to be creative?

In dictatorships this is seldom a problem; producers do as they are told about any serious communication and programmes of entertainment which are not controversial can, if necessary, be bought cheaply from organisations which make them for a world market. In countries where television is largely financed by advertising, the hope of advertisers that they will be able to please everybody and offend nobody acts as a controlling influence. It is normally difficult to get sponsors for programmes which are politically or socially controversial.* Most broadcasting therefore tends to be conformist.

The BBC had never been merely conformist. It had always been prepared in broadcast discussions and debates to give opportunities for the expression of dissident and non-conformist views. But its own freedom was limited by public opinion as expressed through Parliament. If the programmes which it presented offended a large section of the mass public, Parliamentary decisions about the renewal of the BBC's Charter could be affected. This was very relevant in 1963. The current Charter was due to expire in 1964 and a new Charter would probably be in draft by June 1963. The very fact that 'That Was The Week That Was' had aroused the British public meant that much public opinion about the BBC tended to coalesce around their reactions to 'That Was The Week That Was'. It had pleased millions, but there had been widespread criticisms of the amount of 'smut' in the programme. The idea that the BBC had 'gone sour' was being bandied about. Though this was firmly rejected by the Chairman of the Board of Governors, Sir Arthur fforde, whose integrity was unassailable, the accusation was nevertheless made by people who served on the BBC's Advisory Councils, one of whose functions was to reflect public opinion to the BBC.

Another criticism of 'That Was The Week That Was' was that its attacks on leading politicians were 'unfair'. The Director-General and the Board of Governors were anxious not to restrict the programme in its handling of political matters but some Governors tended to feel that those who ran it had—in their endeavours to avoid the usual clichés of political debate—allowed their critical presentations of political figures, which occasionally included their wives, to become too personal.

Presentations of this kind were likely to be resented. A General

---

* Sponsorship was eventually withdrawn in the United States even for Edward R. Murrow's famous 'See It Now' series.

Election was imminent. There was speculation about whether it would take place in the autumn of 1963 or be postponed until 1964. Special factors made it certain that political feelings would run high during the pre-election period. The Leader of the Opposition, Hugh Gaitskell, had died in January 1963 and had been succeeded by Harold Wilson. The Labour Party therefore would have a new Leader. And in the Conservative Party there was the continuing question of whether Harold Macmillan, now nearly seventy, should lead the Conservative Party into another hard-fought General Election.

During the summer of 1963 the Profumo scandal and the ensuing Denning Report caused the leadership crisis in the Conservative Party to be even more acute. The country had become very sensitive to the importance of moral values and much aware of political uncertainties. In all these circumstances it is surprising that the BBC should have been prepared to allow a programme as controversial as 'That Was The Week That Was' to return in September 1963 and to plan to keep it running weekly until the following April.

At the end of the first 'That Was The Week That Was' series the Board of Governors had recorded 'their congratulations to the Television Service on the introduction of an important programme in which the Board had taken a continuing interest and which had their support throughout.'[5] They wanted it to return, but they wanted 'smut' to be eliminated and greater care exercised before personal attacks were made. It was on receiving assurances from the television service that this would be the case that the Board of Governors agreed to the new season of 'That Was The Week That Was'. But the Chairman of the Board was still in a state of some anxiety.[6] And Stuart Hood was asked by the Director of Television to see Ned Sherrin and make it clear that the Board's plans for 'That Was the Week That Was' were not 'suggestions for improving the programme. They were instructions which have to be obeyed.'[7] Alasdair Milne had already been told that he was likely to be asked 'to undertake a rather stricter responsibility when it returns and Ned Sherrin and those most intimately concerned must also be aware of this'.

The discussions during the summer of 1963 about the handling of 'That Was The Week That Was' were a revelation of both the weaknesses and strengths of the BBC. Its strength was its faith in producers. It was relatively easy to find capable administrators whose main function would be to ensure that the rules under which the BBC was permitted by Parliament to operate were observed by the programme staff. It was also relatively easy to find creative people, whether producers or the freelance contributors they employed, who wanted to have access to the money, resources and great audiences which the BBC could make available but who did not respect, understand or want to observe the rules which Parliament had laid down for the conduct of broadcasting.

The BBC's solution had been to give editorial control, not to administrators, but to producers who were themselves creative, who understood the conditions under which creativity flourished, but who also understood the reasons why Parliament had to put limits upon the power of broadcasters and who could interpret Parliamentary rulings effectively to the contributors they employed. Donald Baverstock and Alasdair Milne were two such producers, but a few were not. And the weakness of the BBC was that in such cases it was faced, from time to time, with the disagreeable necessity either of imposing detailed disciplines upon producers in regard to the handling of programmes, which they would resent, or else taking off altogether the programmes for which they were responsible.

During the early autumn of 1963 a feeling was growing up within the BBC that 'That Was The Week That Was' was causing more trouble than it was worth. Nevertheless it returned to the air on Saturday, September 28 as planned. By the following Monday there were fifty-nine telephone calls of criticism and none of praise; forty-one letters of criticism and five of praise. Complaints were that it had been vulgar, smutty, infantile, stupid, boring and dreary.[8]

It had a mixed Press. Monica Furlong in the *Daily Mail* said:

'Can viewers really perceive nothing but the doubtful jokes and Mr Levin's aggression? Do they really never notice how often the first is funny and the second is siding with the angels?'[9]

The *Daily Herald* remarked:

'It came back to BBC screens with the old outrageous mixture of wit, rudeness, cruelty, smut and sheer exuberance. Puncture TW3 at will, riddle it with abuse or contempt and still the thing bounces back with an awesome impregnable vitality.'[10]

Less than two months later, on November 13, the BBC formally announced that

'the present run of "That Was The Week That Was" will end on December 28, 1963 and not continue, as had originally been intended, until the spring.'

The reasons for taking it off, officially, were political. The BBC's announcement stated that

'1964 will be General Election year, and political activity will be mounting to a height as the date of the Election nears. In these circumstances—and as controversy grows over issues which the electors will be called upon to decide—the political content of the programme, which has been one of its principal and successful constituents, will clearly be more and more difficult to maintain. Rather than dilute that content, and so alter the nature of the programme, the BBC thinks it preferable that "TWTWTW" should continue as at present only until the end of the year.'[11]

There was an immediate outcry. The BBC's Head of Secretariat reported on November 19, 1963 that during the previous seven days there had been over 700 letters of protest about the decision to end TW3 on December 28 and only 200 of congratulation. The congratulations came from those who disliked the programme and were delighted to hear that it was going to be taken off. Comments included: 'Why wait until December 28?' The protests came from the programme's supporters, many of whom did not believe that the reasons given by the BBC for ending TW3 were the real ones. A resentful viewer wrote

'Election year—tell that to the Marines.'

and another

'All the world will claim that the Tories have got the show banned.'[12]

It was understandable that viewers should be sceptical about the official statement. The BBC, they said, must have known long before the announcement on November 13 that there would be a General Election in 1964. Why, then, if it was so difficult to continue 'That Was The Week That Was' during the pre-election period had they allowed it to come back on September 28, 1963 with the intention of keeping it running until April 1964?

It was certainly true that the BBC was accustomed to dealing with allegations (and sometimes the realities) of political bias. It was equally true that programmes concerned with politics were difficult to handle during the run-up to a General Election. But these were familiar problems. The new and disturbing factor about 'That Was The Week That Was' was the apparent breakdown of the Corporation's normal machinery for exercising editorial control, of maintaining balance in its political output, and of preventing the frequent use of 'swear words, blue jokes, and obscene gestures'.

Neither the Chairman of the Board of Governors, Sir Arthur fforde nor the Director-General, Hugh Greene, wanted to end 'That Was The Week That Was'. They enjoyed the sharp cutting edge of its mockery; were proud of having given it so much freedom; and defended it when it was attacked. But they did expect that by the autumn of 1963 it would be sufficiently controlled, editorially, to prevent the personal attacks on political leaders which were hard for the BBC to justify, and to ensure that the smut which offended so many viewers would be eliminated.

The failure of these hopes was made clear by the Director-General on November 7 when he recommended to the Board of Governors that 'That Was The Week That Was' should not continue after the end of 1963. He said, 'the programme had assumed exaggerated importance both in public and in the BBC. Senior staff, including himself, had been involved in weekly consideration of the script in detail.'[13]

I was now one of these. The Director-General had summoned me and said that I must take personal responsibility for 'That Was The Week That Was'. He would make himself available on the telephone at any time for consultation.

This, in a sense, was logical. As a result of the impending start of BBC 2, there had been organisational changes. Michael Peacock had been put in charge of the new channel, Donald Baverstock was now in control of BBC 1, and even more remote from the detailed surveillance of 'That Was The Week That Was' than he had been. It remained Alasdair Milne's responsibility but Alasdair Milne was now the Head of one of the four departments in the Group of which I had become the overall Head. It could be expected that Alasdair Milne, as Head of 'Tonight' Productions, would be responsible to me for 'That Was The Week That Was' and that I, in turn, should be responsible for it to the authorities within the BBC. That meant, ultimately, to the Director-General and the Board of Governors.

This may have been logical. But I was dismayed. I felt as if I were being asked to ride a tiger. From the first, TW3 had been treated as a special case. Its remarkable success, the controversies it aroused and the fact that there was a good deal of confusion about its editorial control owing to Donald Baverstock having become Assistant Controller of Programmes just at the moment when TW3 was about to go on the air, meant that almost everybody at a high level had taken a hand in its management. The Director-General talked personally to Ned Sherrin; so did the Director of Television; Alasdair Milne and Ned Sherrin were asked, before the re-start of the programme in September 1963, to discuss their future plans directly with the Board of Governors. Lines of control had, therefore, not been clear. It was impossible, I believed, now to make them so. The producer and the team had achieved so much freedom that this could not be curtailed without undermining the authority of the producer and destroying the morale of the team. But control had become necessary. The Director-General, faced with such constant and powerful complaints about 'That Was The Week That Was', found that he had to deal with a quantity of these himself. He considered that some of the items about which complaints were made were not defensible, so he was forced to try to prevent such items being transmitted. This meant that he personally, against his temperamental inclinations, had to become a kind of censor. And I, under his instructions, became an instrument of censorship.

Ordinary methods of editorial control would not do. We were long past that. So I tried others, none of which was noticeably successful. I arranged a series of lunches with Ned Sherrin, Alasdair Milne and David Frost at which we could discuss, in general terms, their future plans for 'That Was the Week That Was'. These were agreeable occasions. All three were intelligent, informed, courteous and reasonable. There was never any disagreement about what the general approach should be. The problem came later; when the general consensus had to be translated on Saturday into a script for the next edition of the programme.

It was never possible, apparently, in a topical programme which had so many contributors, for a script, even in draft, to be available before late on Friday night. One copy was sent to Alasdair Milne. I arranged that another should come to me. It reached my home between nine and ten p.m. on Friday. Alasdair Milne and I, by arrangement, discussed it on the telephone early on Saturday morning. There was no point in trying to come to hard decisions. The script was only a draft. It could be, and often was, radically changed during rehearsal. But we could agree on possible areas of difficulty.

Alasdair Milne attended rehearsals. I did not want to do so. If I did, it might seem a reflection upon his judgment and, as an innovation, be resented by the team. Yet I was responsible to the Director-General, he to the Board of Governors, and they, ultimately, to Parliament. And I fully understood why the BBC could not allow one of its programmes to transgress the rules which had been laid down in regard to political balance or to offend public opinion by the inclusion of blue jokes and obscene gestures. I was therefore not against the idea of control, only defeated in my endeavours to exercise it without, effectively, destroying a programme which I, like the Chairman of the Board of Governors, the Director-General, and so many others, admired.

The crunch always came on Saturday afternoons when the programme finally took shape. By then it was possible to see how different in tone (or offensiveness) a portrait of a politician or a sketch or the lyric of a song could be in performance as compared with what they had seemed in typescript. Alasdair Milne was not always able to attend rehearsals. In that case I did. And if he did attend and found that an item which we had agreed was doubtful was still being included, he telephoned me. I went across to see it, and if I felt it necessary to do so I consulted the Director-General.

This was very much a hit-and-miss procedure. Too many different kinds of judgment were involved: the producer's, Alasdair Milne's, mine and that of the Director-General, who had not seen the item in rehearsal and was dependent on the information which reached him by telephone. Overtly, there were never any difficulties. Ned Sherrin, if told that a particular item must not be included, did not argue. He was too cool a character to value argument as well as too concerned with the problem of getting the programme effectively on the air. And there were nearly always excuses which he could use to justify changes. The draft script was usually too long. Almost any item could be cut on the grounds that the programme was overrunning.

But the situation was not sensible. Interference was bound to harm 'That Was The Week That Was'. The Director-General had foreseen this and had said to the Board of Governors on November 7, 1963 that under the firmer control which he had instituted 'the programme's own perceptible decline in vitality was likely to be accentuated'.[14] Yet the point had been reached when he had to try to control it or take it off. He decided to take it off.

Many years later he told me that the decision was entirely his own: it was not the result of political pressure but of his estimate of the future reactions of the Board of Governors. Sir James Duff, the Vice-Chairman, a much respected figure, was in a peculiarly responsible position owing to the ill-health and frequent absence of the Chairman. The Director-General considered that Sir James might well resign if TW3 were to continue and that other Governors might follow his lead. The programme partly, as he had foreseen, because of the firmer controls, had lost something of its sparkle and was, he considered, not worth retaining at the high cost of the disruption which would be caused by a number of resignations from the Board of Governors. So he himself took the decision and informed the Board that TW3 would not be transmitted after the end of 1963.

My own experience led me to see things rather differently. I believed then, and still do, that the problems of TW3 were both personal and organisational but at a lower level than that of the Board of Governors. The personal contribution of programme creators such as Donald Baverstock and Alasdair Milne to enterprises like TW3 is immeasurable. They had shaped it just as they had shaped 'Tonight'. But once Donald Baverstock, as a result of his promotion to the post of Assistant Controller of Television Programmes, was removed from direct editorial control, and Alasdair Milne, also promoted, was unable to give it his undivided attention, the programme changed. It was no longer, as had been intended, an offshoot of 'Tonight' operating within the guidelines of the 'Tonight' disciplines, but became, unintentionally, an endeavour to discover whether a group of creative people could work outside the normal framework of BBC editorial control and yet observe, of their own will, the obligations imposed upon broadcasting organisations by Parliament. The experiment failed.

Perhaps failure was inevitable. Perhaps the BBC was expecting too much. Perhaps mockery is indivisible. The hope that the team which produced 'That Was the Week That Was' would refrain from some kinds of mockery of political personalities or some aspects of royalty or of religion, was rather like putting written notices in a field saying 'Keep off the Grass' and expecting the grazing cattle to obey them. To the team, the suggested restrictions were at once incomprehensible and irrelevant. The problems of the BBC were not theirs. Theirs was a kind of private fun which they were sharing with a mass public. That was part of the charm of the programme. Watching it was like going to a private party rather than attending a public performance.

It remained throughout 1963 more innocent than lascivious, its small doubtful jokes paling beside the realities revealed by the Denning Report and a possible connection between a Cabinet Minister and a criminal underworld. It merely, in effect, demanded special privileges. Whatever this particular team found hypocritical, pompous or unreal must be mocked in whatever manner they found effective. It was made available, however, to millions of viewers by a piece of machinery which was ultimately under public control. The BBC was part of that machinery. It had to take account of its public responsibilities, even if this meant limiting the freedom of expression which had been extended to a particular group of privileged broadcasters.

Such responsibilities are profound and go far beyond the special interpretation put upon them in Britain by the BBC or the IBA: they are inherent in the use of any right to broadcast, nationally or internationally, a combination of entertainment and information which reaches millions of individuals in the vulnerability of their homes. TW3 required a particular understanding of this general responsibility since, like 'Tonight', it dealt with politics and entertainment within a single framework, rather than separately under different departmental disciplines.

I was made peculiarly aware, late in 1963, of the loss of the experienced 'Tonight' approach when I attended a TW3 rehearsal. One of the sketches was so humanly offensive that I thought it should not be transmitted and said so to the producer. He simply remarked politely 'Oh, didn't you like it? Then *of course* we'll take it out.' I came away distressed, wondering whether I had been right and ran, purely by accident, into Donald Baverstock. I told him what was in the sketch. He said, 'Oh my God!' There was a pause, then he added slowly 'It's important to understand that if a group of people are expected to go to the limits of what is permissible, they must have it within them to go beyond those limits.'

That kind of understanding of the nature of creativity is rare. It is even more rare when found in combination with a general understanding of the responsibilities of broadcasting. Without the day-to-day exercise of such leadership, and with, as a result, too many different instructions coming from too many different people at too many levels, TW3 died not so much from excessive censorship as from confusion of purpose.

Strangely enough, it disappeared in a blaze of conformist glory. Since it was to continue until December 28, 1963, it was still running in November when, early in the evening of the 22nd, news of the attempt on President Kennedy's life reached the BBC. 'Tonight' was on the air. I was watching it while waiting for Michael Peacock and his wife who were to take me to the Guild of Television Producers' Ball where the Television Awards of the Year would be announced. They were late. My telephone rang. Waldo McGuire, then Head of BBC television news, told me that President Kennedy had been shot in Dallas. It was not yet known that he had died.

Stunned, as was everybody, I rang Lime Grove where Paul Fox, by then Head of Television Public Affairs, was still around. Cliff Michelmore, on 'Tonight', had given the news briefly and closed the programme. Meanwhile Michael Peacock drove me to the Television Centre where I joined Kenneth Adam and Stuart Hood, who had returned from the ball and were rearranging television programmes for the rest of Friday evening and for Saturday.

Paul Fox, a man of decisive action, had already been in touch with the Prime Minister. Sir Alec Douglas-Home was on his way to the country for the weekend but came back immediately to London in order to broadcast. The Leader of the Opposition, Mr Wilson, was making a speech in Wales. Paul Fox arranged for a BBC studio in Manchester to be made available and for an emergency car to bring him across the country so that he also could broadcast. Mr Grimond, the Liberal Leader, was taking part in a debate in the Oxford Union. He was prepared to come at once to Lime Grove but there was no transport which could get him there in time. An undergraduate with a fast sports car offered to drive him. So by eleven o'clock the Leaders of all three British political parties were able to give their reactions to the almost incredible news of the assassination of the young President of the United States.

It is difficult to realise, at this distance in time and after other Presidents have come and gone, what an immense shock the news of the assassination was to British, and to world, opinion. For millions of British viewers that shock was expressed on the following night in 'That Was The Week That Was'. Between ten o'clock on Saturday morning and the transmission of the programme the same night, Alasdair Milne and the production team tore up the prepared programme and wrote a new one, complete with new songs, new music, new speeches. It had a different polish, but it was still polished. For those who were caught in the mood of the time it was immensely moving. Senator Hubert Humphrey, who asked that the complete transcript should be printed in the Congressional Record, said in his speech about the way in which the occasion had been handled:

'This show has been known chiefly for its biting satire and bitter wit on public affairs and figures. On this Saturday night, it scrapped that format and did a program on the United States and the tragedy that befell us. It was a show of reverence and respect. This we might have anticipated from the British; nevertheless we are deeply appreciative. Our feelings however were far more deeply touched by the character and quality of this program. It carried a truly tremendous feeling under a superb, just short of staccato, control. It had penetrating critical power and mordant analysis with such skilfully understated warmth of restraint that made its feeling a piercing and authentic one.
We did not do this for ourselves. We could not at that time. Perhaps these young Britons were in a position to be more objective. But that is not sufficient explanation for me for the excellence of quality and felicity of what they did. Art, said the philosopher Santayana, is the trick of arresting the immediate. This programe did indeed "arrest the immediate" in all its ugly hardness, but also in its searing tragedy, and in its depth of meaning in history, hope, and duty.'

'That Was The Week That Was' was being acclaimed internationally just at the moment when it was disappearing from British television screens. For a brief moment the immense talents of its production team had been used to express not only British but much international emotion. In the face of sudden death there had been no controversy but a shocked condemnation of violence. 'That Was

The Week That Was' reflected this mood. There was no mention of the Bay of Pigs, nor of the start of the war in Vietnam. Controversy was stilled. If 'That Was The Week That Was' had continued it would have had to express controversy and not simply unanimity. When nations are united in their attitudes there is no problem for television. It is when they are divided, not only about ends but means, that television current affairs programmes must reflect this division, and thereby antagonise large numbers of viewers.

This is what happened to 'That Was The Week That Was'. It reflected controversy with the same vivacity, realism and wit as, on the occasion of President Kennedy's assassination, it had reflected unanimity. But whereas unanimity has no enemies, controversy is surrounded by them. Various attempts were made in the United States to translate 'That Was The Week That Was' into programmes which would be satisfactory there. They all failed. No American television network was prepared to offer to those who expressed controversy with the wit and originality of 'That Was The Week That Was' the amount of freedom it had been given by the BBC. And in the end this very freedom had been resented. The various anxieties would have been lessened if public opinion had been wholly behind the programme. But some sections of British viewers, as well as some members of the Board of Governors, were opposed to the vivacious expression of attitudes with which they did not agree and of which from time to time they disapproved.

[14]

Television's Challenge to Parliament
1962-1965

While 'Tonight' and 'That Was The Week That Was' were changing the style and tone of television topical programmes, large questions about the relationship of television to Parliament were being
raised. The most immediate was that of reconciling the wishes of the
Prime Minister, Harold Macmillan, with the rules about Ministerial
broadcasts as agreed between the political parties and the BBC and
recorded in the Aide Mémoire of 1947.

As a result of the Conservative victory in the General Election of
1959 Mr Macmillan was, so to speak, Prime Minister in his own
right. He was no longer merely the survivor of the Suez crisis who
had 'emerged' as the successor to Sir Anthony Eden in 1957. He
appeared to be entrenched and it seemed possible, although he was
sixty-five, that he might lead the Conservative Party into another
General Election.

To him it continued to be inconceivable that anyone should be in
a position to question the right of the Prime Minister to use television, or any other mechanism, to address the nation at moments of
national significance and by 1962 the Director-General of the BBC,
Hugh Greene, arrived at the idea that it might be possible for the
BBC on national occasions to invite the Prime Minister to give
'addresses to the nation' which would not fall within the category of
Ministerial broadcasts and which would not be subject to the rules
about rights of reply by the Opposition or require consultation
between the Party Whips.

The key phrase which made this possible was that these broadcasts would be given 'at the invitation of the BBC'. When 'Press
Conference' was started in 1953 the Corporation had said, in its
internal memoranda, that appearances of Ministers in this programme were not 'Ministerial' broadcasts within the definitions of
the Aide Mémoire, since 'Press Conference' broadcasts were given
at the invitation of the BBC, not when demanded by Ministers.

Moreover the subjects of these broadcasts, as well as their dates and timings, were arranged by the BBC and not dictated by Ministers.

There was therefore a precedent for some broadcasts by Ministers being free from the rules of the Aide Mémoire. But there was a new, and different, factor in the proposed 'addresses to the nation' by Mr Macmillan. This was the absence of questioning. In 'Press Conference' Ministers were questioned by newspaper journalists. In other programmes in which Ministers appeared by invitation of the broadcasting organisations there were questioners, whether newspapermen or television interviewers. But in the proposed 'addresses to the nation' a Prime Minister was being invited to give a 'straight' talk on television without having to submit to interrogation and without having to be subject to the formal procedures which governed the rights of reply by the Opposition to Ministerial broadcasts.

An example of the way in which the new 'addresses to the nation' were handled is revealed in some correspondence about a proposed broadcast by Mr Macmillan after the 1962 Commonwealth Prime Ministers' Conference. On September 17, 1962, when Head of Television Talks and Current Affairs, I wrote to Kenneth Adam, the Director of Television:

> 'You will know that we were instructed some time ago by D.G. to invite the Prime Minister to broadcast, on television if he wished to do so, at the end of the Commonwealth Prime Ministers' Conference. The point about this broadcast was that it was to be an invitation from the BBC to make a statement to the nation on an occasion of national significance. The Prime Minister has not yet made up his mind whether he wishes to accept this invitation or not. I gather from Harold Evans* that, understandably, he wishes to see how the Conference goes before making up his mind, although he feels he ought to accept.'[1]

Although the formal rules about Ministerial broadcasts were not to apply to 'addresses to the nation', the BBC was still required, in general, to preserve political balance in its programmes. So it had to consider the position of the Opposition. I discussed this with the Chief Assistant to the Director-General, Harman Grisewood, who had talked about it to the Director-General. On September 19, I wrote to Harman Grisewood:

* The Prime Minister's Public Relations Adviser.

'I said I would confirm on paper to you the various discussions we have had about the Prime Minister's broadcast and also put on record the conversations I have had with Harold Evans and Mr Grove about it.

Harold Evans let me know on Monday that it was probable that the Prime Minister would accept our invitation to broadcast, although he had not yet made up his mind completely. We had already arranged that Huw Wheldon would produce and that an OB Unit would be available to record him at Admiralty House,* if he should wish to do the broadcast from there.

I had already mentioned, on your instructions, to Harold Evans, that a situation might arise in which the BBC might, in the light of the nature of the Prime Minister's broadcast, wish to invite the Leader of the Opposition to broadcast, probably in the following week. Harold Evans was mildly concerned about this and said that this was, after all, a broadcast by the Prime Minister to the nation on an occasion of national importance and he wondered whether it was necessary for the BBC to *invite* the Leader of the Opposition.

I reported this to you and you asked me to explain to Harold Evans that the situation would be handled by us in the light of conversations that D.G. had had with him in relation to reports to the nation. You asked me to let him know that there would be no question of our approaching the Leader of the Opposition before the Prime Minister's broadcast, but that if, in the unlikely event of the broadcast being so controversial in character that we felt we should have to concede a right of reply should it be demanded, then we would prefer to issue the invitation ourselves rather than have to concede it in reply to a request.

In discussing the practical arrangements with Harold Evans I let him know this and he seemed quite happy about it. His main anxiety was that no approach should be made to the Opposition before the broadcast took place and only afterwards in the light of the nature of the broadcast itself.'[2]

Harold Evans, however, with characteristic realism, said in conversation (and I reported this in my memorandum of September 19),

---

* This was the Prime Minister's temporary residence. No. 10 Downing Street was undergoing repairs. 'OB Unit' meant an Outside Broadcast van with its accompanying facilities and staff.

'the subject itself is now so controversial that the Opposition might well consider any statement of the Prime Minister on it to be something to which they ought to have a right of reply.'[3]

The Prime Minister gave his broadcast on the night of September 20. He did not use the occasion in any way for party purposes. His broadcast was not, therefore, in the party political sense, 'controversial'. But in the wider sense indicated by Harold Evans there was so considerable a difference between the attitudes of the Government and those of the Opposition that the subject in itself was controversial; and the Opposition felt that it ought to have an opportunity of using television to present its views. The BBC therefore, invited the Leader of the Opposition, Hugh Gaitskell, to give a television broadcast on September 21, the night after Mr Macmillan's broadcast.

The situation was delicate. I wrote, on the following Wednesday, September 26, to Mr Grisewood:

'You will remember that it was felt to be extremely important that the Leader of the Opposition should not use this broadcast as in any way a Party occasion, in that the Prime Minister had not, in fact, used the occasion of the broadcast which we had invited him to give as a report to the nation, in any way for Party purposes.

You may also remember that we suggested that Mr Gaitskell should come to lunch with us at Lime Grove before finalising the broadcast. He was proposing to come with some sort of draft at 3 p.m. and we felt that lunch would give us an opportunity of discussing the broadcast with him before it was in any way finalised.

As it turned out, this was a most happy idea. Mr Gaitskell himself came, brought Mrs Gaitskell and Mr Harris* with him and lunched with A.H.T. (C.A.) Tel.† and myself here. This was a most useful opportunity of getting our ideas across to the group as a whole. It was a very pleasant social occasion. The ideas of A.H.T. (C.A.) Tel. and myself were warmly received as a contribution to their thinking and did quite considerably alter, I

---

* His publicity adviser: later (1974) Lord Harris.

† Alasdair Milne: by then one of the two Assistant Heads of the Television Talks Department. He had special jurisdiction within the department over matters of current affairs.

think, the colour of the broadcast. Mr Gaitskell said, at one point, "We get so enclosed in the Party political situation that it is most valuable to have the views of outside people like yourselves, who are thinking differently."

The whole afternoon, and indeed the whole time till eight o'clock, was spent in getting the broadcast drafted, re-drafted, written over, timed and changed. In the course of this procedure the opening paragraph, which I think might have been very unfortunate, was happily dropped.

Mr Gaitskell eventually spoke the broadcast three different times on to tape and chose the final one as the one he wished to have transmitted. He waited to see it transmitted with us at Lime Grove; was very happy about it and eventually dropped me at my flat in Kensington obviously delighted at the way everything was handled.

I must say I was very relieved, since the situation had, as you well know, potential difficulties of a considerable kind.'

In fact this change in the way in which broadcasts by Prime Ministers, and replies by the Opposition, were given on television without recourse to the machinery of consultation with the political parties was a recognition of the change which had taken place in the relationship between television and politics. By 1962 there was, certainly, such a proliferation of political programmes on television that there was no lack of opportunity for Ministers or Leaders of the Opposition to argue their cases on television. But 'addresses to the nation' made possible a different style of political communication. These broadcasts were not merely a reflection of the routine Party Political struggle. By eschewing party arguments they could be endeavours by statesmen to offer to the nation broadly different policies based upon different principles.

During this period, moreover, there was a new and unexpected development in the relationship between television and Parliament. On Monday, October 22, 1962, the Director-General of the BBC, Hugh Greene, gave a dinner at Broadcasting House to some leading members of the Conservative Party. These included Iain MacLeod, MP, then Chairman of the Party; Sir Toby Low, later Lord Aldington, Deputy Chairman; and William Deedes, MP, Minister Without Portfolio. The BBC's purpose in giving the dinner was to gain support for its endeavours to get better facilities within the Palace of Westminster for the broadcasting of Parliamentary affairs and the interviewing of Members of Parliament.*

Neither Iain MacLeod nor Sir Toby Low seemed in the least eager to discuss this particular matter. They were preoccupied with an altogether larger subject. They doubted whether Parliament could survive the challenge of television and believed that the whole future of Parliament in Britain depended upon its proceedings being televised.

Coming from politicians of such experience and standing, these opinions were startling. The idea of televising the proceedings of Parliament was not new. But Prime Ministers had continued to take the line that decisions about the televising of Parliament must be taken by Parliament itself; and the BBC had continued to say that it would be ready to conduct experiments if Parliament requested it to do so. Neither Parliament nor the BBC appeared to be anxious to press the matter.

The arguments against televising Parliament were well known: the presence of television cameras would alter the whole character of Parliamentary debates; some Members of Parliament would play to the cameras; exhibitionists would get more attention than they deserved; much of the daily work of Parliament took place in committees operating in small rooms so that it would be difficult, even if desirable, to show on television this important aspect of Parliament's activities. Then there were the dangers of being misunderstood by a mass audience; a great deal of what happened in the House of Commons was governed by rules of procedure which would be incomprehensible to many viewers; much legislative detail, however necessary, was too specialised to hold the attention of those not immediately concerned. Moreover, if, during a debate, the House of Commons were seen to be sparsely attended, the public might think that Members of Parliament were idle whereas they could well be dealing, outside the debating chamber, with the business of their constituents.

Above all there was the matter of editing. For reasons of timing alone it would be necessary to record the proceedings and to edit them. But who could be entrusted with this responsibility? To leave it to the broadcasting organisations was altogether too dangerous. Bias in editing was obviously possible. Should it be undertaken by a

* BBC representatives at this dinner included the Chief Assistant to the Director-General, Harman Grisewood, and myself.

Committee of the House working to the Speaker? But this would involve delays which would destroy the topical interest of the programmes.

Beyond all these practicalities lay legitimate and profound fears. Would not the intrusion of television destroy the intangible atmosphere which shaped the deliberations of an assembly so rooted in British history? Once destroyed it could not be replaced. Surely it was better to postpone the decision? There would, almost certainly, be technical developments which might make it possible for television to have smaller cameras and less obtrusive lighting. Better make no change for the moment.

Being aware of all these familiar arguments, it was surprising that politicians like Iain MacLeod and Sir Toby Low should put forward their view that Parliament and television must be brought into some sort of an alliance and believed that the televising of Parliament was the most obvious method of achieving this. But the truth was that, without there being any deliberate intention of doing so, the coverage on television of politics and current affairs had already by-passed the formal limitations of Parliamentary debate. Industrial affairs were discussed on television not only by Members of Parliament but by Trade Union leaders, bankers and leading representatives of the Confederation of British Industry.* Budgets on television no longer consisted merely of a statement on Budget Day made by the Chancellor of the Exchequer, followed, on the next night, by the criticisms of the Shadow Chancellor. On television, as the details of the Budget proposals came through on the tapes, there was running comment from bankers and economists, financial journalists and stockbrokers, as well as a reflection of man-in-the-street opinion and of reactions from abroad.

The debate, in fact, had been enlarged. It had escaped from the closed shop of the Parliamentary scene. What was said in the House of Commons by a junior Minister or a lesser Member of the Shadow Cabinet could easily be less important than what was being said on television by the Governor of the Bank of England or by the General

---

* This widening of political argument continued: a notable example occurred during the General Election campaign of 1970 when there was a famous discussion on 'Panorama' between Lord Cromer, Governor of the Bank of England, and Lord Kearton, an eminent industrialist who was not unsympathetic to Labour, and they agreed about the seriousness of the economic situation, a subject of dispute between the contending Parties.

Secretary of the TUC. In the absence of any extensive coverage of Parliament in the mass circulation newspapers, television had become the main method by which the British public was kept informed about the aims and intentions of those who held, or wished to hold, the reins of political power.

An important factor in this development was the effect on television of the Press. The continuing freedom of the Press was a force which made it necessary for television current affairs programmes to deal with matters which had been exposed, or widely canvassed, in the newspapers. This became evident during 1963 when the Profumo scandal shook the Macmillan government and affected the leadership of the Tory Party.

Television current affairs personnel were, of course, well aware of the rumours which had been circulating about the Minister of War, John Profumo, a call girl, Christine Keeler, an osteopath, Dr Stephen Ward, with whom she had taken up residence, and a Soviet Naval attaché, Captain Ivanov. On April 10, 1962, Harold Macmillan had told Conservative back-benchers at a lunchtime meeting, 'I shall be leading you into the next General Election.' If the rumours about Profumo were true, the Opposition might be able to discredit the Macmillan government on the respectable grounds that it had been negligent in regard to its responsibilities for national security.

On May 28 the Prime Minister felt it necessary to announce that there would be an inquiry and that Lord Dilhorne, the Lord Chancellor, would conduct it. On May 31 Lord Dilhorne told Mr Profumo that he would want to see him on the following Thursday, June 6.

Mr Profumo in fact saw the Prime Minister's Principal Private Secretary, Mr Bligh, and the Conservative Party Chief Whip, Mr Redmayne, on Monday, June 3, tendered his resignation and confessed that for four months he had been lying to his colleagues, to his wife, and to the House of Commons. At 6 p.m. that evening Harold Evans released the text of Mr Profumo's statement.

For Mr Profumo all was now over. But the political situation remained. How would this revelation affect the position of Mr Macmillan, the Tory Leadership, and the prospects of the Conservative Government?

These major political questions were discussed freely in the newspapers. It might have been expected that they could be dealt with equally freely in television current affairs programmes. But the difference between newspaper and television journalism made it possible for the political parties to affect the handling of political subjects on television in ways which were not possible in relation to newspapers.

Comment in newspapers did not depend upon the personal participation of the politicians immediately involved. But, since it was possible, and had become the practice, for politicians to appear in television programmes and to be questioned on behalf of the public, any television treatment of the political repercussions of the Profumo crisis was bound to seem inadequate unless it included the questioning of political leaders. The result was that if the political parties thought it inadvisable for senior politicians to be interviewed on television about the Profumo affair, and if party disciplines were sufficiently tight, the political parties could prevent the adequate handling by television of this particular event.

That is what happened for a brief period in June 1963. The first major television current affairs programme scheduled by the BBC to take place between the Profumo confession on June 3 and the Profumo debate in the House of Commons on June 17, was 'Panorama' on June 10. Three Members of Parliament, Angus Maude (Conservative), Emmanuel Shinwell (Labour) and Mark Bonham Carter (Liberal), none of them closely concerned with the handling by the Government of the Profumo affair, accepted invitations to appear and to take part in a discussion chaired by Robin Day. But a number of leading figures in both the Conservative and Labour parties more closely involved in the political handling of the Profumo situation had been invited into 'Panorama' and, as I said in a note to Kenneth Adam,

'everyone we approached either refused immediately, or accepted and then, quite clearly after having checked with Party headquarters, withdrew.'[4]

It seemed likely that this experience would be repeated in regard to 'Gallery' on June 13. It was inconceivable that 'Gallery' should fail to try to deal with a political matter which was filling the newspapers, arousing the country, causing fears about possible negligence in matters of national security and about moral standards in high places.

'Gallery' had been started in February 1961 with the specific purpose of trying to bridge the gulf between Parliament and the individual viewer. Our original idea had been to select subjects likely to be of personal interest to individuals in various parts of the country, illustrate these with film and personal testimony, and then question Members of Parliament about how Parliament was dealing with them. In action 'Gallery' had changed, and by 1963 it was a highly specialised programme in which politicians liked to appear because on it they encountered other politicians and political journalists, who talked their language. Of all the BBC's television current affairs programmes this was the one least able to ignore the fact that the Profumo crisis might bring down the Macmillan government.

I described in my memorandum[5] to the Controller of Television Programmes the detailed negotiations which preceded the eventual appearances of Lord Hailsham, a Member of the Cabinet and Lord President of the Council, in 'Gallery' on June 13, where he was interviewed by Robert McKenzie. I wrote:

'. . . it was clear that no-one of any note in either party would talk in "Gallery" unless they had top level sanction from Party headquarters . . .

. . . In spite of the previous attitudes taken by Party headquarters, Editor, "Gallery", John Grist (who gets on very well with Iain Macleod) telephoned Iain Macleod and asked him whether he would in fact appear in "Gallery". He said that he couldn't, because he was winding up in the Debate on Monday, but said that he would arrange for Lord Hailsham to come in his place. Macleod's office did not seem to be interested in the content of what Lord Hailsham was going to say, but merely made the practical arrangements about getting him to the studios by 10 o'clock and seeing that he would be taken away in time to catch a midnight train.

We thought it quite possible on Thursday that Hailsham, as others had done, might telephone and say that he could not manage the broadcast after all.

In fact, we found out, as a result of a conversation I had with William Deedes at lunch time, that this was a high level decision in that it was a firm commitment.

This arose because "Tonight" had organised a *vox pop* film report from Parliament Square, which would include a number of senior backbenchers and anyone who happened to be significant and around at this time. They felt that the programme might be very hostile to the Conservative Government and asked me if they could invite Iain Macleod to appear in "Tonight", in order to put the Government's view. I explained to them our negotiations for "Gallery" and "Panorama" with Macleod, but said that I would approach William Deedes, who might consider it appropriate to speak on this subject and would be suitable as the spokesman for the Government. He let me know on the telephone at lunch time that he must regretfully decline this invitation because it had been decided at a high level that only one person should speak and in one place. This was to be Lord Hailsham, who would be appearing in "Gallery".'

In a sense, therefore, Lord Hailsham in the 'Gallery' interview was the nominee of the Conservative Party. He himself made this clear to me when he arrived at the television studios. He said, 'Well, here I am. What do you want me to do?' I said, 'It was good of you to come between a dinner party and catching the midnight train.' He said shortly, 'I came because I was asked to come by the Chairman of the Party.'[6]

This did not mean that Lord Hailsham was simply voicing the official party line. The interview was impromptu and he was answering, impromptu and in a highly personal style, the questions put to him by Robert McKenzie. By deciding 'at a high level' that the only person who should speak on television about the Profumo affair would be Lord Hailsham the Conservative Party was merely evincing its trust in his ability to present to the nation on television the combination of legal, moral and political judgments which had governed the actions of the Macmillan administration in its handling of the Profumo case.

The interview was headlined in the newspapers on the following morning. Robin Day had said in his introduction to 'Gallery': 'For the first time since the Profumo scandal burst open last week a Cabinet Minister speaks on television about the Government crisis.'[7] Whatever Lord Hailsham said was bound to be news. But the manner in which he said it on television was as much highlighted as the content of his contribution. The *Daily Herald* stressed the manner. It said:

'Lord Hailsham, Lord President of the Council, got angry last night when he was being questioned on the BBC television programme "Gallery" about the Profumo crisis. He banged his fist and accused interviewer Robert McKenzie of turning the affair into a party political issue.'

On the air Lord Hailsham was certainly rough with McKenzie. We had planned the interview so that it should in no way seem to be a Party Political broadcast, but as I said in my subsequent report:[8]

'We had deliberately envisaged this as a discussion about the Conservative Party and its politics and therefore Bob McKenzie necessarily had to ask in a penetrating and persistent way the kind of questions which were in everybody's mind.'

Some of those questions apparently annoyed Lord Hailsham. In his first reply to Robert McKenzie's query about how it could happen that a man like Profumo was able to rise to high office in the Conservative Party Lord Hailsham denounced Mr Profumo's associations with 'dingy companions' and the fact that he had 'lied to his friends, lied to his family, lied to his colleagues, lied to his solicitor, lied to the House of Commons'.[9] But when McKenzie went on to ask whether it wasn't 'a strange comment on the leadership of your party that a man with his background should for so long have been able to hold onto the position he did?'[10] Hailsham retorted sharply, 'Well, how can we tell? It's silly to make a party issue of this. A scandal can arise in one party or it can arise in another. Let's recognise it for what it is—a scandal.'[11]

The same theme emerged later in the interview. Lord Hailsham said, 'What I say is that when a thing like this has happened, and public morality is seriously upset and confidence is threatened, to try to turn it into a party issue is really, beyond belief, contemptible.'[12] McKenzie pursued this and asked, 'You feel that those who have spoken out—the Bishops, *The Times* and so on—have tried to turn it into a party issue?'[13] Lord Hailsham retorted fiercely, 'I think *you* have.'[14]

That was the end of the interview. Watching it in the studio and talking with both Robert McKenzie and Lord Hailsham before and after it, I came, rightly or wrongly, to a conclusion which I stated in my report to the Controller of Television Programmes and the Chief Assistant to the Director-General. This was that

'whereas Hailsham's general moral indigation about being caught up in so sordid a set of circumstances was genuine, nevertheless as part of the tactics of handling the interview, he had been determined not to be on the defensive but to go out and attack. After the broadcast he was extremely friendly with us all, including Bob McKenzie, and everything went off in an aura of amiability.'[15]

Though we were anxious that this appearance of Lord Hailsham in 'Gallery' should not seem in any way to give him an unchallenged platform, and indeed it had certainly not done so, nevertheless we had had to consider the Opposition. In my memorandum to the Controller of Television Programmes I wrote:

'I understand that there has been a complaint from the Labour Party that this broadcast by Lord Hailsham seems to have done the Conservative Party good and they may wish themselves to speak. In fact, after a good deal of discussion, we had invited Patrick Gordon Walker into this edition of "Gallery". He said that he did not wish to discuss the Profumo affair and its effect on politics. The line on this had been given out by the Leader of the Party, Harold Wilson, before he went to Moscow. Harold Wilson would be taking his own line in the Debate on Monday. He, Gordon Walker, did not want to forestall Harold Wilson's attitude.'[16]

Since a senior member of the Labour Party had been offered a chance of appearing in the same programme as Lord Hailsham and had refused it, there could be no question of any need, in terms of party political balance, to offer special television opportunities to the Opposition in relation to the Profumo case.

But other aspects of the interview threw a considerable light on the changing relationships between television and Parliament.

Behind the whole of Lord Hailsham's treatment of Robert McKenzie there appeared to be a real, or assumed, resentment of the fact that a television interviewer was asking questions of a member of the Cabinet about matters which ought to be left to Parliament.*

But in that case, why had he come? Why did he, the Lord President of the Council, agree to answer questions in a television programme on Thursday, June 13, when the Government's handling of

---

* Many years later Lord Hailsham said, during a discussion with Richard Crossman in the BBC series 'Crosstalk' (January 4, 1973), 'My anger was directed partly against Bob McKenzie and partly against the group who had been discussing the thing and said there was no morality in it.' (Transcript)

the Profumo affair, and the security risks involved, were going to be debated in the House of Commons on the following Monday? He had come, he said, because he had been asked to do so by the Chairman of the Conservative Party. But again, why? Why not leave it to the House of Commons on Monday when the Prime Minister and the Leader of the Opposition would be confronting each other on the floor of the House?

The fact was that the mass public would not be able to see this confrontation nor listen to the arguments put forward. The proceedings of Parliament were not televised and there seemed little likelihood of any change in this situation in the foreseeable future. The vast television audience, in the meanwhile, was gaining its impressions of the handling of the Profumo case from the newspapers and from a number of politicians who, in spite of party disciplines, accepted invitations to appear in one or other of the many television current affairs programmes which were transmitted day by day and week by week. Such political figures were bound to be the most individualistic, the most rebellious or others who simply did not care to toe the party line. Almost by definition they were not representative of central opinion in the political parties. Party attitudes on the Profumo issue, therefore, as far as the mass television audience was concerned, were in danger of going by default.

Public reassurance could not be left until the run-up to the election. Before the debate on Monday, June 17, 1963, something might be done to affect the opinion of the nation. If the Conservative administration failed to convince the House of Commons the result might certainly be disastrous for the party but the worst that could happen would be a change in the Tory leadership or an early General Election. If public opinion were on its side the Conservative Party could survive either. But time was short. There had been mutterings about the need for a change in the leadership even before the Profumo case. It was important, therefore, to restore *now* confidence in the integrity of the Party. And who could do that better than Lord Hailsham? His combination of moral fervour, outspoken language and intellectual dexterity, made him a figure of national as well as party significance. It was possible that he could give a different tone to the discussions about the Profumo affair; influence, in the short run, the debate in the House of Commons and, in the longer run, affect those viewers who would be voting in the next General Election.

The Hailsham interview was in fact a demonstration of the importance of television to political leaders. Whatever the intention, and
however strongly Lord Hailsham felt that these matters should be
left to the House of Commons, the interview was in essence an
appeal to the nation in advance of the debate in the House of
Commons and therefore, in a sense, a by-passing of the elected
representatives of the people assembled in Parliament.

The problem for politicians by 1963 was how to be able to continue to use television for communication with the electorate at times
such as the Profumo crisis and yet keep the activities of television
producers and the broadcasting organisations within bounds so that
their handling of political affairs did not become a threat to Parliamentary institutions. This, in one way, was not difficult because
neither broadcasters nor Parliamentarians wanted a direct confrontation between their interests. Most broadcasters understood,
and had a reverence for, the purposes and practices of democratic
representative government. Parliamentarians respected the need for
freedom of expression in broadcasting just as they respected the
need to maintain the freedom of the Press. Nobody wanted to pursue
a collision course. The issues were too difficult and too grave. So
with neither broadcasters nor Parliamentarians anxious to press the
matter to a conclusion, and few people willing to think about it, the
whole question of the relationship between television and Parliament,
as well as the desirability of televising Parliamentary proceedings,
remained in a kind of limbo.

The possibility of televising Parliament had not, however, been
forgotten. Even in the difficult period between the Profumo debate
in June 1963 and the Conservative Party Conference in October
1963, the Prime Minister, Harold Macmillan, suggested in July that
there should be inter-party talks on the advisability of televising,
daily, a short edited programme of the proceedings of the House of
Commons. And the Leader of the Opposition, Harold Wilson,
agreed to take part in such talks.

Moreover, without deliberate intent, the handling on television
of the Profumo debate in the House of Commons on June 17, 1963,
had been a visual demonstration of the absurdity of the relationship
between Parliament and television as it then existed. Television
cameras were not allowed within the Palace of Westminster and
therefore no facilities existed for the interviewing on television of
Members of Parliament at convenient moments while debates were

taking place. So Paul Fox, by then Head of Public Affairs within the Talks Department of the BBC's Television Service, decided that television producers must use their ingenuity to reflect, as best they could, tonight not tomorrow, the progress of the Profumo debate. In 'Panorama' therefore, on June 17, 1963, though Richard Dimbleby presided as usual over tape machines, commentators, newsmen and visiting political pundits in order to give television viewers a blow-by-blow account of the progress of the debate, in Parliament Square something more unusual was happening. A television camera unit had been set up in this public and open space. There Robin Day, in the pouring rain, interviewed a number of journalists and Members of Parliament. Verbally, these contributions were valuable enough. It was the fact of vision which made the whole situation seem ludicrous. On millions of television screens Members of Parliament, including George Wigg, Woodrow Wyatt and William Rodgers (Labour), Peter Kirk and Gerald Nabarro (Conservative) and Jeremy Thorpe (Liberal) were seen sheltering under umbrellas held over them by Robin Day and his assistants, in order to make it possible for them to give on television their impressions of a Parliamentary debate of national importance.

The absurdity of this attempt to reflect to viewers the deliberations of Parliament could be attributed by broadcasters to the obstinate refusal of the authorities to permit facilities for television interviewing within the Palace of Westminster. Or, by Parliamentarians, to the unreasonable insistence of current affairs producers that they must get as close as possible to the areas where political decisions were being made so that they could provide instant television for the benefit of television viewers.

But behind these trivialities lay a very real clash between the existence of television and the nature of representative Parliamentary democracy. If, for example, the proceedings of Parliament were televised and millions of individual voters were able to see and hear the debates in which different political policies were being advocated, might not these voters consider that they were now able to judge for themselves and be reluctant to leave the ensuing decisions to be made, allegedly on their behalf, by their representatives in the House of Commons? In other words would not the logical conclusion of televising the proceedings of Parliament be government by referendum?

In 1963 such possibilities were remote. Ideas about televising

Parliament were limited to the thought that there might be a short daily edited television programme which gave the highlights of the day's proceedings and, with various safeguards, of making excerpts from such recordings available to the editors of television news and current affairs programmes. And by the autumn the question of televising Parliament was overshadowed by more immediate concerns: the Conservative Party Conference in October; the sudden illness and retirement of the Prime Minister, Harold Macmillan; the fight for the Tory leadership conducted in the full blaze of party-publicity in Blackpool; the struggle between R. A. Butler, Reginald Maudling and Lord Hailsham for the succession; and the surprising emergence as Leader of the Conservative Party and Prime Minister, of the fourteenth Earl of Home, who gave up his historic title and his seat in the House of Lords in order, as Sir Alec Douglas-Home, to seek election to the House of Commons and assume the responsibilities of government.

Television and the Party Leaders

The problems which faced Lord Home in October 1963 were formidable. A fourteenth Earl as Prime Minister seemed an anachronism. And though the way had been paved by Anthony Wedgwood Benn, the whole machinery of Lord Home's renunciation of his title together with the provision of a convenient by-election so that he could become once more a Member of the Commons, appeared so contrived as to be a questionable method of choosing the head of a democratic government. Moreover, the Cabinet had been weakened by the refusal of two prominent Conservatives, Iain MacLeod and Enoch Powell, to serve under the new Prime Minister.

This was the general situation on October 21 when Lord Home was interviewed in No. 10 Downing Street by Robin Day and Robert McKenzie. Robin Day's first question was:

'Prime Minister, when do we start calling you "Sir Alec"?'[1]

Lord Home replied pleasantly, if shortly,

'When the lawyers say so, and this time they've got to move pretty fast. I should think some time this week.'[2]

McKenzie pursued the subject of the succession:

'Could I bring you to the question of how you got your job, which has been really controversial? *The Times* said today "Many Conservatives in high places are extremely angry and resentful at the way Lord Home got the leadership." Now do you yourself think it was a democratic process?'[3]

The questions went on relentlessly if rather less personally, about the reasons for the poor record of the Conservative Party in recent by-elections and about the prospects, if any, for a meeting between Lord Home and Mr Khruschev and with President Kennedy. Lord Home continued to reply with courtesy and even with humour. When Robin Day said:

'Prime Minister, as one who was a pretty good cricketer in your youth, would you not think it likely that when the next general election comes round the British public may feel this—whatever the policies—that the Conservative innings ought to be declared closed, and the other side should go in to bat?'[4]

Lord Home answered:

'Well, one of the things I learned at cricket was how to spot a googly—you know what a googly is—and that is a fellow who twists his hand round one way and the ball comes out the other. No, I'm not going to answer that question, I think.'[5]

This interview, watched by eleven million people, was important. *The Times* reproduced it almost verbatim on the following morning. But its importance lay in its soothing qualities rather than in any new policies which were disclosed. After the political disturbances of the Profumo scandal and the fight for the Tory leadership it was reassuring to find the new Prime Minister, ensconced in No. 10 Donwing Street, apparently unruffled and in control of the situation.

For Lord Home the television broadcast was a personal success. The Downing Street setting suited him. The previous Prime Minister, Harold Macmillan, had seemed to enjoy being seen in No. 10. But his intense appreciation of his historic surroundings gave them an air of being a back-drop for his somewhat histrionic political performances. To Lord Home the setting seemed as natural as his own drawing room. He treated his interviewers as he would any guest in his own house. And, for the television audience, his style was a change; simpler and more direct than that of either Harold Wilson or Harold Macmillan.

Yet I myself was not happy about the interview nor about the way in which current affairs interviewing in television was developing. On the day after the Prime Minister's broadcast I wrote a memorandum to the Director of Television which I copied to the Editor of News and Current Affairs and to the Chief Assistant of Current Affairs, Television. We had been told that the Prime Minister liked the Day/McKenzie approach to television interviewing because he found it stimulating. And we were very conscious of the fact that, in order to maintain political impartiality, we had invited the Leader of the Opposition, Harold Wilson, to appear on television on the night after the Prime Minister's broadcast. That morning I said in my memorandum about the interview with the Prime Minister:

'There is a danger, I think, in BBC interviewers, on occasions of importance of this kind, seeming too much to be "dogs snapping at the heels". In my view this created a sense that the interviewers were attacking and that the Prime Minister was very much on the defensive. This is even borne out by *The Times* talking about the Prime Minister "facing the bowling".

'Obviously whatever treatment was given to the Prime Minister last night must be followed in the interview with the Leader of the Opposition tonight. Nevertheless I think we have to watch this, regardless of what the Prime Minister may have said. It is not so much a question of whether he did or did not find this treatment stimulating; but that we do not want the BBC itself, in its interviewing on major occasions, to seem unable to rise to occasions of this kind. This is not a policy point; it is rather one of manner.'[6]

My main anxiety was that BBC television current affairs interviewing was tending to become something of a closed shop and that the manner was too uniformly accusatory. It was important that political interviews on television should be questioning in order to prevent them being the equivalent of party political broadcasts. And it was equally important to maintain the principle that the choice of interviewers should not be affected by the personal likes or dislikes of those who were to be interviewed.

But by October 1963 the situation was becoming difficult. BBC television current affairs producers believed, with some reason, that Harold Wilson disliked being interviewed by Robert McKenzie. And a few of them feared that pressure might be brought to bear upon them to exclude McKenzie from the interviewing team which would question the Prime Minister on October 21 and the Leader of the Opposition on October 22. Though both the Director-General and his Chief Assistant would have preferred more variety in the style of television current affairs interviewing, no such pressure was in fact brought. But the belief that pressure was possible made television current affairs personnel doubly determined that the Day/McKenzie team should be chosen for the coming interviews with Lord Home and with Mr Wilson.

I had been concerned, as my memorandum showed, about the

questioning of Lord Home. Nevertheless his handling of the questions had been so urbane that the broadcast had remained agreeable rather than embarrassing. I was therefore all the less prepared for the explosion of anger which followed the interview with the Leader of the Opposition.

Mr Wilson had come to the BBC's Television Centre at Shepherd's Bush and the interview took place in a studio there. So he did not have the advantage of the Prime Ministerial setting which Lord Home had enjoyed on the previous night. I knew that leading members of the Opposition, including Hugh Gaitskell when Shadow Chancellor, had been acutely aware that, when speaking on television, Ministers had the benefit of the visual authority conferred upon them by being seen in an official residence such as No. 10 or No. 11 Downing Street. The problems created by such differences of background had been discussed at a high level within the BBC. It had been decided that they could not be helped. Given the British party system the Opposition would one day be the Government and its leaders would then address the nation from No. 10 or No. 11 Downing Street, and their opponents would be seen in a studio.

But on the night of October 22 I knew that Mr Wilson, having watched Lord Home on the previous evening, would be sensitive to any deficiencies in the studio background with which he was provided. And this, in my opinion, was unnecessarily stark. Nevertheless the interview opened smoothly enough. McKenzie started by saying:

'Mr Wilson, about the 14th Earl. Now you've been making a great fuss about the fact the Tories have chosen a peer, and yet you, the Labour Party, were the people who insisted that the peer should have the right to come back to the Commons?'[7]

He went on:

'Is there any reason, therefore, why the Tories shouldn't choose a peer if they think he's their best man?'[8]

Wilson replied:

'None at all. We're not against choosing an earl, an Etonian, or anything else, if he is the best man. What we're against is that an earl—or anyone with a particular educational background—should have a flying start over all the others, and in the particular case of the selection we feel that the method of selection was of such a kind as not to choose the best person, perhaps. And also, of course, it inflicted on the House of Commons someone who was not a member of the House of Commons with all the difficulties we've been facing today.'[9]

McKenzie said:

'When you say "inflicted" someone, after all he was in the House of Commons before, then like Lord Stansgate's heir, Mr Wedgwood Benn, he had to go to the Lords, and now comes back at the first opportunity so really there's no objection to that.'[10]

Wilson answered:

'No, but of course I really cannot accept that there was no-one in the House of Commons that could have been selected and I think many Conservatives take the same view. May I say I've nothing against Lord Home personally at all. We take the view that everyone should be equal in the matter of selection and yet—well, the last three Prime Ministers have all been to one school, and there are forty thousand schools in this country—nearly half the Cabinet comes from that school. I think it still shows that the Conservative Party is out of touch with the times in which we're living.'[11]

The interview continued, predictably, with the degree to which Lord Home did, or did not, understand 'ordinary people'. But after Robin Day moved on to the subject of a British independent nuclear deterrent the atmosphere grew tense. Eventually McKenzie said:

'Mr Wilson, may I bring out here one thing I think that is in the public mind, and there's some uneasiness about your own position in all this, dating really right back to the moment when Mr Gaitskell, three years ago, put up his great fight to save the Labour Party from neutralism and a pure CND policy. Now the fact you ran against him, for the leadership, in the middle of that fight, a moment of great extremity for him, has caused a certain real doubt in the minds of many people.'[12]

Mr Wilson replied at length, but said first:

'Well, it's a question you put every time we're on the air, whatever we're supposed to be discussing, Bob.'[13]

When the broadcast was over Mr Wilson complained bitterly to the Director-General, Hugh Greene, who happened to be giving a dinner that night in the Television Centre, about the questioning to which he had been subjected. He considered that it had been unfair when compared with the questioning of the Prime Minister on the previous evening.

The BBC always sensitive to allegations of bias, called immediately for transcripts and for comments from those responsible for the interviews. I had watched both; and had read the transcripts. It could not be denied that, on the screen, they were different in tone. In my internal reports I ascribed, rightly or wrongly, this difference to the fact that Lord Home had the advantage of speaking from No. 10 Downing Street and that his tolerant manner had taken the sting out of the questioning. When the transcripts were studied the actual questions appeared to be equally tough, even equally, and personally, harsh. But there was no doubt that the Leader of the Opposition genuinely believed that he had been unfairly treated. It was understandable that he should resent this.

The interview on October 22, 1963, was even more important to him than the interview on the previous night had been to Lord Home. He was in the weaker position. Lord Home, after all, was Prime Minister. As Leader of the Conservative Party he had inherited the tradition of Conservative rule which had been created by the Conservative majorities in the General Elections of 1951, 1955 and 1959. The Labour Party ascendancy, established in 1945, had lasted only six years. During the long period from 1951 to 1963, the Labour Party, and Harold Wilson, had been in Opposition. Their great chance must come in the next General Election, which would have to take place, if not in 1963, at any rate in 1964.

The feverish political climate of the run-up to a General Election was, therefore, already in existence in 1963. It would be a disaster for the Labour Party if the Conservative Prime Minister were to postpone the election until the last possible moment and use the period between October 1963 and October 1964 to build up, with the aid of television, so considerable a personal following in the country that the Conservatives would be able to continue in office for a further term of four or five years.

In fact this did not happen. Sir Alec Douglas-Home did not care for television. He particularly disliked being in any way personally involved in the machinery of television presentation. For a Prime

Minister to have to give thought to the question of which camera he ought to look at when he addressed the nation, or be compelled to wait before starting his address until he had received a signal from a television floor manager, and end in sufficient time to allow a boxing match or a dramatic performance to take his place on the screen, was to confuse the processes of government with those of show business.

When persuaded by circumstances, or by his colleagues, that it was necessary for him to appear, he would do so. But only if he could treat such appearances casually. So long as he could walk, without fuss, into a television studio and talk with the directness which he was accustomed to use on a public platform, then television became acceptable. This meant that he preferred to be interviewed rather than attempt a straight address to camera. For him the interviewing situation was the more natural and it spared him the necessity of giving thought to the mechanisms by which his words reached millions of voters. As far as television was concerned, he wished, so to speak, to retain his amateur status.

Meanwhile Mr Wilson, with professional thoroughness, had applied his mind to a consideration of the political uses of television. He mastered the techniques of the teleprompter and was able to give effective 'straight' talks to camera and dispense with the aid of interviewers who might, by their questions, affect not only the manner but the content of his communication. He paid infinite attention to detail, deciding personally upon the length of the music which should accompany the title sequence of a Labour Party election broadcast, and supervising the television backings for his own addresses. He could not yet broadcast from No. 10 Downing Street but he made certain that he should be seen seated at an executive-type desk in front of a Georgian window which created the atmosphere of an office in Whitehall.

The differing television styles of Sir Alec Douglas-Home and Mr Wilson were of importance during the election campaign of 1963/4. The proceedings of Parliament were still not televised; Parliamentary debates were sparsely reported in newspapers of mass circulation; party political broadcasts seldom seemed interesting, largely because they were too narrowly propagandist and failed to match, either in the free exploration of ideas or in the professional skill of their presentation, the political discussions and interviews seen in ordinary television current affairs programmes. It was from these, therefore, that millions of voters derived their main impressions of the competing personalities and policies of the political parties.

By mid-1963, even before Sir Alec Douglas-Home had succeeded Mr Macmillan as Prime Minister, plans for the broadcast handling of the forthcoming election were being finalised. It seemed likely that effectiveness on television would be even more necessary for political leaders during the next campaign than it had been in the past. Not only were there to be thirteen television party election broadcasts (five Conservative, five Labour and three Liberal—each of fifteen minutes), but there was talk of personal 'Confrontations' on television between key members of the main parties. Ever since the Kennedy–Nixon debates in the American Presidential Election of 1960 the desirability of having similar encounters in British General Elections had been canvassed in politico-television circles. Why should important political figures, including party leaders, not appear on the same platform in front of television cameras and answer questions put by impartial interviewers?

This idea appealed to many television current affairs producers who were dissatisfied with the usual arrangements made for broadcasting during a General Election. Because broadcasting plans for the three weeks before Polling Day were decided at a meeting, or a series of meetings, between the political parties and the broadcasting organisations, the parties, when acting in unison, had been able to prevent the free broadcast discussion of electoral issues during the final stages of the campaign. At these meetings the parties not only agreed the number and length of their own election broadcasts, they maintained, since it was agreed that the broadcasting organisations ought not to use the persuasive power of either radio or television to influence the way in which electors cast their votes, that it was for the parties to decide which news and current affairs programmes were likely to do this and which, therefore, ought to be suspended once Parliament had been dissolved.

These decisions were affected by their insistence that they, and they alone, were entitled to determine the issues upon which an election should be fought. It was not for the broadcasting organisations, which had no elective authority, to raise matters which lay outside the political arguments presented by the parties, whose members were the elected representatives of the people, in their manifestos, their speeches, their broadcasts, their posters, or by their candidates in the field. And this might happen if television programmes such as 'Panorama', 'Tonight' and 'Gallery', which included discussions of politics and the interviewing of politicians, continued right up to Polling Day.

In the light of these attitudes, the BBC, anxious to avoid a head-on collision with the main political parties, which, when acting together, in some sense represented Parliament, had accepted severe restrictions upon the programmes which it transmitted between the Dissolution of Parliament and Polling Day. Moreover, for fear of worse, it created its own strict self-censorship. During the last three weeks of the campaign there must be the closest scrutiny of all news and current affairs programmes in order to ensure that each preserved a careful political balance and that none could be attacked on the grounds that it was raising new issues in the electoral battle. Even light entertainment programmes were checked, and occasionally altered, in case some comedian's joke might affect the intentions of voters.

When applied in detail these rules often seemed absurd. But the fears of the parties were understandable. In theory, and perhaps even in practice, it would be possible for a group of producers, interviewers and commentators to present, during the last weeks of an election campaign, emotive programmes which might stampede a significant number of viewers into voting in ways which might have been different if there had been more time for reflection. Such programmes, whether accidental or the result of deliberate bias, could affect the policies which would dominate the country for the next five years. Broadcasting organisations were ultimately responsible to Parliament; but a possible post-mortem after the event was not sufficient to allay the fears of the political parties. To allow broadcasting organisations complete freedom to present whatever programmes they wished right up to Polling Day would give them, or the production staff they employed, unacceptable opportunities to misuse their powers. In a Parliamentary democracy it was necessary to prevent any such possible warping of the electoral process.

Yet the present position was not satisfactory. During the last weeks of an election campaign there was no serious treatment on television of election issues except the one-sided propaganda programmes put on as party election broadcasts by the political parties. And there was no questioning on television of political leaders by impartial interviewers. Voters were accustomed to seeing party leaders questioned on television throughout the year in current affairs programmes. To stop such questioning in the last weeks of an election campaign, just when it seemed most necessary, was surely unjustifiable as well as inept.

'Confrontations' offered a possible way out of this dilemma. As early as May 2, 1963, the Television Talks Department sent to the Editor of News and Current Affairs an internal memorandum about the television handling of the next General Election. This included a suggestion that there should be 'a short series of confrontations between leading figures from the three major parties'.

On October 29, 1963, soon after Sir Alec Douglas-Home had succeeded Mr Macmillan as Prime Minister, I put, as part of a paper for which the Director-General had asked, the case for 'Confrontations' as I saw it. We were all aware by now that whereas the Labour Party was likely to welcome 'Confrontations' the Conservative Party was reluctant to accept them. I said:[14]

'The argument in the interest of the nation and of the electorate is, we believe, formidable. The effect of television upon the electorate is, we are told, and there seems little evidence to contradict it, that voters rely more and more upon the election broadcasts in television, and go less and less to public meetings held during the campaign. This may be deplorable but it is a fact. We live in an age of television and have to see where television fits into the British concept of democracy and the electioneering system which has grown up in this country. It is of no avail to wish that election broadcasts in television did not take place and that the electioneering process were carried out in local meetings in which the local personalities questioned those who wish to be elected. This still happens: but the process has been dwarfed for good or ill by the impact on the nation of television election broadcasts. One of the advantages, and perhaps the essential, of the political public meeting was that it gave an opportunity to any individual to heckle, or at any rate question, the man who was seeking his vote. To the degree to which voters watch television political programmes and go less and less to public meetings where they have the right of questioning, the very existence of television is depriving the voters of the right to question. It can be said that public meetings still occur: that people are free to go to them: that any increase in vicarious questioning by television interviewers and others is a resignation of the individual's right himself to question and an undermining of the duty placed by a democratic society upon each individual to act for himself and not rely on the machine of television to do his acting or his thinking for him. All this is true and not to be denied. Nevertheless we in television have to face the actual and not the ideal facts. And if we relinquish the responsibilities which the existence of television has itself created, we are doing less than our duty. If we confine ourselves, as we are likely to be doing without Confrontations or National Hustings, to the presentation of the Party cases as they themselves wish to present them in Party Election Broadcasts and to reporting in News Bulletins, Campaign Reports and News Election Reports, we are not replacing the right of the individual to question the contenders which we ourselves by the existence of television are taking away.'

In spite of these arguments in favour of 'Confrontations' of the Kennedy–Nixon type I did not myself believe that they would take place on television in this country. Most politicians and party strategists in Britain were aware of the continuous discussion which had followed the Kennedy–Nixon 'Confrontations' in the USA. A number of political commentators believed that Richard Nixon had made an error, in party terms, by appearing on television with the then less experienced John F. Kennedy. Nixon had held the office of Vice-President of the United States: Kennedy was an up-and-coming Senator. By appearing before the vast television audience as rival and equal contenders for the Presidency, Nixon, some people thought, had thrown away the advantage of the authority which his term of office as Vice-President had conferred upon him.

Then there was the fact that 'Confrontations' seemed altogether too chancy and too dependent on trivia. Was Nixon's much publicised 'five o'clock shadow' simply a matter of inadequate make-up? Was it true that Kennedy had been better prepared for the questions which he was asked? Moreover, many people believed that 'Confrontations' over-personalised the political conflict. To accept them would be like thinking that a war could be settled by a duel between two commanders in the field rather than by a struggle between two armies.

Such points as these were not ignored by British Prime Ministers. The undeniable fact in all the post-mortem discussion about the Kennedy–Nixon debates was that Nixon, who had held office, had lost the election and that Kennedy, the challenger, had won.[15] No British Prime Minister wanted to risk a personal encounter on television which might enhance the status of the Leader of the Opposition and put the Prime Minister, who had been responsible for the government of the country and therefore for any mistakes which might have been made, publicly on the defensive.

By 1964 the Conservatives were in a peculiarly difficult position in regard to 'Confrontations'. They had been in office since 1951. At the highest level 'Confrontations' would now have to be between Sir Alec Douglas-Home and Mr Harold Wilson. It could not be expected that a new Prime Minister would be willing to justify in an impromptu session under Opposition attack, everything which had been done in the last thirteen years. In any case 'Confrontations', with their inevitable highlighting of the element of personal conflict between rival political leaders, were not in Sir Alec Douglas-Home's style. He would not be at his best in a medium which he disliked, particularly if the occasion demanded some overt display of his abilities. So the Conservative Party clearly had more to lose than to gain from accepting 'Confrontations' on television. Yet it was not easy to refuse them. Refusal might give an electoral advantage to the Opposition. Labour Party campaigners could make great play with the fact that Mr Wilson had been willing to appear on the same platform as the Prime Minister and answer questions, and that the Prime Minister had refused to accept the challenge.

In spite of all these uncertainties the BBC sent formal letters to each of the three main parties inviting them to take part in 'Confrontations' during the election campaign. On January 21, 1964 there was another meeting between the parties and the broadcasting organisations. No reply to the BBC's invitation had been received from the Conservative Party. By February 25 'Confrontations' were finally rejected.

This situation had been foreseen within the BBC, and not entirely regretted. 'Confrontations' in the style of the Kennedy–Nixon debates were not a wholly satisfactory solution to the problem of how to use television more effectively in a British General Election. Yet it was not easy to suggest a substitute. Broadcasters were unwilling to abandon the idea that there should be *some* questioning of party leaders during the last weeks of an election campaign. The Corporation considered what had come to be called 'National Hustings'. The term 'Hustings' had been used in 1959 for programmes in which candidates appeared in regional television studios, or in local halls in front of outside broadcast cameras, and answered questions put by members of an invited audience. They made it possible for voters in various regional centres to question candidates, and, because they were initiated locally, local viewers were no longer merely at the receiving end of London-originated television electioneering.

But the programmes had not been entirely satisfactory. In order to reassure the parties that there would be no political bias in the questioning, the invited audiences were selected mainly on the advice of the local representatives of the three main political parties. The result was not only that the questions and answers were highly predictable but that each candidate found he was facing questions from an audience two-thirds of which were automatically hostile to him. The parties had therefore asked the BBC to suggest a different method of providing questions in regional programmes of this kind during the 1964 election. In these circumstances, and well aware that at a national level 'Hustings' were certain to be even more difficult than they had been in the regions, the BBC was reluctant to believe that 'National Hustings' were the proper substitute for 'Confrontations'.

The formula eventually arrived at, and put into practice during the 1964 election, was that of 'Election Forums'. These were an adaptation of an idea which I had put up in a rather different form in sound radio before the General Election of 1945. Viewers would be invited to send to the BBC, on postcards, the questions which they would like to have put to party leaders. A trio of experienced television interviewers (Robin Day and Kenneth Harris*, under the chairmanship of Ian Trethowan†), would use the postcards as the source of their questioning. In the 'Election Forums', therefore, television interviewers would simply be the spokesmen of the public; the questions would be what the public, not they, wished to ask. 'Election Forums' were a pale and undramatic shadow of 'Confrontations'. There was no direct encounter between the Prime Minister and the Leader of the Opposition. But, for the first time in a British General Election, there were three major programmes in which the

* Of the *Observer*.

† Journalist and former Lobby correspondent who frequently presented 'Gallery', became Managing Director of BBC Radio in 1970 and succeeded Huw Wheldon as Managing Director of BBC Television in 1976.

leaders of the main political parties answered questions sent in by the public.[16]

The Director-General of the BBC had mentioned 'Election Forums' at a meeting with the parties as early as December 17, 1963. At an internal BBC meeting on February 25, 1964 it was announced that the Director-General had written to each of the three main political parties inviting them to take part in one of three 'Election Forum' programmes to be transmitted on the Tuesday, Wednesday and Thursday before Dissolution. On March 6 senior BBC current affairs producers were told that the Liberal and Labour parties had formally accepted 'Election Forums' and that Conservative agreement was probable. But it was not until June 12 that the Director-General was able to say that the Conservative Chief Whip, Mr Redmayne, had agreed to 'Election Forums', subject to consultation about their length and form.

In the meanwhile the Government had announced, in April, that the election would be in the autumn. Polling Day, it was eventually decided, would be October 15, 1964. The party election broadcasts would start on Saturday, September 26 and end on Tuesday, October 13. The three 'Election Forums' would take place on September 22, 23 and 24, thus finishing before the party election broadcasts started on September 26. The 'Forums' were, therefore, in a sense, the first shots in the locker of television electioneering; important because they offered the public a new chance of comparing the three party leaders as they appeared on the screen on consecutive nights.

As was the practice, the Government would have the last word. The Prime Minister therefore would answer questions on September 24, the Opposition Leader on September 23, and the Leader of the main minority party, Mr Grimond, would appear first, on September 22. Mr Grimond was almost invariably effective on television; but the crucial contrast would obviously be between Mr Wilson and Sir Alec Douglas-Home. One of these two would be the next Prime Minister.

The extra strains which television imposes upon party leaders were already considerable. 'Election Forums' added to them. The impact of the demands which they made upon political leaders varied according to the way in which the party organisations conducted their campaigns. It was clear to those who saw Mr Wilson in action that he gave television a high priority. He had faith in his own mastery of its techniques, and in his ability, through them, to make evident his intention, and that of his party, to communicate as directly as possible with the mass public who were viewers as well as voters.

The Conservative Party's handling of the campaign was very different. Sir Alec Douglas-Home, in eight open-air meetings during a single day, continued to emphasise his dislike of television. His favourite joke was, 'I like to come and see you in person to show you that I'm not exactly what they make me look like on the TV screen.' This went down well. But it was estimated that as a result of the long hours of travelling and talking during one of these energetic days he had been seen and heard by twenty thousand people. For his television 'Election Forum' he had an audience of around seven and a half *million*. No wonder that after the Conservatives had lost the election and Mr Wilson had become Prime Minister a senior Conservative politician said to me bitterly, 'They allowed Sir Alec to exhaust himself talking to hundreds at farm gates instead of making effective use of television where he could talk to millions.' And, indeed, when Sir Alec arrived for his 'Election Forum' programme he seemed not only exhausted but, in comparison with Mr Wilson on the previous night, relatively unprepared.

For us within the BBC, the 'Election Forum' programmes demanded elaborate planning. They were new; nothing like this had been attempted previously in British General Elections. Editorial control was in our hands, not, as with party election broadcasts, in those of the political parties. The key element was the selection of the questions. It must be impeccably fair. The first problem was how to get them in time. Invitations to the public to send in their questions must be given by radio and television broadcasts. Anything else would be too slow. So, from September 16 to September 22 the public were invited at frequent intervals on radio and television to send to the BBC the questions they wished the party leaders to answer.

During the six days between the issuing of the first invitations and the start of the 'Election Forums' on September 22 over 18,000 postcards arrived. They were sorted under headings such as rents, pensions, foreign affairs, defence and so on by a team of current affairs producers and experienced secretaries. The overall idea was to make a preliminary selection which would be handed to the three interviewers who would put those questions which expressed most succinctly whatever the greatest number of viewers seemed to want answered. There was also a selection of questions which could be the basis for supplementaries.

Representatives of the BBC's programme correspondence unit, accustomed to such problems, inspected the cards in order to help detect any signs of organised lobbies which might have arranged for hundreds of cards to be sent on specific subjects. No evidence of any such lobbies was discovered, and there were few of the lunatic fringe questions which might have been expected. What did emerge was that most of those who sent in questions wanted simple answers to complex problems. On the postcards, often underlined, were, again and again, words like 'No hedging on this question please' and 'Please answer Yes or No'. Other questions showed the same desire for an unequivocal answer and the same lack of understanding of, or unwillingness to accept, the complexities of the national and international issues involved. On pensions for example:

> 'Your definite statement, please, on an increased Retire-
> ment Pension:
>
> > How much?
> > This year?
> > Next year?
> > ?   ?'

On Rhodesia:

> 'If Southern Rhodesia declares itself independent what
> would your action be, and why?'

On party politics:

> 'Why must we suffer Party politics to please just a few.
> Why not a *Coalition Government* to please *Everyone*?'

Nevertheless a great number of the questions were shrewd, sharp and well-informed. What we had not foreseen, and probably ought to have, was that if questions were invited from a British mass public the great majority would be concerned with shoe-pinching personal matters and not with broad issues of defence, foreign policy and international affairs. Thus of the 18,050 questions, 4,050 were about pensions, 1,863 about housing and rates, whereas only 660 were on defence and even less, 368, on foreign policy.

The effect, however unintended, was that the high proportion of questions on domestic rather than international issues might have given an advantage to Mr Wilson rather than to Sir Alec Douglas-Home. Yet again, perhaps this was fair enough. Sir Alec was speaking not as Foreign Secretary but as Prime Minister.

It is difficult to assess the degree to which the personal approaches of political leaders to occasions of this kind affect the outcome. Considerable differences were certainly evident even in their reaction to the practical arrangements made for them. Transmission, in each case, was at 9.30 p.m. They were asked to be in the studio by 9 p.m. so that they could familiarise themselves with the set-up and the lighting could be adjusted to suit their individual characteristics. For their convenience we had asked them to state whether they would like dinner beforehand or a cold supper, or drinks and sandwiches. Mr Grimond, coming from Orkney, would like dinner. He arrived with one assistant, enjoyed a good dinner, talked easily to the interviewers, most of whom he knew, and although, as always, there had been no discussion of the questions which would be asked, went to the studio relaxed and in a good humour. He gave brilliantly effective replies to his interviewers even though Kenneth Harris, perhaps anxious to prove that he could be as hard-hitting as any, was uncharacteristically somewhat harsh in his manner.

Mr Wilson did not want dinner; he would prefer a cold supper. He arrived; polite, wary and prepared, with a posse of advisers, ate cold ham and salad with the interviewers and the production staff and went to the studio with the air of a serious politician dealing with an important situation. His technique was to give long answers to short questions. This enabled him to include matters which were in the interest of his party even although they were somewhat on the periphery of the subject raised in the question.

Sir Alec Douglas-Home wished to come straight to the studio; he would dine at home and arrive at 9 p.m. He came, accompanied only by Sir Michael Fraser. He looked so exhausted that his skin seemed to be drawn tightly over his skull. His answers to the questions fired at him seemed totally unprepared: he simply walked into the studio, sat down in the appropriate chair, and answered them, giving authoritative replies on subjects of which he was a master and somewhat threadbare answers to others about which he was less knowledgeable.

The differences between the styles of Mr Wilson and Sir Alec can be seen from transcripts of the openings of their respective 'Election Forums'.

Mr Wilson on September 23, 1964:

TRETHOWAN: Tonight, the second of our 'Election Forum', Robin Day, Kenneth Harris and myself, put questions from you the voters to the leader of the Labour Party, Harold Wilson. Robin Day.

DAY: Typical of many questions, Mr Wilson, is this one, from a gentleman in Nottingham: what are your comments on the accusation that the Socialist Party's leadership is a one-man band?

WILSON: I'm rather surprised at this accusation being made. I remember the last election in 1959 when it was all fought in terms of Macwonder, Supermac and the rest. As far as we are concerned we're a team. We have, first, a democratic constitution. We elect our leader, he doesn't get selected by some mysterious process. But if you take our manifesto, for example, which was issued a week last Friday, this is the work of a team the chairman of which was the deputy leader of the Party, George Brown, and all of my colleagues have played a part in it. I would just say this though, that the Press rather build up this, because if three or four of us make speeches, very often I find that my colleagues who will usually say something far more important than I'm saying, get very small reporting or none at all, and a very long piece about what I'm supposed to have said.

DAY: It does seem to occur to people perhaps in another form—this gentleman from Hendon—who says, although I have no doubt that you will have the ability to capably carry on the Prime Minister's job, do you seriously believe you have a team backing you to form a Cabinet of Ministers able to implement the Labour Party manifesto?

WILSON: Yes, of course. I think a first-class team—of course because we've been out of office for some years, some of them may not be so well known as the Conservative Ministers, but you know, some of us were around in quite senior positions, negotiating with the Russians, with the Americans, and the rest, not without success, long before Sir Keith Joseph, Enoch Powell, Mr MacLeod, were even Members of Parliament. So we have considerable experience there. And we've got some first-class young people coming up as well.[17]

Sir Alec Douglas-Home on September 24, 1964:

DAY: First, Sir Alec, from a lady in Wythenshawe who says why have you not done all these things which you are now promising? This really does baffle people. You've had your chance. Why did you not do all these things?

SIR ALEC: Well I wonder what the lady means by 'all these things'? Of course we have been, during the last few years, modernising Britain very fast. I can only really, I think, name one or two, but, of course, we've re-organised the whole Ministry of Defence, we've re-organised the whole Ministry of Education and the system of education in this country and we've re-organised the research and found much more money for it. Then, of course, all the programmes in the social services and the roads, the hospitals and the rest, we've shown enormous programmes of expansion and, what is more, found the money to pay for them.

HARRIS: Sir Alec, a lady from Trowbridge—does Sir Alec think that a command of economics is essential for a political leader? And if so, is he equipped to be the Prime Minister of this country?

SIR ALEC: Well, he ought to have common sense, and applied economics is, I think, common sense.

HARRIS: A large proportion of the present government are the products of one school, says somebody from Angus in Scotland. Doesn't the Prime Minister agree that this indicates that birth and wealth still confer enormous privilege within the Conservative Party?

SIR ALEC: Well I should think it's . . . I'd like to look at the figures; but of course the Government, for instance, members of the Cabinet . . . wide range of schools and so I would think of the Conservative Party in the House of Commons. I'm all for parents choosing the education that they give to their children. And if parents want to pay for their children, can pay for their children, and want to, to go to a Public School or Grammar School, or wherever they like, that I think is right.[18]

In roughly the same time Mr Wilson answered two questions and Sir Alec three. If Mr Wilson's replies sometimes seemed over-contrived, Sir Alec's sometimes seemed to be thin. To a viewing audience accustomed to hearing discussions about economics week by week in current affairs programmes his answer to the question put to him about the need for a Prime Minister to have a command of economics was not likely to be reassuring.

Too many factors enter into the decision-making processes of an electorate to make it possible to say whether or not 'Election Forums' had any effect on the results of the General Election of 1964. Even the most determined students of the relationship between television and elections find it hard to discover what, if any impact the entire television coverage of an election campaign has upon patterns of voting. And 'Election Forums' were only a fraction of the total political output of television during the election of 1964. Moreover they were BBC, not party, programmes, therefore they were not carried by Independent Television: the result was that large numbers of viewers could choose alternative programmes. Nevertheless on a single channel they had audiences ranging from five million for Mr Grimond to seven and three quarter million for Mr Wilson and seven and a half million for Sir Alec Douglas-Home. They were, therefore, widely seen. Their audiences can be compared with those for party election broadcasts, which averaged twelve million. But these were transmitted simultaneously on all television channels with the result that viewers who hoped to watch television at 9.30 p.m. found that on thirteen evenings between September 26 and October 13 they had, willy nilly, to see party election broadcasts. In the case of 'Election Forums' there was a choice of viewing. So the size of their audience was remarkable.

Because 'Election Forums' were a new departure in television electioneering and because the Conservative Party was concerned about Sir Alec Douglas-Home's lack of conspicuous success on television, it is worth considering some of the observations about them in the BBC's audience research report on the election of 1964. In general, as in all political broadcasting, viewers tended to think that the leader of their own party had done better than the leaders of other parties. But as far as Sir Alec Douglas-Home was concerned this was not invariably the case. According to the report some even of his own followers were not entirely happy about his showing in 'Election Forum'. It was also reported that uncommitted viewers thought that the answers given by Sir Alec were a good deal less satisfactory than those given by either Mr Grimond or Mr Wilson. Putting these factors together it seems possible that 'Election Forums' may have had some significance in relation to the floating vote.

But how important do the political parties consider the floating vote to be? In my experience, the parties during an election campaign are undecided about whether they want to use broadcasting to whip up the enthusiasm of their own supporters or to appeal to the uncommitted. They tend, therefore, to try to do both; to use their election broadcasts from time to time to make an onslaught on their opponents in order to please party loyalists and yet endeavour in other broadcasts to appeal to the electorate as responsible statesmen, the obvious people to govern the country and to represent it abroad.

Such fundamental differences in approach, style and manner may be acceptable in party election meetings where political leaders, hecklers apart, are speaking mainly to their own supporters and where inconsistencies are not readily detectable. But they are highly confusing to a television audience of millions which becomes aware of differences between the nature of individual broadcasts from the same party, which also watches broadcasts from other parties, and which is accustomed to seeing, in current affairs programmes, party leaders discussing political issues in reasonable terms with their opponents. It is hard for an audience of this kind to believe in the sudden transformation of political leaders from fire-breathing dragons today into elder statesmen tomorrow.

The Conservative Party did well in the election. It was astonishing, after the famous thirteen years of Tory rule, the Profumo scandal, the struggle for the leadership and the succession of a new Prime Minister (an earl transformed for the nonce into a commoner) that it should have come so near to winning. But the fact was that it lost, even if only by four seats. Mr Wilson was now Prime Minister. On Monday, October 26, at the invitation of the BBC, he gave a television broadcast from No. 10 Downing Street. This was not a Ministerial broadcast and the Conservative Party did not ask for a right of reply. Mr Wilson, typically, chose to give a straight talk to camera using a teleprompter. There was no nonsense about interviewers. He was in command.

Conservatives, having come so near to victory, could not reconcile themselves to failure. They sought for scapegoats. Television was one of them. Researchers into the effect of television on elections may find it impossible to decide what, if any, effect television has upon election results, but in 1964 many Conservatives were convinced that television was responsible for their having lost the election. In Conservative circles it was widely said that they had lost because 'Sir Alec was not good on television', and that this was due to the BBC's lighting. They seldom said openly that what they alleged to have been poor lighting was deliberate and the result of political bias. But it was hinted.

Gossip became so general that the BBC decided that it was necessary to try to deal with it. Early in 1965 Sir Alec Douglas-Home and a number of officials from the Conservative central office were invited to come to Lime Grove where an experimental session would be arranged. They could then see Sir Alec under different kinds of lighting and judge for themselves. The invitation was accepted. Success for Sir Alec on television was still important. The Labour Party's meagre four-seat majority had been reduced to three by the unexpected defeat of Labour's Foreign Secretary, Patrick Gordon Walker, in a by-election at Leyton. A government majority of three was scarcely viable. Ministers hardly dared leave the House of Commons to attend to the business of their departments in case there were a snap vote.

The Party survived precariously with the help of the Liberals. But this was uncertain. Neither the Labour Party nor the Liberal Party wanted a pact. The Liberals demonstrated their independence by voting from time to time with Labour but did not invariably do so. The Government could not carry on in this way for long. There was bound to be another General Election soon. And Sir Alec Douglas-Home, still the Leader of the Conservative Party, would have to fight it.

This was the position on Monday, February 22, 1965, when Sir Alec, accompanied by a number of representatives of the Conservative central office arrived at Lime Grove. A current affairs producer was in charge of the arrangements, a senior engineer was there to adjust the lighting, an experienced make-up assistant was in attendance; a teleprompter had been made available and monitors were provided so that the group could watch Sir Alec as different kinds of lighting were tried out.

The session started at eleven in the morning. Sir Alec had brought with him the text of a speech which he had delivered in Newcastle the previous weekend. It concerned the case of Rookes versus Barnard—important in relation to trade union law. This was typed on a special machine and laced up on the teleprompter. Sir Alec used his own copy for the other experiments. He was seen giving the speech direct to camera from behind a desk, reading it from a teleprompter, and in an interview. At intervals the lighting and the position of his desk and chair were altered. Sir Alec endured all this with exemplary patience, but clearly disliked it. Notably modest, he did not care for being, so to speak, on display and having his appearance studied.

We stopped for lunch. A cold buffet had been laid out in one of Lime Grove's hospitality rooms. As I took Sir Alec down through the interminable corridors, he said 'It's no use. I'm not good on television and nothing can be done about it.' I said 'That's not true. Do you remember your first television broadcast as Prime Minister when you were interviewed by Robin Day and Robert McKenzie? You were so good that the general comment afterwards was that here at last was a Prime Minister who could answer questions simply and directly. And do you remember walking into the "Panorama" studio and giving a most successful interview without preparation, fuss or rehearsal?' Sir Alec, looking more cheerful, said 'Yes. What went wrong then?' We were now in the luncheon room. The current affairs producer who had been in charge of the studio session and who knew Sir Alec, was standing beside me. He said, with a kind of gay insouciance, 'Well, sir, you were honest in those days.' His remark was heard by the entire party. There was a startled silence, then everyone hastily began to talk about lighting. Sir Alec listened with his accustomed courtesy. Then he turned to me and the producer beside me and said, 'Now let's go on about this business of being honest.' Stepping in, and feeling that it was only honest to try to answer him honestly, I said, 'Well, during that session in the studio you didn't seem to believe a word of what you were saying.' He picked up the Rookes versus Barnard speech which he had been using, threw it on the table and said, 'I didn't. It bored me so much that I didn't change a word of it. I simply used the draft I had been given.'

This, not the lighting, was what had gone wrong. Sir Alec could not pretend an interest which he did not feel. If his advisers insisted upon his making speeches which bored him his lack of interest was disastrously obvious. This was peculiarly important on television. In the early days of his Premiership he had seemed, almost transparently, to be saying what he genuinely thought and felt. He spoke without pretence, with confidence, ease and humour. There was no contradiction between his personality as it was revealed on the television screen and the sentiments he was expressing. He was a success because both seemed genuine. As the election drew nearer this quality of genuineness seemed on television to become a trifle tarnished. At times, as in 'Election Forum', he appeared uncertain, and occasionally, as in the Rookes versus Barnard experimental session, he said what he had to say without conviction.

Long before this session I had suspected that Sir Alec, unwilling to give television the serious thought he devoted to matters which really interested him, was relying too much upon those of his advisers who saw his television appearances as tools which they could employ in the whole grand strategy of the campaign without understanding sufficiently well the nature of television and the complex and varying relationship between the medium and the personalities of those who try to use it.

Whatever the political parties believe it is a kind of tragedy for television producers if political leaders who appear in programmes for which a producer has some responsibility fail to reveal the qualities they genuinely possess. Only if they do so can television assist the electoral process in a democracy. If television becomes a distorting mirror, whether because those within the parties who give advice to the leaders during an election campaign do not really understand television, or because a party leader allows himself to be persuaded to say things on television in which he does not really believe, the whole business of television communication seems to have floundered and the particular television producer concerned is bound to feel that he, or she, is somehow to blame.

In my experience this feeling is a result of professionalism and has nothing to do with the personal political leanings of any producer or technician. No television lighting man would deliberately bungle the lighting because he was opposed to the political opinions of the man he was lighting any more than a surgeon would deliberately bungle an operation upon a patient because the patient happened to be a Labour politician and the surgeon's own views were Conservative.

This professionalism in the presentation of politics on television is, I believe, essential and in Britain it has been maintained, though sometimes with difficulty. It is profoundly to be hoped that it will not be destroyed by mischievous incitements to those who work in communications to sabotage the nation-wide communication of any person who holds political views to which they are opposed. That way lies dictatorship and the denial of freedom.

With all this vaguely in mind, anxious that Sir Alec Douglas-Home—or any other political leader—should reveal himself on television to the millions who were being asked to put him into power as he was and not as a tool of his party machine, I pursued the discussion about honesty in political television. Being acquainted with most of those of his advisers who were present at this curious lunch I thought that I could myself be honest without giving offence. I said to Sir Alec, within the hearing of all, 'You mustn't let these people persuade you to say on television things that you don't believe in.' One of them, intelligent, young and recently appointed, said, 'But there are things that the leader *must* say.' I said, 'Not on television. In meetings or pamphlets if you like. But not on television. The lack of conviction comes over.' He merely laughed and said, 'The party expects them to be said on television.' That was that. Nothing more could be done.

We were soon in the summer of 1965. On July 22 there was a political sensation. Sir Alec Douglas-Home resigned the leadership of the Conservative Party. That evening the BBC mounted a special edition of 'Gallery' in which Robin Day asked Sir Alec:

'Is your decision also a decision to retire from politics?'

DOUGLAS-HOME: 'No. I'm going to stay a Member of Parliament and I hope I shall be able to do some useful work on the back benches.'

DAY: 'Not on the front bench?'

DOUGLAS-HOME: 'Well. I'm not going to say anything about really whether I will return to the front bench, because I think it's absolutely unfair that any successor should feel that he's bound to ask anybody on to the front bench; it's absolutely essential that any successor should be free to choose who he wants in his Shadow Cabinet and who he wants in his government which will follow.'

DAY: 'While appreciating that, you haven't in fact set your heart against not serving in Government again if the opportunity were put to you?'

DOUGLAS-HOME: 'All my political life, on the whole, I've done what I've been asked to do. But I'm not going to suggest that anybody in the future should ask me to do anything. This is their choice and when the time comes, if the request is made then I should make up my own mind.'

But perhaps the most characteristic reply was that which Sir Alec gave in answer to Robin Day when the latter said:

'I'm not going to ask you who you would like as the new Leader because I know you won't tell me, but what do you think the qualities of the new Leader ought to be?'

DOUGLAS-HOME: 'Oh, I don't think I can say that. Different leaders have different qualities, he must obviously have the qualities of leadership, and there are many, and he must be able to command the House of Commons. In the end of the day, the authority of a Leader derives from his Leadership of the House.'

DAY: 'What advice do you give to whoever is the new leader—from your experience?'

DOUGLAS-HOME: 'None.'

[16]

Labour in Power
1964-1970

By the time Sir Alec Douglas-Home resigned the leadership of the Conservative Party in July 1965 the Labour Party had already changed the style of the relationship between Government and broadcasters. The change was largely due to the Prime Minister, Mr Wilson, who was determined to use television to explain his policies personally to the nation. It was also the result of the joyous arrival in power in October 1964 of a Party which had been in opposition since 1951.

Most Labour leaders were accustomed to appearing in television current affairs discussions and in Party Political and Party Election programmes; to having their speeches televised when they attended Party Conferences and to being interviewed in front of television cameras. Now it was their turn to speak from No. 10 or No. 11 Downing Street; or, if they came to the studios at Lime Grove or the Television Centre, to arrive not in taxis but official limousines. It was for them that BBC commissionaires displayed their ceremonial white gloves and policemen were on duty at the doors. The general feeling at high levels within the Labour Party was summed up for me by the wife of an eminent Labour politician who was now a Minister in Mr Wilson's administration. When I said, 'He seems to be enjoying himself,' she answered, 'It's as if you'd had a Jaguar car with its engine running locked up in the garage for thirteen years and at last it's out on the road.'

The sense of released power and achieved privilege was intoxicating. Anthony Wedgwood Benn, a one-time producer in the BBC's overseas service, had become Postmaster General and could exercise considerable authority over all radio and television as well as all postal communications. George Brown, with his occasionally eccentric behaviour, endearing generosity of spirit, high intelligence and, apparently, some continuing resentment of the fact that he had never been to a university and that his talents had not been sufficiently recognised, had become First Secretary of State, Deputy Leader of the Party and Minister in charge of the newly created Department of Economic Affairs.

One day, soon after the Labour Government had begun to operate, my secretary, handing me a list of messages, said, 'And a Mr Brown rang up.' 'Was it Mr *George* Brown?' She replied coldly, 'I didn't ask his Christian name.' But it *was* Mr George Brown. Would I go that very morning and have a pre-lunch glass of sherry with him in his new department. Geoffrey Cox, then in charge of Independent Television News, would be there too.

George Brown received us warmly in his newly-decorated office, explained, with obvious pleasure, his choice of décor, curtains and pictures, then rang a bell to summon his newly-appointed Old Etonian assistant and asked for a copy of the Declaration of Intent which was to be put up in every factory in the country and transform industrial relations. He thought that neither Independent Television News nor BBC current affairs programmes had given it the attention it deserved; he ran through its provisions enthusiastically, and said he hoped that we appreciated its importance and that television would do it justice.

He was amiability itself. What he did not fully understand was that even if we had wanted to change the television coverage of the Declaration of Intent there was little we could do. Within the BBC and ITV there are established procedures by which decisions are taken. Current affairs producers, editors of current affairs magazines, those in control of news bulletins and news programmes, attend routine meetings and discuss plans with their seniors. They have world-wide sources of information and can draw not only upon the agencies but upon their own regional, home, foreign and specialised correspondents. It is in these regular preliminary discussions that television policy is made. If, in subsequent action, editors or producers transgress their obligations to be politically balanced, fair and impartial, they can be reprimanded, dismissed or removed to other programme areas. These are the ultimate sanctions. But they have to be applied carefully. The reasons for applying them, very properly, must be well documented.

Producers and other production staff are seldom disciplined for single mistakes. And they are not given day-by-day orders in regard to the programmes for which they are responsible. The general organisation provides for advance consultation at all levels: and, if there is subsequent criticism, for detailed investigation. A sudden intervention by the head of a group of departments in the existent plans for current affairs programmes was virtually impossible. If I had given instructions that 'Panorama' or 'Gallery' must pay more attention to the Declaration of Intent there would have been immediate revolt. This would have been all the more explicit if it had been known that my instructions were the result of a meeting with George Brown. I would seem to be undermining one of the fundamentals of broadcasting freedom, that is, freedom from Government interference in day-to-day operations.

This freedom had recently been reiterated. A new Charter and Licence had been issued to the BBC in March 1964. It was to run from July 30, 1964 to July 31, 1976. The proposals for the terms of the new Charter, debated in the House of Commons in January 1964, were based upon two Government White Papers which had been issued after consideration of the Report of the Committee on Broadcasting under the Chairmanship of Sir Harry Pilkington. One of the White Papers had assured the BBC of its traditional independence in programme matters and day-to-day administration. It was not so much this fresh assurance of independence as the continued, and now scarcely questioned, tradition of freedom which meant that there was no reason why the Corporation or its staff should give way to Ministerial pressures. In the case of George Brown and the Declaration of Intent the situation was easy. There had been proper Ministerial interest but no undue Ministerial pressure. During the next few years this was not always the case.

Broadcasting had always been more important to the Labour Party than to the Conservatives. Labour believed that the Press, because it was mainly owned by capitalists, was Conservative-orientated. This situation was to some extent redressed by broadcasting. Labour had its own rights to television time for Party Political and Party Election broadcasts. Moreover, in order to preserve political impartiality, broadcasting producers maintained a rough equality in the number and nature of the appearances in current affairs programmes of Labour Party sympathisers and of Conservatives. Labour leaders, conscious of the significance of broadcasting in the Party's struggle for power, were resentful if they suspected that they were being denied any of the broadcasting opportunities which had been allowed to the previous Conservative administration. This became a major problem in regard to

Ministerial broadcasts and eventually led to changes in the rules for 'Ministerials' as laid down in the Aide Mémoire of 1947.

Mr Wilson, like Mr Macmillan, did not want to be trammelled by the agreements between the political parties which had been set down in 1947 and wished to use television to address the nation whenever he thought it proper to do so. But Mr Wilson's approach to Ministerial broadcasting was more considered, more austere and less tolerant than Mr Macmillan's.

Mr Macmillan simply wanted to use television on occasions decided by himself, not by some rules or other, and did not see why there should be any right by which the Opposition could reply to a broadcast by a Prime Minister. Mr Wilson had given thought to the functions of television in a democracy, had not only mastered its techniques so that he could use it effectively, but had concerned himself with the relationship between television, Government and the machinery of party politics. He did not care for the current system of Party Political broadcasts which, like many politicians, he believed to be useless. He wanted, instead, to use television as a means of direct contact between Government and governed; a method by which governments could explain their major policies to the millions of individuals who could be reached through television and to achieve this on occasions when such statements would be accepted as being outside and above the daily party political conflict.

He therefore wished to abolish Party Political broadcasts and substitute a series of 'Fireside Chats' in the Rooseveltian manner. Unlike Mr Macmillan, who was content to ignore the rules, Mr Wilson wanted to have the rules changed. And it emerged that he was willing to have national broadcasts on the lines of his proposed 'Fireside Chats' given also by the Conservative and Liberal Parties. It was not a mere advantage for himself that he was seeking, but a different approach to the use of television in a democracy.

This was refreshing. Many people, broadcasters and politicians, as well as the public, would have been glad to see the end of Party Political broadcasts. Broadcasters found them a burden, the public found them a bore, party politicians found them expensive and thought them ineffective. But it soon became clear that Mr Wilson's proposals had, in reality, little to do with Party Political broadcasts. 'Fireside Chats' were not a substitute for Party Politicals but, in effect, for Ministerial broadcasts. That was a much more serious matter.

The rules about Ministerial broadcasting, in spite of continuing disputes about their interpretation; in spite of modifications (acknowledged and unacknowledged) in the practice of implementing them, were of vital importance. They had been created, and maintained, in order to prevent the abuse of broadcasting by the executive. Ministers, clearly, must have a right of access to the new medium for national purposes. But this right had to be carefully defined in order to prevent Ministers, including Prime Ministers, from making, for personal or party reasons, an arbitrary use of the right to broadcast.

By 1965, though the rules about Ministerial broadcasts had not been materially altered, they had fallen, as far as television was concerned, into desuetude. Prime Ministers had been interviewed in No. 10 Downing Street or in television studios, leaders of the Opposition appeared regularly in television discussions, Ministers and Shadow Ministers took part in 'Panorama', 'Tonight' and 'Gallery'. All this made the formal machinery of Ministerial broadcasts with its consultations with the Whips if there were claims by the Opposition for a right of reply, seem cumbersome and unnecessary. But Ministers, particularly Prime Ministers, were understandably not satisfied by the frequent opportunities offered them of appearing in television current affairs programmes. On such occasions they were questioned by interviewers whom they had neither selected nor approved: in discussions it was the broadcasters, not they, who chose the other participants: the circumstances and the timing of the programmes in which they took part were determined not by them but by others, often members of the broadcasting organisations whom they scarcely knew.

Any politician, certainly, could refuse an invitation to appear on television. But this was a purely negative right. If they did appear, it was within limits imposed by editors, producers and other television personnel over whom they had no direct control. But, above all, the appearances of Ministers in current affairs programmes did not touch the core of the problem with which the rules of the Aide Mémoire had attempted to deal. How was it possible to ensure that a Prime Minister was able to use television to address the nation when he himself, not some member of a broadcasting organisation, thought it proper for him to do so? How could he be prevented from misusing this right? And how was it possible to make certain that the Opposition could claim a right of reply and that this claim would be considered fairly and impartially?

In practice, and without any announcement or publicity, these problems had been dealt with by the new arrangements between the BBC and the Party Whips. There was no change in the rules of the Aide Mémoire about Ministerial broadcasts. But they had been supplemented by 'invitations'. These informal agreements* caused little difficulty during the later years of the Tory administration and the run-up to the General Election of 1964. After 1964, with Labour in power and with Mr Wilson as Prime Minister, the situation was different. Mr Wilson's determination to use television as an instrument of government exposed one of the many weaknesses of the system of 'invitations'. There was, apparently, no provision for what should happen if a Prime Minister wished to broadcast to the nation and the BBC, having regard to the need to maintain political impartiality, did not feel that it should issue an invitation.

Difficulties over this point arose early in 1965. The Labour Party was facing a balance of payments problem. There was dispute between the parties about whether the current crisis was due to the position which Labour had inherited from the outgoing Conservatives or to an aggravation of the situation as a result of the policies which Labour had pursued since it had arrived in office. In January 1965, Mr Wilson, anxious to make the country aware of the gravity of the problems with which he was trying to deal, expressed a wish to give a broadcast on the export situation. The BBC met this wish, in accordance with the informal system of 'invitations', by inviting him to broadcast on television on January 19, 1965.

By February there were greater difficulties. The Government was to make a statement on the economic position of the country in the House of Commons on February 22. It was expected that this would include not only a general review but also an announcement of a reduction in the surcharge on imports which the Labour Party had imposed and which had angered Britain's partners in the European Free Trade Association. 'Panorama' had therefore planned for the evening of February 22 a discussion of the state of Britain's economy and had invited Mr Wilson, Mr Heath (then Conservative 'Shadow' Minister for Trade and Economic Affairs), Mr Paul Chambers (then Chairman of Imperial Chemical Industries), and a Swiss banker, speaking from Zurich, to take part.

Four days before the proposed 'Panorama' discussion I was

---

* For the earlier history of this development see Chap. 14.

telephoned by the BBC's Editor of News and Current Affairs and informed that Mr Wilson did not want to appear in the 'Panorama' discussion on Monday. Instead he had suggested that he should give a broadcast from No. 10 directly *into* 'Panorama'. This offer, I was told, had been accepted by the BBC.

I was dismayed. The inclusion of an unchallenged Ministerial broadcast within the framework of a BBC current affairs programme was surely a disaster. It blurred the distinction between programmes which were under the editorial control of the Government and those which were under the editorial control of an independent and impartial broadcasting organisation. At Lime Grove I consulted hastily with Paul Fox, by then Head of BBC Television Current Affairs, and John Grist, Chief Assistant Current Affairs (Television). We were in agreement—as indeed we were bound to be. If the distinction between BBC programmes and 'Ministerials' was blurred, the assurance of the independence of broadcasting from Government interference in regard to its programmes and day-to-day administration was worthless.

We telephoned our protests. If the BBC wished to invite the Prime Minister to broadcast to the nation, without being interviewed and without taking part in a discussion in which other points of view would be heard, why not invite him to give a broadcast from No. 10 Downing Street before 'Panorama' started? That would make the distinction clear: and 'Panorama' could be presented in the ordinary way.*

Our points were taken. Mr Wilson did not broadcast into 'Panorama' on that Monday, February 22. Instead the Chancellor of the Exchequer, then Mr Callaghan, accepted an invitation to take part in the discussion. But Mr Wilson did not give his broadcast before 'Panorama' either. We were told at a routine Current Affairs meeting on the morning of February 19 that the BBC had invited the Prime Minister to broadcast from No. 10 Downing Street at 9.30 p.m. on Wednesday, February 24. The broadcast was to last

---

* A few days later I received a typically generous note from Oliver Whitley, who had recently succeeded Harman Grisewood as Chief Assistant to the Director-General. Mr Whitley had come from the Overseas Service of the BBC. He was a calm man of wisdom and integrity. He was however less experienced than Harman Grisewood in the continuing negotiations about broadcasting which took place between the BBC and the political parties. His note, dated February 26, 1965 ran:

ten minutes and would be entitled 'Production and Exports'. The
Conservative Party would be informed: so would the Press. The
Director-General said, later in the meeting, that the offer to broadcast was based on three similar invitations to the Prime Minister
during the life of the previous Government. There would be no
question of the Opposition having the right to make a formal claim
for a reply through the Whips' office as envisaged for Ministerial
broadcasts under the Aide Mémoire of 1947. The BBC itself would
decide whether to invite the Leader of the Opposition to broadcast.

The next move came from the Opposition. Two days before Mr
Wilson's proposed broadcast a Conservative Party delegation,
headed by Sir Alec Douglas-Home, visited Broadcasting House to
discuss with the then Chairman of the Board of Governors, Lord
Normanbrook, and the Director-General, Sir Hugh Greene, the
circumstances of the BBC's invitation to the Prime Minister to
broadcast on February 24.

This meeting had been followed by an announcement from Mr
Edward du Cann that Conservatives regarded the present time as a
pre-election period and expected equal opportunity if the Prime
Minister should broadcast in similar circumstances again.

In the event Mr Wilson did not use his broadcast to promote in
any direct way the political policies of his own party. It was almost
clinically national. In considering the economic situation of the
country he certainly hit out at prolonged expense account lunches
but he also denounced demarcation disputes. In a typical paragraph
he said, towards the end:

> 'From now on our approach must be from everyone, whatever his
> position, on whatever side of industry, a full day's work for a full
> day's pay. Good money, yes, but it must be earned. We've got to
> pay for skill and expertise, and use it. In every department of
> management, production, sales, we've got to be a lot more profes-
> sional. In the modern world, the gentlemen can't beat the players.

'Dear Grace,

Don't worry. I take your point about the inviolability of Pan* and Gal†
and won't let you down. The education of the C.A. to D.G. is a *process* I'm
afraid. At least you haven't lost anything, despite a near shave.
Yours,

Oliver'

*† i.e. 'Panorama' and 'Gallery'.

We have to see that wages and salaries, profits, dividends, rents, all incomes, do not get ahead of our rising national production, as they have been doing and are still doing.'[1]

But in spite of the fact that Mr Wilson's address showed no trace of special pleading in a party political sense, the new system of 'invitations' to Prime Ministers had clearly not solved the problems of Ministerial broadcasting. It did not satisfy Mr Wilson, who still wanted 'Fireside Chats': it did not satisfy the Conservative Opposition: and it was viewed with suspicion by many of the BBC's own current affairs personnel who saw in the system, as it was being operated, a possible surrender of the independence of broadcasting to the demands of the executive.

Meanwhile the whole matter was being widely discussed. The Prime Minister, in talk with Lobby Correspondents, mentioned the possibility of 'Fireside Chats' for the Government, the Opposition and the Liberals. At the Friday morning meeting of the BBC's senior current affairs staff, it was agreed on February 26, 1965, that in view of recent development, consideration should be given to the whole system of Party Political and Ministerial broadcasts. At the normal follow-up meeting at which the Director-General and his Chief Assistant were present, the Director-General said, in reply to a question from the Editor of News and Current Affairs, that the invitation to Mr Wilson to broadcast on February 24 was in accordance with the alternative method of providing for the broadcasting of statements by the Prime Minister to that contained in the 1947 Aide Mémoire. This alternative method had been fully discussed with the Chief Whips at the time and had been working satisfactorily since 1961. But the Director-General also said that he had been having further talks with Mr Wilson and that he would be continuing these talks on the following Monday, March 1.

He went on to give an outline of Mr Wilson's ideas about 'Fireside Chats' and asked for the comments of those present. It was nearly half-past twelve and it was Friday. I wanted time to think and asked if I could consider the suggestions and send him a written piece on Monday morning. He welcomed this. So hurriedly, over the weekend, I wrote a memorandum entitled 'The Future of Party Political Broadcasting in Relation to Fireside Chats'.[2] It ran:

'The proposition is the suggestion from the present Prime Minister that the Annual Series (as distinct from Election Party Broadcasts) of Party Political broadcasts should be abolished and that instead there should be a number of 'Fireside Chats', or addresses to the nation, by the Leaders of the Parties on a two, two, one basis: that two from the Labour leaders; two from the Conservative leaders; and one from the Liberal leader should be originated by the BBC and not carried by either ITV or BBC 2: that a similar number should be originated by ITV and not carried by either BBC 1 or BBC 2.'

I went on to give my comments:

'There is nothing sacrosanct about the name "Party Political broadcast". This is merely a term which had been applied to agreed sections of "offered" time on television (and sound radio) over which the Parties, and not the BBC or ITV have editorial control. If the Parties wish to change the name given to their sections of time and to put it to a rather different use I cannot see that we should have any objection. Rather the reverse. The very term Party Political Broadcast conjures up a picture of arid, often apparently irrelevant, party wrangling, and even perhaps encourages the use of time in this way. If the parties wish to make more constructive and illuminating use of their sections of time it cannot be anything but in the national interest to encourage the move.'

I was anxious, however, not to seem to be agreeing with those politicians and members of the BBC staff who wished to see Party Political broadcasts abolished altogether. So I also said:

'This does not in any way alter my own belief (stated in various papers) that the Parties and the Leaders of the Parties should have access by agreed *right* to time under their own control so that they can use this important medium of communication with the country. We are not re-considering therefore, the principle that time should be offered over which we surrender editorial control. Indeed, it would, in my view, not only be undesirable but impossible to do so effectively. If such time were not "offered", it would be demanded. The very difficulties there were over the Prime Minister's broadcast last week were an indication of this. The demand was made: we issued an "invitation". Such situations might recur: they are unhealthy. They must be avoided and the present proposition indicates a way of doing this.'

I added:

'I imagine that the main reason why the Prime Minister did not want his broadcast to be given under the title "Party Political Broadcast" was that he did not wish to talk to the nation as Leader of the Labour Party under a Party Ticket, but as Prime Minister representing the nation as a whole. But this was the very situation which the "Ministerial" type broadcasts were designed to meet. Historically the BBC has always showed in action that it cannot, and should not, try to prevent the Prime Minister, or any Minister nominated by him, addressing the nation as representatives of Government on matters of public importance on particular occasions. This right, however, has to be hedged around with safeguards otherwise it might lead to a monopoly over this method of communication and become a danger to freedom. Hence the complicated arrangements for "rights of reply" in case the Prime Minister (or Ministers) confused deliberately or otherwise his rôle as Leader of a Party with his national status as Prime Minister. The whole system of Ministerial broadcasts has fallen into some desuetude however, partly because in sound radio it was used too often on unimportant occasions (Post Early for Christmas) and it became as a result something of a joke as well as a bore and also because in television there were so many appearances of Ministers in ordinary current affairs programmes that they had an ample number of occasions in which they could present their policies without having to resort to Ministerials.'

I went on to point out that only in formal Ministerial broadcasts were Ministers normally able to give an unchallenged statement of their policies (in current affairs programmes they usually appeared in discussions or were interviewed) and that Mr Wilson's proposed 'Fireside Chats' did not in fact provide a substitute for Party Political broadcasting but for the largely disused 'Ministerials'.

Matters such as these could not be dealt with solely by the BBC and the Prime Minister. If there were to be formal changes in the rules about 'Ministerials' there would have to be fresh agreements between the political parties and the broadcasting organisations. The Director-General was inclined to think that the Corporation should wait for further initiatives from the parties. And the attitude of the Opposition was highly uncertain. Oliver Whitley, in a paper to the Director-General[3] pointed out that it would be difficult for

Opposition leaders to address the nation in the non-controversial way envisaged by the Prime Minister in his proposals for 'Fireside Chats'. The likely problems were also clearly stated by Trevor Lloyd Hughes, the Prime Minister's Press adviser, when he came to a routine lunch at Lime Grove on March 3, 1965. Although the lunch had been arranged some months earlier, it was impossible to ignore the Prime Minister's proposals for 'Fireside Chats'. Trevor Lloyd Hughes, who exuded shrewdness and common sense, made the following points:[4]

1 The Prime Minister wanted at times to use television to speak to the nation. The next time he would wish to do so would be likely to be in June 1965. These would be national occasions used for the national interest and would not contain controversial party material. The Prime Minister would welcome the Opposition being given similar time to be used in a similar manner.

2 The Opposition were in quite a different position from the Government. Even if they did not use the language of Party Political controversy to do so, the Government could argue that the Opposition were making Party capital out of a national situation if, in these television broadcasts, they opposed Government policy in specific matters.

3 The abolition of Party Political broadcasts would be more in the interest of a Government than an Opposition. Moreover both Party machines were likely to think it necessary to put out some hard-hitting Party programmes to encourage their own followers.

On March 26 the Director-General informed the BBC's Friday morning current affairs meeting that the present feeling in the Conservative Party appeared to be, broadly, to retain the present arrangements but to give Party Political broadcasts a different title. No action was, however, taken. The political parties were preoccupied with the need to prepare for another General Election. Mr Wilson's majority in the House of Commons was too small for him to be able to carry on for long, and the Conservatives were trying to adjust themselves to being in Opposition and to the personality of their new leader. In these circumstances the problems of 'Fireside Chats' and the future of 'Ministerials' remained in abeyance. Yet Mr Wilson's proposals were a kind of portent; the Labour Party had served notice that it was not satisfied with existent arrangements for broadcasting by political leaders.

The General Election, widely expected in the autumn of 1965, was not announced by Mr Wilson until February 28, 1966 and took place on March 31. Neither Mr Heath nor the Conservative Party stood a chance. When Sir Alec Douglas-Home resigned the leadership of the Conservative Party in July 1965 he said that he was going because a number of people thought that another leader was better able to win an election. But in March 1966 his successor, Edward Heath, was defeated and the Labour Party came triumphantly back to power with a greatly increased majority, 111 over the Conservatives, with Liberals getting twelve and 'Others' one.

The Conservative Party had not had enough time, even if it had the will, to demonstrate that it could be an effective Opposition, let alone a viable alternative government which would provide anything different from what it had done, or failed to do, during the famous thirteen years of Tory rule. And there was a further difficulty for the Party and for Mr Heath. The Party had to get used to a different style of leadership: Mr Heath had to establish himself as a public figure. In 1966 he was scarcely known to the British voter. In so far as the electorate was aware of him, it was in connection with complicated technical issues; at home, Resale Price Maintenance; abroad, the intricate negotiations in Brussels about the Common Market. He appeared frequently on television where he showed his concern for public opinion by his willingness to take infinite trouble to present viewers with a closely-argued and well-documented case.

Yet success on television eluded him. It was not that he disliked television, as Sir Alec Douglas-Home had seemed to do. His failure to use television to gain a strong personal following among the mass public was rather, I believe, because he seemed to expect each individual viewer to be as much animated by reason as he was himself. The result was that he shared his ideas with them, but not his feelings. So on television he appeared less human and less comprehensible than such obviously human political figures as Harold Macmillan, Aneurin Bevan, George Brown or Lord Hailsham.

Television adds a significant human dimension to political communication. The very fact that the man is there himself in close-up and that every viewer can form his own judgments about him, makes political assessments as a result of seeing a politician on the screen different from those which result from reading about him in newspapers or from studying his writings. Anyone who watches a Party

Conference on television, as distinct from watching the selected bits included in news and current affairs programmes, gets an unmistakable flavour of direct participation in a reality which seldom tallies with the second-hand versions obtained from reading even the best accounts in the best newspapers.

The absurdities, the eccentricity, the fervour which emanate from the floor; the quality of the rulings from the chair; the expressions on the faces of the leaders on the platform; the clamour from youth, as evident in their clothing and their hair styles as in their speeches, are unequalled as a portrayal of that part of British society which is interested in politics. This is the justification for the continuous (or near continuous) 'live' coverage of Party Conferences which was made possible when the BBC acquired a second channel. The succession of conferences held each year in the autumn, starting with the Trade Unions, going on to the Liberals, the Labour Party and Conservative Party Conferences, provide between them a picture of the state of Britain—particularly of the Britain where life is lived away from London and the South-East—which is worth any amount of contrived studio discussion in front of allegedly representative invited audiences.

As always, television is at its best when it is reflecting, through its outside broadcast cameras, a real world which it does not control but can only help to interpret. This is as true of politics as of show jumping. It is the most important argument in favour of the televising of Parliament. Informed comment is certainly as necessary for politics as for sport. But the televising of Party Conferences proved that it was possible (in spite of occasional difficulties) for informed comment to be combined with overall impartiality.

People who do not like television, sometimes because they are successful users of the written word and do not understand the different world of television, tend to say that television's success in reflecting political events such as Party Conferences is due to the fact that television is better at presenting personalities than policies. Behind such allegations there lies, in my opinion, an underestimation of the perceptions of the mass public. Voters do not want 'personalities' (e.g. the flamboyant and the publicity seekers) to govern them. They want men who can do the job and whom they can trust to do it honestly. Policies can change and often do, particularly when a party moves from opposition into office. The limitations upon power which are revealed by contact with a world which is independent of party opinion affects party thinking and changes of thought alter the arguments and the speeches.

The viewing public, aware of this as a result of the difference between what politicians argued yesterday and what they are arguing today, therefore pays attention not so much to what a man says on television as to the total picture of himself which he reveals in every tone, every gesture, every flicker of an eyelid when he answers a question. The mass electorate inevitably therefore judges not so much the changing arguments as the men who continue to put them forward. And trusts or distrusts them accordingly.

No one who worked closely with Mr Heath, as I did on television for many years, could fail to trust him. Highly professional himself, he respected the professionalism of others. Many politicians distrust broadcasters because they suspect them of conscious or unconscious party bias. Mr Heath trusted their professionalism just as he expected them to trust his own. The idea that they would allow their personal political beliefs to affect the lighting of a politician on television would never enter his head. Similarly he would not expect them even to consider the possibility, when he made a suggestion about a television broadcast, that he was trying to obtain a personal or party advantage at the expense of their duty to be impartial.

The problem for the Conservative Party, and for Mr Heath in so far as he considered it a problem, was how to extend to the nation the atmosphere of mutual trust which he created in his dealings with broadcasters. This raised within the party the whole question of party, as distinct from individual, identity. A Party is an embodiment of political principles and attitudes which a mass public can recognise and any Party leader, in addition to being an individual, has to be some kind of living symbol of the Party as a whole and of the voters who give it support.

But Mr Heath was not a recognisable symbol of the Conservative Party. He had not 'emerged' by the curious practice of consultation within the inner ring of the party as a result of which Sir Alec Douglas-Home had become Prime Minister in 1963. He had been elected by the complex system of balloting which had been agreed by the Party after difficulties about the succession had become so obvious at the 1963 Blackpool Conference.

In a sense, therefore, his personal position was strong. There could be no doubt that he was the Party's chosen leader. It had discarded tradition, in the shape of Sir Alec Douglas-Home, in favour of a new man of different origins. Mr Heath did not conform to any obvious Conservative pattern. He was neither a farmer nor an industrialist. He had inherited neither status nor wealth. He had been to a grammar school, not to Eton. He was a musician who had reached Oxford as a result of an organ scholarship. He liked sailing, not hunting. He had no connection with any of the great Tory or Whig families. He was unmarried. He had been a popular Conservative Chief Whip, had shown courage at the Board of Trade, and, during the Macmillan administration, had gained, in Brussels, the respect of his European colleagues. He was untiring, determined, a man of unimpeachable integrity, but an individualist who did not care for some aspects of Tory practice and who particularly disliked the old-school-tie network of influence which gained for some Tories positions of power, wealth and ease.

He was Conservative in politics; but why? In what kind of personal conviction was his Conservatism rooted? Mr Heath kept this to himself. He was prepared to display in public his public but not his private face. So even to Conservatives who loyally supported him as Party Leader he remained something of an enigma.

The four years from 1966 to 1970 were not easy for Mr Heath. After his defeat in 1966 he was expected to devise, in opposition, policies which would give a new look to Conservatism and yet not antagonise those multitudes of Conservative voters who hoped for political victory without significant social change.

Mr Wilson's problems were almost equally difficult: he had to convince not only the Labour Party but the Trade Unions, upon which so much of Labour's support and finance depended, that a party in government had responsibilities to the nation as a whole and not only to those who had worked for it when in opposition.

Both leaders, in a sense, were engaged in the delicate task of trying to educate their own parties without diminishing the enthusiasm of their most hardworking supporters. Television did not help them. They were bound, in a television age, to make policy statements to the nation on television, to appear in television current affairs discussions and to be interviewed in a variety of television programmes. But on television they were talking simultaneously to their own party members, their opponents, the floating voter, and to the world in general. What they said on television could affect financial centres in Paris and New York, cause a cancellation of orders for British goods and so create unemployment at home; increase the risks of war in Africa and the Middle East or heighten dismay in Gibraltar or the Falkland Islands.

Every Minister who appeared on television was aware of these complicated responsibilities. He must, for everybody's sake, watch his words. But if he did so, if he failed on television to give the rousing restatements of party principles which produced standing ovations at Party Conferences, he tended to disappoint his followers and so weaken the whole basis of his authority. When he gave Ministerial broadcasts or 'straight-to-camera' addresses to the nation, he had at least the advantage of being in charge. In discussions, he had to face those who questioned his assumptions and in interviews he had to deal with informed interviewers who could ask persistently for specific replies on subjects which had been omitted from the agenda of a Party Conference or, if raised, dextrously glossed over.

Television therefore tended to increase rather than diminish the problems of political leaders. But whereas the Conservative Party tended to blame Mr Heath, as they had blamed Sir Alec Douglas-Home, for not being 'better on television', the Labour Party, anxious to make use of television for political persuasion and the purposes of government, tended to find a scapegoat for their frustrations in the handling of broadcasting by the existent organisations.

The fact that within the Labour Party between 1966 and 1970 there was a growing desire to abolish both the BBC and the IBA and substitute for them institutions more to their liking did not become apparent until May 1970. But during these four years the party's resentment of the way in which the BBC dealt with political matters was already evident.

The frequent disputes between them were widely reported in the Press. On April 4, 1966, a headline in *The Times* ran 'Top Level Talks on the Prime Minister's Clash with the BBC'. On April 5, Robert McKenzie felt it necessary to write to *The Times* denying that the Prime Minister had any objection to being interviewed by him on television. On April 22, it was reported that Ian Mikardo, the Labour MP who was to be Chairman of the Labour Party Conference in 1971, and Chairman of the Parliamentary Labour Party in 1974, complained in the House of Commons that Ministers had exercised grossly improper influence with producers of television political programmes in order to induce them to include or exclude certain Members of Parliament from their programmes. The implication clearly was that the Prime Minister was trying to prevent representatives of the Left within the Labour Party, of whom Mr Mikardo was one, from making appearances on television. This implication was underlined by reports (e.g. in *The Times* on April 2, 1966) that the Chairman of the Independent Television Authority (then Lord Hill) 'had made some tactful concessions over the use of left wingers in current affairs programmes' and that these concessions had 'sweetened the atmosphere' as far as the ITA was concerned.

A number of separate threads can be discerned in regard to all this anger. One was the existence of important divisions within the Labour Party. As far as broadcasting was concerned the situation in 1966 was very much what it had been in 1951 at the time of the Bevanite split and the difficulties over 'In the News'. Should broadcasting organisations, in trying to present the political scene, pay attention to the different strands of opinion within a political party? Or should they ignore the dissidents and give access to television in current affairs programmes only to those who represented the opinions of the leadership?

To any experienced broadcasting producer the question scarcely required an answer. Broadcasters must reflect situations which exist; they are outside, not part of, the struggle to maintain the unity of any political party; they must therefore give proper, and carefully balanced, opportunities of expression to the different opinions within the party and not only to the central views of the party leadership.

But this inevitably infuriated those party leaders who were trying, with infinite patience and diplomacy, to hold together the differing groups within any political party. To such leaders, broadcasting became a spanner in the works. It was an enemy because it was not on their side. It was not helping them in their battle for unity and for what they felt to be sanity.

A situation of this kind was particularly hard for the Labour Party to bear. With its authority increased by its success in the 1966 election it was touchy about its treatment by broadcasters. There were a number of incidents when Labour leaders considered that they were being treated by television producers with less than the courtesy that they felt due to them. But the main dispute between the Labour Government and the BBC was more serious. It centred on the old problem of Ministerial broadcasts. The leadership of the Labour Party believed that the rules about Ministerial broadcasting had been changed: that during the years of Tory government fewer 'rights of reply' had been granted to Labour than were now being accorded to Conservatives.

Such a belief inevitably involved the BBC. Whether under the rules of the Aide Mémoire of 1947, or the new practice of 'invitations', the Corporation played an important part in making the decision about 'rights of reply'. Disputes about the fairness of these decisions not only drew attention to the inadequacies of the current arrangements for Ministerial broadcasts; they also highlighted the responsibilities of the BBC in regard to them. These were basically indefensible. It was not really acceptable in a parliamentary democracy that a broadcasting organisation should be placed in the position of having to adjudicate between representatives of the Government and of the Opposition about whether a Leader of the Opposition should, or should not, have the right to use television to reply to a broadcast by a Prime Minister. Some way must be found of limiting the responsibilities of the BBC without allowing the abuse by the executive of its legitimate access to television.

A review of the Aide Mémoire, therefore, was generally felt to be necessary. This was important but difficult. Ministerial broadcasts and the rights of the Opposition in regard to them lie at the heart of the relationship between broadcasting and politics. The rules of the Aide Mémoire of 1947, for all their faults, were in a sense an embodiment of the tradition which gave British broadcasting its distinctive quality. This tradition, based upon the recommendations of various Broadcasting Committees and endorsed by the decisions of Parliament, was that though broadcasting in Britain was ultimately responsible to Parliament it must be free from Government interference in its day-to-day running. The differentiation between Parliament and Government was crucial. Parliament included the Opposition. And the inclusion of the voice of the Opposition in major decisions concerning the control of broadcasting was an important factor in ensuring that in Britain no government would be able to dominate broadcasting as governments did in most other countries in which broadcasting was not dominated by commercial interests.

In Britain the need for broadcasting to be free from government domination was a bi-partisan decision. Minister after Minister in both Conservative and Labour administrations had reiterated the policy announced in the House of Commons on November 15, 1926 by the then Postmaster General, Sir William Mitchell-Thomson:

'While I am prepared to take the responsibility for broad issues of policy, on minor issues and measures of domestic policy, and matters of day-to-day control, I want to leave things to the free judgment of the Corporation.'

This freedom of broadcasting was linked to, and largely dependent upon, the British democratic and multi-party system. Under this, every Government must expect at some time to be in Opposition and would then wish to be able to use broadcasting to put its alternative policies to the nation. No party, therefore, wanted political censorship over broadcasting to be exercised by the Government of the day for this would merely recoil upon their own heads when they were in Opposition. Equally, to ensure broadcasting freedom and the broadcasting rights of the Opposition, Governments must not be in a position to appoint or dismiss the staff of broadcasting organisations or dictate to broadcasters how they must handle news or current affairs programmes.

So long as Parliament retained its ultimate power of control over broadcasting, which it did by its regular reviews of the Charters, Licences and Acts of Parliament upon which the very existence of broadcasting institutions depended, and so long as broadcasters observed the terms upon which Parliament insisted (e.g. that broadcasters should be impartial in their treatment of matters of controversy and refrain from expressing their own editorial opinions) an effective balance could be maintained between the power of the Government, of the Opposition and of broadcasters. But if Prime Ministers were able to use their right to broadcast whenever they thought fit to press their policies, however controversial, upon the nation, and if the Opposition were denied any right to use broadcasting to reply, then the control of broadcasting by Parliament as distinct from control by the Government of the day, would be threatened. And so would the freedom of broadcasting. Hence the importance of the rules of the Aide Mémoire of 1947. In effect they set limits upon the broadcasting rights of the Executive, were an assertion of those of the Opposition and gave a significant status to broadcasters.

The question during the years from 1966 to 1969 was whether the principles embodied in the 1947 rules could be maintained if these rules were altered in order to bring them more into line with current thinking. And, if the rules of 1947 were revised, whether it was necessary to provide some opportunity for a Liberal or a representative of any other minority party of similar strength to broadcast if the Opposition claimed, and obtained, a right to reply to a Ministerial broadcast. These negotiations took time. At long last, on February 25, 1969, the BBC circulated to its senior staff the agreed text of a new Aide Mémoire.*

At first glance the Aide Mémoire of 1969 looked very like the Aide Mémoire of 1947.† In fact the changes were radical: Ministerial broadcasts as defined in 1947 were virtually swept away. After 1969 the only Ministerial broadcasts of any significance were those in the 'second category' which, as defined in 1969, were not far removed from Mr Wilson's concept of 'Fireside Chats'. The power of the Prime Minister in regard to these major Ministerial addresses to the nation was increased and that of other Ministers reduced in that they could be given only by the Prime Minister or a member of the Cabinet selected by him; and the BBC was in a sense demoted since it no longer had the responsibility of adjudicating between the political parties when the Whips disagreed about rights of reply.

All these moves could be said to favour the Executive.‡ But one highly important change worked in the contrary direction. This was that the right of reply by the Opposition to a Ministerial broadcast became automatic. It was no longer subject to such hazards as agreement by the Whips or an adjudication by the BBC. There could not be a repetition of what had happened at the time of Suez— a determined effort to ensure that there should not be any formal broadcast expression of policies which were in opposition to those of the Government; after 1969 the views of the Opposition as well as those of the Government could, by right, be broadcast to the nation on those matters of policy which were the subject of Ministerial broadcasts in the important 'second category'.

This constituted a new check upon the possible abuse of the power of broadcasting by the Executive, for within days of a broadcast appeal to the nation by a Prime Minister, and usually on the following night, the official Opposition could be certain of being able

---

* For text of the Aide Mémoire of 1969 see Appendix B.

† For text of the Aide Mémoire of 1947 see Appendix A.

‡ The only limitation upon 'second category' Ministerial broadcasts was the pious hope that they would be 'normally infrequent': Prime Ministers no longer needed to depend upon the fiction of 'invitations' from the BBC when they wanted to broadcast to the nation.

to present its alternative policies to the viewing and listening public.*

Neither the Aide Mémoire of 1969, nor any of its possible consequences, caused the slightest ripple of interest in the Press or among the vast audience of viewers. This was not surprising. The phraseology of the Aide Mémoire seemed to have been designed, almost deliberately, to discourage public attention. And few viewers were likely to care whether the frequent appearances on their screens of Prime Ministers, Leaders of the Opposition and other politicians, were the result of editorial decisions made by those who ran such programmes as 'Panorama' and 'This Week' or a consequence of agreements like the new Aide Mémoire, which in certain cases left editorial control in the hands of the political leaders.

Even television producers, except the few who were concerned with the production of political programmes, were apt to find such matters as the relationship between Parliament and the Broadcasting Authorities remote from their immediate preoccupations with budgets and how to obtain a good 'slot' at a peak time for the programmes of drama, light entertainment, exploration, archaeology, or sport which they were making and which, at long last, seemed to have been agreed by the management.

Television producers, as well as most of the viewing public, had in fact come to take for granted the nature of British broadcasting and the freedoms upon which its quality depended. Even the announcement in May 1970 by the Minister of Posts and Telecommunications,† then John Stonehouse, MP, of the terms of reference of the Committee of Enquiry which was to be set up under the chairmanship of Lord Annan, Provost of University College in London, scarcely disturbed either viewers or producers, though they should have been a signal that the continued existence of the organisations which provided programmes for the public, and in which producers worked, could not be taken for granted.

It was normal procedure for a Committee of Enquiry to be

---

* It is worth noting that the new rules about Ministerial broadcasting continued to provide a viable solution for this central and difficult problem. As late as April 5, 1976, Mr Callaghan, the newly elected Prime Minister, gave a Ministerial broadcast from No. 10 Downing Street: on the following night, Mrs Thatcher, the Leader of the Opposition, replied, and the Liberal Leader, Mr Thorpe, took part in a discussion on April 7.

† The powers formerly exercised by the Postmaster General in regard to

appointed before any renewal of a BBC Charter; and the current
Charter and Licence were due to expire on July 31, 1976. What was
surprising was not the appointment of the Annan Committee but the
fact that its terms of reference were so wide. Whereas the Pilkington
Committee* had been obliged to assume, in making its recommendations, the continuing existence of the BBC and the ITA, no such
obligation had been imposed on the Annan Committee; this body,
therefore, could put the whole of British broadcasting into a melting
pot and recommend to Parliament something quite different from
anything resembling the kind of British broadcasting which so far
had existed.

The whole future of British broadcasting, it seemed, would now
depend upon the recommendations of the Annan Committee and the
attitude of the Parliament which considered them. Their decisions
would affect the quality of the programmes which the public
received; the nature and amount of television advertising; the size
of the licence fee or whatever alternative system of financing was
devised; the output from the regions; the future of local broadcasting; of programmes for schools and of the Open University; the
balance between light entertainment, drama, music, sport and programmes for children, as well as the rights and freedoms of all
producers, not simply those who dealt with news and current affairs.

But politics and broadcasting react upon each other in unexpected
ways. By the spring of 1970 the Prime Minister, Mr Wilson, was
considering June or October as possible dates for the next General
Election. Victory in June was beginning to look possible; the results
of the municipal elections indicated that there might be an overall
Labour majority of 50 in a General Election; and on May 12, 1970
a Gallup Poll showed a 7% Labour lead.[5] Rather than risk waiting
till October, Mr Wilson decided upon June. On May 18 Parliament
was dissolved. Polling took place on June 18. To the astonishment of
almost everybody except Mr Heath,[6] the Conservative Party was
returned with a clear majority of thirty over all other parties. By
midday on June 19, Mr Wilson admitted defeat; at 6.30 p.m. the

---

broadcasting were vested in the Minister of Posts and Telecommunications
in 1969 (Cmd. 4194).

* The BBC's current Charter, for the first time, had been granted for
twelve years, from 1964 to 1976 (Cmd. 2385). It was the result of Parliamentary consideration of the Report of the Committee on Broadcasting
under the chairmanship of Sir Harry Pilkington, set up in 1960.

Queen accepted his resignation; at 6.50 p.m. she asked Mr Heath to form a government.

This had an immediate effect upon the future of broadcasting in Great Britain. The Annan Committee had not yet met; no member, except the Chairman, had yet been appointed and one of the first decisions of the new Conservative Government was that it should be disbanded. To Conservatives, the only pressing matter of broadcasting policy appeared to be the introduction of commercial radio. Otherwise the years following upon 1970 seemed likely to be a kind of interlude in the development of the relationship between broadcasting and politics.

In fact, though in 1970 it was hard to believe, we were entering a period when drastic change began to seem possible, when the standards which the British people had come to expect from British broadcasting and its freedoms from government domination were seen to be in jeopardy, and it became evident that decisions made for short term political reasons might alter fundamentally, and irreversibly, the whole structure of broadcasting in Britain.

[17]

Into the Unknown

1970-1976

By 1970, when the Conservative Government and Mr Heath came into power, I had retired and was no longer actively engaged in trying to relate television to politics. But I found it impossible to stop being concerned about a matter which had occupied my mind for so many years. And I was dismayed by what was happening to that relationship. Indeed when, in 1970, some of my former colleagues in the BBC kindly gave me a dinner and, inevitably, we talked about broadcasting and the future of television, I felt myself to be a Cassandra crying doom.

There was no obvious reason for my unease; it was only that, underlying much of the talk I heard about television as I went around, there seemed to be some kind of resentment, like thunder in the air. Its causes were obscure: perhaps viewers, expecting more and more from television, nevertheless resented, obscurely, being so often at the receiving end of communication; perhaps producers, more and more conscious of their increasing skills, were becoming over-resentful of any sort of control, even of their ultimate accountability to Parliament; perhaps politicians, openly resentful of what they felt to be their over-casual treatment by television personnel, were, in fact, obscurely resentful of the medium itself and of the pressures upon them to make use of it.

My colleagues received my imprecise forebodings with a cheerful disbelief. This in itself was reassuring. *They*, clearly, had no sense of doom. Why should they? Things, apparently, were going so well. The Corporation had survived the shock of Lord Hill's arrival in 1967 as Chairman of the Board of Governors after the death of Lord Normanbrook. This was a Prime Ministerial appointment and the general gossip was that Mr Wilson had made it in order to humiliate the BBC and bring its forceful Director-General, Sir Hugh Greene, to heel. It was certainly an odd move. Lord Hill, once a well-known broadcaster on medical matters, had been a Conservative Minister and, from 1963 to 1967, Chairman of the Independent Television Authority. But by 1970 he was already revealing convictions which he was to declare in the House of Lords in 1974 after he himself had retired. He said:

'I deeply believe that the independence of the BBC is not only a great source of its strength but it is something which the rest of the world would wish us to retain. In my period as Chairman of both bodies (BBC and ITA) I travelled around the world a good deal. They knew, if it is not chauvinism to say so, that the broadcasting services in this country are by far the best in the world, and they also knew that an important element in that success was the independence of their organisations.'[1]

Lord Normanbrook's death and Lord Hill's appointment had, of course, broken up the Normanbrook/Greene team: a remarkable alliance between the wise, shrewd, politically experienced Civil Servant and the adventurous, determined, but equally shrewd and experienced journalist: but Hugh Greene, with some difficulty, had accepted the situation and by 1970 was working with the new Chairman, though not as Director-General but as a Governor of the BBC. So at the dinner which I had been given and during the conversation afterwards he was there, providing, as always, a sense of continuity, a presence of power and of confidence in the creative skill of broadcasters which made a mockery of my predictions of impending disaster.

And there were other reassuring factors. One, strangely enough, though at the time as much of a shock to what Lord Hill called 'both bodies' as his own move from the ITA to the BBC, was a re-allocation of the contracts of the commercial companies which provided television programmes for Independent Television. These changes, which Lord Hill had himself announced while he was still the chairman of the ITA, included the elimination of one existent company (TWW), its replacement by another (the Harlech consortium), as well as the creation of two new groups which would serve, respectively, some areas of Yorkshire which had hitherto been part of the Granada TV empire and London at weekends.

It was natural that this apparently somewhat arbitrary action by the ITA (it was much criticised in the Press) should cause an upheaval within Independent Television and protests from commercial television companies which felt that they had been unfairly treated. The BBC was, however, also affected. Aidan Crawley, who resigned his Parliamentary seat in order to become chairman of London Weekend Television, was joined as head of programmes by Michael Peacock, who gave up a senior post in the Corporation in order to be free to do so. With him went other members of the BBC's television production staff, attracted by the excitement of starting something new, developing their own ideas and also, hopefully, of having the chance, by acquiring shares in the company, of building up a certain amount of capital—something they felt to be impossible on their much-regulated BBC salaries. James Bredin had gone some time earlier to run Border Television. Geoffrey Johnson Smith and Chris Chataway had become Junior Ministers; and now one more of the young lions who had grown up within my erstwhile current affairs unit, Donald Baverstock, having already left the BBC with a good deal of huffing and puffing on both sides, became responsible for the development of programmes in the newly-established York-shire company and took a number of talented BBC people with him.

By 1970, however, all these disturbances had settled down into what was, in practice, a new and welcome stability within British television. There was a greater degree of intermingling between BBC and ITV personnel, a tendency for their standards to grow closer together, and for there to be more informed and less hostile discussion between them of each other's work.

In general the television situation seemed almost incredibly satis-factory. From the earliest days those who had political responsibility for the development of broadcasting in Britain had been haunted by two fears: one was that broadcasting might be dominated by the grosser forms of commercialism which would, they believed, lead to trivialisation and possibly to the corruption of men's minds; the other that it would be government-dominated with a consequent decline in respect for freedom and an essential step in any move towards dictatorship.

Such fears, apparently, were no longer necessary. As far as tele-vision was concerned, whether by accident, good fortune or native wisdom, Britain appeared to have succeeded in getting the best of all worlds. It had achieved a television system which embraced two vigorous bodies, each offering a wide diversity of programmes which fulfilled different needs, which were differently financed and dif-ferently motivated but which complemented each other. The BBC, rooted in its public service tradition, was the more likely to sustain that tradition and to attract those who wished to work in the atmosphere which it had created. ITV, engendered in a spirit of robust commercialism, had forced the BBC by its competition to be more flexible and more attentive to the wishes of its audience but had itself gradually been forced, as a result of public opinion expressed through Parliament, to become more socially responsible and to abandon some of the commercial practices which the television companies had adopted enthusiastically during the Fifties and Sixties when fortunes were being made and commercial television had seemed to be a gold mine. Both bodies could now be said to be operating in the public interest; both were ultimately responsible to Parliament; there was no government domination; and the grosser forms of commercialisation had been prevented.

Moreover, because the BBC was responsible not only for Home but External Broadcasting services, members of the Corporation's staff moved regularly between them; seniors such as Ian Jacob, Hugh Greene and Charles Curran,* before they became Directors-General, spent years in the polyglot world of Bush House, had to consider world reactions to world broadcasting and be sensitive to what was happening in Peking, Washington, Lusaka or Singapore; BBC foreign correspondents contributed both to its World and Home Services, to television as well as to radio; representatives of the External Services attended, along with representatives of sound radio and others, like myself, from television, the Friday morning meetings at Broadcasting House where BBC news and current affairs policy was shaped.

All this meant not only that what went on in the world was of direct concern to the Corporation but that the Corporation's traditions, standards and reputation influenced the world. Because its External Services had inherited from its Home Services the tradition of freedom from government interference in its day-to-day running, these services had never become, as in so many other countries around the world, a propaganda exercise dealing in distorted facts which soon, automatically, came to be disbelieved, but, instead, were regarded as a reliable source of information which millions, even in circumstances of danger, tuned in to hear when they felt that their own government-dominated broadcasts were telling them lies.

* Succeeded Hugh Greene on April 1, 1969.

The result was that British broadcasting was respected throughout the world; its personnel, as I myself found, were warmly welcomed in broadcasting circles wherever they went; what they said and thought mattered; their engineers and their production staff carried weight at every kind of international conference.

In addition to the, so to speak, world-conscious approach of the Corporation there was the rather differently orientated service provided by the IBA. The BBC was increasing its regional and local services but, if only because of its different basic structure, the emphasis of the IBA system upon regional interests was greater. So here, in an important area, ITV complemented the BBC and provided additional outlets for political appearances and political discussion. Although the BBC still continued to be responsible for the origination of Party Political, Party Election, Ministerial and Budget broadcasts, politicians appeared increasingly in Independent Television News and in such outstandingly responsible current affairs studies of people and politics as those transmitted every Sunday in 'Week-End World', a regular feature of the company in which, by 1971, John Freeman had succeeded Aidan Crawley as Chairman.

These developments were valuable. There were different treatments of political matters which threw different lights upon different subjects without any of them having to depart from an essential political impartiality; politicians were less dependent upon invitations from a single broadcasting organisation when they wished to express their views to the nation; and the competition between the BBC and ITV had become stimulating rather than destructive.

All this was true: and in 1970 I recognised its truth. Like Lord Hill, I believed that Great Britain had the finest broadcasting services in the world. And this opinion was not based upon what *he* thought or upon what anybody else thought but upon my own observations. During the long years since 1936 when I had watched the first programme of the first television service being transmitted from Alexandra Palace, again like Lord Hill, I had travelled widely, seeing television programmes being produced and talking to television people not only in France and Germany, Italy, Greece and Portugal, but also in such different Communist countries as Bulgaria, Yugoslavia and Czechoslovakia; I had watched television in Egypt and had been invited to lecture in Cairo to the entire staff of the Egyptian television service; had seen how television was managed in Mexico, attended television film festivals from Alexandria to

Acapulco, and discussed the making of documentaries with television producers from Japan, Argentina, Chile, Algeria and Albania; had spent three months—at the invitation of the State Department—studying the relationship between television and politics in the United States, sat beside Ed Murrow and Fred Friendly in New York while they made one of their 'See It Now' programmes, discussed television programme-making with the news and public affairs producers of the CBS and NBC as well as television policy with representatives of the Federal Communications Commission. And, as I moved slowly across the country from Washington, DC, to Salem, Oregon, I watched television programmes being produced everywhere, in immense studios in Hollywood and small Negro stations in Kentucky, in universities and public libraries as well as, from coast to coast, by shoe-string enterprises run by zealots who hoped to establish some kind of public service television in the USA.

Wherever I went the basic problems seemed to be the same: television services—or rather those responsible for establishing and running them—had made, or were still making, the essential decisions which had been faced by Britain in the late Twenties and early Thirties—should they allow television broadcasting to be dominated by governments or by commercial interests?

The United States had opted for commercial domination but was worried about some of the effects of that decision and was making a conscience-salving attempt to create a viable public service television network. This, though insecurely financed, operated by means of a number of independent stations ranging from the pioneering and highly talented WGBH in Boston to tiny adventurous organisations such as one I visited near San Francisco where I saw a staff of part-time enthusiasts opening the mail 'on camera' so that they could thank their supporters for the postal orders they had received that morning—donations sent to ensure that programmes of a quality which would have been routine in Great Britain might be seen by a handful of American viewers.

In dictatorships there was no problem; government control was taken for granted; and, though enforced with varying degrees of rigidity, was absolute. I knew that this would be so, yet I was startled, when visiting one of the less rigid of the Communist states and being taken on a tour of its studios, to find that on every floor as we got out of the lift we were faced by a soldier in uniform with a rifle slung over his shoulder.

Even in western democracies such as Italy and France government interference in television broadcasting—particularly in news and current affairs—was accepted, sometimes reluctantly and with a shrug of the shoulders, but, nevertheless, as inevitable. In Italy television staff, even down to the office boy, seemed to be changed whenever there was a change of government; in de Gaulle's France, when dining in Paris with an official of the United Nations, I was asked during dinner if I minded having the television set turned on to watch the news. When I replied 'Of course not. But why? We'll only hear what the government wants said', my host's answer was 'That's why I have to see it. It's the best indication we have of what's going on in de Gaulle's mind.'

Television staff envied the freedoms of British broadcasting. Many said, 'We admire your standards: but, of course, they wouldn't work here.' If I said, 'Why?' I got different answers. In commercially run stations a frequent reply was, 'We'd never get a sponsor': in government-dominated countries the reaction was usually simply another shrug of the shoulders and an indication that it would be better not to ask so many questions.

Summarising, in the United States television was business: apart from some of the newsmen, a section of documentary producers who admired the Murrow/Friendly approach and a number of those who produced programmes in universities and libraries, the greatest enthusiasts I met on my travels were the energetic young men who hoped to leave their jobs as television directors or 'front men' and become owners of television stations, thereby making, if not a fortune, at least a good deal of money.

Theirs was a cut-throat world; but their zeal, hard work, dedication and naivety were remarkable and endearing. They did not suffer from governmental pressures, looked vague if such possibilities were mentioned, and talked enthusiastically about getting sponsors for any programmes they might make. Few of them, however, thought about making programmes at all; small television stations took what they wanted from the networks on the best terms they could obtain, while they themselves put together the necessary amount of sustaining material and were interested only in the commercials.

One afternoon as I watched the rehearsal of a sponsored but inexpensive chat-cum-minor-light-entertainment show in a small station on the West Coast, the sponsor's agent, very much in evidence in the control gallery, constantly and peremptorily interrupted the director of the programme in order to give detailed instructions about how a girl singer should, while singing, display more effectively the product which was being advertised. Neither the singer nor the director seemed to mind. It was routine.

When I asked who was responsible for the programme, who had planned it and engaged those who took part in it, nobody seemed to know. The director had only just seen the script himself; perhaps the advertising department?—or the compère? He had no idea; nor, apparently, had anyone else. Control by sponsors was apparently as readily accepted there as control by government was in dictatorships.

In between these extremes came numbers of developing countries in which a television service was a prestige symbol, as necessary to the national pride as a national airline or a plant which supplied nuclear energy. But though necessary, television was expensive; instead of trying to make programmes themselves it was easier and cheaper to buy old American films: so the world was flooded from West Africa to South East Asia with ancient Westerns, hoodlums and gangsters, shootings and American slang.

I had always been conscious of the dangers of television and I had not seen these dangers in purely national terms. As early as 1947 when asked to write the television section of a book on mass communication I had begun by saying:

'Television is a bomb about to burst. Already in radio and film we have loosed upon the world forces which affect men's minds as powerfully, and possibly as dangerously, as the new weapons of war affect their bodies. Now, at a moment when we can still scarcely guess at the long term results of, say, American films upon the Asiatic mind, or propaganda broadcasting upon the inhabitants of Africa, we have upon our hands, and in our midst, this great new force, television.'[2]

This was prophecy—not proof. But awareness of danger had never been far from my mind and my travels abroad had tended to increase rather than diminish it. So, in 1960, I persuaded Richard Cawston to embark upon a mammoth project, a television documentary film which involved a study of the television services of twenty countries and was eventually transmitted in 1961 under the title of 'Television and the World'.

Dick Cawston, in my view, was the only television documentary producer (certainly at that time) who could undertake a task of such proportions; he had rare qualities; one was the total integrity of his approach to his subject. He would present, with a gifted professionalism, the facts as he found them; there would be no bias, no propaganda, no attempt to convince. Yet there would be style and a planned variation of interest, of light and shade and of speed.

He travelled twice round the world; first, by himself, to twenty of the eighty countries which by now had television services and then, with a camera crew, to film in the studios, the homes and the streets of those nine which seemed the most representative of different approaches to television. When I saw the rough cut I knew that the result was an impressive achievement and that we were justified in trying to make the programme.

Few of those, I believe, who saw it—and millions did—will ever forget some of its images; the gnarled fingers of illiterate Italian peasants as they tried laboriously to shape the letters of the alphabet while they were being taught by television to read and write; the hundreds of bewildered, upturned Egyptian faces as they watched in the streets of Cairo on a huge communal screen a sophisticated sex-comedy set in a luxurious penthouse apartment; or television in one of the shanty town shacks above Rio de Janeiro where a man was gazing entranced, like a child at a Christmas tree, at an exquisite blonde girl who sang as if to him alone, and his worn-out wife, sitting on a hard chair beside a bare table, continued to stitch with resigned, stoic, indifference.

None of this was faked; none of it 'reconstructed'; it was what Dick had found. He did not draw any conclusions, simply left it to those who saw the programme to make up their own minds about the impact of television, both socially and politically, upon the world scene. To me it was at once moving and terrifying. Those who watched seemed pathetically vulnerable. Perhaps they weren't. Perhaps they were so rooted in their own way of life, their own cultures, that television, reflecting as it did its own peculiar version of some aspects of the West, made no impression upon them at all. It was impossible to tell. Yet as I saw boats in Thailand drifting at night down the moonlit canals and from each of the quiet houses standing on stilts in the water there came the shattering sounds of gunshots, screams and galloping horses as mothers held up their children to watch an American Western, I felt that all this must be making an impact of some almost unimaginable kind.

I asked Dick for his own impressions. He was, as always, cool and factual. He said that in a remote part of Nigeria, where his film had shown villagers in the evening going to a thatched communal centre to see yet another cowboy adventure, he had talked to some of them. They did not, he said, distinguish between the nations of the West; it was all 'white man's country'; and equally they did not distinguish between fact and fiction or the present and the past. Westerns showed what was happening *now* in 'white man's country'; they were not a fictional representation of an imagined existence years earlier in part of America. One man, asked if he had ever been to 'white man's country', said no; but he would like to. Why? Because there men were strong and took what they wanted. A woman shrank back; no, she didn't want to go. Why? Because in 'white man's country' there was shooting all the time.

'Television and the World' added a new dimension of reality to the fears I had expressed in 1947. It was obvious by 1961 that the television bomb had in fact burst and that the social and political effects of television could not be kept within national boundaries. Those who made decisions about the creation and sale of television programmes had responsibilities which went far beyond any immediate effect upon viewers in their own countries: there seemed to be few correctives to the impact of unbridled commercialism upon peoples who were illiterate or cut off by poverty, distance, dialect and language from other influences, and who might well, as a result, come to believe that the kind of life at once violent and luxurious which the dream-world of television presented to them was not only existent and desirable but attainable.

But the main alternative to an unbridled television commercialism was an even greater evil: television used as an instrument of the will of a dictator. Commercialism, uncontrolled, might be harmful, but at least it was innocent; the harm it did was not intentional, simply an accidental by-product of television entertainment seen purely as a means of selling goods. Dictatorships were not in the least innocent; whether they were of the right or of the left, whether absolute or partial, whether intended to ensure the rule of a régime or an individual, whether reasonable or megalomaniac, they deliberately tried to use the instruments of communication, of which television was probably the most important, to ensure that no opinion other than their own should be heard, to limit the freedom of men's minds, to prevent facts being presented which did not endorse the validity of the courses they were pursuing, and above all to suppress, harshly, any expression of critical, let alone dissident, opinion.

It was with all this in mind that, during the years after 1970, I studied the developments of broadcasting in Britain, the ways in which television was being affected by political decisions and, in a changing political climate, how television was affecting politics. The more I saw of television, the more I compared the nature, standards and disciplines of television in Britain with those which obtained elsewhere, the more I became convinced that it was impossible to separate a consideration of television from a consideration of the political systems in which it operated, and, indeed, which it helped to create.

There seems, even though this is neither wished nor demanded, to be an inevitable interaction between television, political power and the way in which nations are governed. In the United States, with its almost obsessional hatred of government intervention in means of communication and its reverence for the forces of the market, television advertising techniques affected elections and were used during the 1968 Nixon campaign for the Presidency in ways which, as Joe McGinniss revealed in *The Selling of the President*,[3] shocked even some of those who were employed to put them into practice. They certainly shocked even such an experienced observer as Alastair Cooke, who described the McGinniss book as a 'terrifying account of what happens to a Presidential candidate in an age which regards the advertising man as an important and natural ally of the politician'.

The methods actually used, and vividly described, were certainly terrifying in the Orwellian sense: here, in a democracy, was a deliberate attempt to manipulate men's minds in order to ensure the placing of a particular individual upon a pinnacle of power. It was easy to dismiss such methods as something that couldn't happen here. But British political parties had already employed advertising men to assist in the making of their television election programmes.[4] In any case, was not the use of television advertising techniques to sell a President or a Prime Minister simply a logical development of a triumphant commercialism?

In 1970 the Conservative Party, now in power, was committed to the introduction of commercial radio and was campaigning for the allocation of a fourth television channel to commercial interests. I did not for a moment believe that the Party wanted television adver-

tising techniques to be used in Britain in the way they had been used
by the Nixon team during the 1968 Presidential election: what did
alarm me was the possibility that Conservatives might pursue policies and set up institutions which, however unintentionally, might
bring television electioneering practice in Britain nearer to that
which was already operating in the United States.

And I felt a similar, but opposite, alarm about the attitudes to
television of the Labour Party. Labour leaders constantly said that
they rejected any operational system for radio and television which
was based upon government censorship. Yet, however sincerely this
might be held as a principle, it seemed to me that, given the disapproval which some of them made no attempt to conceal about the
way in which the mass media handled political matters, their
resentment of criticism and their continued allegations that Conservatives were given a better television showing than those who led
or supported Labour, they might, when in power, not only seek to
destroy such existing institutions as the BBC and the IBA but replace
them by others, which, however unintentionally, might result in
government censorship of all the main means of communication,
including television.

Crucial decisions were likely to be taken soon and would certainly
be political. It was important that they should be made by Parliament for long-term national and international reasons rather than
taken in a hurry by whichever party happened to be in power in
order to serve immediate or future party interests. Parliament, over
the years, had shown great wisdom in its handling of broadcasting
matters; it had laid down conditions for the use of the 'national
property' which made certain that broadcasting and broadcasters
should be ultimately responsible to the representatives of the people
assembled in Parliament and yet had made equally certain that they
should be free from government interference in the making of programmes and day-to-day running; it had accepted a degree of
commercialisation but had forbidden sponsorship and ensured that
commercial television practices should be in the overall charge of a
body acting in the public interest. Parliament, surely, could be
trusted to be equally wise at this important time when each of the
main political parties, acting separately, might be tempted to try to
placate those elements within the party which wanted strong action
in regard to broadcasting, whether this action was to give greater
freedom to commercial interests or a greater power to a political

party, when in government, to create institutions which would ensure the perpetuation of the kind of society that particular party had approved when in opposition.

Much depended upon whether the basically bi-partisan policy which Parliament had displayed in regard to broadcasting for something like fifty years could be maintained at a moment of high political tension at home and revolution abroad. That remained to be seen. Meanwhile the new Conservative Government, as might have been expected, pressed on with its plans for commercial radio. During 1970 and 1971 there were conversations about them between the Chairman of the Governors of the BBC, Lord Hill, and Christopher Chataway, by then Minister of Posts and Telecommunications,[5] and in March 1971 a White Paper was published which proclaimed the Government's intention to authorise the setting up of sixty commercial radio stations in addition to the twenty local radio stations already in existence. In June 1972 a Sound Broadcasting Act extended the functions of the Independent Television Authority (now renamed the Independent Broadcasting Authority) to include the provision of local sound broadcasting services.

There were other urgent broadcasting problems: the allocation of the so-called fourth television channel; the continuing, but unsettled, question of the televising of Parliament; the clamour for a more complete and more effective radio and television coverage in English rural areas as well as in Scotland, Wales and Northern Ireland; and the need to consider what should be done, now that the Annan Committee had been disbanded, about the renewal of the BBC's Charter and Licence.

Some of these matters were dealt with at speed; but on the whole the Conservative Party, always more interested in government than in communication, seemed ready to leave broadcasting to the professionals and to those sections of the party which hoped that it would be possible for money to be made not only out of commercial radio but from a fourth television channel.

So the campaign for the allocation of the so-called 'spare channel' to the existing television commercial companies continued, apparently with official Conservative blessing; and television professionals continued to cope with the normal but exacting task of adjusting television services to the rapidly changing social and technological circumstances in which they operated.

There was a greater devolution of programme authority to the regions and to local stations, the need for which was emphasised by the Report of the Crawford Committee* and which, as the Committee pointed out, was more necessary for the BBC than for ITV since the latter's structure, in any case, was more regionally based; multitudes of 'talk-in', 'phone-in' and 'Open Door' programmes were created in order to give viewers a chance of presenting their own cases, putting their own questions and their own opinions; there was the remarkable development of the Open University, a government-backed alliance between the BBC and the academic world which enabled students to gain degrees by means of courses in which television broadcasts played a major part; there were all the problems of the demand for the extension of colour, with its engineering, programme, design and financial implications; there had to be an assessment of the value of cable television; there was the need to estimate the impact both upon scheduling and party political broadcasting of the home recording of television programmes which cassettes already made possible and video discs might make differently possible in the future, of the increasing opportunities for satellite broadcasting and the political dangers of direct broadcasting by satellite into people's homes; the finalising of such devices as CEEFAX which allowed viewers with suitable attachments to their sets to punch up at will (and without any interruption of ordinary programme transmission) a variety of tables of information ranging from the latest news and sports results to the most recent weather forecasts.

These routine duties kept television professionals busy enough. But there was no longer any immediate threat of a major disruption of the kind which the wide terms of reference given to the now disbanded Annan Committee had seemed to foreshadow. The Conservative Government, as far as broadcasting was concerned, seemed anxious to avoid trouble. In 1971 it consulted the Television Advisory Committee, that high-powered body which could be called upon for information about technical matters, and by 1972 the Committee reported that no major technical developments were likely before the early 1980s. So by 1973, the Government was able to announce that a major enquiry into broadcasting was not necessary at the present time and that it intended to extend the Charter of the BBC and the period covered by the Television and Sound Broadcasting Acts, all

* See below.

due to expire in the near future, until 1981. The result was an almost audible sigh of relief: the essential but orgiastic rite of pulling broadcasting up by its roots every now and then to see how it was getting on would apparently not now start till around 1978: everyone could settle down to getting on with their work.

The Government certainly, in May 1973, set up a special broadcasting Committee under the Chairmanship of Sir Stewart Crawford 'to examine the Broadcasting Authorities' plans for the coverage of television and sound broadcasting services in Scotland, Wales, Northern Ireland and rural England, bearing in mind the particular needs of the people in those areas'. This was, however, an enquiry with a precise and limited objective, a necessary recognition of the fact that parts of England, as well as Scotland, Wales and Northern Ireland, wanted less 'Londonisation' in their broadcasting and more say in determining the nature of the programmes which they received.

It was interesting, however, that, according to the Committee,[6] the pressure 'for television to help to assert and reflect national or regional identities' came not from viewers 'but from those concerned with policy, whether political parties, language societies, regional associations or Government authorities'. What viewers wanted was something rather different. The Committee made this clear by saying, 'The availability of television services has come to be considered as a condition of normal life, and people now expect these services as they do those of basic public undertakings, such as electricity or water' and that people living in areas which did not have good television services felt deprived. The sense of deprivation in such circumstances was emphasised. 'The central point made to us . . . taking the country as a whole, was the importance attached to good reception of television services' and it went on to say, ominously, 'the fillip given by the availability of colour reception has made those who are still not served feel increasingly resentful at their deprivation and those who have a poor service . . . increasingly bitter at being required to pay the full licence fee'.

The demand for television and the sense of deprivation if it should not be available were understandable. Few people who live in cities and move in sophisticated circles are able to comprehend the degree to which television, for those living in any kind of isolation, whether rural or urban, the elderly, the immobile, the poor and the lonely, mothers anywhere who cannot leave their young children, provides not only entertainment and information but a sense of being in contact with the world and with other people. This was what made television seem a necessity rather than a luxury. But it was clear from the Crawford Report that viewers not only wanted television but expected the best services (in colour) and were sensitive about cost.

This sensitivity to cost at a time of inflation presaged difficulties for the future, not so much for the IBA as for the BBC, since the IBA, as had been pointed out to me many years earlier, could itself put up revenue by increasing advertising rates, whereas the BBC could not, without Government permission, increase the size of the licence fee upon which its finances depended. In July 1971 the Government authorised an increase in the licence fee to £7 a year for monochrome and £12 for colour. This meant that, with the rapid growth in the demand for colour, the BBC at the end of 1973 was in the black instead of being in the red.

But the respite could only be temporary. The costs of television were rising alarmingly. A main cause was inflation: but another was the expectation of the British public that television would get better and better, not only technically but in the nature, quantity and variety of the programmes which were transmitted. This apparently insatiable public demand was strengthened by the power of the creative producer in British television. Producers with ideas (and there were few who did not believe that their ideas were valuable and that it was their right, rather than their privilege, to use television to express them) wanted to stretch television resources to the limit and felt frustrated if what they believed to be essential resources were denied or if the budgets for their programmes were restricted.

The combination of public and producer demand for more resources for more and better television and therefore for more money posed great problems for the political parties in their handling of broadcasting issues. If there had been no, or only minimal, inflation the increasing costs of television might conceivably have been contained. But during a period of rapid inflation the financing of television became an acute national difficulty. If viewers really wanted, as the report of the Crawford Committee seemed to indicate, television on the cheap but not cheap television, the end of the road must be an increase in commercialisation. No political party wanted to face the country with the need for a continual rise in the licence fee and, since the revenues of commercial television came not from licence fees but from advertising, its costs were concealed from the individual viewer and its expenditure could be increased without causing any public disturbance.

This situation was less difficult for Conservatives than for Labour. There was no sign that Conservative leaders wanted to abandon the public service principle in British broadcasting or to destroy the BBC: but, equally, there were few signs that they would be broken-hearted if their policies for increasing the commercialisation of broadcasting had, in practice, this result. Anyway, in 1973 they could forget the matter: major decisions about broadcasting had been postponed; and the campaign for a second commercial channel could be continued without any need to be bothered about the possible consequences of its success.

For the Labour Party the future of broadcasting and the methods by which it was financed were of altogether greater concern. The prospect of any further abandonment of systems of communication to commercial interests was anathema. Not only that. Many Labour leaders believed not only that the Press but existing broadcasting organisations were tilted against Labour. So, shocked by their unexpected defeat in 1970, and just as convinced that 'the media' must have been one of the causes of defeat as the Conservative Party had been in 1945 and 1964, they were not content to accept any kind of stability in broadcasting arrangements; they wanted, instead, complete change.

In 1972, therefore, the powerful Home Policy Committee of the Labour Party under the chairmanship of Anthony Wedgwood Benn 'convened a meeting to discuss the media and communications and their relevance to a democratic socialist society'.[7] These meetings continued throughout 1973 and the early months of 1974 under the chairmanship of Mr Benn until, in March 1974, he was appointed Secretary of State for Industry in the new Labour Government (and for a few weeks was also Minister of Posts and Telecommunications).

During the years between 1972 and 1974 the ideas which were being engendered within Labour's Home Policy Committee began to leak out but were not taken very seriously by broadcasters. It was said that a group of those on the left of the Labour Party hoped to abolish not only the licence fee but the BBC and the IBA and take over the running of all broadcasting in Great Britain. They intended, so the story went, to finance broadcasting by seizing the revenues of the commercial companies and distributing these to whatever suitable groups they selected to produce radio and television programmes.

Tales of this kind were discounted: they couldn't be true: anyway it could never happen: the country would never allow a great national asset to be destroyed in this way: British broadcasting was admired throughout the world: here, at least, Britain was pre-eminent: these stories were absurd, or at least a wild exaggeration.

The full truth did not begin to appear until after the victory of the Labour Party in the General Election of February 1974. The Conservative defeat was more absolute than it looked on paper: Labour, certainly, had gained only four more seats than Conservatives and fewer votes had actually been cast for Labour than for Conservatives in the country as a whole; but in the House of Commons the Opposition parties were fragmented (37 seats were held by Liberals, Scottish and Welsh Nationalists and others) so that the Labour Party, in practice, was now, very firmly, the Government. Moreover it looked like being so for some time. For in the hope of confirming Labour's position as the party of government, Mr Wilson called another General Election in October 1974, and once again defeated the Conservatives.

The Conservative Party, twice defeated in a single year, was also in considerable disarray. Mr Heath's leadership was challenged and after two ballots in February 1975 he was replaced as Party Leader by Mrs Margaret Thatcher. The Party, once more, had to reshape its policies and accustom itself to a new style of leadership. Meanwhile the Labour Party, triumphantly if precariously in office (precariously since its overall majority still depended upon how the various minority parties in the House of Commons chose to vote on any particular issue) pursued vigorously in Government the policies it had developed when in Opposition.

One of these was its policy about broadcasting. No time was lost. The Home Secretary, Mr Jenkins,* announced in the House of Commons that the BBC's Charter and the Broadcasting Authority Acts, instead of being extended until 1981 as the previous Conservative Government had suggested, should now, he proposed, last only until July 1979. He also announced immediate action of another

---

* The broadcasting responsibilities of the Minister of Posts and Telecommunications had been transferred by the new administration to the Secretary of State for the Home Department.

kind—the re-appointment of the disbanded Annan Committee. Its terms of reference were no less wide than those which it had been given in 1970:* its deliberations were expected to take about two and a half years and another two and a half years would be spent in a consideration of its findings and the enactment of legislation.

By 1974, therefore, British broadcasting was back in the melting pot. Moreover the respite for broadcasters was shorter than it looked: preparation of both oral and written evidence for the Annan Committee had to begin at once since the whole future of broadcasting in Britain might depend upon the Committee's recommendations and those presumably would be finalised towards the end of 1976. So between 1974 and 1976 'preparing for Annan' occupied a good deal of the time of broadcasters and, for anyone who had studied the history of the relationship of broadcasting to politics, it was evident that behind these necessary labours lay another and disturbing possibility.

This was that when the Committee's recommendations were made public the Government might ignore them or use them as an excuse for the policies it was in any case determined to pursue. After all, the Conservative Government in 1954 had largely ignored the majority report of the Beveridge Committee and had based its introduction of commercial television and its breaking of the BBC's monopoly upon the minority report of a single member of the Committee, that eminent Conservative, Mr Selwyn Lloyd. Might not the Labour Government in 1977 behave in a similar manner and select from the Annan Committee's report whatever suited its own broadcasting intentions?

In May 1974 these intentions were laid open for public discussion. The Labour Party published a pamphlet entitled 'The People and the Media' with a foreword by Ron Hayward, the Party's General Secretary. The suggestions put forward dealt with the organising and financing of the Press and of broadcasting and differed very little from the conclusions arrived at by the Party's Home Policy

---

*The terms now ran:

'To consider the future of the broadcasting services in the United Kingdom, including the dissemination by wire of broadcast and other programmes and of television for public showing; to consider the implications for present or any recommended additional services of new techniques; and to propose what constitutional, organisational and financial arrangements and what conditions should apply to the conduct of all these services.'

Committee. Moreover since, shortened, they were presented to the Annan Committee as the Party's evidence, there was every likelihood of their becoming the official policy of the Labour Government.

In essence the plan proposed for broadcasting was that the BBC and the IBA should be replaced by two 'agencies', a Communications Council and a Public Broadcasting Commission. The Communications Council would be government-funded, would 'keep the operation, development and inter-relation of all the mass media under permanent review',[8] have its own staff and resources, and, although not an executive body, would be able to investigate issues involving more than one medium 'such as a possible subsidy of one medium by funds levied from another'.[9]

How this Council should be appointed and how its members should be chosen was not made very clear, but it was indicated (see page 5 of the Press Release under the heading 'Accountability') that it should be composed of 'elected representatives from major sections of the community' and that it would include 'representatives from trade unions and from local government as well as some MPs'.

In contrast, the Public Broadcasting Commission *would* be an executive body. Its major responsibility would be the collection and allocation of broadcasting finance (including the collection of advertising revenue). The licence system would be 'phased out, commencing with the freezing of the licence for monochrome TV, followed later by its complete abolition'. The Commission, at a later stage, could 'review the position of the colour TV licence'.

Neither of these bodies, however, would do any actual broadcasting or itself be concerned with making programmes, with detailed scheduling or with transmission. Indeed the essential questions of where programmes were to come from, who was to make them, how they were to be transmitted, on what days, at what length and in what order they were to be presented to the public, seemed scarcely to have been considered, let alone answered. It was said (page 4) simply that 'Programme-making itself would be carried out by a wide variety of dispersed programme units reflecting the creative talent of all parts of the UK'. And the document went on to say 'One possibility, suggested in "The People and the Media", would be to organise the output of these dispersed programme units through two television corporations, each responsible for running one national and one regional channel. The PBC* would provide

* i.e. The Public Broadcasting Commission.

minimum co-ordination to avoid duplication of programmes, and would supervise the broad allocation of programming in different categories.'[10]

The whole aim of the scheme in so far as it was possible to judge from the documents, was to separate the control of broadcasting in Great Britain from the making, organisation and presentation of programmes. This was what had already happened to a large extent in countries where broadcasting was dominated by an unbridled commercialism. In such cases the ultimate control was the desire to make money; therefore the making of programmes was subordinated to the controlling powers of the accountants, the businessmen, the sponsors and the advertisers, whose decisions about programmes were paramount and whose judgments were based on the money-making potential of any particular programme idea.

In considering the new scheme for broadcasting put forward by the Labour Party it was necessary to judge what desires lay behind the ultimate broadcasting controls which were proposed. I believed that it was possible to discern a number. Some were bound up with general party attitudes and, indeed, with changing world attitudes, to authority, tradition and the exercise of power. Broadcasting, and in the 1970s this increasingly meant television, was regarded by a number of politicians and by the politically minded as a method of exercising power in order to change society rather than as a new method of communication which allowed mankind to see things happening at distances beyond the reach of the human eye.

Hence the emphasis in the Labour Party documents upon controls rather than upon programmes. Those who drew up these plans were, apparently, less concerned with television's ability to extend experience than with the ways in which it could be used to ensure the creation and perpetuation of social systems which the Labour Party approved.

I use the term 'perpetuation' with some deliberation in order to emphasise what I considered to be the most important aspect of the Labour Party's broadcasting proposals as made public in 1974: this was their insistence upon the creation of new institutions rather than the modification of old ones. Changes must be root and branch: there must be no opportunity for backsliding: the creation of new institutions could make any basic alterations in the proposed new controls over television as difficult as denationalising a nationalised industry.

The Labour Party, in fact, by its proposals, was facing Parliament and the British people with the task of deciding whether existing broadcasting institutions such as the BBC and the IBA were, or could be made, capable of adapting themselves and their output to the changing social and political needs of the last years of the twentieth century or whether the radical changes outlined in the Labour Party's plans would, in practice, result in an improved broadcasting service and one more attuned not only to present but to future demands.

This task was momentous enough, since, as I had discovered and have tried to show in this book, it is virtually impossible to separate the methods by which television is controlled in any country from the way in which that country is governed. Each, inevitably, affects the other. Labour Party plans for the reorganisation of broadcasting had, therefore, to be considered not only from the point of view of how they would affect the freedoms of broadcasters and the nature of broadcasting programmes but, more importantly, of how they might affect the conduct of politics in Great Britain.

The essence of the British system in both politics and broadcasting was the ultimate authority and responsibility of Parliament. Could it be that this was now, in effect, being questioned? Could the desire, evident in some sections of the Labour Party, that the National Executive, expressing the wishes of the Labour Movement as a whole rather than the Parliamentary Labour Party, should determine the actions of a Labour Government, be linked with the wish to set up new television institutions? The BBC and the IBA were expressly and clearly responsible, ultimately, to Parliament, and through Parliament to the electorate. Was it significant that in the Labour Party's broadcasting plans there was so little mention of Parliament or the need to maintain Parliament's ultimate responsibility for broadcasting? Were these new broadcasting plans, in fact, intended to ensure that broadcasting would be responsible not to Parliament but to the National Executive of the Labour Party? And that broadcasting should be an instrument of the National Executive in its struggle for political authority in the country?

Speculations of this kind, however wild, were bound to be created by the tone of some of the Party's publications about its plans for broadcasting. What was certain, however, was that the crucial decisions following upon the publication of the Annan Committee's Report would in fact be made by Parliament and that many of the statements in the Labour Party's documented plans were reassuring. A main example occurs on Page 8 of 'The People and the Media';[11] it was 'reiterated that the Labour Party absolutely rejects any policy for the mass media, or any system for operating it, that is based upon government censorship or central control. It is equally opposed to the monopoly domination of the media by direct or indirect commercial influences whether through advertising, or other concentrations of power which interfere with free communications.'

But these were the established principles which had governed the practice of British broadcasting since 1926. It was valuable that they should be reasserted in 1974. As I have tried to show, however, the problem does not lie in the acceptance of this aim but in how to achieve it and how best to resist the day-to-day pressures from both political and commercial interests, which, if not resisted, could prevent that achievement. What was now required was that an informed Parliament, with this declared aim firmly in mind, should decide how the proposed new institutions would be likely to assist rather than to hinder the achievement of so firmly stated a purpose.

I myself believe that the problems of the relationship between television and politics are more profound, more deeply rooted and perhaps more disturbing than any of the manifestations of dissatisfaction with existent broadcasting organisations set down in 'The People and the Media'. The fact is that a number of politicians of all parties, backbenchers as well as leaders, and some of the men and women who speak for industry and the unions, feel diminished by the need to appear on television and resentful of the circumstances in which such appearances take place. They carry great responsibilities: in normal circumstances, outside television, the scale of these responsibilities is recognised by the way in which they are treated and the accustomed formalities with which they are encompassed. Parliament has its mace-bearers, the Speaker his robes; at Party Conferences and Trade Union Congresses leaders sit on the platform; a good speech receives an ovation and even a poor one can be expected to be greeted with polite applause.

Much of all this, no doubt, is nonsense and some of the trappings are false, ridiculous and unnecessary. Nevertheless they are a reminder of the importance and responsibilities of the office to which the holder, temporarily, has been appointed (or elected) rather than an attempt to flatter the ego of the fallible human being who happens at this moment, rightly or wrongly, to be in occupation of that office.

On television such visible signs of office and such reminders of responsibility normally do not exist: Her Majesty's Secretary of State, a member of the Cabinet as well as a Member of Parliament, whose decisions can affect war and peace, the life or death of individuals, the prosperity, pensions and education of millions, on television is simply another figure who appears on the screen in the sitting room, often an elderly gentleman who answers questions, more or less well, put by a professional interviewer, or reads, more or less satisfactorily from a teleprompter, a somewhat stilted and often obviously biased speech.

The fact is that, on television, it is almost impossible for politicians to reveal the great qualities they frequently possess. Viewers in the main are not aware of these qualities, have no experience of carrying the weight of vast political responsibilities and little understanding of what is involved in trying to do so. To them, watching comfortably at home, it all seems easy. Why can't politicians speak more frankly and say just what they mean? They're only being asked to talk: anybody can do that. Why make everything so complicated and quote so many statistics? Why do they always blame someone else for what goes wrong? Politicians are pretty boring anyway; do switch him off and try another channel; there might be football or snooker, or 'Come Dancing' or 'Top of the Pops'.

To politicians, often working long hours seven days a week, travelling, sitting on committees, attending meetings in their constituencies, listening to grievances, looking up facts, preparing to make speeches which are seldom heard, replying to attacks by their opponents, shaping policies to which they hope someone will pay attention, or, if in office, making decisions which are often intolerable, since right is on both sides, and the true facts about which cannot be revealed since they might jeopardise delicate negotiations, television appearances often seem the last straw. They are forced to accept almost any invitation from the television organisations. Television is too important (or is felt to be so) to be ignored, and the medium being what it is, that means appearing, however embarrassing, tiresome and exhausting such appearances may be.

And the rewards are dusty: it is difficult for a political leader to tell whether a television interview or speech has been a success: at the end there is no ovation, no applause, probably only an unconvincing murmur of congratulation from the producer, an invitation to go to his dressing-room and have his make-up removed, possibly a drink and a sandwich, while the studio is being re-set for tomorrow's light entertainment show, and while viewers at home hail with relief the end of his vital message to the nation since they can now settle down to watch 'Match of the Day'.

Dissatisfactions of this kind create a disturbing situation. By 1976 a significant number of leading politicians, resenting the increasing demands which television made upon them, occasionally feeling, as a few of them said, 'pushed around' by the professionals, angered by the self-righteous tone of some television interviewers and by such lapses as the BBC's 'Yesterday's Men'[12] (a foolishly-clever undergraduate-type programme presented ostensibly as a serious study of Labour in Opposition which seniors in the Labour Party never forgot or forgave) tended to blame neither the medium nor their own desire to make use of it, but the organisations to which Parliament had delegated its broadcasting responsibilities for everything that went wrong in their attempts to use television to communicate with the nation.

On the other side of this coin was the attitude of viewers who, with little experience of the complexities of the problems governments have to deal with, nevertheless made important judgments about political leaders which were based very largely upon what they saw of them addressing the nation, or being interviewed, on television.

The result was that powerful sections of the Labour Party, at a time when Labour was firmly established in office, had become so impatient that they wished to abolish existing broadcasting institutions; and that there seemed to be a great deal of cynicism about politics among a mass public already disposed to be cynical.

By the spring of 1976 it appeared to me, therefore, that the most vital question in the whole relationship between television and politics in Great Britain was whether the conditions in which politicians made their political appearances on television, and the form which these appearances normally took, were an aspect of the medium itself and could not be altered, or whether they could be modified or complemented so that television reflected more accurately the difficulties political leaders had to deal with in their exercise of power and by doing so was able to give viewers more complete and comprehensive evidence upon which to base their judgments.

Making such an assessment involves a return to first principles. Television is not likely to go away: the reasons why politicians are bound to make use of it, particularly in democracies where governments rely on persuasion rather than force, is that, alone among the media, it allows them to appeal simultaneously, directly, visually and orally to millions of individual voters in their homes.

I have argued in earlier pages that television is essentially a democratic medium since it extends to millions privileges which in the past were available only to the few and gives every individual voter a chance of judging in close-up the quality of those men and women who are seeking his support. Nobody, I believe, can deny that, as a result, television has made a new and valuable contribution to the machinery of democracy. But very little attention has been paid to the limitations upon communication which are imposed by the domestic nature of television reception.

Most television is watched either by single individuals or small groups on small screens in their own sitting rooms. From the earliest days of television, as I have tried to show, this meant that communication on television could be, and much of it *had* to be, direct, informal and friendly, and that its style was bound to be appropriate to the appearance of the speaker as a temporary guest in somebody's house, one who could be dismissed, without discourtesy, by the turn of a knob if he became boring, bombastic or supercilious, or went on too long.

This informal style has been adopted, therefore, by most givers of television news, by the weathermen, by studio commentators, by those who introduce or compère programmes, and, inevitably, by politicians who use television to address the millions of viewers who compose, virtually, the nation. The way in which television interviews and discussions are conducted, again from the first, has been influenced by this style: the individual viewer at home is not physically present but he is always there, an unseen and unheard participant, and the circumstances of these interviews and discussions are designed to make him feel that this is so. Such occasions, therefore, are also informal; when taking part in them Ministers of the Crown do not wear knee-breeches, bishops their vestments or soldiers their medals. Authority and responsibility are not signalised by any outward forms: an interviewer may call a Prime Minister 'Sir' but in the main he is treated simply as another human being.

Occasions of this kind are of value; they assist the voter in making his political judgments because they allow him to assess political leaders in areas which are very much within his own competence and experience. I have said earlier that because the individual viewer, who is also a voter, has to make judgments about people every day of his life his judgments about politicians as people to be trusted or distrusted—judgments made as a result of seeing them being interviewed or taking part in television discussions—are likely to be shrewd.

But what the viewer gets in this way is a very limited view of politics and politicians. This is because politicians are so frequently seen in specially organised television situations and so seldom in action in their own working surroundings. It is as if followers of football were asked to judge the calibre of a footballer from the television interviews he gives before or after a match, and from the opinions of journalists and 'experts', without having any opportunity of seeing him play.

Yet such opportunities could be as available for politicians as for footballers. They are a commonplace in every kind of television programming which involves the use of outside broadcast television cameras to reflect actual events of which each viewer, by means of television, simply becomes an additional spectator who happens to be watching at home. They include not only royal occasions of all kinds but every variety of sport from cricket and football to squash and show jumping, every kind of activity from ice-skating to tossing the caber. Many of these activities, previously considered too specialised for majority audiences, have become popular because production skills have improved and commentaries become more lucid and informative.

It is astonishing that these facilities are not used more often in the communication of politics. But politicians have been nervous of the effect which the intrusion of television cameras might have upon their labours and broadcasters afraid that viewers would be bored and audiences disappear. The only important occasions when politicians can be seen when engaged in essential action and for the lengths of time automatically given to football, cricket or tennis, operatic performances or Promenade Concerts, are the annual Party Conferences and Trade Union Congresses. And even these are usually shown 'live' in their entirety only during the day; in the evening they are normally compressed into unrevealing news items or given in short, highly edited late night 'specials'. There is no attempt to give them the lengthy treatment which is regularly accorded to evening versions of 'Match of the Day'.

It is clear that the televising of Party Conferences and Trade Union Congresses will continue. Yet in the 1950s when I first approached the Conservative and Labour Party organisations with the proposition that they should open their Conference halls to television cameras there was great resistance (particularly from the Labour Party) and I then heard most of the arguments which, twenty years later, were still being used by those who opposed the televising of Parliament.

In practice politicians found to their surprise, in relation to Party Conferences, that television lights are *not* intolerably dazzling, that the publicity seekers among them do *not* play to the cameras and that the general atmosphere has *not* been ruined by the presence of television. So they have come not only to accept but to welcome the televising of their Conferences; and these occasions certainly provide a valuable insight into the behaviour of political leaders when they are dealing with the realities of their relationship with their supporters.

But there is still little opportunity of seeing them in action when they are handling the other side of their complex task, that is, the way in which they deal with the problems of government as distinct from those involved in securing their base. It is essential to provide such opportunities if the mass public are to make more informed judgments of political leaders. But how is it to be done? In spite of all the popular talk about the need for 'open government' it is obviously neither possible nor desirable for television cameras to be present at meetings of the Cabinet or of the Economic Policy Committee of the TUC or when Foreign Secretaries are talking to visiting statesmen or Chancellors of the Exchequer discussing balance of payment problems with Governors of the Bank of England. But it *is* possible, and many people think it desirable, for television cameras to allow viewers to watch the proceedings of the Houses of Parliament.

This is an old and much discussed question; but many of the familiar arguments for and against the televising of Parliament are becoming out-of-date. There has never been any real objection in principle: debates in the House of Commons can be watched by anyone who is able to reach the public gallery, so why not by viewers at home? Technical problems are disappearing as more sensitive cameras and lighter outside broadcast equipment become more available and fears of boring mass audiences are lessened by the increase in the number of television channels and separate television stations which will be there to provide alternative viewing.

And the advantages could be enormous. Politicians would gain in stature and their responsibilities be emphasised by their being seen in the historic surroundings of the Palace of Westminster: constituents would be able to watch their members in action; political leaders would be less dependent upon the invitations of the broadcasting organisations for their television appearances; informed commentaries could illuminate the issues and the procedures just as they have done, and continue to do, when television presents the results of a General Election. Above all, viewers would be able to see for themselves what was happening; their experience, as in a dozen other spheres, would be first-hand: they would no longer have to depend upon the printed or verbal reports of others.

Already great Parliamentary occasions, such as the Budget speeches of Chancellors of the Exchequer and the responses of the Opposition, are reflected on television, instant by instant, as news comes in and every fresh item is commented upon by expectant economists, bankers, industrialists, trade unionists and 'men in the street'. But these events are, in a sense, made absurd, because instead of hearing what the Chancellor says and watching the reactions of the House as he speaks, the vital news is read aloud from bits of paper torn off tape machines by whoever happens to be compèring the programme. And the reactions to each item are conveyed at second hand by breathless reporters who dash out of the House of Commons in order to give their impressions to millions of viewers.

It is no longer necessary for Members of Parliament to comment from under umbrellas held over their heads in Parliament Square by television interviewers as had happened at the time of the Profumo debate. What is astonishing is that similar improvised situations are still occurring nearly fifteen years later and that the televising of Parliament has been so long delayed.

The real reasons for the delay, I surmise, are almost unrecognised and largely subconscious. For the fact which is emerging is that the televising of Parliamentary procedures would force politicians to change their attitude to the function of television in political communication. They would no longer be able to regard it as an instrument to be used in their endeavours to persuade voters to entrust them with power: they would have to see it as a method of providing evidence and an extension of the experience of the individual voter, by whom, inevitably, they will be judged.

That is hard to accept, but there is virtually no alternative. Already, under the pressure of circumstances and as a result of the growing demand, partly created by television itself, for wider access to the decision-making processes which affect the lives of individuals, all kinds of institutions, from the Stock Exchange to great industrial complexes such as Shell, are throwing open their doors so that television cameras and commentators can observe and interpret the forms which decision-making in practice takes within them.

Is Parliament to be left out? That could only mean that other organisations less vital to the nation would increase their significance in the minds of the public and that the authority of the elected representatives of the people asembled in Parliament would be diminished.

This had become so unthinkable, but so likely, that in the spring of 1976 Parliament, having decided that the experiment of broadcasting in sound radio, 'live' as well as recorded, reports of its proceedings had been successful, announced that reporting of this kind was to continue on a regular basis. It cannot be long before similar permissions are extended to television.

What is now required, or so it seems to me, is time; time to assess the results of the inevitable televising of Parliamentary procedures; to see how it affects, if at all, Ministerial broadcasts and rights of reply by the Opposition; how it complements existent television political coverage and in what way excerpts can be used in local stations when local issues are being dealt with in the national Parliament.

Above all, it will take time to modify the tones and styles of television political interviewing. Such interviewing is bound to continue. What the viewer sees of Parliament in action can be only one facet of the political communication which television makes possible. And just as the 'live' television presentation of Party Conferences is supplemented by interviews and discussions so, I believe, the questioning of party leaders by informed and impartial interviewers will be necessary to complement the different, because largely party-motivated, speeches, arguments and disputes taking place in the House of Commons. But there can be little doubt that each will affect the other. And the consequent modifications will have to grow out of experience. This will require not only time but wisdom on the part of politicians as well as of broadcasters.

Time is also required for considerations even larger than these. Millions are growing up in a world in which television is a normal means of communication, no more dangerous or peculiar than the printed word. It is for *them*, in time, to decide what type of television institutions they consider necessary for Great Britain in the last quarter of the twentieth century; and for *them* to determine not only the national but the global nature of their television responsibilities.

Time is also required for the next generation to become accustomed to the shock of seeing the realities behind the words and to find ways of accepting and dealing with them. Television, by making it possible for mankind to see events and people at great distances yet in close-up, is a cruel destroyer of myths, illusions and fictions. It forces reality upon every viewer, brings events in distant lands almost too close to be borne, so that the epidemics, tortures and oppressions, the starving children, dying cattle, and the victims of war and earthquakes, once simply paragraphs in a newspaper, now sear your eyeballs every evening as you sit at home.

Small wonder that millions of British viewers, troubled and made to feel guilty by what they see on television, took refuge in 1976 by means of television from the appalling nature of the world and were among the 350 millions who watched in 83 countries the amiable imbecilities of 'A Song for Europe'.

Perhaps British television, in fact, is not too frivolous but too serious to be endured. I do not think so: I believe that the good sense of the British will enable a new generation to cope with this problem just as the good sense of previous generations found methods of preventing the domination of television by either an unbridled commercialism or the tyranny of governments and managed to combine the ultimate authority of Parliament with an almost un-paralleled freedom for broadcasters.

When I consider these things I can only wonder at the great distances we have come since, in 1936, I watched at Alexandra Palace the first television programme being transmitted and be glad that in Britain the great and ancient institution of Parliament is still linked with the strange new medium of television and that each in its own way has endeavoured to promote throughout the world the freedom of the individual.

Thankfulness, however, is not enough. Hope is also necessary: hope that the qualities of British broadcasting will be able to survive and be developed in a world of dizzyingly rapid technical, social and political change, the speed of which television itself increases by the mere act of reflecting it.

APPENDICES
NOTES
AND
INDEX

Appendix A

Political Broadcasting:
The Aide Mémoire of 1947

This is the official record of the terms of the agreement reached in February 1947 between the Government, the Opposition and the BBC. It was submitted by the BBC in 1947 as part of the Corporation's evidence to the Beveridge Committee and was published for the first time in the Report of that Committee (Cmd. 8116 and 8117) 1950–1951.

The text runs as follows:

1 It is desirable that political broadcasts of a controversial character shall be resumed.

2 In view of their responsibilities for the care of the nation the Government should be able to use the wireless from time to time for Ministerial broadcasts which, for example, are purely factual, or explanatory of legislation or administrative policies approved by Parliament; or in the nature of appeals to the nation to co-operate in national policies, such as fuel economy or recruiting, which require the active participation of the public. Broadcasts on State occasions also come in the same category.

It will be incumbent on Ministers making such broadcasts to be as impartial as possible, and in the ordinary way there will be no question of a reply by the Opposition. Where, however, the Opposition think that a Government broadcast is controversial it will be open to them to take the matter up through the usual channels with a view to a reply.

    i As a reply if one is to be made should normally be within a very short period after the original broadcast, say three days, the BBC will be free to exercise its own judgment if no agreement is arrived at within that period.

    ii Replies under this paragraph will not be included in the number of broadcasts provided for under paragraph 4.

    iii Copies of the scripts of broadcasts under this paragraph shall be supplied to the leaders of each Party.

    iv All requests for Ministerial broadcasts under this paragraph shall be canalized through the Minister designated for this purpose—at present the Postmaster General.

3 'Outside' broadcasts, e.g. of speeches at Party Conferences which are in the nature of news items, shall carry no right of reply by the other side.

4 A limited number of controversial party political broadcasts shall be allocated to the various parties in accordance with their polls at the last General Election. The allocation shall be calculated on a yearly basis and the total number of such broadcasts shall be a matter for discussion between the parties and the BBC.

5 The Opposition parties shall have the right, subject to discussion through the usual channels, to choose the subjects for their own broadcasts. Either side will be free, if it wishes, to use one of its quota for the purpose of replying to a previous broadcast, but it will be under no necessity to do so. There will, of course, be no obligation on a party to use its whole quota.

6   i Paragraphs 4 and 5 relate to controversial party political broadcasts on issues of major policy on behalf of the leading political Parties. For the ensuing year the total number, excluding Budget broadcasts, shall be 12—divided as to Government 6, Conservative Opposition 5, Liberal Opposition 1. Reasonable notice will be given to the BBC.

      ii The BBC reserve the right, after consultation with the party leaders, to invite to the microphone a member of either House of outstanding national eminence who may have become detached from any party.

     iii Apart from these limited broadcasts on major policy the BBC are free to invite members of either House to take part in controversial broadcasts of a round-table character in which political questions are dealt with, provided two or more persons representing different sides take part in the broadcasts.

     iv No broadcasts arranged by the BBC other than the normal reporting of Parliamentary proceedings are to take place on any question while it is the subject of discussion in either House.

7 Where any dispute arises an effort shall be made to settle it through the usual channels. Where this is not possible, the BBC will have to decide the matter on its own responsibility.

8 These arrangements shall be reviewed after a year, or earlier if any party to the conference so desires.

6 February 1947.

Note: The above agreement was revised in July 1948, when Government and Opposition agreed with the BBC that 6(iv) should be construed as:

    a that the BBC will not have discussions or *ex parte* statements on any issues for a period of a fortnight before they are debated in either House;

    b that while matters are subjects of legislation M.P.s will not be used in such discussions.

Appendix B

The Aide Mémoire of 1969

The Aide Mémoire of 1947 was revised and a fresh agreement reached between the Government, the Opposition and the BBC in 1969. The text runs as follows:

1 In view of its executive responsibilities the Government of the day has the right to explain events to the public, or seek co-operation of the public, through the medium of broadcasting.

2 Experience has shown that such occasions are of two kinds and that different arrangements are appropriate for each.

3 The first category relates to Ministers wishing to explain legislation or administrative policies approved by Parliament, or to seek the co-operation of the public in matters where there is a general consensus of opinion. The BBC will provide suitable opportunities for such broadcasts within the regular framework of their programmes; there will be no right of reply by the Opposition.

4 The second category relates to more important and normally infrequent occasions, when the Prime Minister or one of his most senior Cabinet colleagues designated by him wishes to broadcast to the nation in order to provide information or explanation of events of prime national or international importance, or to seek the co-operation of the public in connection with such events.

5 The BBC will provide the Prime Minister or Cabinet Minister with suitable facilities on each occasion in this second category. Following such an occasion they may be asked to provide an equivalent opportunity for a broadcast by a leading Member of the Opposition and will in that event do so.

6 When the Opposition exercises this right to broadcast, there will follow as soon as possible, arranged by the BBC, a broadcast discussion of the issues between a Member of the Cabinet and a senior Member of the Opposition nominated respectively by the Government and the Opposition but not necessarily those who gave the preceding broadcasts. An opportunity to participate in such a discussion should be offered to a representative of any other Party with electoral support at the time in question on a scale not appreciably less than that of the Liberal Party at the date of this Aide Mémoire.

343

7 As it will be desirable that such an Opposition broadcast and discussion between Government and Opposition should follow the preceding broadcast with as little delay as possible, a request for the necessary facilities by the Opposition should reach the BBC before noon on the day following the Ministerial broadcast. This will enable the BBC to arrange the Opposition broadcast and the discussion as soon as possible.

Notes

[1] Prelude: The Essential Decisions
1934–1936

1 Cmd. 4793/1934–35.
2 Cmd. 5091.
3 Cmd. 1822.
4 Cmd. 5329.
5 Cmd. 5091/1935–36.
6 Cmd. 1951.
7 Cmd. 1753.
8 Government Memorandum Cmd. 1893/Dec. 1962.
9 Cmd. 2599.
10 Cmd. 5091.
11 Cmd. 5329, Clause 4 (3).
12 Cmd. 1951.
13 Cmd. 5091.
14 Ibid.

[2] Pre-War Television
1936–1939

1 Cmd. 1951.
2 Cmd. 2599.
3 Cmd. 5091.
4 Ibid.
5 Cmd. 5337.

[3] Television Starts Again
1946–1950

1 Hankey Report on Television, Non-Parliamentary Papers. 1945.
2 Cmd. 6852.
3 Cmd. 5091.
4 'The Public Influence of Broadcasting and the Press', Memoirs and Proceedings of the Manchester Literary and Philosophical Society, Vol. xcv: Session 1953–1954.

[4] Television Gets Closer to Politics
1947–1950

1 *Made for Millions* (Contact Publications, 1947).
2 Extract from Chester Wilmot's papers, lent by his widow.

[5] 'In the News', and Pressure from the Parties
1950–1954

1 Conversation between Sir David Maxwell Fyfe, later Lord Kilmuir, and the author, 1950.
2 Conversation between Michael Balkwill and the author, 1968.
3 BBC file.
4 Television Policy File 1951. Political Broadcasts—'In the News'. Memorandum dated February 15, 1951 from the Director of Television to the Controller of Television Programmes.
5 BBC Policy File 1951. Political Broadcasts—'In the News'. Memorandum of October 21, 1953 from the Secretary of the Director of Administration setting out a Minute registering attitude of Board of Management to paper B7. 124/53. Minute 423 (c).
6 BBC Policy File 1951. Political Broadcasts—'In the News'. Memorandum of February 14 from Michael Balkwill to Director of Television. List was from October 6, 1950 to January 19, 1951 inclusive.
7 Memorandum dated May 11, 1951 from M. Balkwill to the Director of Television referring to John Boyd-Carpenter as being on 'the Maxwell Fyfe list'. Television Policy File 1951. Political Broadcasts 'In the News'.
8 BBC Television Policy File 1951. Political Broadcasts 'In the News'. Memorandum May 11, 1951 from M. Balkwill to the Director of Television.
9 BBC Television Policy File 1951. Political Broadcasts 'In the News'. Note by Director-General G.105/53. Reference to Minute 115/51.
10 BBC Television Policy File 1951. Political Broadcasts. 'In the News'.

[6] Members of Parliament as
Television Commentators
1950–1959

1 Memorandum from GWG, September 11, 1952.
2 Memorandum from GWG, November 14, 1952.

[7] The First Television Party
Election Broadcasts
1951

1 Cmd. 5091.
2 BBC File. Policy: Party Political and Ministerial Broadcasts. File 1. 1949–1954. Memorandum from Grace Wyndham Goldie, Room 214, Marylebone Road. October 10, 1951, to Director of Television.
3 BBC File 1. 1949–54. Policy. Political Broadcasts. Party Political and Ministerial Broadcasts. Memorandum from Mrs Wyndham Goldie,

27 Marylebone Road, to Controller of Programmes, Television. Copy to Director of Television. October 15, 1951.

4 November 10, 1951.

[8] The Breaking of the BBC's
Television Monopoly
1952–1954

1 October 15, 1956.
2 Cmd. 8291.
3 BBC File. Meeting with the Parties—4 April, 1950.
4 Cmd. 8116.
5 Cmd. 8291.
6 Cmd. 8550.
7 Cmd. 8550, Para. 7.
8 Cmd. 8570.
9 Cmd. 8550, Para 7.
10 Cmd. 8550, Para 9.
11 Cmd. 8550, Para. 9.
12 Cmd. 9005.
13 Cmd. 8550.
14 Cmd. 9005, Para. 1.
15 Cmd. 9005, Para. 10.
16 Ibid., Paras 1 and 2.
17 Television Act, 1954.
18 Ibid.
19 Conversation between Sir David Maxwell Fyfe (later Lord Kilmuir) and the author.

[9] Developments in Television
Political Broadcasting
1952–1955

1 Quotation from transcript of the broadcast.
2 As for 1.
3 BBC file. G.47/53.
4 BBC file. G.15/52.
5 Broadcasting Committee Report 1949. Page 109. Paper 8, BBC Memorandum. Political Broadcasting. Aide Mêmoire.
6 Political Broadcasting: Aide Mémoire. Published as Appendix H of the Beveridge Committee Report. Cmd. 8116/8117. 1950/51. Note 1.
7 BBC file. G.47/53.
8 BBC file. Policy: Political. 1947 Agreement with the Parties.
9 BBC file. G.15/52.
10 BBC file. Ministerial broadcasts. 1954.

[10] The Power of the Producer
1952–1955
1 Cmd. 5091, Para. 89.
2 March 16, 1954.

[11] The New Style: Eden Succeeds Churchill
1953–1956
1 Transcript of the programme.
2 Minutes of Meeting of Board of Governors of the BBC: April 14, 1955.
3 Article by the Director-General of the BBC, Sir Ian Jacob, in the BBC Quarterly: Autumn 1954.
4 Minutes of the Meeting of April 12, 1956.
5 Extracts from transcript of the Ministerial broadcast by the Prime Minister, Sir Anthony Eden, August 8, 1956.
6 Extract from transcript of Sir Anthony Eden's Ministerial broadcast on Wednesday, August 8, 1956.
7 Extract from transcript of Mr Menzies' broadcast of August 13, 1956.
8 Hutchinson, 1968.

[12] 'Panorama', the News and the Rise of the
Television Interviewer
1956–1959
1 ITV 1967. A guide to Independent Television. Published by the Independent Television Authority, January 1967. Pages 29 and 30.
2 Memorandum dated March 16, 1956 from Head of Television Talks (Leonard Miall) to Assistant Head of Television Talks (G.W.G.) with copies to others. 'I am assuming that Macmillan will be broadcasting on television on April 18 and that it will be an O.B. from Downing St. He has requested that you should produce this yourself.'
3 Memorandum dated April 5, 1956 from A.H.T.Tel. (G.W.G.) to Huw·Wheldon: with copies to H.T.Tel. (Leonard Miall) and others.
4 Memorandum from Huw Wheldon to the Head of Television Talks, Leonard Miall. Dated March 19, 1957.
5 Ibid.
6 Memorandum from Rex Moorfoot to the Head of Television Talks. March 20, 1957.
7 Memorandum from Huw Wheldon to the Head of Television Talks, July 8, 1957.

[13] 'Tonight' and 'TWTWTW'
1957–1963
1 BBC Year Book.

2 BBC File. 'That Was The Week That Was'. Policy Memorandum from A.C.P.Tel. to C.P.Tel. Nov. 15, 1962.

3 BBC File. 'That Was The Week That Was'. Policy Memorandum. Jan. 11, 1963.

4 BBC file. 'That Was The Week That Was'. Policy Memorandum January 14, 1963, from A.C.P.Tel. to A.H.T.(C.A.)Tel.

5 BBC File. 'That Was The Week That Was'. Policy Memorandum from D. Tel. to C.P.Tel. April 30, 1963.

6 Ibid.

7 Ibid.

8 BBC File. 'That Was The Week That Was'. Policy Memorandum from the Head of the BBC Secretariat to the Controller of Television Programmes. Sept. 30, 1963.

9 *Daily Mail*. October 1, 1963.

10 *Daily Herald*. September 30, 1963.

11 BBC File. 'That Was the Week That Was'. Policy Memorandum from Day Press Officer to Press Agencies. November 13, 1963.

12 BBC File. 'That Was The Week That Was'. Policy Memorandum from the Head of Secretariat to the Controller of Television Programmes. November 19, 1963.

13 Minutes of BBC Board Meeting, November 7, 1963: following upon paper G. 135/63: a draft minute of the discussion of the General Advisory Council.

14 Ibid.

[14] Television's Challenge to Parliament
1962–1965

1 Memorandum from Head of Talks and Current Affairs Television to D.Tel. through A.C.P.Tel. September 17, 1962.

2 Memorandum from Head of Talks and Current Affairs Television to Mr Harman Grisewood. Subject: Broadcast by Prime Minister. Date September 19, 1962.

3 Memorandum from Head of Talks and Current Affairs Television to Mr Harman Grisewood. Subject: Broadcast by Prime Minister. Date September 19, 1962.

4 Memorandum from Head of Talks Group, Television (G.W.G.) to Controller of Television Programmes. Subject: The Profumo Case: Lord Hailsham in 'Gallery': June 13, 1963.

5 Ibid.

6 Ibid.

7 Transcript of 'Gallery': June 13, 1963.

8 Memorandum from Head of Talks Group, Television, to Controller of Television Programmes. Subject: The Profumo Case: Lord Hailsham in 'Gallery': June 13, 1963.

9 Transcript of 'Gallery': June 13, 1963.

10 Ibid.

11 Ibid.

12 Ibid.

13 Ibid.

14 Ibid.

15 Memorandum from Head of Talks Group, Television, to Controller of Television Programmes.

16 Ibid. Memorandum from Head of Talks Group, Television, to Controller of Television Programmes. June 13, 1963.

17 Transcript of interview.

18 Ibid.

[15] Television and the Party Leaders

1 Transcript of television interview: The Prime Minister, Lord Home. Monday, October 21, 1963.

2 Ibid.

3 Ibid.

4 Ibid.

5 Ibid.

6 Extract from Memorandum from Head of Television Talks to the Director of Television. October 22, 1963.

7 BBC Telediphone Transcript of interview with the Rt Hon. Harold Wilson: questioned by Robin Day and Robert McKenzie. Recorded from transmission Tuesday, October 22, 1963.

8 Ibid.

9 Ibid.

10 Ibid.

11 Ibid.

12 Ibid.

13 Ibid.

14 BBC Memorandum: from Head of Talks Group, Television. Subject: The General Election in Television. October 30, 1963.

15 There were no similar 'Confrontations' between Presidential candidates for sixteen years. The Kennedy/Nixon encounters took place in September 1960. In September 1976, as a result of a challenge issued in August by President Ford during his acceptance speech at the Republican Convention, a series of 'Confrontations' with the Democratic candidate, Jimmy Carter, were arranged, the first to be on September 23. As in 1960, these were not to take the form of direct debates; each candidate would answer questions put by a panel of journalists. The new factors were that for the first time an incumbent President would be taking part; that the encounters would take place

not in a television studio but in a public hall, and that the sponsor was the League of Women Voters, relying, for finance, upon the subscription of its members.

16 A major difference between 'Election Forums' and the Kennedy/ Nixon 'Confrontations', was the element of public involvement. In the American 'Confrontations', the interviewers put their own questions to the candidates. In 'Election Forums' the interviewers were limited to putting questions sent in by the public.

17 Transcribed from a TV telediphone recording. 'Election Forum'. Recorded from transmission September 23, 1964.

18 Transcribed from TV telediphone recording. 'Election Forum'. Recorded from transmission. September 24, 1964.

[16] Labour in Power
1964–1970

1 Transcript of the Prime Minister's television broadcast, February 24, 1965.

2 Memorandum from Head of Talks Group, Television, to D.G., March 1, 1965.

3 BBC Memorandum from Mr O. J. Whitley to D.G., March 3, 1965.

4 Notes made by the author at the time of the lunch.

5 See *The British General Election of 1970* by David Butler and Michael Pinto Duschinsky. (Macmillan 1971.)

6 Ibid. See also *Behind the Screen* by Lord Hill. (Sidgwick and Jackson, 1974.) Lord Hill, Chairman of the BBC's Board of Governors in 1970, says that when he went to Television Centre on the night of the election to see the preparations for the transmission of the results, 'I asked Robert McKenzie what he thought the result would be and he forecast a Labour Party majority of eighty. Everybody I met thought the Labour Party would win.'

[17] Into the Unknown
1970–1976

1 January 23, 1974. Parliamentary Debates (Hansard), House of Lords. Official Report.

2 *Made for Millions.* (Contact Publications Limited, 1947.)

3 (Andre Deutsch, 1970.)

4 For details of the use of advertising agents by the Conservative Party during the General Election campaigns of 1959 and 1964, see references to Colman, Prentis & Varley on pages 75–8 of *Communication and Political Power* by Lord Windlesham (Cape, 1966).

5 For details see Lord Hill's account in *Behind the Screen*.

6 Cmd. 5774. Report of the Committee on Broadcasting Coverage.

7 *The People and the Media*. (The Labour Party, 1974.)

8 News Release. *The Labour Party and Broadcasting. Evidence to the Annan Committee*. (Issued by the Labour Party Information Department, Transport House.)

9 Ibid.

10 Ibid.

11 Ibid.

12 Transmitted on June 17, 1971. For one account of the circumstances see *Behind the Scenes* by Lord Hill (Sidgwick and Jackson, 1974) and extracts published in the *Sunday Times* on September 15, 1974.

Bibliography

Very little has been written about the relationship between television and politics. Much of what exists has to be disinterred from official publications, books of reference, and a number of specialised works, some of which are mainly about politics but deal also with aspects of television, others of which are mainly about broadcasting in general but are necessary to an understanding of television development. There are also many agreeable personal statements based on the experiences of politicians and broadcasters—biographies, diaries, reminiscences—which throw light upon the interaction between television and politics at various times.

All I am doing here is to list those in each category which I myself have found essential, useful or illuminating, at the same time indicating some additional and more comprehensive bibliographies for those who wish to go further. I have also added a note about recorded visual material.

ESSENTIAL DOCUMENTS (Published by Her Majesty's Stationery Office)

Reports of Committees on Broadcasting (including television)

Sykes. Cmd. 1951 (1923): *Crawford.* Cmd. 2599 (1926): *Selsdon*, on Television. Cmd. 4793 (1935): *Ullswater.* Cmd. 5091 (1936): *Hankey*, on Television (1945): *Beveridge.* Cmd. 8116 and 8117 (1951): *Pilkington.* Cmd. 1753 (1962).

These papers contain between them a statement of the principles upon which British broadcasting is based. They also embody evidence of the condition of broadcasting (including some comparison with broadcasting in other countries) at the given dates. The dates are those of the publication of the reports not of the appointment of the Committees. The official title of each publication is 'Report of the Broadcasting Committee of . . .' with the date of publication.

OTHER KEY PUBLICATIONS (also HMSO)

Memorandum on the Report of the Broadcasting Committee 1949. Cmd. 8291.
  Comment by the Attlee government on the Beveridge Report of 1951.
Memorandum on the Report of the Broadcasting Committee 1949. Cmd. 8550.
  Comment by the Churchill government on the Beveridge Report (1952).
Memorandum on Television Policy. Cmd. 9005. (Nov. 1953).
  Statement by the Churchill government redefining the policy stated in Memorandum of 1952.
Television Acts: 1954 and 1964.
  These five pronouncements are vital to an understanding of the official processes which permitted a degree of commercial competitiveness in

353

British television and also of the subsequent history of the relationship between the ITA (later IBA) and Parliament.

Report of the Committee on Broadcasting Coverage (Chairman Sir Stewart Crawford). Cmd. 5774 (1974).

Investigation into the broadcasting needs of Scotland, Wales, Northern Ireland and rural England.

WORKS OF REFERENCE AND SPECIALISED STUDIES

British Political Facts 1900–1975. David Butler and Anne Sloman. (Macmillan 1975).

In addition to its comprehensive political material this contains a brief section on broadcasting which gives basic facts about the BBC and IBA together with a short bibliography.

BBC Handbooks (Published by the BBC yearly since 1928).

The Handbook for 1976, which incorporates the Corporation's Annual Report and Accounts, contains sections on the BBC's constitutional position, its relation to Parliament, the text of its Charter and Licence and information about its current affairs and news programmes.

Independent Television Handbooks (Published by the ITA, later IBA, yearly since 1954).

TV and Radio 1976 contains a summary of the history of Independent Television, its constitutional position, the relationship between the Authority and the commercial companies, its methods of advertising control and code of advertising practice.

The History of Broadcasting in the United Kingdom. Asa Briggs.

Vol. I. The Birth of Broadcasting (1961). II. The Golden Age of Wireless (1965). III. The War of Words (1970). IV. Sound and Vision (in progress). (Oxford University Press).

Nuffield Election Studies.

The British General Election of 1950 was written by H. G. Nicholas.

David Butler has been author or co-author of the Nuffield election studies since 1951. Each contsains a television section. Titles are *The British General Election of . . .* with dates of elections, 1951, 55, 59, 64, 66, 70, Feb. 1974, Oct. 1974 and the Referendum of 1975. (Macmillan).

Television and the Political Image. J. M. Trenaman and D. McQuail.

The impact of television on the 1959 General Election. (Methuen 1961).

Communication and Political Power. Lord Windlesham. (Jonathan Cape 1966).

Pressure Group: the campaign for commercial television. H. H. Wilson. (Secker and Warburg 1961).

The People and the Media. (Labour Party 1974).

Includes a statement of Labour Party broadcasting policy.

British Broadcasting, 1922–1972.

A comprehensive bibliography. (A revised edition under consideration). (BBC 1972).

The Selling of the President. Joe McGinnis. (Deutsch 1970).

The Making of the President, 1972. (Jonathan Cape 1974). *Breach of Faith.* (Jonathan Cape 1976). Both by Theodore H. White.

The People's Films. A Political History of U.S. Government Motion Pictures. R. D. McCann. (Hastings House, New York 1973).

Includes comment upon television for President and Congress.

PERSONAL STATEMENTS, REMINISCENCES, ETC

Ariel and All His Quality. R. S. Lambert. (Gollancz 1940).

Made for Millions (Includes television section by Grace Wyndham Goldie). (Contact Publications 1947).

Into the Wind. J. C. W. Reith. (Autobiography). (Hodder & Stoughton 1949).

The Reith Diaries. Edited by Charles Stuart. (Collins 1975).

The Public Influence of Broadcasting and the Press. (The Clayton Memorial Lecture). Sir William Haley. (The Manchester Literary and Philosophical Society 1954).

One Thing at a Time. Harman Grisewood. (Hutchinson 1968).

Particularly for the Suez reminiscences.

Moshe Dayan: Story of My Life. (Weidenfeld & Nicholson 1976).

For his account of the Suez negotiations.

Behind the Screen. Lord Hill. (Sidgwick & Jackson 1974).

Covers his experience as Chairman both of ITA and of the Board of Governors of the BBC.

Day by Day. Robin Day. (William Kimber 1975).

Richard Dimbleby. Jonathan Dimbleby. (Hodder & Stoughton 1975).

The Way the Wind Blows. Lord Home. (Collins 1976).

RECORDED VISUAL MATERIAL

At the end of a book which has emphasised the difference between the impact of what is seen and what is only heard or read I would wish to refer any reader not only to printed sources but to what has been visually recorded. Though desirable this is difficult. Access to television recordings is not easy. There is no national television archive. Until the time when such an archive can be created (and paid for) those who wish to consult television records have to make do with what exists. The British Film Institute— which came into existence primarily to further the art of the film—contains in its film archives a selection on film of television material. Most broadcasting organisations, national and international, keep television material in their own libraries for their own programme purposes. Sometimes this material can be hired, or purchased. Television material is, however, not only enormously more expensive to copy than the printed word but also more fraught with technical, contract and copyright problems. Information can be obtained from such bodies as BBC Enterprises and commercial television companies. But it should be said that even viewing is normally charged for (and not always possible) since making provision for viewing is a costly process.

It is to be hoped that as soon as the national economic situation improves steps may be taken to create a national television archive (with possible international connections) for the use of future historians.

Index